Namibia

The Two-

ONF

Namibia's Liberation Struggle
The Two-Edged Sword

COLIN LEYS
& JOHN S. SAUL

WITH CONTRIBUTIONS BY
SUSAN BROWN • PHILIP STEENKAMP
SIPHO S. MASEKO • CHRIS TAPSCOTT
LAUREN DOBELL

JAMES CURREY
LONDON

OHIO UNIVERSITY PRESS
ATHENS

James Currey Ltd
54b Thornhill Square
Islington
London N1 1BE

Ohio University Press
Scott Quadrangle
Athens
Ohio 45701

2 3 4 5 99 98 97 96 95

British Library Cataloguing in Publication Data
Leys, Colin
  Namibia's Liberation Struggle: Two-edged
  Sword
  I. Title. II. Saul, John, S.
  320.966884

ISBN   0–85255–375–7 (cased)
       0–85255–374–9 (paper)

Library of Congress Cataloging-in-Publication Data
Namibia's liberation struggle ... the two-edged sword / by Colin
  Leys and John S. Saul.
     p. cm.
  Includes bibliographical references and index.
  ISBN 0–8214–1103–9. -- ISBN 0–8214–1104–7 (pbk.)
     1. Namibia--Politics and government--1946–1990. 2. Namibia-
  -Politics and government--1990- 3. Guerilla warfare--Namibia.
  4. South Africa--History, Military--1961- 5. Swapo--History.
  I. Leys, Colin.   II. Saul, John S.
  DT1645.N37   1995
  320.966884--dc20   94-8024
                                                            CIP

Typeset in 9/10½ Palatino by Opus 43, Cumbria
Printed and bound in Great Britain by Villiers Publications, London N3

Contents

III THE LEGACY

Preface

This book is the product of a research project conceived in August 1989 during Namibia's transition to independence. It was clear then that the fact that Namibians had been forced to fight a 23-year war in order to achieve their independence had marked profoundly both the country's main liberation movement, the South West African People's Organization (SWAPO), and the emerging Namibian polity as a whole. It seemed important, while memories of the struggle were still fresh, to try to register what had been involved in this crucially formative experience, especially in relation to its impact on post-independent development. Accordingly, this book is not a history of Namibia's independence struggle in all its many facets. It is, rather, a study – and a preliminary one at that – of the way the war affected both the liberation movement itself and the political culture bequeathed to the country at independence.

The project drew together a group of researchers which included, besides the authors in this volume, Somadoda Fikeni of Queen's University and the University of the Transkei. We were also fortunate in being able to enlist the involvement of a group of Namibian law students, under the direction of Andrew Corbett at the Legal Assistance Centre in Windhoek. We sought, in addition, to find colleagues who could contribute detailed studies of the roles of such actors in civil society as women and the labour movement, but without success (the major studies of the labour movement by Pekka Peltola of the University of Helsinki and Gretchen Bauer of the University of Wisconsin were unfortunately still in progress when this project had to be finalized). In seeking to examine the changing role of the state in war and peace, it would have been as relevant to look at the military or the civil service as at policing (studied in Chapter 7). These important subjects are, however, touched upon in the chapters which follow (notably, aspects of the politics of both women and workers in Chapters 3 to 5).

Funding was provided by a research grant from the Canadian Social Sciences and Humanities Research Council, for which we are much indebted. We are also grateful for financial support from Atkinson College, York University, and Queen's University, Kingston. In addition, funding was provided to Lauren Dobell by a grant from the Canadian International Development Agency, and to Sipho Maseko and Somadoda Fikeni by the Southern Africa Education Trust Fund in Ottawa. In Namibia, invaluable support was provided by the Namibian Institute of Social and Economic Research under the direction of Professor Chris Tapscott, who also contributes to this volume. At Queen's University we were ably and generously helped by Mrs Bernice Gallagher and Mrs Shirley Fraser of the Department of Political Studies.

Namibians who have assisted us are too numerous to thank individually, although the many names cited in our notes will give some indication of the range of those who often went to great trouble to give us invaluable information and advice. We are very grateful to them all. The chapters, written by Leys and Saul, that bear most directly on SWAPO's own history were circulated in draft to all our principal respondents and we are particularly grateful to those who replied to our request for criticisms and comments.

A study of this nature is inevitably somewhat controversial and we appreciate the encouragement to persevere with it we received from many leading Namibians – not least from the Hon. Theo-Ben Gurirab, Namibia's Minister of Foreign Affairs, who encouraged us in our efforts to understand the history of Namibia's liberation struggle with the comment, 'It is the nature of enquiring minds to make connections.' Needless to say, neither he nor any other Namibian bears any responsibility for the connections made or interpretations advanced in this volume.

C. L. and J. S. S.

About the Contributors

Susan Brown, who worked for many years as a journalist for various newspapers in South Africa, Namibia and Britain, is presently a development consultant in Namibia.

Lauren Dobell conducted research in Namibia while a graduate student at Queen's University, Kingston, Ontario. She is presently at Oxford University studying Namibia's post-independence development.

Colin Leys teaches politics at Queen's University, Kingston, Ontario. His publications include studies of development in Zimbabwe, Tanzania, Uganda, Kenya, the Caribbean, the Atlantic Provinces of Canada and Britain, and various papers on the theory of development. He is currently working on a book on the relation between the market and democracy in Britain.

Sipho Sibusiso Maseko teaches politics at the University of the Western Cape. He carried out research in Namibia while a graduate student at Queen's University, Kingston, Ontario. He is currently studying the role of black businessmen in South African development.

John S. Saul teaches social and political science at York University, Toronto. He was a founding member of the Toronto Committee for the Liberation of Southern Africa and is an editor of the Toronto-based periodical *Southern Africa Report*. He has published extensively on development theory and on the political economy of a range of countries in eastern and southern Africa. He is presently working on a book about the 'Thirty Years War' for southern African liberation, 1960–90.

Philip Steenkamp holds a post-doctoral fellowship and teaches history at the University of Victoria, British Columbia. He is completing a book on the role of the churches in Namibia's independence struggle, and conducting research on the history of agrarian resistance to white rule in South Africa.

Chris Tapscott is Director of the Namibian Institute of Social and Economic Research at the University of Namibia. He has published numerous papers and reports on development in Namibia. He has also worked on the relation between theory and practice in South African development policy.

Chronology
Namibia's Liberation Struggle, 1959–92

EXTERNAL	INTERNAL
1959	Old Location massacre
1960 Sharpeville massacre	OPO becomes SWAPO. Nujoma leaves for Tanganyika
1961 SWAPO office opened in Dar es Salaam	First SWAPO Congress at Rehoboth?
1963 First trainees sent to Algeria OAU Liberation Committee formed	Second SWAPO Congress at Windhoek?
1964	Odendaal Report recommends bantustanization of Namibia
1966 ICJ rejects Namibia case	Omgulumbashe camp destroyed Repression begins
1967 Army Cmdr Hainyeko killed	
1968 Kongwa crisis: SWAPO HQ moves to Lusaka	
1969 (–1970) SWAPO Congress at Tanga	SWAPO Youth League formed
1971 ICJ rules South African mandate ended	Contract workers' strike National Convention formed
1972	SADF called in to Namibia
1973 UNGA declares SWAPO 'sole and authentic representative' of the Namibian people	Ovambo elections boycott: intensified police repression
1974 Coup in Portugal: Vorster–Kaunda detente: MPLA–FNLA–UNITA conflict develops	Exodus from north begins SADF becomes officially responsible for security in north National Convention dissolved
1975 MPLA gains control in Angola	Ovambo chief Elifas murdered Army repression in north escalates
1976 Soweto uprising 'Shipanga' crisis: enlarged Central Committee meeting: new constitution, programme adopted: move of SWAPO HQ to Angola begins	SWAPO 'Congress' in Walvis Bay
1977 'Contact Group' starts negotiations	SWAPO Conference in Katutura (Windhoek)
1978 South Africa 'accepts' UNSC Res. 435, attacks Cassinga PLAN formed, grows to +/- 8,000, incursions mount	Abortive SYL efforts to convene internal Conference begin Koevoet formed 'Internal' elections for Constituent Assembly won by DTA
1979 P. W. Botha's 'total strategy' begins	Constituent Assembly becomes 'National Assembly'. Meetings banned in north SWAPO National Executive at home dissolved
1980 Reagan replaces Carter: 'constructive engagement', 'linkage' policies begin CANU splits from SWAPO	DTA-controlled Council of Ministers formed
1981 Operation Protea leaves SADF in southern Angola, PLAN pushed 150 km from border 'Spy drama' develops	SWAPO meetings banned in south, activity declines Drought begins
1983	Community-based organizing develops National Assembly and Council of Ministers abolished
1984 'Insurrection' begins in South Africa	'Spy drama' becomes widely known in Namibia
1985	Transitional Government of National Unity formed
1986	/Ai-//Gams Declaration
1987 Gorbachev's 'new thinking' Cuito Cuanevale battle begins, ends in stalemate	
1988 Peace Plan agreed (December)	
1989 Ceasefire (1 April)	SWAPO wins November elections to Constituent Assembly
1990	Independence (21 March)
1991	Land Conference and SWAPO Congress held in Windhoek
1992	SWAPO wins regional elections

Abbreviations

AG	Administrator General	OAU	Organization of African Unity
AME	African Methodist Episcopal (church)	OBS	Otto Benicke Stiftung
ANC	African National Congress	OPC	Ovamboland People's Congress
Angop	National News Agency of Angola	OPO	Ovamboland People's Organization
ASO	Academy Students' Organization	PLAN	People's Liberation Army of Namibia
BC	Black Consciousness	PO	Protection Officer
CANU	Caprivi African National Union	POIC	Private Overseas Investment
CBIE	Canadian Bureau for International		Corporation
	Education	PPRAC	Police Public Relations Advisory
CCN	Council of Churches in Namibia		Council
CEB	Ecclesial base communities (Latin	PPRC	Police Public Relations Committee
	America)	PUM	Patriotic Unity Movement
CHQ	Command Headquarters	REC	Regional Executive Committee
CIA	Central Intelligence Agency		(NANSO)
COSATU	Congress of South African Trade Unions	RELC	Rheinisch Evangelical Lutheran Church
DTA	Democratic Turnhalle Alliance	SAAF	South African Air Force
ELC	Evangelical Lutheran Church in SWA	SACBC	South African Catholic Bishops'
ELCIN	Evangelical Lutheran Church in		Conference
	Namibia	SACC	South African Council of Churches
ELOC	Evangelical Lutheran	SADF	South African Defence Force
	Ovambo–Kavango Church	SAP	South African Police
FAPLA	People's Armed Forces for the	SNM	Somali National Movement
	Liberation of Angola	SRC	Students' Representative Council
FNLA	National Front for the Liberation of	SWANLIF	South West Africa National Liberation
	Angola		Front
Frelimo	Front for the Liberation of Mozambique	SWANU	South West African National Union
GELC	German Evangelical Lutheran Church	SWAPA	South West African Progressive
GSC	General Student Congress(es)		Association
ICJ	International Court of Justice	SWAPO*	South West Africa People's Organization
IDAF	International Defence and Aid Fund	SWAPO-D	SWAPO-Democrats
IUEF	International University Exchange Fund	SWAPOL	South West Africa Police
JMC	Joint Monitoring Commission	SWASB	South West African Student Body
LWF	Lutheran World Federation	SWATF	South West African Territorial Force
MPC	Multi-party Conference	SWC	SWAPO Women's Council
MPLA	Popular Movement for the Liberation of	SYL	SWAPO Youth League
	Angola	TGNU	Transitional Government of National
MUN	Mineworkers' Union of Namibia		Unity
NABSO	Namibian Black Students' Organization	UCT	University of Cape Town
NACOS	Namibian Council of Students	UDF	United Democratic Front
NAFAU	National Food & Allied Union	UDI	Unilateral Declaration of Independence
NAM	Non-Aligned Movement	UELCSWA	United Evangelical Lutheran Church of
NAMPOL	Namibia Police		South West Africa
NAMSO	Namibian Students' Organization	UN	United Nations
NANSO	Namibian National Students'	UNDP	United Nations Development
	Organization		Programme
NANTU	Namibia National Teachers Union	UNHCR	United Nations High Commissioner for
NAPWU	Namibian Public Workers' Union		Refugees
NASEM	Namibian Student Education Movement	UNIN	United Nations Institute for Namibia
NC	National Convention	UNIP	United National Independence Party
NDF	Namibian Defence Force	UNITA	Union for the Total Independence of
NEH	National Executive at Home		Angola
NEPRU	National Economic Policy Research Unit	UNSCR	United Nations Security Council
NGO	Non-Governmental Organization		Resolution
NIP	Namibian Independence Party	UWC	University of the Western Cape
NISER	Namibian Institute for Social &	VEM	Vereinigte Evangelische Mission
	Economic Research	WCC	World Council of Churches
NNC	Namibian National Congress	WHAM	Winning Hearts and Minds
NPA	National People's Assembly	WRP	Workers' Revolutionary Party
NSC	National Student Congress(es)	YWCA	Young Women's Christian Association
NSCC	National Schools Crisis Committee	ZANU	Zimbabwe African National Union
NUNW	National Union of Namibian Workers	ZIPA	Zimbabwean People's Army
NWV	Namibia Women's Voice		

* Over the years as SWAPO became a household name it tended to be written 'Swapo', and when 'South West Africa/Namibia' became just 'Namibia' at independence, Swapo officially became 'Swapo of Namibia'. SWAPO has been retained throughout this text purely for consistency.

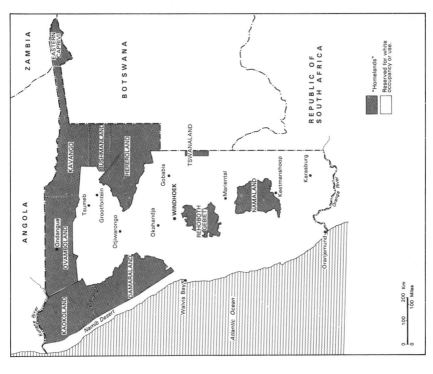

MAP 1 NAMIBIA: PRINCIPAL TOWNS
Source: R. H. Green *et al., Namibia: The Last Colony* (London: Longman, 1981)

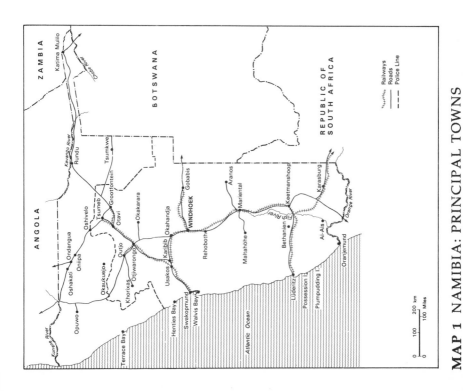

MAP 2 NAMIBIA:
COLONIAL LAND DISTRIBUTION

MAP 3 NAMIBIA: POPULATION DISTRIBUTION
Source: E. Leistner and P. Esterhuysen (eds), *Namibia 1990: An Africa Institute Country Survey*
(Pretoria: Africa Institute of South Africa, 1991).

1
Introduction

COLIN LEYS & JOHN S. SAUL

Namibia, David Soggot has memorably said, is a small nation that was 'plucked from the shadows of history by calamitous fate'.[1] If this is so, we would have to say that since 1990, when it won its independence, the country has been cast back into the shadows again, while fate has moved on to pull other small nations, each in its turn, briefly into the limelight: Lithuania, Bosnia, Somalia.... But this formulation risks confusing history – what happened, and what it means – with the inconstant attention of the media. For it was not fate that brought Namibia out of the shadows of history, but the Namibians' own obdurate refusal to remain there – their hundred-year resistance to colonial rule.

Their struggle was immensely costly. The Namibians were, to begin with, a collection of small agrarian and stock-keeping peoples, divided by language, culture, and competition for land, and dispersed over great distances by a harsh climate. They were confronted by industrialized powers – first imperial Germany, then South Africa – armed with the latest military technology and willing to use it ruthlessly. They themselves were at first armed only with a passionate sense of injustice, powerfully reinforced by Christianity, leading to a refusal to bow to their oppressors, no matter how overwhelming their power. Their first desperate effort at military resistance was met by genocide – the systematic slaughter of three-quarters of the Herero and half of the Nama peoples between 1904 and 1908. In the following two decades other, more local rebellions were also violently suppressed. And yet, after the Second World War, the Namibians gradually rebuilt their resistance movement, taking their case to the UN Trusteeship Council, the International Court of Justice, the Organization of African Unity and – last but not least – the two sides in the Cold War, eventually resuming armed struggle from bases outside Namibia in the mid-1960s.

It was not fate, then, but the Namibians themselves who forced their case onto the agenda of world history. They did so in another, deeper sense. As Soggot has also noted, the aura of 'Gothic megalomania' surrounding the infamous 'extermination order' issued by the German Chief of Staff, Von Trotha, against the Herero in 1904, and the systematic barbarity with which it was carried out, displayed a mindset which ultimately would lead to Nazism and the carnage of the Second World War.[2] Apartheid, and the carnage it has induced both within South Africa and throughout the southern cone of the continent, is a product of the same fundamental perversion. The Namibians thus have the distinction of being among the first to resist both these evil forces, doing so for long periods when the rest of the world was not anxious to be concerned.

The Two-Edged Sword

It was partly to honour this, the Namibians' real history, that the research presented in this book was undertaken. There is a dearth of serious accounts of the Namibian liberation struggle. The history of the South West Africa People's Organization (SWAPO), the liberation movement that came to lead that struggle, has been particularly prone to either demonization or canonization. For South African historians of the struggle SWAPO have been 'terrorists', 'communists', 'hapless bunglers', while too much of the solidarity literature presents a SWAPO incapable of error and free of all shortcomings. There is, then, a more illuminating history of the Namibian struggle to be written, one that takes seriously the grim nature of SWAPO's enemy, the South African colonial regime in Namibia, and the nobility of SWAPO's cause, while nonetheless surveying realistically the costs of the struggle, including those incurred by some of SWAPO's own political practices.

For 'the essence of war is violence', and the Namibians, in being forced to fight one, could not come out of it unscathed: the sword they took up was unavoidably two-edged. Their war was fought on grossly unequal terms, and the other side rarely took prisoners. The Namibians fought with limited equipment and training, little or no medical or other support, and limited security of communications. The combatants carried their equipment for days or weeks through mosquito-infested bush, to carry out missions of sometimes doubtful immediate value, and, as the years went on, with decreasing chances of survival. Inside the country, as the war escalated, repression mounted until jailing, brutality, torture and killing became routine.

In these conditions the liberation movement's own strengths and weaknesses were tested to the limit. During the period of armed struggle it was understandable that scholars sympathetic to the cause of liberation should stress the former rather than the latter; it was understandable, too, that at independence many, perhaps most, Namibians should want to forget the war and its costs. Santayana's dictum that those who forget the past are doomed to repeat it is valid, however, and forgetting the real history of the struggle also means forgetting the voices of those who lost out in the struggle's inner contradictions and conflicts. Yet these voices also have important things to say to the succeeding generation.

This, then, was one major reason for undertaking this study: not to write a definitive history of the Namibian struggle – this will require more time, and more distance – but to help to place the story, in its real complexity, back on the historical agenda; to help to keep it from slipping back into the shadows. A second reason was to look at the liberation struggle in terms of the legacy it bequeathed to post-independence development. This has relevance beyond the Namibian case. Every route to independence is unique, but there are lessons in the differences and the similarities between them. How might the nature of the independence struggle affect the subsequent balance between authoritarianism and democracy, property and people, church and state? These are hotly debated issues, especially as regards the claims that have sometimes been made for the liberating impact of independence achieved by armed, as opposed to purely political, struggle. Are there lessons to be learned from the Namibian experience, not only for Namibia but for South Africa and the region as a whole?

THE SOUTHERN AFRICAN CONTEXT

The Namibian liberation movement constituted in an important sense one front of a much broader struggle – the 'Thirty Years' War' against white minority rule that fanned out across the region between 1960 and 1990.[3] This epochal struggle began in the early 1960s with the first outbreak of armed resistance in Angola, the massacre at Sharpeville, and the subsequent banning of the nationalist movements in South Africa. Over the following three decades it became a regional war, fought in Mozambique, Angola, Zimbabwe, South Africa and Namibia. Its end was gradual – from the independence of Zimbabwe in 1980 to the troubled ceasefire in Angola in 1992 – and inconclusive in many ways, as the ends of prolonged wars perhaps always are. It is incontestable, however, that the release of Nelson Mandela in February 1990 and the launching of the politics of negotiation in South Africa marked a decisive turning point.

It was also in 1990 that Namibia, Africa's 'last colony', emerged as an independent state with SWAPO – itself founded, significantly enough, in 1960 – forming Namibia's first post-independence government.

SWAPO had played a distinctive role in driving this regional struggle forward, but it was also borne along by it. Indeed, regional and global politics determined the outcome in Namibia in crucial ways that SWAPO could not influence. It is no accident, for example, that when, in the late 1980s, the negotiations occurred that paved the way for 'independence elections' in Namibia under UN supervision, SWAPO was not actually present at the bargaining table. The new balance of power between the United States and a fast-retreating Soviet Union, the military stalemate between the South Africans and the Cubans in southern Angola, and the shifting equation of domestic politics inside South Africa itself: all these factors were crucial, indeed preponderant, in finally bringing the United Nations into Namibia to oversee a resolution to the long-standing stalemate there.

In contrast, as Chapter 2 shows, the war waged by SWAPO could have only a limited degree of success (even though in a guerrilla war to survive is a kind of success, and SWAPO did survive). Moreover, it was largely external circumstances that dictated SWAPO's acceptance, in the end, of a more formally democratic constitution for an independent Namibia than its ideological stance in the 1970s had led many observers to expect. And these circumstances also encouraged SWAPO's acceptance of a distinctly neo-colonial economic structure that contrasted with its left-leaning pronouncements in the days of armed struggle.

SWAPO'S ACHIEVEMENT, AND ITS COST

For all the external determinations of events, the fact remains that SWAPO was there at the end, ready and able to replace the departing South Africans. It stands as a remarkable achievement that a small group of Namibians living and working in Cape Town in the later 1950s could set in motion a movement that would, over the next thirty years, so challenge South Africa's illegal presence in South West Africa and so establish its own political coherence, military presence and international credibility as to emerge, by 1990, as the governing party of an independent Namibia. Even if many of the developments that produced this outcome were outside SWAPO's control, it is also true that SWAPO's role as the unremitting antagonist of South Africa – politically inside the country, diplomatically on the world stage, and militarily – was crucial. For the South African state made every effort to legitimate its rule – including, from the mid-1970s onwards, the attempt to secure a post-independence settlement in which Namibia would be ruled by a coalition of elected ethnic leaders dependent on Pretoria. It was SWAPO's struggle that, in the final analysis, foiled such plans.

Skilled footwork was necessary in order to produce this result. Stitching together the resources necessary for maintaining SWAPO's operations – often, in the early years, a real bootstraps effort – and 'working' both sides of the Cold War; moving gingerly on the slippery terrain provided by the front-line states that provided sanctuary and bases for forward operations; winning friends and neutralizing enemies internationally in order to sustain a convincing presence at the United Nations; weathering South Africa's sustained and determined military offensives and its ubiquitous 'security' operations; helping to keep the cost to South Africa sufficiently high to figure significantly in Pretoria's final decision to withdraw; managing the tensions involved in balancing the needs of the internal and the external struggle and of civilian versus military concerns: SWAPO's achievement on all these fronts was by any standard substantial.

Much more could be written about many of these subjects than is to be found in the present volume. Little is said here, for example, about SWAPO's diplomatic accomplishments, although this is an intriguing theme that deserves more research. Even Susan Brown's history of the more strictly military aspects of the war itself in Chapter 2 is less detailed about both that war's complex logistics and the immediate human drama of waging it on a day-to-day basis than another presentation might be. It is, instead, an account tailored to the central purpose stated in our preface: examining how the fact that Namibians were required to fight a war in order to achieve their independence marked both the country's leading liberation movement, SWAPO, and, more generally, the emergent Namibian polity itself.

For it is clear that against the political accomplishments of their struggle – independence, democratic elections, a SWAPO government – must also be set the fact that Namibians paid a heavy political price for the manner in which that struggle was won. It is a price, this book argues, that must also be acknowledged and carefully assessed. It included, notably, the fact that in exile hundreds of SWAPO's own members were detained, starved, tortured or even killed, and their claims to a democratic voice within the movement silenced. To study seriously events like SWAPO's crisis of the mid-1970s (the mis-named 'Shipanga crisis'), or the 'spy drama' that played itself out in Angola in the 1980s is to realize the need to modify the picture of SWAPO's development presented in SWAPO press releases and support movement literature over the years.

To date the most pungent statement of a 'counter-history' of the struggle that foregrounds this aspect has been put forward by some of those who had been imprisoned by SWAPO in Angola. In their view,

> SWAPO experienced throughout its development a whole number of crises that emerged basically as a result of the incompetence and the undemocratic and junta character of its leadership.... [The] leadership of SWAPO always resorted to using violent means including armies of the host countries in suppressing anybody who dared to complain about the problems within the organization. Hence it has always been operating like a paramilitary organization where force is the order of the day. The failure by the leadership of SWAPO to courageously tackle internal problems in the movement not only delayed the struggle but also led to the loss of many lives and undermined greatly the unity of our people.[4]

This account has been in disrepute since the issue of SWAPO's detainees was seized upon by South African agents, and by the conservative Democratic Turnhalle Alliance (DTA) opposition to SWAPO, for use in their bid to discredit SWAPO during the 1989 election of Namibia's new constituent assembly. Nonetheless, the ex-detainees' interpretation of the history of SWAPO contains a real measure of truth.

Indeed, these detainees were among those casualties of the struggle's inner contradictions and conflicts whose views must be considered in any balanced assessment. This was a point forcefully brought home to us as we pursued our research; on numerous occasions, when we interviewed those who had found themselves on the 'wrong' side of debates and conflicts within the movement, they emphasized that they now spoke, precisely, to be heard, and not for personal reasons alone. Independent Namibia offers a relatively open liberal-democratic terrain. How is that to be safeguarded most effectively? Many former dissidents expressed the hope that having their story told publicly would help make people more alert than they would otherwise be to any tendency on the part of SWAPO to revert to the negative practices of its past; with this aim even some SWAPO-aligned respondents agreed.

There is something else. While a formally democratic system has indeed emerged in Namibia, it seems fair to say that little popular empowerment has been realized. As noted above, the SWAPO leadership seems to have felt it had little choice but to accept a 'neo-colonial' niche within the regional and global economic system. The almost inevitable complement to a neo-colonial economics is a 'neo-colonial politics' which limits popular demands for radical social and economic policies. SWAPO appears to have accepted the resultant pattern of popular disempowerment with more comfort than its democratic declarations during the days of anti-colonial struggle led many of its supporters to expect.

Yet the continuity of SWAPO's political practice in this respect is actually quite striking. In exile, the leadership developed a political culture that frowned on spontaneity and debate, increasingly defined criticism as disloyalty, and eventually gave free rein to those in charge of the movement's 'security'. Moreover, this political culture had a significant impact inside Namibia, too, as the external leaders gradually came to make 'internal SWAPO' into an instrument of their external strategy, and increasingly discouraged militant activism even in those parts of the country where it was still possible.[5]

The suppression of democratic politics inside SWAPO also affected the movement's social and political thinking. Throughout the history of the struggle there were rank and file demands for accountability, majority rule, and the right to debate major policy issues. Had some of these demands been conceded it might have produced a different, more expansive political climate within the movement. Responding to the requirements and demands of a popular constituency would have been more necessary and, perhaps, more fundamentally radicalizing than the 'progressive' pronouncements of a handful of intellectuals within the movement could ever be. This, too, is a point to which we return in the chapters that follow.

LIBERATION AND DEMOCRACY IN THE 'THIRTY YEARS' WAR'

The paradox of 'liberation without democracy' that seems to stalk SWAPO's development may also be viewed instructively from a comparative perspective – highlighting similarities with and differences from the histories of other liberation movements fighting brutal racist dictatorships elsewhere in southern Africa (to go no further afield). For the possibility exists that the very process of struggling for liberation, especially by resort to force of arms, almost inevitably generates political practices that prefigure undemocratic outcomes. The imperatives of solidarity – the determination not to give aid and comfort to South Africa – certainly encouraged observers to blur this issue at the time. Even with the benefit of hindsight, however, some temptation exists to downplay this paradox, to write off any pull towards authoritarian practices within the liberation movements – and, by extension, within the new nations-in-the-making that these movements come to embody – as being not worthy of any special attention; or to see it, at worst, as being the inevitable if regrettable price of any liberation struggle.

Yet much of the literature on armed liberation struggles of 'progressive' provenance has posited a pull in the opposite direction, seeing guerillas involved in 'people's wars' as embedding their politics in popular aspirations in a novel, radicalizing and even democratizing way. The logic of protracted struggle, it was argued, made the politics of armed liberation movements more democratic and radical than those of other nationalist movements and more likely to lead to genuinely socialist outcomes in the post-liberation phase. Looking back at the experience of anti-imperialist struggles (both in southern African and elsewhere), can we now see such formulations to have been, to a significant extent, the stuff of myth?

Some revisionist literature would now suggest as much. For example, the second thoughts of Gerard Chaliand, expressed in the revised (1989) edition of his well-known 1977 volume, *Revolution in the Third World* (a book based primarily on his own first-hand experience with numerous anti-imperialist guerilla movements), make sobering reading in this regard.[6] For he argues that a misguided brand of Third Worldism tended, over many years, to mask contradictions within liberation movements and encourage a rather romantic reading of their political practice and potential. Such revisionism can lean too far in the opposite direction, of course: there were radicalizing, consciousness-raising effects that flowed from the SWAPO leaders' durability, tenacity and international success. Yet Chaliand is correct in drawing critical attention to the climate of the times that, during the 'Thirty Years' War' for southern African liberation, shaped much of the discourse of the liberation movements themselves and of their supporters around the world. Can there be any doubt that during those years of relative success (within the southern African region and beyond) both the movements and their international supporters too often allowed the rightness of their cause (and their preoccupation with the truly evil nature of the apartheid enemy) to dull their democratic sensibilities? The left really must know better in future;[7] seen in this light, SWAPO's experience may be instructive, perhaps even typical.[8]

Yet there also seems to be something *sui generis* about the SWAPO case – at least as regards the 'spy drama' that led to the detention and torture of hundreds of SWAPO members in prison camps in Angola in the 1980s. Of course, grim tales are emerging from the histories it is now becoming possible to write about liberation movements throughout southern Africa. For example, recent revelations of abuses within some of the ANC camps – most notably Quatro camp in Angola – suggest the existence of a pathology of liberation politics that may be general, if not universal.[9] But the ANC's concern to acknowledge and make some amends for what happened seems to distinguish it from SWAPO, which in the name of national reconciliation has refused any public enquiry into what happened at Lubango, transferred security personnel from there to the post-independence security apparatus, and appointed the Chief of Security at Lubango to high office.

It is important, then, to make a finer discrimination between the practices of the different liberation movements.[11] And this is also relevant to the discussion of the different degrees of radicalization that their struggles have evoked. For example, Frelimo – at least in the years before South African destabilization took its full toll in Mozambique – produced out of its liberation struggle a 'progressive' development project more sensitive to the needs of its popular constituency than did many other movements in southern Africa, including SWAPO. True, in subsequently establishing a 'developmental dictatorship' in independent Mozambique, Frelimo's often high-handed approach to politics helped to dash some the promise of its undertakings. One could certainly see in this – although there were many other factors making for such an outcome in Mozambique – a manifestation of the arrogance of power that seems to recur so frequently in the politics of liberation struggles. But there are distinctions to be made, nonetheless, and only a careful exploration of each case can begin to account for them.

Other cases further afield also offer interesting comparisons. For example, there is a suggestive analysis of the Somali National Movement (SNM) by Hussein Adam, published in mid-1992, that suggests that the SNM's practice of 'decentralized fund-raising [has given] the movement relative independence while enhancing accountability to its numerous supporters'. Here was an armed movement that had 'evolved a semi-democratic approach: it ... held popular congresses periodically to elect its leaders and decide its policies. Until recently, at least, contradictions among its leaders and supporting clans were handled politically rather than militarily.'[12] Within the Eritrean liberation struggle, too, there is evidence of a semi-democratization, with clearly hierarchical tendencies balanced against real space for dissent and an opportunity for substantive discussion at congresses;[13] one may legitimately wonder whether either the original escalation of the SWAPO crisis that occurred in Zambia in the mid-1970s, or the victimization of 'dissidents' that followed it, could easily have occurred had SWAPO accommodated dissent in a similar way. To extend such comparisons further would fall beyond the limited compass of this introduction. However, enough may have been said to underscore the importance of additional comparative work on such themes – and also to further warn against casting the discussion too rigidly in terms of ineluctable outcomes.

Moreover, there is another good reason for not seeing any one outcome of the politics of the Namibian liberation struggle as somehow inevitable. For many Namibians were as little inclined to yield to authoritarian practices within the liberation movement as they were to yield to South Africa's racist dictatorship. Anti-democratic practices were imposed on SWAPO's members, literally at gun-point, at a number of crucial moments in the movement's history, and some actually lost their lives in defence of a different approach. To affirm, at least as a working hypothesis, that things might have gone differently, that a range of alternative possibilities was open to SWAPO, will help us to give such moments – and such members – the kind of hearing at the bar of history they deserve.

MORAL QUESTIONS

Here we have begun to touch on some of the broader moral and political considerations alluded to earlier. Those who undertake to fight evil are themselves constantly confronted with difficult moral choices. In SWAPO's case, for example, combatants were often inadequately fed and equipped, and their security was vulnerable. If they were sent on missions in these circumstances, many would lose their lives: but were no missions to be undertaken? Inside the country, among a desperately poor population, the South African security forces could buy information easily, and had a large corps of pliant chiefs and headmen on the payroll to reinforce their efforts to intimidate the population: was no action to be taken against informers and quislings? The movement stood for liberation, equality and democracy, but it could not wish out of existence the ethnic, regional, age and other divisions within its ranks; were hierarchy, discipline, and even authoritarianism too high a price to pay for unity in face of South Africa's overwhelming military strength and lavishly funded propaganda machine?

These are delicate issues for outsiders to deal with, but even had we felt inclined to avoid them, our informants – their views strongly held, and often honed by bitter experiences – constantly challenged us to face them. We would, in any case, have found it impossible to avoid them. It is not that we feel able to pass judgements on the arguments and conflicts which these issues aroused; more often than not the outside researcher is left with the feeling that in similar circumstances he or she would not have acted with equal courage or commitment to principle. It is, rather, that no way of presenting the story can be innocent of a moral standpoint. Also, the people who have shaped Namibia's movements, parties, churches, community organizations and the like, in exile and at home, are fewer and far more accessible than they would be in a larger country, and often they alone know what happened, since so little documentary evidence exists. The result is that the way people felt, their sensibilities, their sense of justice, their fears and hopes – at least as they remember them – are part and parcel of the evidence, impossible to ignore.

It also needs to be borne in mind that, in seeking and being given a unique responsibility for liberating the country, the SWAPO leadership assumed unique obligations, especially towards all the members of the movement in exile. In late 1976, after intensive lobbying, the UN General Assembly recognized SWAPO as the 'sole and authentic representative of the Namibian people'. From this point on most Namibians in exile became almost totally dependent on SWAPO. In any case of conflict between individual members of SWAPO and the leadership, governments sympathetic to SWAPO, UN agencies and non-governmental solidarity organizations all naturally tended to defer to the views of the SWAPO leadership. To do otherwise would have seemed to question an authority that had been conferred on the SWAPO leaders by the international community, not just one they claimed for themselves.

This gave SWAPO a status that the ANC and other African liberation movements did not enjoy, and it left SWAPO's rank and file very much in the hands of the leadership. They had no passports, and could only live outside Namibia – as combatants, students, or camp residents – on the basis of arrangements made between SWAPO and foreign governments. To go back to Namibia was not always possible, and in any case meant almost certain punishment by the South Africans; to return on South African terms (renouncing violence and giving information about SWAPO abroad) led to self-hatred and probable ostracism within their own communities.

The leadership was well aware of its responsibility for members in exile. For example, a major reason for convening a 'Consultative Congress' in Tanga in 1969, that took far-reaching decisions in spite of the absence of any representatives from inside Namibia, was recognition of the need to give legitimacy to PLAN combatants, whom the South Africans were treating as mere criminals and terrorists when they captured them.[14] Yet the fact remains that the leadership was not really accountable for the way it exercised this responsibility: especially after 1966, there was no one else to whom members could appeal if, for example, SWAPO unreasonably separated them from their husbands or wives, withdrew their educational scholarships abroad or imprisoned them as suspected spies. Thus it is also necessary to consider the way the SWAPO leadership exercised its extraordinary power over the Namibians who put themselves under its protection in exile, however much weight must always be given to the exigencies of the war that affected all their actions.

Thus the standpoint from which we have tried to present the story reflects (we hope) the contradictions that Namibians themselves experienced in the struggle: a commitment to liberation, and with it, for many within SWAPO, a commitment to the twin ideals of democracy and socialism; but, tempering this commitment, the recognition that what struggling for these goals demanded in practice was often far from obvious. The old revolutionary dilemmas about the use of force and terror, the nature of leadership, the balance to be struck between inner-party democracy and the need for discipline, the tension created between the building of a nationalist movement embracing all regions and classes and a revolutionary movement with broader transformatory goals: all these are echoed in the Namibian struggle. And besides such issues of high principle there was, of course, also a range of less altruistic motives at work within the liberation movement, no doubt often intensified by the claustrophobic and alienating nature of exile life: ambition, the drive for power, greed, personal rivalry, fear and the rest.

Namibia's History: Some Key Themes

Although the chapters that follow assume no prior knowledge of Namibian or South African history, there are some themes that recur in many of them which it may be useful to highlight at the outset, both to set the stage and to minimize the need for repetition.[15] These themes are settler colonialism, the nature of the colonial economy, the role of the churches and the school system, the 'north/south' distinction, and certain distinctive features of Namibian nationalism.

A SETTLER COLONY

Namibia's colonial history is distinctive in several important respects. Owing to the country's extreme dryness – there are no year-round rivers in Namibia, apart from the Cunene and the Kavango on its northern border, and the Orange River on its southern – it was sparsely populated from the first (and to this day contains barely 1.5 million people). Hence it was relatively vulnerable to the well-armed foreigners – individuals and groups – who began entering from the south as the nineteenth century advanced, in search of cattle land or minerals on the plateau lying inland from the Namib desert. The Orlam and the Basters, who established themselves east and south of Windhoek respectively, were the most noteworthy distinct groups of newcomers (though eventually the Orlam were assimilated by the Nama), but white settlers from South Africa were also present by the end of the century, as were German traders and missionaries. German colonial control was established in the 1880s, and finally consolidated with the genocide of the Herero and the Nama between 1904 and 1908.

The result was a 'highland clearance' on a grand scale. The surviving black populations of central and southern Namibia were systematically pushed off the productive plateau onto its edges, where overcrowding on lands with at best marginal rainfall gradually led to soil exhaustion. These so-called 'communal lands' are easily recognized today by the near-disappearance of ground cover, their little towns and settlements surviving on remittances from family members working on white settler farms or in town, and on the older generation's old-age pensions.

The essence of German colonial rule has been summed up succinctly by Katjavivi:

> First, land was taken from the Namibian people and made available to German settlers. Second, traditional structures were destroyed. Third, Namibians were used as forced labourers on the now white-owned land and the new mines and early industries.... [16]

The butchery of the Herero and Nama was so devastating that not enough labour could be obtained from the southern peoples, even though working for the settlers was made virtually obligatory through pass and vagrancy laws. From early on, therefore, most migrant workers were recruited from the Ovambo and Kavango in the north. The Ovambo and Kavango peoples, and the Makololo groups in eastern Caprivi, living as they did on relatively well-watered land, accounted for about two-thirds of the total population. The German authorities essentially left them alone, so long as enough migrant workers were forthcoming, drawing an official 'red line' between them and the areas of white settlement to the south. Law and order in the north was left in the hands of the chiefs, the colonial police confining their attention to the area south of the red line, which was known as the 'police zone' down to independence in 1990. Although the colonial border between German South West Africa and Portuguese-controlled Angola ran along the Cunene and Kavango rivers, the Ovambo and Kavango peoples were ethnically and economically linked to the peoples on the Angolan side of it;[17] whereas their connection to the peoples of the police zone in the south was established only gradually through the effects of migrant labour, urbanization, and the emergence of modern nationalist politics in the late 1950s.

In 1915 South African forces fighting on the British side in the First World War seized control of South West Africa from Germany, and in 1920 South Africa assumed a mandate for the territory under the League of Nations. German settlers were largely replaced by Afrikaner settlers, and the process of evicting Namibians from the highlands was resumed. Eventually a tidying-up operation, in the spirit of apartheid, was conducted in the late 1960s, in which the remnants of non-white farming in the central plateau were all extinguished (except for the Rehobothers); and so-called 'second-tier authorities' – in effect bantustan administrations – were set up on the now more than ever reduced and impoverished margins of what had once been the indigenous people's homelands (see Map 2, p. xi).

The German policy of violent repression was continued under South African rule: at various times between 1917 and 1932 the Kwanyama-speaking and Kuambi-speaking Ovambo in the north, and the Bondelswart and Rehobothers in the south, were all disciplined through punitive expeditions. From the 1930s to the late 1950s there was a sort of respite, but with the evolution of apartheid in South Africa in the 1950s, and the emergence of new forms of resistance in Namibia, the violence resumed, on an increasingly appalling scale. No one who has not at least read David Soggot's account of the final phase of South African colonialism in Namibia can begin to understand what routine state violence against a civilian population really means.[18] A political activist who fell into the hands of the police, the army, or the counter-insurgency unit, Koevoet ('Crowbar'), was very likely to be beaten, if not systematically tortured, and quite likely (especially when taken by Koevoet) to be killed. To read how men, women and even children were routinely beaten, kicked, jumped on, whipped, cut, torn, burned, electrically shocked, suffocated in water, buried in the ground, hung from chains, ropes and wires ... is to be brought up short, once again, by what Hannah Arendt called 'the banality of evil'. It is hard to remember that this happened, over many years, to some of the very people one is talking to today, and their close relatives and friends: it is also essential to remember that SWAPO had to deal with an enemy capable of this, one that, in the end quite explicitly, regarded Namibians as inferior human beings, who could be treated inhumanly.

A final dimension of Namibia's distinctive experience of colonialism is that, from very early in the history of white penetration onwards, Namibian leaders were remarkably alert to the international context. As soon as the United Nations came into existence they began an energetic process of petitioning in New York, first to thwart South Africa's effort to incorporate the country into South Africa, and later to get the UN to declare South Africa's continued occupation illegal, and to have the UN supervise a pre-independence election and a South African withdrawal. Petitioning was begun in 1946 by Namibian chiefs, especially Chief Hosea Kutako of the Herero, but was continued and intensified, in a more 'modern' register, by the nationalist organizations SWANU and SWAPO from the early 1960s onwards. As we will constantly see, the armed struggle, which SWAPO took up in the mid-1960s in face of the meagre results produced by petitioning and UN diplomacy, was never a substitute, but always a parallel strategy (in SWAPO parlance, a military 'front' alongside the diplomatic 'front'). In this respect the Namibians' struggle had a different character from that of other oppressed peoples who also took up arms but did not enjoy the enormous additional leverage that Namibia's trusteeship status conferred.

THE COLONIAL ECONOMY

Some of the essential features of the colonial economy have been mentioned. First, there was a so-called commercial farm sector on the inland plateau, consisting of enormous white-owned ranches employing very low-paid black labour and accounting for 10–20 per cent of national income prior to independence. Second, a fishery based in Walvis Bay in its heyday accounted for almost a quarter of the national income, before ruthless overfishing by South African and foreign fleets cut the staple pilchard and mackerel catch from over ten million tons annually in the 1960s, to 100,000–200,000 tons annually since the end of the 1970s. The fish processing plants, which were and are mainly South African-owned, also employed significant numbers of Namibians. Third, there was a mining sector (also owned and controlled by South African and Western multinationals), based mainly on diamonds (found in a vast, closed Diamond Area, covering the entire south-western coastal region) but including uranium, copper, lead, zinc, and other less important minerals. Fourth, an essentially food-producing communal farm sector, overwhelmingly dominated (numerically speaking) by the Ovambo and Kavango peoples, contributed critically to the subsistence of these population groups but exported to the rest of the country, or anywhere else, virtually nothing at all. Fifth and last, a state sector accounted by the 1980s for some 30 per cent of total national expenditure, including, at that time, massive military outlays, especially in the north (these in turn generated a bizarre consumer economy of supermarkets and bottlestores whose post-independence future was, to say the least, problematic).

The key support of this whole structure was the system of migrant labour, overwhelmingly drawn from the Ovambo. Until 1972 it was based on contracts which bound the workers to work for wages worth about 5 per cent of white wages, and to live in bleak and insanitary 'compounds', returning home to their families only at two-year intervals. Hatred of this system was the central issue prompting the formation of SWAPO's predecessor, the Ovamboland People's Organization (originally the Ovamboland People's Congress) in 1959; and it continued to fuel the nationalist movement until the general strike of contract workers in 1971–2 brought about its gradual abandonment (although migrant labour persisted).

This economy was not only dominated by foreign ownership, mainly South African (the South African share of total assets was estimated at 91 per cent in 1980); it was also virtually completely integrated into the South African market, taking most of its imports from the Republic, and exporting virtually all its non-mineral exports, and all its diamonds, to it. Moreover Walvis Bay, Namibia's only deep-water port, was initially retained as a South African enclave at independence. The constraints to be overcome in any future effort to achieve economic independence were thus very real.

THE CHURCHES AND EDUCATION

It is commonly estimated that more than 90 per cent of Namibians belong to a Christian church, the highest rate in Africa. The Christian churches have had an enormous impact on Namibia, even if the educational system for black Namibians, which both the German and the South African colonialists left largely to the missions (and hence funded very inadequately), was and is miserably inadequate even by South African standards. Christian moral feeling and biblical imagery permeate the history and language of the liberation struggle to a striking extent, while the demand for education, and the political skills and ambitions it generated, are constant themes. In their chapters Steenkamp and Maseko provide much information on the churches and the education system; only the broad outlines need be indicated here.

The initial Christianizing effort came from German Lutherans of the Rhenish Missionary Society, starting in the early nineteenth century. They concentrated on what became the police zone. The Rhenish missionaries were conservative and paternalist, but amid a social catastrophe culminating in the genocide described above the church did provide stability and support of a kind, and as a result there was eventually a wholesale acceptance of Christianity. Later, however, reacting against the church's complicity in the racist social and political system, large numbers of 'southerners' converted to the African Methodist Episcopal church (AME), introduced from the USA in the 1940s, which soon became the leading church in the south. Later still, a further split occurred in the remaining Lutheran church in the south, with the formation of an African-controlled Evangelical Lutheran Church, separate from the white-controlled German Evangelical Lutheran Church.

The north, by contrast, was Christianized by Finnish Lutherans from the 1870s onwards. The Finns were less closely linked to the dominant white community in the south, and had some ideas – such as the provision of educational opportunities for girls as well as boys – which contained many seeds of change. They were also quicker than any of the other denominations (except the African-led AME) to hand over control to Africans: the first African Bishop of the Evangelical Lutheran Church in Namibia (ELCIN), as the Lutheran church in the north was eventually called, was appointed in 1960. ELCIN was much the biggest denomination, and as the military struggle intensified it emerged as in some ways a religious counterpart to SWAPO in the north. Eventually all the popular churches were obliged to come out against the apartheid state, and in 1978 they converged to form the Council of Churches in Namibia, which 'threw its weight behind the opposition to Apartheid and the South African government'.[19] Indeed, in the 1980s the CCN became almost a leading arm of SWAPO inside Namibia, employing various SWAPO office-bearers and activists and channelling external funds to SWAPO-approved development projects.

Education for non-white Namibians, and especially for 'blacks' (i.e., excluding the so-called coloureds and the Rehoboth Basters), remained extremely limited and rudimentary until very late in the colonial period. Paradoxically, it was under the 1964 Odendaal Plan for separate development that a belated expansion of African education began, with the state taking over responsibility from the missions. Total school enrolments rose from just under 44,000 non-whites (of whom perhaps a quarter were coloured or Baster) in 1960, to just under 350,000 in 1987; and, especially in the 1980s, there was a significant expansion of high-school places for non-whites, even though the quality of this education, much of it provided by untrained teachers, was often very low.[20] Not surprisingly, the new school classes became important arenas of struggle in the 1980s, especially in the north where serving members of the South African Defence

Force were increasingly put into the classrooms as teachers. From the 1970s onwards, as well, the trickle of non-whites who succeeded in qualifying for higher education in South Africa gradually widened into a modest but definite stream, and these students later returned, with their higher training and their exposure to the escalating struggle in the Republic, to galvanize the internal resistance in Namibia and – from the late 1970s onwards – to raise the demand for a much wider internal political mobilization, and greater inner-party democracy in SWAPO itself.[21]

'NORTH' AND 'SOUTH'

Since independence, Windhoek has become the political centre for SWAPO, not just for its opponents: and the 'south' refers more and more to the Nama and Rehoboth areas south of Windhoek. Historically, however, the 'north' was the area north of the 'police zone' and, from the vantage point of that north, the 'south' included Herero and Damara country to the north-east and north-west of Windhoek respectively, as well as Nama and Rehoboth territory to the south. During the struggle these distinctions were important, and remain so to some extent today, even if the referents of the terms are shifting.

In the first place, the experience of colonialism was very different for the Nama and the Herero – and in general all the peoples of the police zone – on the one hand, and the northern peoples, above all the Ovambo, on the other. Early in the colonial period the 'southerners' lost their stock, their homelands and, in the case of the Nama and Herero, the lives of most of their people, after fighting desperate and hopeless wars of resistance. Their social systems were dissolved, and they were forced to integrate into the white economy as cheap labour, while their own economies stagnated on the infertile margins. They adopted Christianity, and they got the greater part of such education as was provided by the missions for blacks. Proximity to South Africa was also important: they were more likely to go there, or to get there earlier, than the northerners, and they went as individuals rather than as contract workers bound to a designated employer. They were also more likely to be allowed to live in townships, as workers in the white towns; and, besides their mother tongues, they spoke Afrikaans.[22]

Among the Herero many people never gave up their sense of having once been the largest and richest people of the southern plateau, and the Herero produced a distinguished line of leaders who were prominent at all stages in the nationalist movement. Yet even these Herero activists, for all their concern with Herero cultural traditions, tended also to be strongly influenced by Christian individualism and apt to think in terms of modern associational politics, and of careers and status in the modern public sphere, rather than of accumulation and status in the ethnic homeland.

People who grew up in the north, by contrast – and most significantly the Ovambo, numbering over half the total population – tended to remain more strongly grounded in their ethnic culture and social structure, in spite of the changes produced by Christianization and by migrant labour. The Ovambo, Kavango and Caprivi peoples had not lost land, stock, or population under colonialism, and they were later in getting schooling on a significant scale. Their chiefs might be seen increasingly as puppets of the South African regime, but not all were. Traditional respect was still accorded to many of them, even after 23 years of war; traditional justice was still sought from them. Moreover, though northern men might learn Afrikaans in the mines or in the Walvis Bay fish factories, it was not the *lingua franca* of the north, and was rarely spoken by northern women; it is significant that when the Ovambo 'homeland' government became responsible for education in the mid-1970s, even they opted to make English the language of instruction, rather than Afrikaans, as was the case throughout the south.

In other words, northern society remained in many ways intact and distinct, in spite of being subjected to enormous stresses. People from the north tended to retain a strong corporate spirit, though Ovambo, Kavango or Caprivian society was not without internal conflicts. Quite to the contrary, intense 'clan' rivalries existed, such as that between the Kwanyama- and the Ndonga-speaking clans of the Ovambo, or the Subia and the Fwe in eastern Caprivi. These rivalries no longer had any real southern equivalent, because the dynamic principles of southern society were no longer to be found in traditional relationships. By the same token, southerners do not seem to have had any concept exactly equivalent to the Oshivambo term *mbuiti*, meaning someone who has not been raised in the homeland – that is, a second- or third-generation urban Oshivambo-speaker.

Last but not least, as the struggle intensified, especially after 1974 when the SADF took over control of security in the north from the police, the north became a theatre of war. Life became increasingly insecure. Many of the young fled into exile, and their parents and elders lived under a curfew, in constant danger from land-mines, and subject to an increasingly ruthless competition for their allegiance between PLAN guerillas and the security forces. Meetings were banned, repression was absolute. Southerners who were active in the struggle, and thought they had seen enough of police brutality, were stunned by the scale and violence of the military repression in the north when they occasionally managed to go there in the late 1970s and after.

It is difficult to know how much to make of these distinctions. On the one hand, from its inception the SWAPO leadership was drawn from both south and north, and in spite of the numerical preponderance of the Ovambo, especially in the movement in exile, unity and the transcending of traditional divisions was a principle constantly reiterated by the leadership. At the same time, the external observer cannot but be struck by how much informal political analysis in Namibia turns on issues of ethnicity. This is particularly marked in discussions of SWAPO where, as we will see in the next section, there seems to be a great temptation to explain SWAPO's internal politics in just such terms – either with reference to Ovambo hegemony within the movement or, even more pointedly, with reference to the role played by a clique of senior Kwanyama-speaking leaders said, from time to time, to have self-consciously developed and advanced its own agenda within and through SWAPO. These are difficult matters to judge – especially for outsiders – and some Namibian commentators may feel we have underestimated their significance.

THE NATIONALIST CHALLENGE

All the above factors helped to define Namibian nationalism in ways to be pursued in more detail in the chapters that follow; only a few of the most central features are sketched here.

There was, first, the relatively overwhelming strength of the South African presence. South Africa could not be 'driven out' of Namibia; on the contrary, South Africa's military weight, the outright defeats it was able to inflict and the constant pressure it exerted by means of its elaborate security operations (including the penetration of SWAPO by spies and the sowing of disinformation), eventually affected the liberation movement in exile in subtle and increasingly negative ways. Of course, the day-to-day financial and political costs of the armed presence that South Africa was forced to sustain in northern Namibia were significant, even though these costs were partly determined by South Africa's larger war aims in Angola. However, as Chapter 2 shows, it was the broader geo-political and military dynamic of the region, in which SWAPO's military activity could play only a limited role, that ultimately dictated South Africa's acceptance of the UN-supervised transition, and SWAPO's accession to power.

SWAPO did, however, achieve impressive diplomatic successes. Finessing the entry of the UN into the Namibian political process became, as we have seen, SWAPO's central strategy and it proved, ultimately, to be a winning one. Was it, for Namibians, also an ambiguous one? Certainly, the cause of Namibian liberation gained great credibility from the steps by which the United Nations came to grant SWAPO status as, first, the 'authentic' and, later, the 'sole and authentic' representative of the Namibian people. But a second consideration – one we will explore further in Chapter 3 – seems inevitably to intrude: did this externally defined ascendancy also help encourage the SWAPO leadership's all too high-handed disregard of other voices, both within the movement and without?

The United Nations connection had one further implication: it meant that South Africa never felt sufficiently confident to ban outright SWAPO's legal political presence inside the country. Of course, South Africa may have had additional grounds for adopting this tactic, feeling constrained, perhaps, to keep just enough of a semblance of open political activity alive in Namibia to lend some credibility to its various attempts (the Turnhalle initiative of the late-1970s, the 'transitional government' of the 1980s) to create an internal settlement tailored to its own interests. In any case, it certainly felt no qualms about the most brutal kinds of harassment of the movement, depriving it of any real above-ground existence in the northern war zone and comprehensively hounding it further south.

Still, the fact that the movement retained a formal legality, combined with its inability to shake the grip of South Africa's military on the north, meant that SWAPO politics inside Namibia did not take place in liberated areas. Instead, in some parts of Namibia – and by the late 1970s this meant the centre and south of the country, away from the northern 'war zone' – SWAPO politics developed out in the open, attaining a real public presence. Was this relatively open political terrain adequately exploited? Certainly, some have argued that the pursuit of exclusive diplomatic standing and armed struggle drew SWAPO too far away from from what was possible closer to home (especially after 1978); such critics have even suggested that SWAPO's 'militarist' emphasis was actually to become something of a self-fulfilling prophecy, justifying a level of South African militarization of Namibia that Pretoria might otherwise have had difficulty in legitimating. Others, more modestly, have argued that at the very least the preoccupations of SWAPO's external leaders led them to rein in excessively the kind of popularly based 'politics of confrontation' that were feasible inside Namibia itself, with some significant negative consequences for post-independence political life.

That some significant instrumentalization and demobilization of internal SWAPO by the external leadership did occur is documented in Chapter 4. The diverse ways in which this fact can be interpreted, however, are particularly revealing of the complexities that confront any analyst of Namibian politics. The suggestion that certain broad strategic calculations shaped the external SWAPO leadership's relationship to SWAPO inside Namibia has merit, but other explanations are also plausible, not least one that would highlight the external leadership's reluctance to see a new cadre of SWAPO leaders emerge, as potential rivals, from a vibrant and relatively autonomous political process inside the country.

Of course, one might also emphasize the importance of the fact that, whatever terrain may have existed for open political struggle inside Namibia, it did not include the northern 'war zone': yet this was where SWAPO's original core support had sprung from, and where more than half the country's population lived. Was the external leadership's principal objective in seeking to control internal politics not, perhaps, to offset – in the interests of sustaining a broadly national project – any too exclusively southern tilt to the internal movement's activities, one that would inevitably tend to 'disenfranchise' those Namibians held under the repressive control of the South African security apparatus in the north? Plausible enough, perhaps, yet the fact remains that such an explanation – cast primarily in terms of 'nation building' – would be considered by other observers to be merely naïve: prone, precisely, to underestimating the extent to which the narrower power calculations (of the kind alluded to above) guided the external leaders' attitudes towards internal political developments.

Many of these observers would argue that the 'nation building' explanation also underestimates the force of narrower ethnic considerations – Ovambo-centred or more narrowly Kwanyama in thrust – in premissing the north/south calculations of at least some of the external leaders. We have alluded to the difficulty of identifying and attaching appropriate weight to such variables and we must reiterate the point here. Nonetheless, the fact remains that the diversity of Namibia – in terms of ethnic background, regional origin, religious affiliation, educational attainment and the like – is a constantly recurring factor in Namibian politics. While SWAPO has achieved some real success in knitting together its diverse constituencies, we have noted that it is commonplace inside Namibia to explain tendencies towards authoritarianism within SWAPO in terms of social divisions, and of ethnic divisions in particular. For some commentators it is precisely Ovambo society's inherited undemocratic norms and the supposed persistence, among an older generation of nationalist leaders, of a predilection for quasi-traditionalist (chief-centric?) structures of authority that needs to be emphasized. We are reluctant to go so far and indeed adumbrate many other possible factors by way of explanation in the chapters that follow. But if, as we will argue, an authoritarian political culture can be seen to have crystallized out of the practices of SWAPO in exile over three decades, we cannot altogether avoid the question of how much explanatory weight should be given to the ethnic factor.

Ethnic explanations have also proved tempting in relation to the 'spy drama' of the 1980s, when so many of the victims were known to be southerners. Certainly, some survivors have testified to their own conviction that, judging from the attitudes of their jailers, their ethnic backgrounds told strongly against them. At the same time, many victims were not southerners at all. As we will see in Chapter 3, generational differences and differences in educational attainment levels were also important. This was even more true of SWAPO's 1976 crisis. Then, most of the main targets of the leadership's crackdown were themselves Ovambo – but they were also, on the whole, younger and relatively more educated, as well as being the products of political experiences and expectations very different from those of the senior SWAPO leaders. In short, the politics of diversity, within Namibia and within SWAPO, are extremely complicated.

SIMULTANEOUS CHRONOLOGIES

Such are some of the complexities that will confront us. More generally, it is evident that one of the most difficult challenges facing any historical inquiry is the existence of several different time lines – different 'histories', each with something of its own logic and momentum – that nonetheless intersect and jointly affect the situation under study. Every historical event, every historical process, is in this sense over-determined, making it virtually impossible ever to hold enough other strands of determination constant so as to reach, confidently, some definitive account of any one of them. As, during the research, we traced the complex weave of factors that helped shape the thrust and, ultimately, the impact of SWAPO's liberation struggle, this problem presented itself in an acute way.

The regional and global dynamics of southern Africa's 'Thirty Years' War', and the evolution of South Africa's own domestic politics, rolled on, often shaping Namibian outcomes in quite fundamental ways. We have alluded, in this respect, to the crowded conjuncture that produced the final denouement of SWAPO's struggle: the UN-supervised elections of 1989. Or consider other such external developments as John Vorster's attempt to ensnare Zambia's Kenneth Kaunda in a dialogue in the 1970s, or South Africa's decision (taken in collusion with the Americans) to carry the war aggressively into Angola in the 1980s and to link a settlement in Namibia to Cuban withdrawal from Angola: these developments also fundamentally affected SWAPO's struggle.

Conversely, Namibians in the resistance took many cues from struggles in South Africa, and beyond.[23] It was no accident, for example, that much of the impetus for establishing SWAPO's predecessor organization, the Ovamboland People's Organization (OPO), came from Namibians resident in South Africa and was inspired by the dramatic political upheavals there during the 1950s.[24] At various other decisive moments the actions of South African students, township residents and workers became key points of reference for the resistance efforts of young Namibians, many of whom had their own first-hand experience of such South African developments in any case.[25] In parallel fashion but on an even broader stage SWAPO's decision in the early 1960s to take the route of armed struggle was framed by the general ambience supportive of such a strategy to be found in Dar es Salaam, and in OAU circles, at that time. Such crucial intersections of different historical time lines could be multiplied and indeed will be alluded to frequently in the pages that follow.

And yet – to return to where we began this introduction – it remains the case that the Namibians were also making their own history. The broad sweep of this reality is, at one level, quite clear. SWAPO emerged in the 1960s as the key expression of nationalist resistance to South Africa's illegal presence in Namibia, and slowly but surely established sufficient military presence, diplomatic credibility and political visibility on the ground inside Namibia to make it difficult for South Africa to enforce its rule or give that rule any novel brand of legitimacy. Thus, from modest beginnings in Dar es Salaam when SWAPO's military effort was still quite notional and its international presence still fledgling, SWAPO grew slowly, and shifted its centre of gravity to Zambia. There, enlarged by the spill-over from the dramatic student and worker activism experienced inside Namibia in the early 1970s, and facilitated by the collapse of Portuguese colonialism in neighbouring Angola, the organization developed more rapidly, shifting its headquarters to Luanda in 1978. By the turn of the decade military confrontation with South Africa had reached its peak.

This success proved extremely difficult to sustain in the 1980s, such was the nature of the South African backlash. SWAPO continued to advance diplomatically, however, both in further isolating South Africa on the Namibia question and in establishing its own credentials as the Namibian answer. Inside Namibia itself SWAPO exercised a strong pull on the loyalties of the great majority of those those who continued to resist South African occupation and white domination – whether in the churches, the schools or the workplaces. In short, this history of nationalist accomplishment, with SWAPO at its core, constitutes one central theme of the story that follows.

As indicated earlier, however, this story has another side. Indeed, we have felt a responsibility to identify as clearly as possible the ways in which mounting a nationalist challenge by force of arms has proven to be a 'two-edged sword' for Namibians. Since some of the new information we have collected – difficult if not impossible to come by so long as the liberation war was in progress – throws light on the grimmer side of SWAPO's story, some may feel we have leaned too far in a revisionist direction. We hope not: we have sought to recognize SWAPO's deservedly central place in the history of Namibia's liberation struggle, but at the same time to grasp its history whole: as being complex and fugitive, fraught with moral and political dilemmas, heroic and horrific by turns.

Certainly, it is no part of our intention to give aid or comfort to any who wish Namibia ill, or who seek to detract from the achievements of its struggle. We doubt that this can be the primary result of attempting to tell the story as honestly and accurately as possible. In any case, our work makes no claim to be definitive, but should be regarded as an invitation to others, not least Namibian scholars and activists them-selves, to sustain a debate about the country's past – whether, in the process, they find themselves confirming anything we say, or contradicting it. One index of how liberated Namibia has actually become will be the extent to which such debate continues.

The Chapters

The first part of this book, Chapters 2–5, presents an historical overview of Namibia's struggle for independence, with principal emphasis on the role of SWAPO as the key military, diplomatic and political actor, both in exile and inside Namibia itself. Thus in

Chapter 2 Susan Brown, while not ignoring South African sources, presents what is first and foremost a thorough account of the ebbs and flows of SWAPO's own war of liberation. The two chapters by Saul and Leys that follow survey the development of SWAPO's political practice, without and within Namibia, and in doing so pay considerable attention – for reasons this introduction has already explained – to the complex pattern of the movement's own inner-party politics. Finally, Philip Steenkamp reviews the role of the churches in the Namibian struggle, a history that intersects with SWAPO's history in ways that are, by turns, both inspiring and unsettling.

The next part poses questions about the impact of the liberation struggle on civil society and the state in Namibia. In Chapter 6 Sipho Maseko looks at the role of students as an active force both within the independence struggle itself and subsequently, as students have tried to redefine their role in post-independence society. In Chapter 7 Colin Leys surveys the problematic area of policing in the transition from repression to the goal of 'policing by consent', while in Chapter 8 Chris Tapscott explores the way in which the Namibian class structure has helped define the conflicts that cut across society, while also being inflected in its development by those very conflicts.

Finally, we attempt in the last part to reflect on the legacy for Namibia, present and future, of the struggle whose inner history is explored in the previous chapters. In Chapter 9 Lauren Dobell surveys SWAPO's first years in office, while in a brief afterword we try to capture something of the range of questions about Namibia's future that are posed by our analysis of both the accomplishments and the contradictions of the country's liberation struggle.

Notes

1. David Soggot, *Namibia: The Violent Heritage* (London: Rex Collings, 1986), p. ix.
2. *Ibid.*, p. x.
3. For an overview of the broad dynamics of this 'Thirty Years' War', see John S. Saul, 'The Southern African revolution', in his *Recolonization and Resistance: Southern Africa in the 1990s* (Trenton: Africa World Press, 1993), Chapter 1.
4. The document produced by the Parents' Committee from which this quotation is drawn is republished in Nico Basson and Ben Motinga (eds), *Call Them Spies – a Documentary Account of the SWAPO Spy Drama* (Windhoek and Johannesburg: African Communications Project, 1989).
5. Like so many other interpretations of SWAPO's history, this observation regarding the relationship between 'internal' and 'external' SWAPO is bound to be controversial. The point is amplified, with appropriate documentation, in Chapter 4, while some significant ambiguities that must attach to any discussion of the internal/external dialectic in the Namibian liberation struggle are further discussed at a later point in this introduction (pp. 14–15).
6. Gerard Chaliand, *Revolution in the Third World: Currents and Conflicts in Asia, Africa and Latin America*, revised edition (New York: Viking Penguin, 1989).
7. Undoubtedly, a variant of myopic self-righteousness concerning such matters has also characterized the political right, both then and now, and is, if anything, even more dangerous: ignoring the importance of class differences and trumpeting the unalloyed virtues of the market, this view heralds, in the name of democracy, a version of 'political pluralism' that is itself fundamentally disempowering (see Chapter 10, below). But this fact should not excuse the left from some hard thinking of its own on the question of democracy.
8. For an interesting case study that suggests the way in which the pursuit of a particular kind of international recognition – in some ways parallel to SWAPO's attempt to establish its international legitimacy over and against the South African claim in Namibia – affects liberation movement politics, see Jeffrey M. Shulman, 'Wars of liberation and the international system: Western Sahara – a case in point', in I. L. Markowitz (ed.), *Studies in Class and Power in Africa* (New York and Oxford: Oxford University Press, 1987). Shulman, who also finds similar tendencies at work in the case of the Algerian struggle, suggests that 'in order to fulfil the functions of statehood and solicit recognition of its announced state, the liberation party creates a hierarchical political and military command' (p. 75).

9. On this subject, the reports of the ANC's two commissions of enquiry in 1992 and 1993 respectively bear noting. For an evaluation of the first of these, see Tom Lodge, 'Spectres from the camps: the ANC's Commission of Enquiry', *Southern Africa Report/SAR* (Toronto), 8, 3–4 (January–February 1993); and for an instructive reflection from within the ANC on both of these enquiries and their implications, see the interview with Albie Sachs (' Serious abuses ') published in *SAR*, 9, 2 (November 1993).

11. For the case of the Zimbabwean liberation struggle, see the ongoing work of David Moore, for example his paper 'The Zimbabwean People's Army and ZANU's interregnum: innovative military, ideological and political strategies' presented to the Uppsala Seminar on Religion and War in Zimbabwe, Uppsala, Sweden, March 1992 and his 'Marxism, militancy and militarism in the Zimbabwean liberation war: debates on democracy and the Zimbabwean People's Army (ZIPA), 1975–1977', presented to the workshop of the Canadian Research Consortium on Southern Africa, Queen's University, Kingston, December 1992.

12. Hussein Adam, 'Somalia: militarism, warlordism or democracy?', *Review of African Political Economy*, 54 (July 1992), p. 19.

13. Personal communication with cadres involved. As it happens, relatively little of analytical substance has been written regarding the *internal* politics of the Eritrean movement. However, at least one Eritrean cadre with whom we spoke qualified his emphasis on the various positive features we have mentioned by suggesting that participants have nonetheless tended to romanticize the achievements of the Eritrean movement in this sphere; significantly, he also stated that the movement has been 'the victim' of an unhealthy conspiracy of silence amongst its friends on such issues.

14. The Hon. Ben Amathila, interview with the authors, 6 July 1992, and personal communication, 5 January 1993.

15. Interested readers are urged to consult two outstanding histories to which this book is indebted throughout: David Soggot, *op. cit.* and Peter Katjavivi, *A History of Resistance in Namibia* (London, Paris and Addis Ababa: James Currey, UNESCO and the OAU, 1988). See also the brief historical chronology in the present volume, p. viii.

16. Katjavivi, *op. cit.*, p. 11.

17. There were also important links between the peoples of Eastern Caprivi and the Lozi of south-west Zambia that were very important so long as Swapo was based principally in Zambia.

18. Soggot's account, *op. cit.*, is the most important because it rests heavily on first-hand evidence collected by him as defence counsel in the many cases he defended during these years; its almost laconic style enhances the immediacy of the savagery he reports. Other relevant accounts are cited in Chapter 7, note 17, below.

19. E. Leistner and P. Esterhuysen (eds), *Namibia 1990: an Africa Institute Country Survey* (Pretoria: Africa Institute of South Africa, 1991), p. 236.

20. Notoriously, the ratio of expenditure per student for whites and blacks was more than 5:1; see Minority Rights Group, *The Namibians* (London: MRG, 1985), p. 22.

21. An Academy for Tertiary Education, including a University of Namibia as its biggest component, was established by the South African regime in 1980, and was said to have about 5,000 students (including many part-time) at independence. Its colonial origins and style, however, and its high proportion of coloured (relative to 'black') students, made the Academy politically suspect to many nationalists down to independence and indeed beyond it.

22. Moreover, Afrikaans was and is the mother tongue of Rehoboth Basters and of coloured Namibians.

23. Of course, for much of this period Namibia was considered by Pretoria to be an integral part of South Africa.

24. Dr Kenneth Abrahams, interview with Colin Leys, August 1990.

25. Not that the pull was entirely one way, by any means. In the early 1970s, for example, the powerful strike action by Namibian workers had considerable exemplary impact on workers inside South Africa itself as they readied themselves, in turn, for the wave of strikes that were soon to transform South Africa's own labour scene.

I THE STRUGGLE

2

Diplomacy by Other Means
SWAPO's Liberation War

SUSAN BROWN

Phase 1, 1959–66: From Exile to Omgulumbashe

In independent Namibia, the beginning of the liberation war is commemorated on Omgulumbashe Day, 26 August. On this date in 1966 the South African Police launched a helicopter-borne assault on the first base established in the country by SWAPO's armed wing, the People's Liberation Army of Namibia (PLAN). Two of the guerillas who had made the long trek from southern Zambia through south-east Angola to the Ovambo region in northern Namibia were killed; nine were captured, together with 45 of their recruits from the surrounding area.

The Omgulumbashe attack marked the end of the beginning of the Namibian war. The earliest stirrings of Namibian nationalism in the late 1950s combined labour and popular organization with petitions to the United Nations and appeals to the International Court of Justice, which had rejected South Africa's attempts to incorporate the mandated territory as a fifth province. SWAPO's early leaders were organizing as the Ovamboland People's Organization when Sam Nujoma and other leadership figures went into exile at the beginning of 1960. Others were initially involved in the South West African National Union (SWANU). It was this small group of exiles, based in Dar es Salaam, who reconstituted OPO as SWAPO in April 1960; the aim was to transform an ethnic and regionally based organization into a national one.

Two months later Nujoma, as president of SWAPO, appeared before the United Nations' South West Africa Committee. International diplomacy was the first key strategy of Namibian nationalists in exile – indeed, the ability to deploy this strategy outside the ambit of South African repression was a central reason for the early exiles leaving the country. In the early days, it was directed primarily at the UN and newly independent nations, and would remain a major theme of SWAPO's activities in exile for the next three decades.

The era of decolonization was under way. In the early 1960s, none of the Western nations (except for some of the Nordic countries) would consider supporting anti-colonial movements. In that early Cold War heyday, this was left to the Soviet bloc and China, who were in bitter competition for the allegiance of anti-colonial movements. The favoured model of decolonization, among these sponsors and those former colonies who had formed the Non-Aligned Movement, was one achieved by a popular movement engaged in armed struggle. In the 1950s an anti-colonial ideology of struggle owing much to Maoism emerged: guerilla insurrection, it was argued, was a key strategy for liberationist mobilization in nations not yet decolonized; the Cuban and Algerian struggles were held up as prime exemplars. Armed struggle would also bleed the recalcitrant colonial power financially, the ideology went, engendering divisions in the colonial ruling clique and exacerbating class tensions: the effect on France of the drawn-out Algerian and Vietnamese insurrections – and French leftist thinking on the subject – was a prime influence. By the 1960s, armed struggle was becoming an essential accessory for any nationalist movement's legitimacy with sponsors in the Non-Aligned Movement, the OAU, the Eastern bloc and China.

This is not to say that armed struggle was merely an ideology imposed externally on the Namibian struggle: in a secret SWAPO congress within Namibia in 1961, it was proposed for the first time.[1] By 1962, SWAPO's first combatants began receiving military training in Egypt, where the movement had opened an office; the following year SWAPO gained representation and training in Algeria. Also in 1963, both SWAPO and SWANU joined the OAU at its inception and began receiving funds channelled through its African Liberation Committee. However, the fact that SWAPO had men in training – at this stage they could be counted in tens rather than hundreds – gave it an advantage in achieving one of its early and enduring priorities: to be accepted as the *sole* movement representing Namibia in the international arena. SWANU lost OAU Liberation Committee support in 1965, largely because, after OAU attempts to get the two organizations to merge failed, it was SWAPO which was committed to armed struggle. For the same reason, the movement had begun to receive Soviet support in the previous year. This did not mean that SWAPO was committed exclusively to the Soviet side in the Sino–Soviet competition for protégés: it would send cadres for training in China, too, in the course of the 1960s. Guerilla training sponsored by the Liberation Committee was provided at Kongwa in Tanzania.

However, the movement's central concern by the mid-1960s was the International Court of Justice's long-awaited ruling on the challenge to the legality of South Africa's mandate over Namibia, of which SWAPO had high hopes. SWAPO was unwilling to launch armed struggle publicly before the Hague decision.[2] Shityuwete indicates that guerillas were in fact being sent into Namibia from the end of 1965. Shityuwete himself was in the second group of ten fighters told to start moving south into Namibia via Angola, with orders not to start fighting, but to be in position if things 'did not go well' at the Hague. They left Tanzania in February 1966, moving through Zambia, Caprivi and Angola. Five of them were captured in Kavango in March 1966.

Great bitterness within and outside Namibia followed the Court's denial of the right of Liberia and Ethiopia to bring the case. SWAPO's response within a few days was a 'declaration of war': 'We have no alternative but to rise in arms to bring about our own liberation. . . .'[3] The following month saw the attack on Omgulumbashe.

The SWAPO leadership in exile seem to have had a clear awareness that undertaking armed struggle was a *diplomatic* necessity with few military prospects, though this was seldom publicly stated at the time. According to a hostile account accompanying the 1968 resignation from SWAPO of a small group of Namibian exiles:

> Propelled by selfish ambitions, some SWAPO leaders . . . tried to make SWAPO appear to be a revolutionary movement waging armed struggle. The motive behind the move was and still is to seek more money and more recognition. Another reason is to instigate the UN to action. In one of the SWAPO papers it is plainly put. 'SWAPO also accepted the fact that we could not possibly win a decisive victory against South Africa. However, we realized that we could create certain conditions within the country which would activate the United Nations to intervene on our behalf. Thus SWAPO launched an armed struggle on the 26th August 1966.'[4]

SWAPO's military operational headquarters and political head office were in Dar es Salaam from 1962. In 1963, according to Shityuwete, there were fewer than 100 trained guerillas when he arrived in Tanzania for training. Groups were also being trained in Ghana, Egypt and Algeria during that period. In the course of 1964, numbers of trained recruits increased to about three hundred based at Dodoma in Tanzania, with more awaiting training.

The average age of PLAN recruits at that time seems to have been higher than it was to be later, partly because recruits who were leaving Namibia had often been activists for some years, and partly because SWAPO's recruiting of migrant labourers returning from South Africa via Francistown in Botswana meant they were recruiting men of working age, rather than the teenagers and students who would become PLAN's main source of recruits in the 1970s.

According to South African versions the first six insurgents slipped into Ovamboland to begin basic political mobilization as early as September 1965, and had trained some 30 young men before sending them home to await a call to arms.[5]

The February 1966 group, presumably Shityuwete's, is alleged to have killed 'two Angolan shopkeepers and an itinerant Owambo' on the Angolan side of the border before being captured.[6] In the South African version, in July 1966 a third group launched the armed struggle 'in no uncertain terms by attacking a number of Ovambo tribal chiefs, firing at a white farmer's house in the Grootfontein district just south of Ovamboland, and shooting up the South West African border post at Oshikango'.[7] The same group had set up the base at Omgulumbashe which was attacked a month later. In September, a retaliatory PLAN attack burned down government buildings at Oshikango on the northern border.

Another group of guerillas arrived in December 1966, undertaking politicization and recruiting in both Ovamboland and Caprivi. (Since SWAPO's 1964 merger with the Caprivi African National Union – CANU – it had Caprivians in its ranks.) Again, headmen were attacked, and a white farmer in the Grootfontein district was wounded.

A major security police crackdown followed. By April 1967 up to 200 Namibians were in detention in Pretoria, including almost the entire internal leadership of SWAPO: such people as Andimba Toivo ya Toivo, Eliaser Tuhadeleni, Nathaniel Maxuilili and John Ya-Otto. Eventually 37 of them were charged under the new Terrorism Act and the Suppression of Communism Act. One died during the trial; in February 1968, the remaining 36 were given sentences of up to 20 years on Robben Island.

This ended the war in Ovamboland until October 1975, when the Portuguese decolonization of Angola opened up the front again. Meanwhile cooperation between the South African and Portuguese colonial forces was shutting off the route westward from Zambia through south-eastern Angola, while tribal authorities and police in Kavango seem to have been an effective block to guerillas moving westward within Namibia from Caprivi.

Phase 2, 1966–74: The War from Zambia – 'Hit and Run' in the Caprivi

With the routes through Angola and Kavango blocked, eastern Caprivi, bordering on and accessible from Zambia, was to become the main theatre of war, following something of a lull during the two years following Omgulumbashe. SWAPO's main aim here was to strike into Caprivi, with classic guerilla sabotage and assassination – not, as later, through the tribal homelands to white settler areas. PLAN Chief of Staff David 'Ho Chi Minh' Namholo refers to the 'hit and run tactics' used in this phase.[8]

SWAPO did not move its political headquarters to Zambia from Dar es Salaam until 1972, but by early 1968 PLAN was targeting the Caprivi for systematic infiltration from Zambia: there were vigorous clashes, and police claimed to have captured 160 combatants by March 1968. In October two large groups entered the Caprivi and the police counter-insurgency unit, which had left the area, returned. By the year's end a total of 178 PLAN members had been killed or captured, the remaining combatants having withdrawn into Zambia.[9] The years 1969 and 1970 were quiet in the Caprivi, which may have been a result of uncertainties within the PLAN leadership and the 1968 purge, discussed below.

It was not until 1971 that the first Russian made land-mine blew up a police vehicle near Katima Mulilo in the Caprivi: the land-mine tactic, a central military element for the next decade, was brought into play. During 1971 and 1972 five policemen were killed and 35 wounded in land-mine explosions. Land-mine incidents, ambushes of police patrols and an attack on a police camp took place in Caprivi in 1973.

As well as land-mines, during this phase PLAN's most common tactics included attacks on tribal leaders (who were paid government employees, the administrative and judicial arm of South African-style indirect rule) and on official buildings such as police and border posts. The strategic objective seems to have been armed propaganda: to supply an inspirational symbol to the still fluid nationalist movement, while generating fear among whites, and in theory willingness on their part and that of other government supporters to make concessions. This was the same rationale as the ANC had at the beginning of its armed struggle. A secondary aim was the destruction – of the legitimacy if not the structures – of the 'traditional' political and judicial networks personified by chiefs and headmen. As indicated above, penetration outside tribal areas was not yet the dominant strategic objective.

Possibly as a result of the restriction of the war to the well-defended Caprivi theatre, organizational strains in the SWAPO exile movement were intensifying. In May 1967, Tobias Hainyeko, the Commander in Chief of PLAN, was shot dead by South African police who had intercepted his boat crossing the Zambezi to Caprivi. SWAPO's version is that he was betrayed by the local Caltex manager who ran the barges along the river;[10] Shityuwete's account is that he was betrayed by his deputy Castro (the combat name of one Leonard Phillemon), who had been detained by the South Africans in February 1966 and who was 'played back' to SWAPO as an agent.[11]

Indeed, Hainyeko was briefly succeeded as PLAN Commander in Chief by Castro, but following a number of captures of guerillas entering Namibia he was detained by SWAPO in 1968 and held in a Tanzanian prison for 17 years. Shipanga's version is that while Nujoma and Peter Nanyemba wanted to promote Castro to field commander of PLAN, the soldiers refused to accept the appointment because they did not trust him.[12] Castro was succeeded by Dimo Hamaambo, who held the position of PLAN Commander to the end of the war and is now head of the new Namibian Defence Force.[13]

Beyond this PLAN crisis, there seems to have been some loss of faith in SWAPO leadership in general. Certainly the seven China-trained SWAPO guerillas who resigned in 1968 were critical of the leadership as a whole. One of the allegations, in addition to inertia and low morale, was that the leadership was at that stage reluctant to encourage Namibians to leave for exile and guerilla training.[14]

However, while military activities were localized and sporadic, and confined to the remote Caprivi (which is not to minimize their organizational and inspirational impact, especially on the youth within Namibia) political events were broadening SWAPO's internal support and attracting a new generation into the organization.

In 1971 the International Court of Justice reversed its 1966 stance and declared South Africa's occupation of Namibia illegal. In a rising tide of nationalism, there were student boycotts and the Namibian churches for the first time addressed an anti-government open letter to the South African Prime Minister, John Vorster. This foreshadowed the important role both the youth and the churches were to play in nationalist protest from then on. Another key event was the massive strike of mostly Ovambo-speaking migrant workers at the end of 1971. The colonial state's repressive response intensified the climate of resistance in northern Namibia.

The student boycotts marked the beginning of the important organizational and politicizing role the SWAPO Youth League was to play throughout the 1970s. Again in 1973, a police crackdown, probably in response to the successful campaign for a boycott of bantustan elections in the north, put many SWAPO leaders in prison, and drove many politicized youths to leave the country in the 'exodus' of 1974.

In 1973, too, Vorster gave a public undertaking that the bantustan independence programme would not go further, and that the territory's people would decide its future. It was at that point that the South African government's long search for a co-optive alternative to the Odendaal Plan began. After this concession, the South African Prime Minister's Advisory Council was set up, which would organize the Turnhalle Constitutional Conference in 1975. This led to the creation of the Democratic Turnhalle Alliance, the spearhead of policies designed to co-opt nationalist and socialist popular impulses.

Meanwhile, however, the South Africans, were expanding their defensive forces. Although the conduct of the 'border war' in Namibia was under the overall direction of the South African Police (SAP), elements of the South African Defence Force (SADF) were becoming involved: in 1968 a small air component of the South African Air Force (SAAF) was stationed at Rundu, on the Angolan border in Kavango. The following year the army became involved, when 1 Military Region was designated, with its headquarters at Rundu; infantry companies were stationed in a couple of strategic places for protection of bases and as a reserve.

Counter-insurgency, however, was at this time primarily the function of the SAP, who also used the South West African Police (numbering a mere 600 at this time) in their anti-PLAN activities. The SAP was picking up this trade rapidly in Rhodesia, where they were deployed against the liberation movements there. Similarities with the tactics used by the Rhodesian forces include the phenomenon of captured guerillas being 'turned' to work in the security forces, which continued throughout the war. Another adopted tactic was the use, beginning this early, of black (or 'blackened') soldiers in PLAN uniforms to entrap guerilla units.

However, by 1973 the SAP was arguing that it was unable to supply a contingent to fight in Rhodesia as well as on the Namibian border. The result was a secret decision in 1973 to hand over command of the counter-insurgency campaign to the SADF.

P. W. Botha, as Minister of Defence, was saying by March 1974 that there was only one answer to the long-term war being waged on the borders: 'a military solution with highly trained people and effective weapons. It is something I have been saying for six years, since I became Minister of Defence.'[15] The second half of 1973 had already seen increasing numbers of military personnel and equipment arriving in what was already termed 'the operational area' along Namibia's northern border. By 1 April 1974, the SADF was in command of the operational area – just in time for the quantum shift in the parameters of the war signalled by the Portuguese coup during the same month.

Phase 3, 1974–8: SWAPO's Offensive from Angola – Targets beyond the Red Line

Portugal's decolonization process would transform the politics of Southern Africa. Angola's independence shifted the Namibian theatre of war westward. PLAN now had access across the common border with Angola into the Ovambo region, home to SWAPO's primary support base among the half of the country's population who lived there. Indeed, for more than a year before Angola's formal independence in November 1975, Portuguese commanders were allowing Namibian exiles passing through Angola free passage to Zambia where SWAPO by then had its exile headquarters. Thousands of young Namibians left in this period, providing a massive injection of new blood to the somewhat stultified PLAN of the time. As well as opening up new military possibilities with an upsurge in PLAN successes and the intensity of the war, however, this also brought new stresses to SWAPO. A time of realignments and great structural change for all sides in the war was ushered in: within SWAPO, the SADF, UNITA and Angola as a whole.

There were three main waves in 1974, the first in June. The South Africans estimated that up to 3,000 young people left Namibia by the year's end, while exile estimates were higher. Many of these were scholars activated by the SWAPO Youth League, who were bearing the brunt of military and police repression in the north. Several other factors came into play: The MPLA was broadcasting with the support of the new Portuguese regime that Namibians would be granted safe conduct, and Nujoma had issued a call in neighbouring Botswana for Namibians to leave the country and join the struggle.[16] According to Shipanga, Jannie de Wet, then Commissioner for the Indigenous Peoples, had told police border guards not to stop people leaving the country, believing this way he would be rid of political 'troublemakers'. ('What a miscalculation!' Shipanga says of de Wet's order.)

Limitations placed by the Zambian government on activities from that country in 1974 – the short-lived but effective result of Vorster's detente policy following a meeting between him and Kaunda – also contributed to the galvanizing effect of the opening of the Ovambo and Kavango fronts.

Accommodating and training thousands of new recruits was a massive strain on the SWAPO exile structures. This was aggravated by the Zambian government's detente with Vorster – and Kaunda's fear of the Soviet-backed MPLA in Angola. Together with the limitations of SWAPO's internal decision-making structures, this led to the severe crisis in Zambia in 1976 which is discussed in Chapter 3. It was also true, however, that SWAPO's move into Angola to take advantage of the new opportunity for action across the Ovambo-Kavango border meant extricating itself from its hitherto close relationship with UNITA, the loser in Angola's pre-independence civil war. Prior to the South Africa–UNITA alliance leading to the South African invasion in October 1975, there had been amicable cooperation between UNITA and PLAN. It made military sense. UNITA had been in south-eastern Angola since 1966, on one of SWAPO's routes into the Caprivi. Between Oshivambo and Ovimbundu, UNITA's power base, there was an ethnic 'cousinship'. Indeed there are some references to PLAN units being seconded to operate with UNITA at this time, and one key commander in Ongiva was a member of both UNITA and SWAPO.

It does seem that the PLAN High Command, however open to criticism levelled by the dissidents in the mis-named 'Shipanga crisis' of 1976, was beginning to gear PLAN training up to take account both of the increased numbers and the probable increase in weaponry budgets. PLAN's Chief of Staff, 'Ho Chi Minh' Namholo, who had left Namibia as a young activist in the June 1974 exodus, recalls that by September 1974 he and about eighty others were sent to the Soviet Union for guerilla commanders' training. This was very much along the lines of classic guerilla theory – positively Maoist, in fact:

> We were taught a typical guerilla warfare [with] semi-regular forces. So we had to study all these typical guerilla tactics: conduct ambushes, and sabotage too – bridges, railways, communication means.... The formation of your forces [at first] is mostly very small groups.... In the semi-regular [stage] you have some bigger forces, and you establish radio communications [between them] and ... where you may have some vehicles for supplies and so forth.... [In theory] the national liberation movement starts with organizing in small political cells within the country, and then up to uprising in certain cities.

On their return in 1975, with the civil war starting in Angola, Namholo and his co-trainees were sent to SWAPO camps in Zambia to train others. In early March 1976, they were sent to Angola: 'Since this was now the most favourable front, most of those who came from training were sent here.' PLAN army headquarters were transferred to Angola in 1976.

According to Namholo, with the opening of the Angolan front PLAN's strategy changed. Instead of 'hit-and-run attacks' in Namibia close to the border (mostly in Caprivi up to that time), the objective now was to across the 'Red Line' (the veterinary *cordon sanitaire* dividing the Ovambo, Kavango and Caprivi regions along the northern border from the white farming areas): '[Strategy] was changed to cross into farming areas, going to urban areas rather than just being in the north or in Caprivi or in Kavango – to bring the war to the farming areas.'

By 1977 there were three 'fronts' – northern, north-eastern and north-western – each a military unit targeting different sectors of the border. Each front had a commander, a chief of staff, and a political commissar; heading different sections were a chief engineer, chief medic, chief of anti-air defence, chief of artillery and chief of logistics. The fronts also operated forward command posts close to the border, which launched operations into Namibia:

> We had detachments, which were mostly maybe two or three kilometres from the border. First they received instructions, then they operated. If we set up an operation, it means the chief of staff and the chief of operations had to go to a forward command post, and command from there, far from the regional headquarters.

Contemporary media reports indicate that PLAN activities in the Ovambo region were intensifying from mid-1975. In a speech in London in June Nujoma said the armed struggle was to be stepped up.[17]

August 1975 saw the assassination of Chief Philemon Elifas, the 'Chief Minister' of Ovambo, where another round of ethnic elections was scheduled. Elifas was an important mover in the planned Turnhalle talks, as an ethnically oriented alternative to SWAPO, and his death was a severe propaganda loss to the South Africans. On 2 September the Turnhalle Constitutional Conference was scheduled to begin in Windhoek, assembling ethnic representatives from around Namibia.

In August, too, SWAPO and UNITA were closing in on the Calueque barrage and pumping station on the Angolan side of the border. The SADF sent infantry and armoured cars to occupy the site, which was crucial to the water supply for the canal system in Ovamboland. Two months later, SWAPO was reported to have established several holding and training camps in Angola with UNITA's help.[18]

In the first report of military action in Ovamboland since the 1960s, on 14 October the SADF announced that seven people had been killed and two were missing in a raid by SWAPO across the Angolan border.[19] The dead included a tribal headman, the first to be killed since Chief Elifas's assassination in August.[20]

In December 1975 the new 'Ovambo Chief Minister', Cornelius Njoba, said that insurgents had been seen as far into Namibia as Ondangua and Oshakati, the regional capital some 60 km from Angola.[21] Just before Christmas a white woman and child were shot by two blacks with automatic weapons near Grootfontein. There was massive local coverage of the search for guerillas.[22] In January a British immigrant and an Ovambo woman were shot by a 30-strong SWAPO unit. Construction workers at Onunu were also shot at, and guerillas took medical supplies from the Oshandi clinic.

The picture from this time on is of regular land-mine casualties among troops in Ovamboland, abduction or assassination of Ovambo headmen, construction workers shot at or injured (South Africa was constructing tarred roads, water towers, pipelines and canals), white construction foremen abducted, stores raided and burned – in one case guerillas took a large stock of provisions and distributed them to onlookers before burning the store. Troops were fired on from across the border. Citizen Force and Commando Battalions were being called up regularly to man bases and escort convoys. All episodes at this time seem to indicate crossings near to the Oshikango area on the central Ovamboland border.

The strange thing about the obvious increase in the PLAN presence along the Angolan border with Namibia, and its intensifying military activity at this time, is that late 1975 to early 1976 saw South Africa's largest military exercise since the Second World War: its invasion of Angola via northern Namibia. Namholo's explanation is that while South Africa was striking deep into Angola, PLAN was able to operate almost with impunity in 'shallow Angola' – the area near the border.

The fall of the Caetano regime had taken the South Africans by surprise. An early response was to build up the numbers of troops along the border, but in the course of 1974 Vorster concentrated on his detente strategy. A number of meetings between South African officials and Zambian President Kenneth Kaunda followed in 1974, part of the build-up to the Victoria Falls meeting of August 1975. In effect, the Vorster–van den Bergh offer was to pressure Rhodesia towards a settlement in return for a Zambian undertaking to withdraw SWAPO's right to use Zambian territory as a guerilla springboard.

Shipanga's version is that Zambia undertook to persuade SWAPO 'to declare themselves a party not committed to violence, provided the South African government allows their registration as a political party and allows them to function as such'.[23] In other words, to become hooked into the nascent Turnhalle co-optive tactics, while abandoning the international clout that conducting an armed struggle provided. The Vorster–van den Bergh scenario was aimed at depriving SWAPO of bases by political leverage as opposed to military action, thereby forcing their participation in the Turnhalle Conference, designed to create an ethnic alternative to the UN's demands for unitary independence. At this time the main South African strategy stressed the importance of the political solution via detente, did not see SWAPO and PLAN as a threat, and refused to believe in their growing strength in southern Angola. However, the faction in the South African state which favoured military dominance of the region was growing in strength.

In September 1975, according to the *Financial Times*, the Zambian government ordered SWAPO to cease all military activities from Zambian soil. SWAPO was also ordered to vacate its farm outside Lusaka, where about 500 people were based, by the end of September. SWAPO sources were reported as claiming that Zambia had, in addition, intercepted all arms supplies to SWAPO. This was denied a few days later by Katjavivi, SWAPO's Secretary of Information, in London, and by the Zambian foreign minister. However, it seems that the Vorster–Kaunda connection was beginning to pay off in the form of severe pressure exerted by Zambia.

All this changed when the South African invasion of Angola became public knowledge in November 1975. From July 1975, the MPLA had forced the FNLA and the small UNITA presence out of Luanda, and was soon in control of most sizeable urban centres – where its support base in any case was concentrated. From that time both the CIA and US Secretary of State Henry Kissinger were urging the South Africans to intervene against the MPLA. Savimbi and Holden Roberto, leader of the FNLA in northern Angola, were also sending appeals to Pretoria. On 14 July Vorster agreed to supply arms to the two movements, as P. W. Botha and the generals had been urging since April. By 1976, Botha and his generals favoured giving SWAPO a military *coup de grâce* in Angola, and forcing the rest of the region to accept this by military destabilization – the strategy which was to dominate the 1980s.

In September 1975 trainers and advisers were sent by Pretoria to Savimbi. On 5 October a South African battle group with UNITA forces clashed with FAPLA for the first time between Lobito and Nova Lisboa. From then on the SADF operated alongside UNITA and the FNLA in four mixed task forces, pushing to just south of Luanda. By early November the first Cuban troops had arrived (probably indicating that their intervention had been planned for some months, given the logistical necessities of such an operation). On 7 November an FNLA attack on Luanda met with a crushing defeat from which it never recovered. On 14 November Reuters published unambiguous reports about the South African military involvement.[24]

The chief consequence of the short-lived South African invasion of Angola (September 1975 to March 1976) was to swing the previously divided members of the OAU, including Zambia, behind the MPLA and against UNITA. It forced SWAPO out of its alliance with UNITA into one with the MPLA. UNITA's defeat and the withdrawal of a small core group, temporarily deprived of South African and US support, deep into the bush of southern Angola, made it possible for SWAPO to move through southern Angola to base itself close to the border of Ovambo, the heartland of its support. For most of the two further years that Vorster held power he resisted his generals' urging of operations into Angola, and they had to make do with cross-border 'hot pursuit'.[25]

SWAPO's ability to deploy into Namibia from shallow Angola would be relatively unfettered until South African 'external operations' and major air and bombing attacks started in 1978. Now PLAN could go on the offensive. Meanwhile, its activity in Caprivi was falling away, partly because of the newly created tracker battalion based there (made up of San trackers inherited from the Portuguese and imported wholesale into Namibia by the SADF, it became 201 Battalion when the South West African Territorial Force (SWATF) was formed), but mostly because PLAN was now able to concentrate on the Ovambo region.

PLAN troops in Angola in 1976, according to Erastus Negonga, operated from bases close to the border in groups of 40–60 men, which were divided into smaller squads, all under the same platoon commander. Supplies were meagre:

> In fact all of our logistic supplies were only concentrating on ammunition at that time – 1976 – and it came from Zambia.... There was no combat food.... We had no proper uniforms.[26]

Still, the classic guerilla advantage held. Within Namibia, Negonga says:

> [D]uring that time the enemy had no influence among the masses.... During that time we had no problem.

His assessment of the SADF:

> During that time, even the SADF were under-trained. They were not specialized in guerilla tactics. That is why they found it difficult to track down guerillas during that time; they were not in a position to move in the areas where we used to operate, and they got demoralized. At that time we had the upper hand.

Operating in bases so close to the border, PLAN cadres were also easily able to move unobtrusively into Namibia to undertake politicizing work among local people – in guerilla theory, an essential prerequisite to military action and sabotage. Proximity made intelligence work easier, too.

The South African pull-out from Angola had enabled SWAPO, backed by the MPLA's logistical system, to begin accessing and distributing Soviet supplies more successfully. It set up a network of training camps for its recruits, and command centres for the northern and north-eastern regions in Angola, with forward command posts and border base camps.[27]

Hot pursuit of PLAN units across the Angolan border by South African forces was starting to be routine. Angola claimed South Africa had crossed the border in July 1976 and razed three villages. Three days later, Zambia accused South Africa of having attacked the village of Sialola, killing 24 civilians and wounding another 45, and took the matter to the UN, as the culmination of 14 'provocative acts'; South Africa claimed Sialola was a SWAPO transit camp.

By October 1977 the SADF was claiming that contacts between security force patrols and PLAN were averaging about 100 a month, with some 300 insurgents in Namibia at any given time, some 2,000 grouped in Angola for deployment into Ovamboland, and another 1,400 in Zambia to target the Caprivi. Between 1966 and the end of 1977, official SADF figures said 88 security force members and 363 insurgents had died – still relatively modest numbers.[28] But the intensity of the conflict was about to escalate, as PLAN started to use its Angolan springboard more effectively and South Africa, in reaction, moved into the phase of external operations.

In 1976–7 UNITA was almost dormant, though some South African supplies were probably still trickling through. It was only when P. W. Botha became Prime Minister at the end of 1978 that large-scale support to UNITA resumed. However, the South African militarists were getting ready to go on the offensive. In July 1977 General Jannie Geldenhuys, a shrewd political general, had been appointed to command all troops in Namibia 'in accordance', P. W. Botha said, 'with the policy to build and develop an independent and complete defence force for SWA'.

Geldenhuys's doctrine was threefold. First, he aimed to win the 'hearts and minds' of the local population, especially in the war zone along the border, in keeping with the planned Turnhalle strategy of co-option and minor reform in the rest of the country. Related to this was the 'Namibianization' of the military forces opposing SWAPO. The core of the ethnic battalions of the SWATF already existed; by the early 1980s its units, manned by black Namibians and officered by whites, and usually using armoured vehicles, were playing a growing part in combat against guerillas. Geldenhuys's point here was to avoid a war of white occupiers against black guerillas – Namibians should begin 'fighting their own battles' against the 'communist threat'.

Second, intensified counter-insurgency was important. Colonel Hans Dreyer of the SAP would found Koevoet, the police counter-insurgency unit, in 1978. Geldenhuys himself, Namibian-born, was a professional who thought terrorism and butchery counter-productive, and favoured real reform well beyond the cosmetic alterations P. W. Botha would countenance. He did not anticipate and could not control Koevoet's and the SWATF's development of a more brutal approach, since he was promoted to head of the South African army early in the 1980s. Further, counter-insurgency among a populace massively opposed to occupation by its nature cannot be, or remain, humane.

The third, and key, aspect of his doctrine was the destruction of SWAPO's logistical bases and supply lines in Angola, rather than reacting in Namibia to a guerilla force that was on the offensive.[29] Geldenhuys, together with Vorster's other generals, was arguing that the insurgency could not be stopped by fighting an essentially defensive war. 'What that implied was pre-emptive attacks on selected PLAN concentrations in Angola, employing far larger force levels than had been used since Operation Savannah.'[30]

Vorster approved in principle, with the proviso that such 'external operations' be subject to top-level political approval. This was the shape of things to come. The South African military and police began to put together counter-insurgency structures and operatives in the wake of the Angolan invasion. It would take another four years or so for these to ripen to full destructiveness against PLAN.

The nucleus of the South West Africa Territorial Force (SWATF), made up of ethnically recruited battalions, had begun to take shape in 1974, when traditional leaders in northern Namibia were granted permission to form armed bodyguard units. These *omakakunya* – scavengers or ragpickers, as local people called them – were also a source of recruits four years later when Koevoet was formed. PLAN's most stubborn, effective and vicious enemies would be recruited from these traditional loyalists. In 1974 1 Ovambo Battalion was formed and 1 Kavango Battalion followed in 1975. These would become 101 Battalion and 102 Battalion respectively.

This was the beginning of what became the SWATF in 1979. At demobilization in May 1989 the SWATF consisted of eight full-time combat battalions, in addition to a number of other units. Commanded by South Africans but manned mainly by Namibians, by the end of the war it was 30,000 strong.

San trackers, whether imported from Angola or recruited in Namibia, would also be hideously effective against PLAN guerillas. As one PLAN commander put it: 'The trouble with guerilla war is that you have to walk, and if you walk, you leave spoor....'[31] The 'cut-line' along the Angolan border was cleared of trees and under-growth, and its kilometre-wide soft sand was patrolled daily for tracks. The chevron-soled combat boots used by PLAN throughout the war were absolutely distinctive and immediately recognizable – a boon to the occupying power's trackers.

From left-over allies of its Angolan invasion, the South African military put together 32 Battalion, which would also operate extensively in southern Angola. Colonel Jan Breytenbach, who had liaised with the southern or Chipenda faction of the FNLA (itself a break-away faction of the MPLA) put together 32 Battalion from these soldier-refugees, with the explicit intention of using them as a counter-guerilla force in 'shallow Angola'. Breytenbach had fought in Rhodesia, and knew the tactics of disguise and entrapment used by the Selous Scouts and similar counter-insurgency forces. Like them, 32 Battalion would often operate in PLAN uniform, scout out PLAN units or bases, and guide in air-borne attacks.[32]

Colonel (later General) Hans Dreyer, Koevoet's founder, had also served in Rhodesia, and learned the tactics employed there. Used in Namibia and Angola in the course of the 1980s, these tactics would prove increasingly effective.

Phase 4, 1978–84: High Tide for PLAN – Followed by Enemy Escalation

Early 1978 saw still more intense PLAN activity, with large-scale clashes between the SADF and groups of 80–100 PLAN soldiers. In 1978 'incidents' – sabotage, assassination, land-mine explosions – would increase tenfold over the previous year. PLAN fighters based in 'shallow Angola' were able to operate intensively as political activators and intelligence gatherers as well as guerillas. Earlier difficulties of supply to PLAN bases near the border were being solved; groups of fighters operating in northern Namibia could easily resupply from bases a day's march at most from the border.

From time immemorial, northern pastoralists had grazed their cattle back and forth across the border, which was still a line on a map rather than a factor in daily life. Ammunition, grenades, mortars and land-mines did not always have to be carried into Namibia on the backs of PLAN fighters: local supporters would drive herds of cattle behind PLAN groups to conceal their spoor, and often heavy material was loaded on the cattle as well. Local homesteads supplied food and shelter, as did many parish churches. A few churchmen also helped fighters to cache arms. Local businesspeople with vehicles provided transport to take guerillas and their equipment into the white farming areas south of the Red Line, where PLAN units could cache arms and begin political activation of local people.[33] Political activation by PLAN units – which remained in the area for periods of up to three months establishing cells of supporters – was also under way in the Kavango region from 1979.

At this stage, between 1978 and 1980, there were no-go areas for the SADF in parts of Ovamboland. The presence and mobility of PLAN units was one reason; another was the increasing use of land-mines. Fighters would plant these in the dirt roads networking the region, and warn local people about them; in turn locals would warn friendly travellers, who had to enquire at each stretch. The SADF, government administrators and members of the bantustan authority had to travel in convoys. One result was that the administration began tarring the main road; construction teams and equipment then became PLAN targets. Morale was high in PLAN and among SWAPO supporters countrywide between 1978 and 1980, since it seemed that a UN settlement was imminent, with SWAPO dominating both the war and the diplomatic arena.

PLAN would lose the strategic initiative, however, when South Africa began striking at will into Angola. The raid on Cassinga on 4 May 1978 ('Operation Reindeer' to the SADF) foreshadowed the phase of South African 'external operations' – raids and sometimes full-scale invasions – which by 1981 amounted to occupation of key areas of the south-western quadrant of Angola by the SADF, an occupation that would last for years in some cases.

Cassinga was a town 250 km into Angola which had been given over to SWAPO for processing people newly arrived in exile, as well as SWAPO members in transit through Angola to or from other countries. A number of United Nations Institute for Namibia (UNIN) graduates had arrived from Lusaka only days before the attack, for example,[34] and a number of candidates selected to attend UNIN that year died there, too. The official South African reason for the attack was that it was believed to be the PLAN command headquarters. It is true that PLAN's commander, Dimo Amaambo, and some troops were based there.[35] It could be argued that SWAPO should not have combined military and refugee centres, but at that time the notion of an unprovoked attack into Angola – let alone 250 km into that country – was unthinkable.

South Africa's version is that its paratroopers had a hard fight against numerous PLAN combatants, following a 'softening up' bombing raid. SWAPO's is that there was only a small armed force present, and that those who died were overwhelmingly women, children and non-combatants. Certainly photographs and videos of the mass graves at Cassinga show almost exclusively corpses of women and children. All interviewees who were Cassinga survivors remember it as a civilian massacre. Two other networks of SWAPO bases close to the Namibian border were also attacked, including 'Vietnam' base near Chetequera, a complex housing the North-western Front regional command (from which a large number of very youthful, newly exiled prisoners were taken back to Namibia to spend years in a prison camp), and other nearby bases.

The timing of these attacks was also significant, coinciding almost exactly with a potentially significant round of international negotiations. While Vorster, embattled with scandal and soon to lose the South African premiership, was still engaged in negotiations, Defence Minister P. W. Botha and his generals were convinced that a military solution was the only one. After P. W. Botha took over the premiership from Vorster later in 1978, SADF raids and operations into neighbouring countries were repeatedly timed so as to do maximum damage to any prospects of a negotiated settlement.

Cassinga engendered an upsurge of fury among all SWAPO supporters inside and outside the country. In August 1978 PLAN fighters based in Zambia mortared and rocketed the Caprivian town of Katima Mulilo in revenge for Cassinga. The South Africans counter-bombarded the Zambian town of Sesheke, following up with a raid.

However, PLAN was still scoring significant successes. One South African conscript, a mortarist in the infantry from 1979 to 1980, said:

> Also of course at that time, 1980, SWAPO was winning the war. They had an enormous presence in Namibia, they were doing some really daring attacks. I mean they once mortared Ondangua and knocked out a radar station there.[36]

In 1978, Erastus Negonga became Chief of Engineering, in charge of explosives and sabotage, of the North-western Front regional command. Its headquarters at the 'Vietnam' base were some 25 km south of Xangongo, or some 75 km from the border. In 1978 the North-western Front had some 60 trained men, plus 500 new recruits, an indication of the impact of that year's exodus of Namibians into exile. (More than 100 of these, as we have seen, were taken prisoner by the SADF in the series of raids that included the Cassinga attack. Most were held in a prison camp in southern Namibia for up to seven years.)

Negonga's main target was the transmission lines connecting southern Namibia, served by one overloaded power station, to the Ruacana hydroelectric scheme. The Calueque water supply scheme, carrying water south-west in a canal through Ovambo, was also a potential target, 'but in fact [I] was very reluctant [about this], because I knew that it was endangering the lives of the population of the northern part of the country. This is why here and there we were not that serious with the water pipeline. But we were supposed to cause expenses to the budget of the colonial masters – that was the strategy.'

Prior to Cassinga, according to Negonga, '[t]hese heavier bombardments from the ... planes were not a normal occurrence; the enemy at that time concentrated on the helicopter gunship attacks'. Before Cassinga, the SADF used aerial bombing mainly against targets on the border; the Cassinga attack marked the onset of attacks into Angola, and the bombing of targets there. These targets, the South Africans have asserted consistently, were SWAPO bases, not Angolan military or civilian targets – though SWAPO began to place its personnel, installations and bases in close proximity to Angolan ones, the South African version goes, thus causing 'side-effect' damage to Angolan property, troops or people. However, the Angolans' account and those of numerous other observers assert that bombing and strafing of towns, villages and, indeed, anything which showed a light at night in southern Angola were increasingly indiscriminate in the four or five years after 1978.[37] The aim was to cause enough damage to drive a wedge between SWAPO and its host and ally.

The PLAN strategy during 1979 and 1980 centred on the 'escalation of battles within

Namibia itself',[38] striking at economic targets, infrastructure and communication equipment. The intention was ultimately to expand PLAN's area of operation into 'the depths of the country' – indeed, there was a designated Southern Region, which included the whole of Namibia south of the Red Line.[39] In addition to the Otavi–Tsumeb–Grootfontein 'Death Triangle', a white farming area that was a consistent PLAN target, fighters did carry out some sabotage in central and southern Namibia, and made contact with activists there, but such activity was highly risky and not intensive.

It was quite easy for PLAN units to move in and out of northern Namibia even after 1979. Negonga says that once he was promoted to Chief of Staff of the North-western front towards the end of 1979, he used to go into Namibia to contact his unit commanders and to give them directives. It was increasingly difficult, however, to maintain PLAN headquarters in southern Angola with any safety. From being chief of staff of a regional front, Ho Chi Minh Namholo was appointed Chief of Staff of PLAN as a whole in mid-1979, and was also nominated to the Military Council of PLAN, which met yearly to decide on policy and strategy, unless called in response to an emergency. Once he became PLAN Chief of Staff, Namholo's immediate superior was Amaambo, the PLAN Commander, and the two headed up the PLAN headquarters, the top military command post. (Above the PLAN headquarters, in the common hierarchy, was the policy-making Defence Headquarters at Lubango, where the SWAPO Secretary of Defence and the Military Council were based; Peter Nanyemba was Secretary of Defence until his death in April 1983, when he was succeeded by Peter Mueshihange.)

PLAN headquarters was constantly under attack after it was bombed at Cassinga. That was not the only difficulty. According to Namholo:

> Amaambo was also detained by the Angolans one time, from Cassinga ... the control and establishment of a proper headquarters was not always there. [After Cassinga] we went to Cahama – it was detected, bombed again; we came to Shitumba – it was detected and bombed; and then ... we changed to another place where we stayed for eight months or so, and then we were bombed again in 1980.
>
> They came with planes, bombed, and with ground forces. Of course, in these battles we shot down many planes, because the headquarters had sufficient anti-air defence means. On the ground we also had entrenched ourselves, because the base now was organized in a semi-regular form, not in a guerilla mobile; because we knew that the enemy was following us up and down, so we had to organize it in a more semi-regular form, with trenches and with bunkers, and with outposts, who engaged the enemy before they reached the main headquarters.

Thus, with air attacks and mechanized column raids by the SADF and SWATF, the South African strategy was escalating the conflict increasingly toward a conventional war. PLAN had to respond accordingly. As Namholo indicates, from operating in small mobile units, PLAN was adopting more conventional military structures and tactics, at least for defence. In the next few years, PLAN would also begin to develop mechanized brigades – which, by that time, would often have to be used defensively against UNITA attacks on SWAPO bases, transport convoys and, potentially, the refugee camp at Kwanza Sul.

The new South African Prime Minister, P. W. Botha, was beginning to implement a threefold military strategy: aggressively attacking SWAPO's bases and lines of communications in Angola, with the aim of destroying PLAN's ability to mount offensive operations; simultaneously, by bombing and 'side-effect' damage, causing Angola's civilian population and army enough grief to motivate the MPLA government to curb or ultimately ban SWAPO's operations; and increasing military and logistical support for UNITA to the point where, from its base area in the south-east, it began from 1980 to launch raids into virtually the rest of Angola (though an undetermined number of 'UNITA' sabotage operations were actually carried out by South African 'recce' commando units).

SWAPO's ability to strike at will into the Ovambo area of Namibia now began to diminish rapidly. PLAN combatants, previously based within a few kilometres of the Namibian border, were forced hundreds of kilometres back into the Angolan hinterland. The PLAN headquarters and regional command points came under constant air and ground attack. Forward command posts, from which guerillas operated into Namibia, became increasingly insecure if close to the border, with their lines of supply disrupted. When SWAPO could no longer establish bases close to the border, this imposed on combatants the need to carry land-mines, mortars, automatic rifles, medical equipment and so on hundreds of kilometres on their backs before they even entered Namibia, let alone crossed into white farming areas. This long trek south was impossible without water, so PLAN operations became restricted to the rainy season between November and March.

At the same time, counter-insurgency activity within northern Namibia intensified. It was designed to intimidate and render PLAN's civilian supporters passive. Koevoet, police and military action against actual or suspected PLAN suppliers and supporters was a deliberately ruthless imposition of terror to erode SWAPO's priceless advantage of practical civilian support of guerillas. PLAN activity in the Caprivi effectively ended in 1980, when the Caprivi African National Union (CANU), and SWAPO, which had merged in 1964, split with mutual recriminations. CANU then took the Turnhalle option, and became part of the DTA.

Apart from the military problems engendered by this increased South African aggression in the years after 1980, the clearing of guerilla bases from 'shallow Angola' and the concomitant logistical problems cut into the time combatants were able to stay in Namibia. This crucially affected their ability to conduct political work among the local population. After 1982, the politicizing role of guerillas who moved continually and easily among the people of Ovamboland, often in civilian clothes, able to communicate and convince, began to wane. The role of combatants was increasingly forced into an exclusively military mould.

Nonetheless, 1981 saw PLAN combat groups break through to white farming areas during the rainy season, and large numbers – between 500 and 600 – active in the war zone. Again in 1982, PLAN's Typhoon/Volcano unit was active in the Tsumeb white farming area for two months, with high casualties before the remnant withdrew. Political activation continued in the Kavango area and began ripening into military action. The 1983 rainy season was the last substantial PLAN military strike south of the Red Line, though the following year saw heavy concentration in the Kavango. Also in 1984, the Ondangua airbase in the Ovambo region was mortared, with some sabotage and other activity north of the Red Line still continuing. In 1985, though activity in the Kavango was declining (in part due to UNITA's expanding presence along the north-eastern border), hundreds of PLAN guerillas were active in the Ovambo region, with a base at Eenhana mortared, and other sabotage – of a bridge and communications – carried out. In short, despite the obstacles, and losing the advantage of surprise by being increasingly confined to activities in the rainy season, PLAN units did get through to northern Namibia. Despite high attrition, they did keep on coming.

Diplomatically, after 1980 the game had also changed radically with the election of an aggressively conservative US government. The author of the 'constructive engagement' policy, Chester Crocker, argued in 1981 that, far from the Cuban and Soviet presence in Angola being justified by South Africa depredations in the 1975 invasion, and by its occupation of Namibia, it was the other way round:

> Angola is the focal point for policy. It is in Angola, after all, that anti-communist forces are effectively engaged in trying to liberate their country from the new imperialism of Moscow and its allies.
>
> This process should be encouraged with the aim of getting the Cubans out so that genuine political reconciliation can take place. As for Namibia, while a settlement is

important there, it will not by itself end the Angolan strife, because Savimbi is by no means the tool of South Africa. He could continue to operate with the active support of other African states and governments elsewhere.

Accordingly, the West should back UNITA until such time that the MPLA is prepared to negotiate and expel the communist forces from Angola. Namibia, according to this argument, is a separate and less important issue.[40]

And so 'linkage' came into being: the linkage of Cuban withdrawal from Angola to a Namibian settlement. In terms of SWAPO's original vision of the armed struggle as a means of increasing diplomatic leverage, the military developments of the early 1980s were heading towards a stalemate in the military arena, while the Reagan and Thatcher governments were to ensure years of deadlock in the diplomatic arena. This would have dramatic organizational ramifications, notably in the party purges of 'spies' in the course of the 1980s.

Almost every year after 1978 saw at least one large-scale South African 'external operation'. These took advantage of the SADF's strengths: its conventionally trained personnel, its heavy weapons and its control of the air. Until the mid-1980s, South African dominance of the skies over Namibia and Angola gave it a major advantage, and air power and bombardment were typically used to soften up a target, which would then be attacked by mechanized and infantry units. June 1980 saw Operation Sceptic, a 'pre-emptive attack' on the Smokeshell complex of heavily defended PLAN bases which occupied some 65 square km of southern Angola. Air attacks and artillery bombardment were a prelude to attacks by mechanized columns. The battle lasted three weeks, and PLAN semi-mechanized elements were used in battle against the South Africans for the first time. On their way out of Angola, South Africans ground forces deliberately attacked an Angolan column, which was also a relative novelty. According to a South African military correspondent, 1980 saw 100 'security force' fatalities, the highest-ever figure, while 1,447 PLAN fighters were killed, an annual casualty rate to be surpassed only once in the succeeding years.[41]

In August 1981, Operation Protea, South Africa's most elaborate external operation so far, took place. It was an infantry operation against PLAN bases around Ongiva, 70 km from the border, which the South Africans then occupied until 1985. Protea began with an air strike on the radar installations at Cahama, some 300 km to the north-west. The town of Xangongo was occupied after joint resistance from PLAN and FAPLA. It, too, remained a South African base until 1985.

Operation Daisy took place in November 1981. Despite a challenge from Angolan MiGs, the South Africans set up headquarters 120 km into Angola and raided the Chetequera area, some 30 km from Namibia. In 1982 there were a series of raids to the north-west and northwards 150 km into Angola: PLAN commands, it was claimed, were disrupted in several sectors. In 1983, South African intelligence detected an unusually large 'infiltration', in preparation for the 1984 rainy season, and a pre-emptive attack was launched.

Operation Askari was much larger than previous operations, fielding four South African mechanized groups of about 500 each and various infantry elements, with thousands of PLAN and FAPLA troops opposing them. Both sides used artillery, and the SAAF bombed PLAN headquarters near Lubango, 300 km from the border. For the first time tanks were used in a war which was now definitely moving into the conventional arena, with southern Angola its main battlefield, as FAPLA-Cuban armoured forces attacked one of the South African mechanized groups.

One result of Operation Askari, from the South African viewpoint, was that apart from damage done to PLAN, 'the Angolans had been hurt badly enough to talk about peace'.[42] On 14 February 1984 South African and Angolan representatives met in Lusaka for talks brokered by the US. The result was the Lusaka Accord, which created the South African–Angolan Joint Monitoring Commission (JMC) which in theory would monitor the removal of foreign troops (South African, Cuban and SWAPO) from most of southern Angola.

In fact, South Africa had no intention of shifting UNITA out of south-eastern Angola, nor did Angola intend to stop PLAN from moving through the area south of the 16th Parallel. According to Negonga, the aim of the Lusaka Accord from the South African point of view, that FAPLA should prevent PLAN from operating south of the line demarcating the demilitarized area, was not attained: 'our forces were operating south of that line; they were not affecting us at all, but sometimes it was only creating some obstacles and difficulties in communicating with fighting forces from the rear'. Also, he adds, aerial surveillance was not effective in the southern Angolan terrain (with its numerous trees, presumably); hence the need of the JMC to deploy foot patrols.

The South Africans had pulled back as far as Ongiva when the JMC was disbanded in February 1985, after much wrangling. In fact it appears that the South Africans were willing to agree to the JMC because they were confident that UNITA (whose strength and geographical scope had been increasing rapidly over the past five years with their support) was strong enough to be an effective surrogate, able to block PLAN from western Caprivi, Kavango and eastern Ovamboland. The South African 'recce' Commandos were providing sabotage operations ostensibly carried out by UNITA, as was indicated by the Angolan capture in May 1985 of Captain Wynand du Toit of the First Reconnaissance Regiment while on a mission to sabotage the Gulf Oil installation in northern Angola.

Similarly, while urging the Lusaka agreement in 1984, the US was eager for a settlement for show in an election year, and at the same time was hinting at the prospect of the repeal of the Clark Amendment forbidding the US to supply arms to UNITA – which eventually took place the following year.

Phase 5, 1985–8: Conventional War to Cuito Cuanevale: the Settlement Stalemate

PLAN operations into Namibia by now faced considerable difficulties: a long route to the border, difficulties in transporting and accessing supplies for attacks into Namibia, and the need to divert increasing numbers of fighters for offence or defence against UNITA. PLAN units had to carry most of their material hundreds of kilometres to heavily camouflaged bases near the Namibian border, from which they operated into the country mostly during the rainy season from January to March.[43] Casualties were high. It took extraordinary tenacity on the part of ordinary fighters to keep coming, year after year during the 1980s right up to the ceasefire in 1988; the combined SADF–SWATF–Koevoet forces took few prisoners, and captured guerillas could be sure of torture to follow.

Not surprisingly, then, the number of 'incidents' does appear to have declined after 1983–4. SWAPO's support heartland was under heavy counter-insurgency pressure, mostly carried out by Koevoet. Civilians aiding guerillas were taking extraordinary risks; the civilian detention and disappearance rate was high.[44] In addition to this, routes of return and supply through southern Angola were fraught with risk.

At the same time, activists within Namibia were being drawn into sabotage and bombing operations: a bomb in Oshakati in 1985 killed a US military attaché; the cities in central and coastal Namibia were targeted for bombings, though the most severe in terms of casualties was another in an Oshakati bank in 1988.

Thus, although PLAN continued to be active in Namibia during and after the JMC, the focus of the war by now was southern Angola, where the South Africa–UNITA *entente* was attacking an alliance of FAPLA, PLAN and Cuban forces. Mechanized and other conventional forces were as a result becoming increasingly necessary to PLAN, which also had to guard its refugee camps in Kwanza Sul province and its lines of supply from Luanda to Lubango.

On the other hand, from late 1984, South Africa was also contending with a massive domestic uprising and concomitant economic problems: the 'total strategy' of destabilizing the region as a defence against 'domestic subversion' was demonstrably a failure, while international sanctions were beginning to bite. Despite all this, after the collapse of the JMC the P. W. Botha government resumed its strategy of air, armoured and infantry attacks deep into Angola, coupled with sufficient support to UNITA to enable it to control much of eastern Angola.

Negonga believes that the Angolans and their allies attained air superiority in 1987 (which agrees with pro-South African reporters like Heitman and Bridgeland). Also: 'The missile build-up in areas like Cahama, Xangongo, Xankete, was a concern in the mind of the enemy, because the enemy was trying to infiltrate planes deep into Angola, which was countered by the missiles.' Enhanced radar facilities at these centres near the Namibian border, from which the South Africans had withdrawn in terms of the Lusaka Accord, were also important in eroding South African air superiority. Between 1985 and 1987 major imports of Soviet military equipment also made a considerable difference to Angola's ability to contain UNITA. This was offset by the fact that by 1985 the strategic airfield at Mavinga, together with routes through Zaïre, were bringing UNITA large-scale US weapons and logistical support. UNITA was now launching sabotage and conventional attacks across a large area of Angola, and controlled the eastern border as far north as Zaïre. (As well as South Africa, Morocco, Zaïre and France had been supplying UNITA; from 1985, with the repeal of the Clark Amendment, the US publicly joined them.)

On Soviet advice, the MPLA government now determined on a strategy against UNITA which was similar to the SADF's against PLAN: to launch massive conventional attacks on UNITA's home base, rather than merely contending reactively with a spreading insurgency. Their main target would be Mavinga because it was crucial to UNITA's supply lines, and its capture would open UNITA's headquarters at Jamba to attack.

In September 1985, when the first major assault on UNITA began, with the first of the MPLA brigades pushing to within 25 km of Mavinga, Savimbi considered withdrawing, because his weaponry was not up to engaging FAPLA in conventional combat. That was when the SADF intervened

> on an unprecedented scale on UNITA's behalf. It sent in a troop of its new radar-guided long-range G-5 guns, which together with Mirage F-1AZ fighter-bombers and Canberra bombers, pounded the advancing MPLA soldiers unmercifully. The MPLA was stopped in its tracks and then withdrew several hundred kilometres to avoid being trapped by the approaching rainy season.[45]

This turned out to be something of a dress rehearsal for what would be a series of crucial battles in 1987–8. An Angolan offensive did not really get under way in 1986 because of the previous year's setback. It was March 1987 before South African reconnaissance commando teams deep in Angola reported big movements of Angolan, Cuban and PLAN troops southeastwards, as the campaign began to get rid of UNITA once and for all.

In 1987, four Angolan brigades, supported by PLAN and Cuban troops, engaged UNITA on several fronts. The SADF again deployed air support, but with less success than in 1985, since the Angolan Air Force now had MiG-23s and Cuban pilots, which provided air superiority. The South African G-5 and prototype G-6 mobile artillery pieces were sent in, as were mechanized units, armoured vehicles and tanks. Four FAPLA brigades, also with tanks, were deployed.[46]

In essence, what appears to have happened was that the South African–UNITA forces had considerable success in the early battles in late 1987, destroying one FAPLA brigade almost to the last man. Then, in retreat towards Cuito Cuanevale, the speed of the Angolan–Cuban forces took the attacking SADF–UNITA commanders by surprise. Once within the defensive parameters of Cuito Cuanevale, the Angolan–Cuban defenders – stiffened by thousands of Cuban veteran troops, four senior generals and large quantities of arms imported from November 1987 on Fidel Castro's direct instructions – managed to bring the SADF–UNITA forces to a halt.

The conduct of this series of battles between September 1987 and May 1988 was affected by the awareness of the political leaders of all sides that the battles were a counterpoint to international diplomacy. SADF commanders in the field complained that their high command would not permit an attack on Cuito Cuanevale in late 1987 while its defences were still weak;[47] the reasons concerned diplomatic contacts being made in New York. A failed South Africa–UNITA attack in March 1988, which aimed to drive the FAPLA–PLAN–Cuban forces back over the river into Cuito Cuanevale before blowing the bridge across it, led to a stalemate, with both sides holding their positions. But it also enabled Fidel Castro and the MPLA to claim a glorious victory – which in turn made it possible for Cuba to convince the MPLA to participate, and make concessions, in negotiations. The participants were Angola, Cuba and South Africa, under the chairmanship of US Assistant Secretary for State for Africa, Chester Crocker, with Soviet observers present.

At the same time, despite the news blackout in South Africa, rumours began filtering through to undermine the white public's – and the politicians' – morale. According to a speech by Fidel Castro at the end of May 1991, Cuban reinforcements were sent to Angola in 1987 when thousands of SADF troops attacked FAPLA units carrying out military operations in the south-east of the country. By 15 November 1987 there were 50,000 Cuban troops in the country. Cuito Cuanevale resisted and South African attacks were repulsed. The combined FAPLA–Cuban forces 'became more powerful with the addition of SWAPO units', until South Africa was persuaded it could not gain a military victory.

> That was how the doors opened for a negotiated solution which would include the fulfilment of UNSCR 435 for the decolonization and independence of Namibia. Without Operation Carlota, the agreements of December 1988 signed in New York would have been unthinkable. The schedule adopted as an annex to the Cuban–Angolan bilateral agreement on a phased withdrawal ended one day ahead of time in May 1991.[48]

In his memoirs, Chester Crocker has a version of events that tallies closely with Castro's.[49] 'We might still be at the [negotiating] table today were it not for the Cuban factor,' Crocker concludes. He represents the P. W. Botha administration as arrogant, double-dealing, divided among itself, incompetent, out of touch and given to bouts of 'appallingly bad public behaviour'.

On the other side, says Crocker, Castro sensed that he was being sucked into his own Vietnam by the ineptitude of his Angolan and Soviet allies. So he declared a fictional victory over the SADF at Cuito Cuanevale. According to Crocker, it was against Cuban advice that the Soviets planned the offensive against UNITA strong-holds in 1987 as 'a lumbering, tactically complex conventional thrust … which was decisively smashed by UNITA and the SADF at the Lomba river.'

In November 1987 Castro worked out a battle plan with Angolan premier Dos Santos, then informed the Soviets. Over the next three months 15,000 fresh Cuban troops were deployed to Angola, together with elements of other crack units and pilots, as well as four highly competent generals. They shored up the defences of Cuito Cuanevale, then in early 1988 launched a flanking manoeuvre southwestwards.

When this was complete, in May 1988, some 11,000 Cuban troops, backed by FAPLA and PLAN, had established a 400 km southern front running parallel to, and in some cases only 20 km from, the Namibian border. It was protected by the MiG–23s and helicopter gunships at the newly upgraded airbases at Cahama and Xangongo, plus 200 tanks, artillery, air defence radar and five different systems of surface-to-air missile systems.

According to Crocker, the SADF commander, Jannie Geldenhuys, also wished to bring his political masters to some lasting agreement. His 'help' to the Cuban political military strategy was to deploy his troops in such a way as to make them appear more numerous to the Angolans – reinforcing Cuban pressure on them to negotiate.[50]

By May 1988, the Soviet Union, Cuba and the US were pressuring the belligerents towards negotiation under Crocker's chairmanship. In the following months, a series of negotiations followed, though the war fizzled on. Essentially, the phase of conventional war had boiled down to a stalemate – the only circumstance which could have kept all parties coming back to the negotiating table.

By July 1988, Castro's chief representative at the Governor's Island talks in New York proposed a statement of agreement to open the way to 'peace without losers'. He said that for Cuba, nothing could be more honourable than leaving Angola 'of our own free will and in the context of Resolution 435 so that a new nation is born'. This was the crucial breakthrough essential to the success of the subsequent talks that led to a South Africa–SWAPO ceasefire and the SADF withdrawal from Angola in August 1988. The series of meetings between Angola, Cuba and South Africa between August and December under US chairmanship, with Soviet observers present, culminated in the Tripartite Agreement signed in New York in December 1988. This provided for implementation of Resolution 435 – UN supervised elections for Namibia – and SADF withdrawal from Namibia. A bilateral agreement between Angola and Cuba provided for Cuban troops to be withdrawn, first northwards, and then by stages from Angola.

Conclusion

The Namibian war lasted 23 years. Official South African figures set the combat-related deaths at 715 security force members (encompassing the SADF, the SWATF and members of both the South African and South West African Police forces) as against 11,291 PLAN fighters and Angolan soldiers.[51]

These figures (if accurate; SWAPO does not appear to have estimates) do not take into account non-combatants caused to disappear by both sides, though another South African estimate is that civilians killed in the course of the Namibian war number 2,000. By the end, the Namibian war, with its last phases taking place extensively in Angola, was estimated to have cost South Africa some R8 billion (under US$3 billion) to wage, while Angolan estimates for a single year's material damage (in 1981, a year of major South African penetration into southern Angola) were US$570 million, some 2,000 dead and 160,000 homeless.[52] In the early 1990s, Angola set the number of its war-displaced persons at 900,000, a substantial proportion of whom would have been affected by the action of South Africa or its proxy, UNITA.

Figures show only dimly the social upheaval which disrupted the lives and social structures of predominantly rural people living in Namibia along the northern border, and in southern Angola – those displaced, disabled, impoverished and traumatised. Nonetheless, for a war lasting 23 years, which culminated in pitched conventional battles, casualty and financial figures on this scale indicate that it was for long periods a low-intensity war.

Attrition by guerilla war, then, was far from forcing South Africa to its knees. That SWAPO was conducting an armed struggle, however, and able to keep recruits voluntarily coming over a generation to take part in it, was crucial to its international and diplomatic campaign. As we see, the origins of the armed struggle were political and international necessity. In the same way, its conclusion was diplomatic and political, rather than military.

Notes

1. J. Putz , H. Von Egidy and P. Caplan, *Namibia Handbook and Political Who's Who* (Windhoek: The Magus Company, 1989), p. 254.
2. H. Shityuwete, *Never Follow the Wolf* (London: Kliptown Books, 1990), p. 101. The SWATF's official version of the war concurs, as does Katjavivi: see P. H. R. Snyman, *Beeld van die SWA Gebiedsmag* (Pretoria: Promedia Drukkery, 1989), p. 11; and Department of Information and Publicity, SWAPO of Namibia, *Swapo: To Be Born a Nation* (London: Zed Books, 1981).
3. See Katjavivi, *op. cit.*, or S. Armstrong *In Search of Freedom: the Andreas Shipanga Story* (Gibraltar: Ashanti Publishing, 1989), p. 80.
4. A. A. Kamati, *et al.*, 'The Statement of our Resignation', mimeo of letter dated 13 November 1968.
5. Snyman, *op. cit.*, p. 11.
6. Willem Steenkamp, *South Africa's Border War: 1966–1989* (Gibraltar: Ashanti Publishing, 1989), p. 21. Shityuwete speaks of his conviction that an Angolan shopkeeper was expecting them and had radioed ahead his group's arrival to a Namibian border post. In fact, he is convinced that from the Zambian border his group of ten was continuously monitored by informers for the South Africans. *Op. cit.*, p. 104 ff. The official history of the SWATF draws a picture of a number of small guerilla groups active in the months before Omgulumbashe: 'In the very first incident in which the terrorists were involved, two shops near Oshikango were plundered and two civilians – a shop-owner and an Ovambo shop-assistant – were murdered.... Other small groups infiltrated the Kavango and individuals got as far as Tsumkwe in Bushmanland to the white farming areas.' Snyman, *op. cit.*, p. 11.
7. Steenkamp, *op. cit.*, p. 21.
8. Interview in 1991 with David Phillips Namholo, PLAN Chief of Staff, combat name Ho Chi Minh, now Chief of Staff of the Namibian Defence Force.
9. Steenkamp, *op. cit.*, pp. 23–5.
10. Katjavivi, *op. cit.*, p. 60.
11. Shityuwete, *op. cit.*, p. 168. A statement by the SWAPO ex-detainees refers to a PLAN 'purge' of PLAN recruits conducted by the Tanzanian military in 1968, giving as a reason not suspicion engendered by an allegedly renegade commander, but persistent complaints by guerillas based at Kongwa that they were being kept on ice in Tanzania rather than being sent to fight in Namibia – an issue which could also reflect problems at command level. See 'A report to the Namibian people: historical account of the SWAPO spy-drama', mimeo, 1989, p. 5.
12. Armstrong, *op. cit.*, p. 94.
13. Almost all SWAPO accounts date Dimo Hamaambo's accession as Commander of PLAN to the 1960s. However, one senior PLAN commander, the political commissar and deputy military commander of the élite Typhoon/Volcano unit in the early 1980s, says that one 'Pondo' – a combat name – was the top commander of PLAN until 1981 or 1982, when he died in a land-mine explosion and was succeeded by Hamaambo. Interview with Johannes 'Mistake' Gaomab, 1989.
14. Kamati *et al.*, *op. cit.*
15. Steenkamp, *op. cit.*, p. 26.
16. Putz, Von Egidy and Caplan, *op. cit.*, p. 256.
17. *Morning Star*, 14 June 1975.
18. *Telegraph*, 15 October 1975.
19. *Cape Times*, 14 October 1975. Later reports said there were eight dead, including six tribal policemen, in a raid on a border post near Oshikango.
20. *Windhoek Advertiser*, 16 October 1975.
21. *Cape Times*, 17 December 1975
22. *Cape Times*, 22 December 1975. The South African Minister of Justice arrived in Windhoek to supervise the search. The almost hysterical coverage of this incident may reflect the fact that the South African and Namibian media were barred from reporting on the contemporaneous (October 1975–March 1976) invasion of Angola, though they were well aware that it was taking place.
23. Armstrong, *op. cit.*, pp. 114–8.
24. See Steenkamp, *op. cit.*, p. 36 ff., and F. Bridgland, *The War for Africa* (Gibraltar: Ashanti Publishing, 1990), pp. 3–12. Bridgland was the Reuters reporter who put the South African invasion in the public domain; he has published favourable analyses of Savimbi.
25. Steenkamp, *op. cit.*, pp. 59–75.
26. Erastus Negonga, officer in PLAN North-western regional command, now in the Namibian

Ministry of Defence. Interviewed 1991.

27. Interview with Ho Chi Minh Namholo.
28. Steenkamp, *op. cit.*, pp. 70–1.
29. Author's interview with General Geldenhuys, 1984. The occasion was his promotion from Army chief to head of the SADF. Interestingly, his successor was General Kat Liebenberg, who had been in command of special forces, which involved overseeing the formation and development of the 'recce' regiments whose specialty was intelligence, scouting, sabotage and assassination in Angola and the rest of the region. Their 'specialist' role was growing in importance, and Liebenberg's promotion reflected this.
30. Steenkamp, *op. cit.* p. 71. Operation Savannah was the SADF term for the 1975–6 Angolan invasion.
31. Interview with Johannes Gaomab, 1989.
32. See Jan Breytenbach, *They Live by the Sword: 32 'Buffalo' Battalion – South Africa's Foreign Legion* (Alberton: Lemur Books, 1990).
33. Johannes Gaomab: 'About 80 of us crossed the Oshivelo gate about September 1980 and entered the Tsumeb-Otavi-Grootfontein area. We were strangers, and at times we had problems with the local population reporting us, so that we clashed with the Boers a few times. But after a while we became established in the area. We had gained support from some local people, including a few whites. Again we brought in arms which we cached, but this time not only on our backs. A lot came down in lorries, Bedfords and Ford Customs, with the help of businesspeople in the north. Some helped us freely, others we had to bribe.'
34. Interview with Simon Zhu Mbako, 1991.
35. Interview with Ho Chi Minh Namholo.
36. Pieter Van der Riet, 'The South African Defence Force in Namibia 1974–1989', African Studies Honours dissertation, UCT, mimeo, 1990, p. 38.
37. Interview with Natanael Shilongo, PLAN platoon commander and platoon secretary of information (intelligence) 1979–1986, in 1991.
38. Interview with Erastus Negonga.
39. Interview with Johannes Gaomab.
40. C. Crocker, M. Gresnes and R. Henderson, 'Southern Africa: a US policy for the 80s', *Africa Report*, January–February 1981.
41. Steenkamp, *op. cit.*, p. 96.
42. W. Steenkamp, 'The politics of power – the border war' in A. J. Venter, (ed.), *Challenge: Southern Africa within the African Revolutionary Context* (Gibraltar: Ashanti Publishing, 1989), p. 205.
43. Interview with Natanael Shilongo.
44. See 'Human rights violations published in *The Namibian* 1986–1989' in M. Hinz and L. G. Leuven Lachinski, *Koevoet versus the People of Namibia* (Utrecht: Working Group Kairos, 1989).
45. Bridgland, *op. cit.*, p. 17.
46. See Bridgland, *op. cit.*, also Helmoed–Romer Heitman, *War in Angola: the Final South African Phase* (Gibraltar: Ashanti Publishing, 1990). According to the South Africans, there were never more than 3,000 of their personnel in Angola at any one time.
47. Bridgland, *op. cit.*, p. 232.
48. *The Namibian*, 18 June 1991. Operation Carlota was the Cuban military designation covering the entire period of its presence in Angola.
49. Chester Crocker, *High Noon in Southern Africa: Making Peace in a Rough Neighbourhood*, quoted in *Sunday Times*, Johannesburg, 25 October 1992: 'Crocker's amazing attack on SA envoys', 'Crocker: the big lie of the Angolan war'.
50. Geldenhuys's version of the war is as follows: 'The objective of the MPLA, the Cubans and the Russians, to take Jamba, was not attained. They did not even manage to get past the Lomba river. Our objective, and that of UNITA, was to thwart their objective. If you think of the war as a rugby match, it comes down to the fact that our opponents never even came near our line: that was Jamba. They did not even cross the half-way line: that was Mavinga. They barely managed to cross their own 25-yard line: that was the Lomba river. Our team was leading by 50-0 and we were busy trying to score a pushover try at Tumpo during injury time when the final whistle blew. Then our opponents went and bragged that they had beaten us by fending off that last try, or by winning one or other lineout.' Jannie Geldenhuys, *Die Wat Wen: 'n Generaal se Storie uit 'n Era van Oorlog en Vrede* (Those Who Win: A General's Story of an Era of War and Peace: English translation forthcoming) (Pretoria: J. L. van Schaik, 1993).
51. Steenkamp, *op. cit.*, p. 185.
52. Angop (National News Agency of Angola): *The War Against the Angolan People* (Agencia Angola Press, 1988), p. 48.

3
SWAPO
The Politics of Exile

JOHN S. SAUL & COLIN LEYS

SWAPO in exile became the main bearer of Namibian nationalism and the cutting edge of Namibia's liberation. As Susan Brown has documented in the preceding chapter, SWAPO wielded – virtually exclusively and with whatever mixed record of success – the sword of armed struggle that was one essential feature of resistance to South Africa's overweening colonial presence in Namibia. Of at least equal importance, SWAPO's exile leadership came to articulate the voice of Namibians that was most clearly heard in international fora, notably at the United Nations: by the 1970s, SWAPO president Sam Nujoma and his colleagues had even managed to establish their movement as the 'authentic' (1973) – soon, 'the sole and authentic' (1976) – representative of the Namibian people in the eyes of the world body. Finally, the exile leadership also remained linked to the process of above-ground popular mobilization that ebbed and flowed inside Namibia itself. Indeed, as Chapter 4 will demonstrate, it was to stake out a position of considerable influence – as stimulus but also as arbiter of what was to be considered politically appropriate – over activity, carried out in the name of liberation, at home.

There were both benefits and costs to the role President Nujoma and the core SWAPO leadership thus came to play at the heart of the Namibian liberation struggle. In our introduction, we spoke of SWAPO's record of 'remarkable accomplishment': the creation, by a small group of Namibians living and working in Cape Town, of a movement that, over the next thirty years, would so establish its own credentials and so challenge South Africa's illegal presence in South West Africa as to emerge the governing party of an independent Namibia. Any careful study of SWAPO in exile must reinforce that judgement. And yet, as we will see, SWAPO's internal politics had its own dark side: demands for more democratic procedures and practices were denied and many innocent members of the movement were imprisoned, tortured, and even killed. Responsibility for these abuses of power is as certainly to be laid at the door of the SWAPO leadership as is credit for the movement's undoubted successes. In the introduction we posed a number of questions as to how such a contradictory reality is best to be interpreted and evaluated. There is a prior task, however: to identify, as accurately as possible, the diverse and cross-cutting forces actually at work within the exile movement over the entire thirty-year period of its existence up to the winning of independence in 1990. This is a task of historical retrieval that is only just beginning to be undertaken with the seriousness it deserves; the following account of the exile movement's own chequered history seeks to contribute to it.

Preeminence and Presidentialism: Tanzania and the 1960s

The 1960s saw both the formation of SWAPO and its rise to a position of preeminence within the Namibian liberation movement. The scale of activity was still modest.[1] The leaders, as they settled into Dar es Salaam over the decade, merely moved from small rooms in places like the Twiga hotel to residence in unprepossessing houses around the city; their offices remained a small, cramped establishment in one or another of Dar's back streets, and their military camp, once established, was also small, tucked away alongside the camps of other movements at Kongwa, in central Tanzania. Yet the fact remains that the seeds of armed struggle were sewn during this period and, of at least equal importance, the essential foundations were laid for SWAPO's considerable diplomatic achievements.

The 1960s also saw the consolidation of Sam Nujoma and his closest associates in positions of virtually unassailable preeminence within SWAPO itself. This was to prove a fateful development, and it was not unchallenged. But the dissent expressed at SWAPO's Kongwa camp in the late 1960s was dealt with peremptorily (with the assistance of the Tanzanian army) – a foretaste of things to come, in Zambia in the 1970s, when demands for democratic accountability within the movement would swell much more dramatically. Was this to be a case of 'liberation without democracy', as we have posed the question elsewhere?[2] Certainly, the 1960s began to witness the gestation of a notably authoritarian political culture within SWAPO – even as the movement was also developing a novel and promising range of strategies to counter South Africa's illegal occupation of Namibia.

What were these strategies? From the outset the distinctive international status of South West Africa/Namibia forced a certain strategic dualism on the emergent Namibian liberation movement. Thus, when it first began to gather fresh momentum in the 1950s, much Namibian resistance to South Africa's illegal occupation focussed on lobbying the United Nations in order to move that body to ensure the territory's safe passage to independence; figures like Fanuel Kozonguizi, representing the South West African National Union (SWANU) and Dr Mburumba Kerina, representing the Herero Chiefs' Council (and, for a time, SWAPO), became particularly prominent on this front. And SWAPO, itself sensitive to the international/United Nations-centred dimensions of the Namibian struggle, was soon able to develop, beyond Kerina, a strong team of external representatives of its own. Deftly positioned – in the US, the UK, Scandanavia, Germany, Eastern Europe and in various parts of Africa, as well as at the United Nations – these representatives were able to establish, most often from scratch, effective networks of contact and support in the countries in which they worked.[3] Over time, they were to have striking success in further isolating South Africa diplomatically.

However, as SWAPO established itself in exile in Dar es Salaam in the early 1960s, its cadres also found themselves operating in a milieu in which, on all sides, preparations for armed struggle against the recalcitrant white minority regimes of southern Africa – the Portuguese colonial presence in Angola and Mozambique, the white settler regime in Rhodesia, the apartheid state in South Africa itself – were the order of the day. This latter approach was not foreign to the emergent SWAPO leadership, the possible need for such a strategy having already been a subject of discussion in the circles that produced SWAPO's predecessor organization, the Ovamboland People's Congress (OPC)/Ovamboland People's Organization (OPO), in Cape Town in the late 1950s.[4] Thus, the idea did not need to be created out of whole cloth for consumption by the Organization of African Unity (OAU) when the latter, shortly after its formation in 1963, created its own Liberation Committee and prepared to back armed struggle in southern Africa.

There was an additional factor at work. SWAPO president Sam Nujoma and his colleagues, centred in Dar es Salaam and not New York, were quick to grasp that independent Africa would prove at least as important a terrain as that of the UN itself in establishing the primacy of SWAPO within the ranks of the Namibian nationalist movement.[5] Thus, after a short-lived attempt at establishing a united front (the South West Africa National Liberation Front/SWANLIF) between SWAPO and SWANU, in 1963 the two movements continued on their separate ways. SWAPO, pledging itself to armed struggle and already beginning to arrange the military training of some of its cadres abroad,[6] was then able (by mid-1965) to win exclusive backing from the OAU as *the* Namibian liberation movement of standing. And it was this kind of acceptance that SWAPO was ultimately to parlay, at the United Nations General Assembly, into its privileged international status as 'sole and authentic representative of the Namibian people'.

Some critics have seen SWAPO's turn to armed struggle, under such circumstances, as merely opportunist. What is certain is that there were differences of opinion within SWAPO from the outset as to what this military effort might entail. Some, like Kenneth Abrahams, advocated a 'people's war' strategy, arguing for the rooting of military action in a mobilization of popular resistance within Namibia itself. Nujoma and others seem to have been more inclined to see military activity as being primarily a matter of 'armed propaganda', designed to push the United Nations into more assertive action.[7] Nonetheless, SWAPO did start preparing for armed action, ultimately using the World Court's 1966 rejection of a case regarding Namibia's status as the signal for its first significant military undertaking in the same year – the attempt to establish a base at Omgulumbashe in northern Namibia.

SWAPO increasingly realized, after Omgulumbashe, that the carrying out of an armed struggle in Namibia from as far away as Dar es Salaam was a logistical nightmare and prepared, as the decade wore on, to shift the centre of its operations to Zambia. Moreover, the leadership had already helped facilitate a merger, as early as 1964, between SWAPO and the recently formed Caprivi African National Union (CANU). This was an alliance destined not to last, collapsing, finally, in 1980 with the withdrawal from SWAPO of Vice-President Mishake Muyongo and many of his followers (amidst charges that they were being victimized, in ethnic terms, by 'the Ovambo leadership'); at this point, however, it did bear the promise of opening up the eastern Caprivi as an important front for military activity. Still, throughout the 1960s the mounting of the military effort remained loosely organized, much to the frustration of some SWAPO combatants, as we will see. In this, SWAPO's military wing tended to mirror the still somewhat improvised character of the organization more generally.

Yet, as noted, enough was accomplished during this decade to establish SWAPO's preeminence in the eyes of the OAU and more widely. More or less simultaneously, a second crucial attribute of SWAPO in exile was also beginning to be locked into place. SWAPO had emerged out of the OPO, a body linking Ovambo migrants resident in South Africa with others operating within the migrant labour community inside Namibia itself (for example, ex-railway worker Sam Nujoma who was a key leader in the resistance to the enforced removal of Africans from the Old Location to Katutura that led to the 1959 massacre of 13 demonstrators). OPO became SWAPO in 1960 in part because Kerina, by then its chief lobbyist at the United Nations, felt the organization's credibility – both *vis-à-vis* the UN and in competition with its chief rival, SWANU – demanded the projection of a national image, but many OPO leaders were eager to establish a Namibia-wide profile for their organization in any case.[8]

Nonetheless, some observers have argued that SWAPO was never to lose, at the top, its Ovambo-centric tilt – in spite of the integration over the years of many members from other regions of Namibia within its ranks. As noted in the introduction to this book, the question of what weight to give to ethnic variables in interpreting developments within SWAPO is a difficult one and their significance can, perhaps, be overstated. What does seem clear, however, is that the members of the OPO old guard who now grouped around Nujoma within SWAPO – Peter Mueshihange, Peter Nanyemba, Maxton Joseph, Mzee Simon Kaukungua, and Dimo Hamaambo are most often mentioned – carried over a certain sense of personal ownership of the movement from the pre-SWAPO days. After all, they had, to a very significant extent, been self-selected as leaders by virtue of their own boldness and initial self-assertion. They accepted the necessarily prominent role granted to the younger, better-educated and often non-Ovambo 'SWAPO ambassadors' who gave the movement so much resonance abroad. But they were equally intent on keeping SWAPO's political and military levers of power firmly within their own grip.

As for Nujoma, it seems clear that in the rather *ad hoc*, rough and tumble politics that had characterized the OPO in Namibia his own appointment as president (shortly before leaving Namibia for exile) involved an element of chance, in addition to reflecting his own personal standing in the movement; at one time, for example, there were as many as five claimants to the title of president and there is a range of differing accounts as to how Nujoma ultimately won the ascendancy. Once he was in place, however, it was not long before the movement's notables came to accept maintenance of the sacrosanct character of Nujoma's position – as, in effect, the 'Headman' of SWAPO[9] – as crucial to preserving their own sense of the organization's true nature. True, the desire to preserve their own positions of power within the movement may have encouraged this attitude. But it also seems to have proven quite easy for them to conceive the safeguarding of both the movement's unity and its high purpose as requiring an unquestioning acceptance of the established leadership and its chosen priorities. Soon Nujoma was bearer of the informal, honorific sobriquet, 'the Old Man', and woe betide any 'youngsters' who sought to undermine this order of things with any novel notions of accountability or the like.

Add to this another essential ingredient: once established as SWAPO president, Sam Nujoma found himself elevated to membership in the league of African presidents, and this, too, was crucial to firming up the hold he and his closest associates were developing over the movement. Nujoma came to expect, even demand, the deference and largely unquestioned loyalty that his fellow presidents, such as Nyerere and Kaunda, received. Equally important for the immediate future was the fact that these other presidents came to feel committed to backing up, with the same ruthlessness with which they defended their own positions, the presidential person of Sam Nujoma. Thus, in the successive crises that marked SWAPO's internal politics in the 1960s and 1970s, when the established SWAPO leadership requested direct action by the Tanzanian and Zambian military, police and prison services against challenges arising from within SWAPO's own ranks, invariably such assistance seems to have been forthcoming.

The significance of such trends cannot be overestimated. Peter Katjavivi has said, nostalgically, that SWAPO in the 1960s still functioned a bit 'like a club',[10] which does capture something of the small scale and rather casual atmosphere of the movement's undertakings at that time. Yet the pull towards a hierarchical style of 'presidentialism' already defined a great deal of the ambience of that 'club'. Not that such trends passed unnoticed, some of the movement's members seeing the leadership's actions as having all too arbitrary a flavour. Did some such actions also manifest incompetence, or even corruption, on the part of some of those in high places? Certainly, rumblings along these lines were heard, from Namibians studying in Dar es Salaam (at Kurasini), for example, and, most notably, from members of the military rank and file. The latter – still a relatively small group (probably no more than a few hundred throughout the 1960s) – were mostly being held, especially after Omgulumbashe, in a state of relative inactivity in Kongwa Camp in central Tanzania. And the stagnation they experienced there had led, amongst other things, to a continuing trickle of desertions (principally to Kenya).

As noted in Chapter 2, such stagnation on the military front was partly traceable to the activities of the army's own commander, Leonard Phillemon (combat name 'Castro'). Castro was widely suspected of being in close contact with the South Africans and combatants felt their lives to be endangered by the passive attitude adopted towards him by the movement's leadership.[11] It was just such a situation that confronted a group of seven soldiers who arrived at Kongwa, in mid-1968, from (SWAPO-sponsored) training in China. Beyond the Castro question, this group felt there to be little clear understanding of military strategy and tactics within the leadership – and they were unhappy at their own growing sense that, indeed, armed struggle was valued merely as a rather token brand of 'armed propaganda'. They also saw in the lack of availability of weapons and other essentials sure signs of corruption.

Sam Ndeikwila, who had arrived at Kongwa from Namibia, via Zambia, a year earlier, found himself similarly disillusioned: by the low level of organization he felt prevailed in the camp, by the evidence of tribalism he found (directed, in particular, against Caprivians in the movement), and by the alacrity with which SWAPO commanders would call on the Tanzanian authorities to place in preventive detention any critics from within SWAPO ranks.[12] He was to throw in his lot with the 'China-men' (or 'Seven Comrades', as they also came to be termed within the movement) when they eventually brought into political focus the discontent within the camp.

Ndeikwila recalls drawing up a memorandum, read to officials in the camp, that called not only for Castro's dismissal and an end to Ovambo-rooted tribalist behaviour within the movement, but also, notably, for the holding of a congress at which the problems of the movement could be discussed fully. Finding their recommendations unfavourably received by the leadership and fearing arrest, the seven finally resigned from SWAPO, critiquing once again – in a 'Statement of our Resignation' – the weaknesses of the movement's military project and alleging that

> Being the founders of the 'Organization', SWAPO leaders consider themselves to be special beings. Holding a position in SWAPO is regarded as an inherited right, and a person may cling to a post as if he had conquered the whole world. Taking advantage of their positions, SWAPO leaders reject and suppress criticism from the people. Correct and constructive ideas from the people concerning the improvement of our struggle are always being sabotaged by the leadership.[13]

The manner in which SWAPO dealt with the resignation of the 'China-men' is also revealing. They were not even allowed to resign from SWAPO. Handed over almost immediately by the SWAPO camp commanders to the Tanzanian army,[14] they were shuttled to Dar es Salaam, arrested and taken directly to the Central Police Station where they were held in extremely harsh conditions for six months without charges. Eighteen months in Keko jail followed before they were rusticated to a low-level security camp (Ndabaro) in a remote region of Tanzania, from which they eventually found their way to Kenya.[15]

Ndeikwila argues that the subsequent Tanga Consultative Congress was, in effect, a response to the demand for one by the 'China-men', though it was held without their presence and, in his eyes, stage-managed in such a way as to render it 'a sham'. One can understand readily enough his sentiment, although he may overstate the case. There were, in fact, others in the movement who felt the need for a congress quite independently of the Kongwa events.[16] Some may have seen it as generally desirable that the executive should be more accountable to the membership. What is certain, however, is that many saw that a major change had taken place regarding one of the movement's constitutionally expressed aims – a commitment to armed struggle – and that this change had never been constitutionally ratified. Finally, there was a need, self-evident to some, for tightening up the movement's procedures, not least in the area of financial accounting. In the event, some 30 people, including 'SWAPO's External Executive Committee, members drawn from the military wing, students, women and the representatives of SWAPO's foreign missions', gathered in Tanga in December, 1969.[17]

There were, of course, ambiguities. Recall that SWAPO, however much a target of the South Africans inside Namibia, was never actually banned throughout the entire period that it also acted from exile. In these complicated circumstances it continued to be said, even at Tanga, that external SWAPO was merely acting in the name of SWAPO inside the country. In truth, the centre of gravity within the organization was already swinging in the direction of the external leadership and, in any case, the delegates at the congress felt they had no option but to proceed with the discussion of pressing matters as if this apparent impediment were not a crucial one.[18] Nonetheless, the issue was not, in the longer run, to be so easily shuffled aside.[19]

Equally striking was the leadership attitude towards whatever measure of democratic procedure the Tanga Congress might be said to have exemplified. Thus, more than one delegate has described Nujoma's discomfiture when asked, as a mere formality, to step down momentarily from the presidential chair in order to facilitate the election of the new slate of officers (which, of course, bore his name); only coaxing by Peter Nanyemba, one of Nujoma's closest senior colleagues within the movement, persuaded the president to accede to this request. At least one person present has suggested that this was due merely to the foreignness of the notion of 'accountability' to Nujoma and his immediate entourage.[20] Less charitably, Andreas Shipanga (then Acting Secretary for Information and Publicity and admittedly a hostile witness) believes that Nujoma determined, there and then, not to countenance the 'risk' of another congress.[21]

In the event, the Tanga Congress left much unfinished business. True, its resolutions reaffirmed 'that armed struggle is the only effective way to bring about the liberation of Namibia' and it did formally elect a new National Executive Committee. But action on a number of crucial issues was merely postponed, notably the drafting of a new constitution for the movement that would help firm up its structures. Participants we have talked with agree that this task was delegated to a committee of the leadership that would bring its proposals back to the next congress. It also seems generally accepted – and, in the light of subsequent events, this is particularly important – that there was a statement of intention by the Tanga meeting that another congress would be held in five years' time (by the end of 1974), and that a special organizing committee would be appointed, at least a year in advance of that date, to make preparations for it. In the event, no such draft constitution and no such congress were forthcoming.

Some of our respondents who were involved during this period suggest that time and circumstances (including SWAPO's move to Zambia) did not permit these promises to be fulfilled. Critics, on the other hand, believe that Nujoma and his senior colleagues merely agreed to them in order to bring the meeting to closure. Certainly, in the years following the Tanga congress, structures – of decision making, accountability and financial control – continued to be as rough and ready as previously. If anything, financial accounting systems became even more notional than previously (especially with the departure of Acting Treasurer Joseph Ithana for further studies in the United States), while the movement's Executive Committee appears to have met seldom, if ever. Thus, fully six years later, and in the immediate wake of SWAPO's severe internal crisis of 1976, the movement's own Ya-Otto Commission could still emphasize the 'dire need for the restructuring and reorganization of the Party administration to ensure', inter alia, 'optimal efficiency and effectiveness', 'revitalization of dormant and inactive departments e.g. Foreign Relations, Information and Publicity and Labour' and 'restoration of the office of Treasurer-General and the establishment of a sound, centrally controlled system of receiving, expending, accounting and auditing of Party funds'.[22] It is therefore not too surprising that during the crisis of the mid-1970s disaffected cadres, finding themselves operating within an organization that was run so imperfectly, were prepared to take seriously charges of corruption and abuse of power in high places – one more reason for their placing high on the list of their demands the calling of a congress that might deal with such matters.

Yet SWAPO continued to have political weight abroad, in large measure because of the increasing effectiveness of its 'external loop' of diplomatic representatives, alluded to earlier. Reinforced by Nujoma's tireless presence on this world stage, these 'SWAPO ambassadors' were increasingly able to deliver resources and ever-enhanced credibility to the movement from networks they had established in their host countries and at the United Nations. Closer to home, the armed struggle advanced more slowly; as Brown has shown, prior to the 1974 Portuguese coup that would eventually open up southern Angola (and hence northern Namibia) to renewed operations, SWAPO's activities were largely reduced to hit and run operations into a well-defended Caprivi. Nonetheless, the shifting of SWAPO's centre of gravity, from the late 1960s on, out of Tanzania and into Zambia marked an important development and it is therefore to Zambia that we must next turn our attention.

Crisis and Consolidation: Zambia and the 1970s

SWAPO, it will be clear, was still a small and relatively fragile organization as it made its move to Zambia. It was unprepared for the massive exodus of Namibians from inside the country in 1974. As we will see, the opening up of the border with Angola as a result of the coup in Portugal suddenly made it possible for thousands of young Namibian men and women to leave the country and join SWAPO in exile. Ultimately this dramatic growth in numbers would enhance SWAPO's credibility in international circles and greatly increase, for a time, its ability to fight effectively against the South Africans inside Namibia. But in the short run (between 1974 and 1976) it also produced a crisis in the movement of substantial proportions, during which, for example, a very large percentage of the movement's combatants (up to 2,000 in number) were placed under arrest. In fairness, handling such an exodus would have presented a staggering challenge to any liberation movement. Yet it was not merely logistics that were at stake: crucially, the question of leadership accountability was also to be posed more dramatically than ever before by the new cadres who now joined the movement.

On first moving from Tanzania to Zambia, SWAPO maintained a relatively modest operation: facilities for representation and administration in Lusaka, a reception centre for arriving recruits at the Old Farm (some 15 kilometres from Lusaka), a military centre called Central Base (near the town of Senanga in south-western Zambia) and some smaller bases closer to the Caprivi frontier.[23] With the substantial growth of numbers after 1974, the changes occurring in Angola in the wake of the Portuguese coup, and the increased availability of funds as the southern African struggle became more visible internationally, SWAPO's infrastructure expanded. The Old Farm was replaced in 1976 by the Nyango settlement (about five hours west of Lusaka), while Central Base was complemented from 1974 by a nearby reception and training facility called Oshatotwa. Services, however, remained quite rudimentary down to the mid-1970s,[24] and, as noted earlier, military operations remained relatively low-key during this period.

More immediately important was the political explosion occurring inside Namibia itself. At the centre of this upsurge, as documented in the following chapter, was the SWAPO Youth League (SYL) which stepped forward in the early 1970s, with remarkable militancy and courage, to lead the internal resistance. Young people confronted school authorities, mounted public rallies, helped in organizing the 1971 general strike and contributed centrally to a subsequent challenge, in the north, to the authority of the largely government-appointed Ovambo chiefs. When the chiefs called for help the administration, seeing that the police were already stretched to the limit, gave way to the South African Defence Force (SADF) and barbarous repression followed.

In March 1974, the coup in Portugal threw open the border to Angola, while in April the SADF formally took control of security in the north, later formally declaring it a war zone. Most of the SYL activists who were not still detained or jailed left Namibia for Zambia (via Angola) in June or July 1974, and in the following twelve months several thousand young Namibians would do the same, though not before the Youth League had held a congress of its own at Oniipa. There, amongst other things, delegates elected Pelao Nathanael Keshii as President and Reuben Shangula as Secretary General in a meeting that evidenced, in its very occurrence, something of the democratic spirit that had affected so many of those swept up in the dramatic mass resistance of the previous few years.[25] It was this spirit that was profoundly to inform subsequent events in Zambia, events in which Keshii and Shangula were also to play important roles.

Meanwhile, the opening up of the Angolan border also facilitated the movement of military traffic in the other direction. SWAPO fighters were now able to gain access through Angola to Ovamboland. In doing so, however, SWAPO was drawn even further into cooperation with UNITA, despite the fact that contradictions were rapidly coming to a head between UNITA and MPLA (ostensibly SWAPO's closest Angolan ally as a fellow member of the Soviet-supported 'club' of liberation movements). The link to UNITA (with its control over the area of south-eastern Angola most proximate to central Caprivi and Ovamboland) had been inescapable while SWAPO was obliged to conduct its armed struggle from Zambia, and had also been acceptable to the extent that UNITA's efforts were, at least in appearance, directed against the Portuguese; moreover, UNITA's ethnic base (the Ovimbundu) had very close ties to the Oshivambo-speaking people of northern Namibia. At the same time, it is clear that there were tensions, cast in ethnic, ideological and strategic terms, within the SWAPO leadership over the UNITA question; some leaders (Hamaambo, for example) began quite early to forge the military ties with the MPLA that were to become so important later, while others remained more oriented to the longer-standing UNITA link. This issue was soon to come to a head, as UNITA attached itself in an ever more compromised and unqualified manner to South Africa's regional purposes.

New developments in regional politics, closely linked to the fact of the Portuguese coup, now aggravated these difficulties acutely for SWAPO. The Zambian President, Kenneth Kaunda, had always been a somewhat reluctant recruit to the cause of militant struggle in southern Africa. He was caught between the expectations of his fellow African leaders that he should play a front-line role in that struggle, and his awareness of Zambia's economic vulnerability *vis-à-vis* the redoubts of white power. Moreover, in the words of Barber and Barratt, 'Zambia was host to the two rival Zimbabwean nationalist movements and SWAPO. Apart from constantly having to intervene in factional squabbles within and between these movements, Kaunda was faced with an increasing number of armed men in Zambia who were not under his control, and with the threat of Rhodesian retaliatory attacks.'[26] In short, Kaunda walked a tightrope in the region. Small wonder that he found himself open, in the wake of the Portuguese coup, to the blandishments of South African President John Vorster as the latter sought to introduce his policy of regional 'detente'.

Was this to be 'peace at any price' in southern Africa? Many of Kaunda's critics thought so at the time, and certainly SWAPO leaders worried about the implications of Kaunda's machinations (largely focussed though they were, in the first instance, on the situation in Rhodesia/Zimbabwe) for their own cause.[27] Moreover, the complexity of the situation for SWAPO was compounded by the congruence of Vorster's and Kaunda's positions on the Angolan question. Here the lure of detente combined with Kaunda's strong anti-Soviet prejudices to draw him to the side of UNITA.[28] According to Shipanga, Nujoma and Nanyemba were informed by Zambia in October 1974 that they must stop fighting from Zambia.[29] Whether this is true or not, the SWAPO leaders themselves were hardly less paralysed by the impossibility of foretelling the outcome of the intensifying conflict between UNITA and the MPLA. The conjuncture was thus fraught with problems that would have challenged the ingenuity of any liberation movement. The truth of this observation does not, however, obviate the need to assess how the problems were in fact handled by the SWAPO leadership.

For the leadership suddenly found itself facing a dramatic challenge to its authority from within the organization.[30] The ensuing crisis has been termed misleadingly 'the Shipanga crisis' because of the alleged central role of the senior SWAPO leader Andreas Shipanga within the dissident circles of the time. In fact, he remained a relatively minor player in the ensuing drama, while three substantial groups of 'dissidents' were far more important: soldiers who were in PLAN before the exodus, including some commanders; soldiers who came out in the exodus, trained, and were sent to camps in western Zambia or Angola; and a group of SYL leaders who were also part of the exodus and continued to act as SYL leaders in Lusaka.

Soldiers already in PLAN found the confusion over detente and the UNITA/MPLA links extremely frustrating,[31] and morale was undermined further by the weaknesses in PLAN's general logistics: food, clothing and medicine were often lacking, as well as arms; people suffered and died without adequate support; and allegations that corruption was responsible were widely believed.[32] There was a growing demand to investigate abuses of authority, to clarify what the organization was fighting for, and to have a clear constitutional base ('we are fighting as terrorists and bandits because we have no programme').[33] To be sure, not all the experienced PLAN combatants took these complaints as far as demanding the holding of a congress; indeed some, especially among the commanders, continued to support the leadership in spite of all criticisms. Still, it seems likely that most of this group of combatants supported the idea of a congress by the end of 1975. The second group of PLAN members, newly recruited from the 1974–5 exodus and much larger in numbers, had not yet experienced combat, nor the ambiguities of the situation on the ground in Angola and Zambia, and initially most of them were eager to get to the front. Some, however, were soon persuaded that the problems were dangerously real, and as time went on more and more of them also came to support the demand for an investigation and a congress.

The Youth League leaders were in a special category. Having spearheaded the struggle inside Namibia and having been duly elected to office there, a core group of them anticipated taking their place within SWAPO in exile as a body.[34] Eventually a group of them did manage to establish themselves as 'SYL representatives' in Lusaka, with some office space in the Liberation Centre, while also maintaining contact with other SYL members at the Old Farm settlement and, later, at Nyango. For their part, the SWAPO leaders in exile expected the Keshiis and the Shangulas to accept subordinate roles under the authority of the Director of Youth, Homateni Kaluenja, who had been elected to his position at the Tanga Congress and was still based in Dar es Salaam. The newcomers, however, saw themselves with some justice as significant members of the internal leadership of SWAPO, in whose name the external leaders were supposed to be acting, according to the Tanga Congress resolutions. They wanted a place in the leadership in exile in Lusaka, and they had the character and education to shine in it. They also came from a background of participant urban politics unfamiliar to the old OPO leaders. They lacked deference; moreover, they were often quite well known among the new arrivals from Namibia, whereas the old leadership was not.[35] Ambitious, but also increasingly concerned at the weaknesses they perceived in the workings of exile-SWAPO,[36] they now took the lead in publicly articulating the growing demand that a SWAPO congress be held.

Ultimately, several meetings in 1975 between the SYL leaders and various senior members of the SWAPO Executive Committee found the latter agreeing on many of the Youth Leaguers' points (that a constitution should have been drafted, that a congress was overdue) and even, ultimately, accepting the demand for the early holding of such a congress.[37] Concretely, however, nothing was done and, in any case, the SWAPO leadership was soon taking steps to disperse the Youth Leaguers[38] and limit their political activities; eventually (in April 1976) they were to have the Zambians arrest them. The leadership was, in any case, being moved towards repressive action by a far more dangerous challenge to its authority than that represented by the Youth Leaguers: that from the soldiers themselves.

The efforts of the SYL to get a congress called were known to the soldiers at the camps in western Zambia,[39] but the soldiers' actions that were to precipitate the final explosion within SWAPO were independent of the SYL. By late 1975, PLAN had 2,000–3,000 trained combatants in camps in south-western Zambia, many if not most of whom were still inadequately armed and inactive, as well as being poorly fed and clothed, and direly in need of a calibre of political and military leadership that was not forthcoming. Rumours abounded and no steps seem to have been taken to keep them well informed. At this point, the demand for a congress was enjoying wide support among the PLAN troops in SWAPO's main military camp, Central Base, and at other smaller bases, and these combatants also (in early 1976) elected a set of committees to investigate the movement's situation, draft statements and call for a congress.[40]

They also rejected the authority of their commanders, and even placed two of them under arrest. Fifteen representatives then went to Lusaka where they met with OAU and Zambian government representatives (SWAPO officials refused to attend). They agreed to establish a temporary command structure for themselves, and articulated their demands, echoed in a range of documents produced by the soldiers' committees during this period. 'We are not a splitting group,' they were to write in a statement addressed to Nujoma. 'At the same time we would like to assure you of our determination to rid the party from the evil of corruption. We believe that the party will represent the people's aspirations only when it is reorganized through the Congress.'[41] As another undated document of the time (produced by the 'anti-corruption fighters' and headed 'We Demand the Party Congress') explained, this would be a democratic congress, in which 'delegates … from the soldiers will be elected by the soldiers themselves (to exclude the nomination of persons by the commanders or Planning or Military Council)', and it would be preceded by a 'commission of enquiry' composed of 24 members, eight from the Zambian fronts, eight from the Angolan fronts, and eight from non-military branches of SWAPO, and likewise directly elected; and this commission would conduct a full and rigorous review of every department in SWAPO headquarters and at the two fronts.[42] In short, the soldiers were after a real accounting from the leadership,[43] and a democratic congress with power to, among other things, make changes in the Central Committee.[44]

Events now moved rapidly to a climax. There were various scuffles (between soldiers and commanders loyal to the leadership) at the bases and soon Central Base was surrounded by three or four battalions of the Zambian army. The dissidents were told to surrender their guns, and that a committee was to go to Lusaka. Forty-eight commanders, members of the soldiers' 'main' committee, were chosen, and driven to Lusaka on about 23 April; there they were arrested by Zambian soldiers. After a spell in Mwinilunga prison camp in the far north-west of the country they were taken to Mboroma detention camp near Kabwe, where they joined some 1,600–1,800 other combatants who had also been arrested by the Zambians at Central Base and elsewhere.

In the meantime Nujoma and Muyongo[45] had also invoked Zambian assistance to move against the SYL leaders (including Keshii and Shangula) and those within the SWAPO leadership who had been most willing to give them a hearing (Shipanga, Solomon Mifima, and Immanuel Engombe for example, all of whom were on the Executive), 11 persons in all. Ferried to prison in Tanzania, where President Nyerere obligingly kept them in order to help evade a writ of Habeas corpus secured in Zambian courts on Shipanga's behalf, they were eventually freed, under international pressure, in 1978. The fate of the detainees at Mboroma was grimmer, because the outside world was for a long time ignorant of their fate, and because most of the detainees were unknown. Hardship was severe,[46] until finally (in April 1977), after an extraordinary feat of endurance and courage, two escaped detainees, Hizipo Shikondombolo and Sakarias Elago, reached Nairobi via Dar es Salaam.[47] In Kenya they met a small community of earlier Namibian 'exiles within the exile' (among them Sam Ndeikwila) who helped them draft a press release.[48] This at last focussed international attention on Mboroma itself.

With the situation now more fully out in the open, the Zambians felt constrained to intervene and gave the detainees the choice of either accepting the protection of the United Nations High Commissioner for Refugees (UNHCR), or returning to SWAPO for rehabilitation. Two to three hundred chose to leave SWAPO and were taken to the UNHCR refugee camp at Maheba in north-western Zambia, where most would remain until 1989. The majority, some 1,200–1,300, opted for 'rehabilitation' by SWAPO; this was carried out at Mboroma.[49] There some 45–50 commanders who had been active in the 'anti-corruption' leadership, most of them having been among the 48 taken to Lusaka and arrested in April 1976, are widely believed to have been taken out of the camp singly or in small groups and killed in the following weeks or months.[50] About 600 of the remaining 'rehabilitees' were eventually moved to Nyango, while others were transferred to Angola, some of them arriving in Cassinga just before the May 1978 attack by the South Africans, in which many of them are believed to have died.

The SWAPO leaders were faced with a difficult dilemma during this period, of course. Where some would see the soldiers as making legitimate democratic demands, these leaders were inclined to smell 'mutiny'; this may, in fact, be an inevitable ambiguity in an organization that is on the one hand a political party/state-in-the-making, and on the other a military structure. Nonetheless, to leave the matter there would be to underestimate the impact on events of the leadership's decision to adopt a purely authoritarian stance. Perhaps the dissidents were not sufficiently sensitive to the full complexity of the challenges facing the SWAPO leadership, but what is most significant is that they were never really invited by the SWAPO leadership to understand such things. 'No questions' was the order of the day: and, most fundamental to the moment, 'no congress'.[51] For, when all is said and done, it was the holding of a reasonably democratic congress that served as the core demand for both soldiers and Youth Leaguers alike (and even for Andreas Shipanga himself, it would appear).[52] In contrast, as we will soon see, in the aftermath of the crisis the SWAPO leadership was to lock into place a political culture, the basis for which had already been established well before the crisis of course, that frowned on open debate within the movement, sanctified (as the 'mother body') a largely untransformed SWAPO and gave free rein to those who safeguarded its 'security'.

Did this apparent suppression of democratic politics within SWAPO have the long-term effect of compromising the movement's ideology in other important ways? One possibility, certainly, is that a more enthusiastic acceptance of the notion of popular empowerment, so central to the dissidents' critique, might have produced a very different and potentially quite radicalizing political climate within the movement. The dissidents had mixed opinions on ideological matters, but the fact remains that some of their documents do much more than merely hint at the possible intersection of democratic and socialist demands:

> We got information from reliable sources that there are people in the SWAPO leadership who are having farms, hotels, shops and bank accounts, that is why they are less interested in the liberation struggle. When we demand the National Congress where a clear, socialist line be drawn, they consider us enemies, this is because we believe that socialism is a better society. We are against exploitation of man by man....This is one of the reasons why they don't want the Congress to be held, because they know that in a socialist Namibia, there will be no room for private owned shops, hotels, etc.[53]

Meanwhile, however, the SWAPO leadership had weathered the crisis, thanks, in large part, to the role played by the Zambian military. Nonetheless, its international credibility was momentarily shaken. Various foreign backers, the Scandinavians in particular, waited to see what would happen next. Things were also on the boil at the United Nations. January had seen the unanimous adoption of Security Council Resolution 385 condemning South Africa's illegal occupation of Namibia and calling for 'free elections under the supervision and control of the United Nations'. Now, too, the lobbying to advance SWAPO's own position – at the end of the year, it would be embraced by the General Assembly as the 'sole and authentic representative' of the Namibian people – had become particularly intense. A first step to recuperate any lost ground had to be to render an official account of the events in Zambia. This was the principal task of the Ya-Otto Commission, made up of ten prominent SWAPO members (including Theo-Ben Gurirab, the movement's highly respected Chief

Representative to the United Nations) and chaired by Central Committee member John Ya-Otto.

The Ya-Otto Commission – which, it must be noted, did not hear evidence from any of the dissidents themselves – was to play a major role in naming SWAPO's democratic crisis 'the Shipanga crisis'. Presenting the crisis as springing from a mere play for power within the SWAPO leadership, it portrayed Shipanga, 'being naturally opposed to armed struggle', as 'determined to wreck the entire leadership of the Party to ensure the success of the international imperialist-South African conspiracy of which he was the witting agent' (p. 9).[54] In fact, the case made for his central role in the crisis is, in light of the evidence, largely fictional, its main function being to trivialize the democratic thrust from below that was the real issue at stake.[55] 'The Commission [was] convinced', for example, 'that Shipanga's connections with the Youth League turned its leadership into a hostile group against SWAPO leadership.' Furthermore, 'with the same intention of creating dissension and disruption in the Party, this time in the People's Liberation Army of Namibia, he manipulated some receptive cadres to carry out his machinations' (p. 8).

When not directly traced to Shipanga's 'machinations', troubles in the military camps and elsewhere were presented in the report as the product of spies and 'misguided elements' who 'capitalized on people's ignorance and political immaturity'. The Youth League leaders did come in for some special condemnation of their own, of course. The report sought not only to caricature their activities inside Namibia and to query their credentials:[56] their disloyalty in exile to the 'mother body' of SWAPO was another constantly reiterated theme. Yet the statement that 'they were neither prepared nor willing to reconcile whatever differences might have existed between them and the mother body' (p. 10) makes no reference to the fact that the chief demand of the Youth Leaguers, like that of the military dissidents, was for a congress at which, precisely, differences might have been resolved. Easy, then, for the Commission to charge, in conclusion, 'that the motive and ultimate aim of these dissidents was to seize power' (p. 11), thereby equating the wish to get new leaders elected at a representative congress with 'seizing power'!

Yet the Ya-Otto Commission, despite its misrepresentation of the nature of the democratic challenge the 1974–6 crisis represented for the movement, actually conceded many of the points the rebels had been making. Thus the 'enemy agents' were said to have utilized 'the existing loopholes and shortcomings of the Party e.g. the delayed Congress, lack of political programmes, official incompetence, corruption and shortage of arms and ammunition to further their sinister mission'(p. 16). And this admission was complemented by a stinging, more detailed, litany of 'official shortcomings and incompetence' that were said to mar SWAPO practices (including 'insensitivity on the part of some members in the leadership and their unwillingness to admit mistakes and solicit advice from colleagues. In the absence of self criticism', the report continued, 'leaders tend to disregard their accountability to the people they lead' (p. 12)).

To be sure, there is no evidence of self-criticism on the part of the commissioners regarding SWAPO's handling of the immediate crisis at issue. Indeed, the extensive list of movement 'shortcomings' reads rather oddly when situated with reference to the misrepresentation of events that otherwise surrounds it in the text. Did this reflect a judgement on the part of some of the younger SWAPO leaders that they had little option but to accept the political hegemony of Nujoma and the 'old guard' (and even cover for them), yet also wish to see a movement that would operate with greater effectiveness and probity, a movement more credible both to its own members and to a concerned international constituency? A dangerous game, of course. Those who sought so to modernize the movement without more fundamentally democratizing it exposed themselves to the very considerable risk that they themselves might become targets of elements within an unreconstructed top leadership clique when circumstances shifted against them. In short, by condoning the abuse of power that marked the period 1974–6, such cadres may merely have been sharpening the knife that would later be pressed to their own throats in Angola.

Beyond the Ya-Otto Commission, Nujoma and his closest colleagues also sought to rationalize their manner of coping with crisis by demonstrating the strong mandate they retained from home. Crucial to this was the congress organized by SWAPO's internal leadership at Walvis Bay, on 29–31 May, a congress initially intended to deal with the necessary reconstruction of the internal party. Now, as we will document in more detail in the following chapter, this congress found itself inserted into the broader crisis of the movement, with the external leadership taking a major interest in, and even manifesting some nervousness about, its likely outcome. There was, in fact, much confusion inside Namibia about the events in Zambia. In the end, however, the internal party felt it had little choice but to endorse the top leadership and call upon them, in turn, to appoint the rest of the outside leadership.[57]

This was done (and exile-SWAPO's *de facto* primacy within the organization more forcefully confirmed than ever) when the external leadership held what they apparently hoped might pass for a kind of 'congress' of their own, an 'Enlarged Central Committee Meeting' held at Nampundwe near Lusaka between 28 July and 2 August. Here, in the absence of those now safely in confinement and without any real election of delegates, the SWAPO leaders met to confirm themselves in their positions, to seek to streamline, to some greater degree, the movement's administration and to adopt a new constitution and political programme.[58] If very far from being, as Katjavivi would have it, an 'occasion to address the roots of the 1976 rebellion', Nampundwe was at least an occasion at which the 'modernizers' were allowed to have their day.[59]

Some present at Nampundwe have also claimed that the Political Programme adopted there, notable for its strong leftist thrust, represented a bow in the direction of the concerns of 'the youth' (notwithstanding the fact that the youth, as an active political force, had by this point been brought to heel, with many promising cadres lost, and much of the possibility of a serious debate on SWAPO's long-term project irretrievably foreclosed).[60] For the document was remarkably left-leaning (albeit in a somewhat Stalinist register), pledging SWAPO to 'unite all Namibian people, particularly the working class, the peasantry and progressive intellectuals, into a vanguard party capable of safeguarding national independence and of building a classless, non-exploitative society based on the ideals and principles of scientific socialism'.[61] Some in SWAPO took this commitment to be a serious one at the time,[62] others now speak retrospectively of the more opportunist considerations that were at play in its adoption. But if such considerations were important it must be emphasized that this was opportunism designed not merely (or even primarily) to help SWAPO refurbish its radical credentials in the eyes of young Namibians. Increasingly, the intended audience was those Eastern European backers whose assistance to a revived SWAPO military offensive from Angolan soil was likely to be crucially important, as well as the 'Marxist-Leninist' government of Angola itself.

In any case, the Nampundwe documents may be less important in epitomizing the direction of development of the movement in the wake of the 1976 crisis than a second set of documents, much less well known, that were adopted by SWAPO's Central Committee only a year later: the various 'Revolutionary Decrees' identifying 'crimes against the Namibian People's Revolution' and specifying their generally draconian punishment. Crimes? The central decree is defined as relating 'first and foremost to political crimes, i.e. felonious acts aimed at obstructing the accomplishment of the objectives of the revolutionary and liberatory struggle of the people of Namibia waged by the SWAPO and other friends of the movements and patriots. These objectives are and shall be reflected in various documents of the SWAPO movement which is the only authentic representative of the Namibian people.'[63] Here the two-edged nature of SWAPO's hard-won designation as 'sole and authentic representative' – so useful, positively, in undermining the legitimacy of South Africa's hold over Namibia – reveals most clearly its potentially negative side. Were such decrees also to be the real legacy of the crushing of criticism that had marked the climax of the 1976 crisis: a small élite of leaders confirmed in their unaccountable power and a movement, a political culture, a country-in-the-making, in which critics were to be deemed, with little hesitation, criminals and spies?

Of course, one must not trivialize 'security concerns'. The world of the southern African liberation movements of the period was honeycombed with intelligence operatives from many countries, East and West. Not least important were agents of South Africa itself who managed either to penetrate the movements' own ranks or to get quite close to them;[64] moreover, South African intelligence agencies soon became expert at modes of disinformation designed to suggest a more extensive degree of penetration of southern African movements than was actually the case. In short, the foreign pressure bearing down on a movement like SWAPO was intense. At the same time, it seems clear that the fetishization of security also fed the paranoia and the power drives of some leaders in ways that had a dynamic and logic of their own, and that within SWAPO were to spawn practices infinitely more destructive of the health of the movement than any actual South African penetration of it could possibly have been. The further degeneration of the internal politics of SWAPO in the 1980s – the riding roughshod over the constitutional niceties of the Nampundwe documents and the cruel abuses of power that marked the movement's 'spy drama' – must be understood, to a very marked degree, in these terms.

In order to confirm this, and to make the connection between the distinctive political culture that by now had crystallized firmly within SWAPO in exile and its final, grim denouement in the torture camps of Lubango, it will be necessary to track SWAPO, in the following section, to Angola. Already, as the 1970s wound down, SWAPO had recentred the bulk of its military activities there and its political centre of gravity was now shifting there as well. It may bear noting that there also remained some residue of SWAPO's political presence in Zambia right up to the coming of Namibian independence. There was still the Nyango settlement, a haven for a declining but still significant number of civilians, mainly women and children, throughout the period. And there was also the United Nations Institute for Namibia (UNIN), founded in 1976 as a training centre for functionaries of a future independent Namibian state and a research base for developing policies and programmes for a new SWAPO government. Indeed, UNIN remained an important hub for the group of SWAPO intellectuals (alluded to above) who had a modernizing, developmentalist, if not particularly radical, vision for SWAPO. This was a group, including the UNIN director Hage Geingob (later to become Prime Minister of Namibia), who seem themselves to have come under threat from the security apparatus as it became increasingly powerful within the movement in Angola. Ironically, by the late 1980s, Zambia may well have come to seem some kind of relatively safe haven from SWAPO's authoritarian tendency.[65]

Liberation ... and Lubango: Angola and the 1980s

What, then, of SWAPO in Angola? As noted earlier, some sections of the SWAPO leadership – army Commander Dimo Hamaambo chief among them – had been prepared to throw in their lot with the new MPLA government quite early on, well before others could quite decide how best to balance the respective claims of UNITA and the MPLA or to cope with the machinations of President Kaunda. Indeed Hamaambo, as Army Commander, seems to have made this move as early as 1974 and had even set up a PLAN Command Headquarters (CHQ) at Cassinga, in southern Angola, by 1976. By 1977, however, Nujoma and Nanyemba were also working hard to repair their relationships with the victorious MPLA leaders, who remained somewhat bitter over SWAPO's failure to break earlier with UNITA. They were sufficiently successful in this to secure the moving of SWAPO's Headquarters to Luanda in 1978.[66] Now, too, PLAN's training camps and SWAPO's Defence Headquarters (DHQ), together with Secretary of Defence Nanyemba, were moved to bases near Lubango in south-west Angola – a siting also necessitated by the infamous South African attack on Cassinga of May 1978 that had claimed some 600 civilian lives.[67]

In the wake of the Cassinga massacre, a new civilian settlement was also created at Kwanza Sul, much further north, with perhaps 35,000 residents by the mid-1980s.[68] There was also a smaller civilian settlement, originally for children and later a vocational training centre, at Ntalandando, between Luanda and Kwanza Sul, and a substantial transit camp on the edge of Luanda for SWAPO personnel waiting either to be sent abroad or for a posting after returning from overseas. SWAPO headquarters staff were housed in town. As noted earlier, the settlement at Nyango in Zambia continued to function as well, and there were several thousand Namibian students studying throughout the world on scholarships obtained through SWAPO, including over a thousand in Cuba, hundreds in Ghana and Sierra Leone and other African countries, and larger or smaller numbers in numerous other countries including the USSR, the GDR and other Eastern bloc countries, the Scandinavian countries, India, Britain and the USA. Meanwhile, of course, the war against South Africa continued; indeed, as Brown shows in Chapter 2, PLAN activities reached a peak in 1981, with semi-conventional units penetrating the settler areas in the Otavi triangle, and guerillas operating throughout Ovamboland and even as far south as Windhoek and beyond. Only a few years later there were said to be some 8,000–9,000 combatants in PLAN.

Considering the parlous state of the organization in 1976, its relocation in another country and the establishment there of a quasi 'state-in-exile' with an active army, a well-developed health system and a far-flung education and training programme were impressive achievements, even when the exceptional levels of international financial and technical assistance that had gradually become available to SWAPO are taken into account.[69] The critics of 1974–6 had been silenced; it might well also appear that their criticisms had been proved unjustified.

The evidence presently available indicates otherwise, however. In the first place, the habits of authoritarianism that the critics had challenged unsuccessfully were now apparently widespread. Contrary to the solidarity literature of the time, the civilian camps were not run by elected councils, but by commandants with absolute authority.[70] In Angola there was, certainly, a serious security threat, above all from UNITA as it gradually extended its effective control over the countryside towards Kwanza Sul (specialized PLAN units were created to defend bases, including Kwanza Sul in 1982, against UNITA attacks). Yet the accounts of camp residents (and also of civilians under SWAPO's jurisdiction abroad) seem to show that this was not the only cause of the 'no questions' regime. Even before the move to Angola 'it was not good to ask questions', and the atmosphere in the camps and in SWAPO circles overseas seems often to have been charged with anxiety and suspicion.

In the military the problem was different. Strict discipline was essential. Those in command, however, from Nanyemba and Hamaambo downwards, came from a generation that had had few educational opportunities.[71] Some, including Nanyemba, were highly intelligent, but others, drawn from the migrant workers recruited in Botswana in the 1960s and early 1970s, were neither educated nor always especially able. They often seem to have felt threatened by the more educated youngsters under their command. They tended to deal with this by expressions of contempt for intellectuals, and by refusing to share information or explain their decisions. The problem was aggravated in 1980 when the South Africans introduced conscription in the south of Namibia. From then on a high proportion of those coming out were southerners, still more highly educated than the exodus of 1974–6, so that anti-intellectualism became mixed with anti-'southern' feeling on the part of those in command.[72]

Paradoxically this was also aggravated about this time by the decision of Nanyemba, as Defence Secretary, to upgrade the PLAN command (and perhaps also, for his own political purposes, to strengthen his DHQ *vis-à-vis* the Command Headquarters). He coined a slogan, remembered by several as 'We can no longer have an illiterate army', and set about recruiting able new arrivals, who were mostly southerners, into his Defence Headquarters. The old guard under Army Commander Dimo Hamaambo may well have felt threatened by this trend. However, on the eve of a Central Committee meeting in April 1983 – when it seems that Nanyemba was hoping to get support for a radical reconstruction of the PLAN command structure which would have put power decisively into the hands of a reduced general staff recruited by himself – he was killed in a car crash. Hamaambo in effect succeeded to Nanyemba's authority and introduced something very like the new structure envisaged by Nanyemba, but staffed with his own people.[73]

In the meantime, as Chapter 2 shows, South Africa had committed enormous resources to its military effort, their sheer weight determining that the war should start to go badly for SWAPO. Cassinga had been PLAN's Command Headquarters since 1976; after the May 1978 attack, in which Hamaambo escaped but a number of his staff died, new Command headquarters were established successively at Cahama, Shitumba, Mongwa and elsewhere, but each one was attacked until Hamaambo was finally driven to relocate his headquarters near Nanyemba's Defence HQ outside Lubango. By 1982, in fact, the South Africans had occupied all of 'shallow Angola', and all PLAN bases had had to be withdrawn some 100–150 km north of the Namibian border, while in Namibia locally recruited battalions of Namibians under South African command, and the Koevoet counter-insurgency force created in 1978, began to inflict terrible casualties on any PLAN operation across the border. These developments severely reduced PLAN's capacity to threaten security inside Namibia. From 1984 onwards PLAN was mainly involved in operations against UNITA in Angola itself, with brief and costly incursions into Namibia confined to the rainy season from January to March.

The demoralization caused by this situation as it developed after 1981 was aggravated by a widespread awareness that the South Africans had extremely accurate knowledge of PLAN movements and intentions. This was largely due, Brown suggests, to their ability to monitor PLAN radio communications to an extent that PLAN's field commanders did not grasp, but some information also undoubtedly came from spies, which afforded a plausible rationale for the establishment in 1981 of a new SWAPO Security Organization under the control of the Deputy Army Commander, Solomon Hawala. And the new exodus of young Namibians from the south, fleeing conscription, coincided with this development.[74]

All the ingredients were now in place – military reverses, declining morale, misgivings about the competence of the army command, insecurities extending to rivalries between successive generations of exiles and between different ethnic groups, the arrival of a new wave of exiles from the south, and a pervasive tradition of authoritarianism, reinforced in the aftermath of the 1976 crisis – for the institution of the system of organized terror which now enveloped the entire organization, and which was halted only by the peace accord of 1988. In the ensuing 'spy drama' almost a thousand SWAPO members in exile were arrested, taken to Lubango, and forced to 'confess' to being South African agents, if necessary by being beaten or otherwise tortured to the point of death, and then detained, with poor food and little or no medical care, in covered pits in the ground where some, certainly, died.[75] It is a story that remains to be fleshed out in further detail. What we are concerned with here is to understand how it happened, and why it was not stopped.

In the first place, the new security organ seems to have been created on the initiative of Nanyemba, probably on Russian advice. Key personnel are said to have been sent to the USSR to be trained in security work some time before the Central Committee formally decided in 1980 or 1981 to establish a separate Military Security Organization of up to 250 men, under Hawala's control and answerable only to the president. This development must also be seen in the context of the fact that by 1980 PLAN itself had become effectively autonomous. Apart from Nanyemba and Nujoma himself, only three other members of the Central Committee appear to have been allowed to visit Lubango.[76] Now a new security organization was established in Lubango under the sole control of the Deputy Army Commander, who was not even accountable to the Secretary for Defence. Extraordinarily enough, even Nujoma's wife was interrogated by it for some weeks in 1988,[77] and in 1989 Aaron Muchimba, his brother-in-law and a Central Committee member, was also taken to Lubango and detained.

The personnel of the new organization were recruited largely from older PLAN combatants, most of whom had only limited education. Their mode of operation was unvarying. Detainees who refused to admit to being 'sent' (i.e. by the South Africans) were tortured until they confessed to various crimes that their captors wanted to hear, and gave the names of other people allegedly involved with them.[78] It is said that anyone implicated by three such 'confessions' might in turn be detained. Those who were detained were, for the most part, never released, partly because they had had to confess their guilt in order not to be killed, and partly because keeping them in Lubango prevented the rest of the exile movement from knowing what was happening. People were afraid, because others were constantly being arrested; but the full truth about what was happening was not known, even if it was feared. As the net widened, no one could feel secure.[79] More and more of the movement's brightest and most critical minds disappeared from their posts.[80] Letters were read by 'Security', and fear of being denounced by personal enemies or even neighbours became general throughout the exiled community, from the USSR to Scandanavia, Britain and Cuba. By 1988 the 'spy' question had become a matter of officially fostered paranoia, mentioned in all speeches in Angola, at all camp parades, in every issue of the SWAPO newspaper.

At first people were shocked to hear that so-and-so was accused of being a spy, but refused to believe that SWAPO would have arrested him (or her) without strong grounds for suspicion. But eventually everyone knew someone who had been arrested and who they could never bring themselves to believe had been a spy, and finally it was obvious that the arrests had a deadly irrational momentum of their own which had nothing to do with spying: in truth the revolution was consuming its own children.[81]

Those in the leadership who were kept out of Lubango grew more and more alarmed.[82] In 1984 Geingob is even said to have raised the issue at a Central Committee meeting: Hawala is said to have shouted him down.[83] It is also stated that Lucas Pohamba, SWAPO Chief of Operations in Luanda, tried again later, but was told it was a military matter, not to be discussed by the Central Committee. Eventually it became too dangerous for anyone to protest.[84] After the interrogation of his wife and the arrest of his brother-in-law, for example, even Nujoma looked vulnerable. It is even said that Hamaambo himself, fearing the eventual disabling of PLAN, once contemplated a military assault on Hawala's headquarters; short of that, it is hard to feel confident that 'SWAPO Security' would not in the end have destroyed the movement abroad. As one senior cabinet minister acknowledged to us, 'There was fear everywhere. The Central Committee could not act. We were saved by [the implementation of Security Council Resolution] 435'.

Ironically, the dissidents of 1976 had, at the time, been called the 'destroyers of the party'.[85] In retrospect, however, the rejection of their demand for accountability and democracy, and the repression of their leaders, can be seen to have eliminated the one internal force that might have broken SWAPO's tendency towards authoritarianism; as a result, the organization now came very close to being eliminated as a significant actor in the final rounds of the liberation struggle by a Stalinoid monster of its own creation. Stalinoid? Here we touch on one of the chief paradoxes of the southern African revolution more broadly considered. For the growth of SWAPO's links to the Eastern bloc was crucial (as was true for most liberation movements in the region) to its military credibility. At the same time, as suggested above, the growing Eastern European presence within the movement nurtured practices that reinforced tendencies already apparent in the SWAPO security apparatus. Increasingly, too, such practices were defended in the name of socialism, of 'Marxism-Leninism', vanguardism and a one-party state in the making. Small wonder that 'socialism' came to seem to many within and without SWAPO to be a project little worth defending.

Of course, other historical processes were sweeping the situation forward in the last days of the Angolan war and, as Susan Brown has demonstrated, in ways that were often beyond SWAPO's ability to influence. But here, too, timing was all. On the one hand, SWAPO had not yet had time to self-destruct. On the other, the movement remained an important player during this, the culminating moment of its years in exile, despite the fact that it was not actually present at the bargaining table that would decide Namibia's fate. That it did so is, of course, an index of the remarkable successes that had actually been achieved (especially in the diplomatic sphere) by the movement during its three decades of exile. Such were SWAPO's links with the Cubans, the Angolans and the Soviets, for example, that the latter were not likely to abandon Namibia's cause altogether during the negotiations described by Brown. Such was the credibility SWAPO had earned for itself at the United Nations and in other international circles (the world of the churches, of the anti-apartheid network broadly defined, of the more 'progressive' Western countries) that its concerns could not be ignored during the internationally monitored winding-down of South Africa's occupation of Namibia. And such was SWAPO's continuing political legitimacy inside Namibia itself, particularly in the populous north, that South Africa and its acolytes within Namibia would not prove able to finesse electoral victory away from it when elections for a constituent assembly finally came, under UN supervision, in 1989.

SWAPO had won. To be sure, the movement (or, put more precisely, some within it) paid a price for its excesses in exile. From the mid-1980s, as we will see in Chapter 4, voices were heard inside Namibia exposing the plight of the detainees. In addition, the impact of the release of detainees from the dungeons on the eve of the elections, coupled with the fact that several hundreds of other suspected victims remained unaccounted for by SWAPO, undoubtedly weakened the movement's electoral appeal in southern Namibia. Without the salience of the detainees' issue – also seized upon by South African propagandists for their own electoral purposes, of course – SWAPO would probably have won the two-thirds majority in the elections for the constituent assembly necessary to give it the formal power to dictate constitutional outcomes. Would the SWAPO security establishment then have been empowered to inflict its authoritarian politics on an independent Namibia?[86]

Perhaps not. Other factors than electoral numbers were at play during the transition period: the Soviet model and regional presence in retreat, the regional hegemony of a global capitalism that brooks not even the mildest left postures firmly in place. Already, in the run-up to independence, the kaleidoscope of power within SWAPO was being shaken up and the imbalance that had come to privilege the hard-line 'securocrats' – with their cruel arrogance and their Stalinist mind-sets – was being redressed by circumstance. As we will see in our concluding chapter, the transition was now to be framed by acceptance of the dictates of various avatars of international capitalism and comfortably sealed by constitutional compromise with the DTA opposition. A more democratic outcome than might have been anticipated was thus wedded to a less transformed socio-economic structure than might have been expected on the basis of SWAPO leaders' pronouncements in exile.[87] It was the kind of transition that drew SWAPO's UNIN team and diplomatic corps personnel to centre stage.

It was this group who, at least for the moment, were to become firmly established in ministerial office,[88] their own left formulations of the 'Political Programme' days mothballed as they moved out of exile and into power, and their own past acceptance of many of SWAPO's authoritarian tendencies down-played. Their preferred status (over both 'securocrats' and other leaders, dubbed 'hardline', who were close to the military) in the diplomatic and entrepreneurial circles that now 'really counted' in Windhoek thus became the key to their ascendancy. Of course, Nujoma was to be President, ever the survivor. Consider, however, the senior SWAPO leader (of the ex-UNIN, ex-diplomatic type) who told us he was especially pleased with the fact that the blending of SWAPO's military wing (PLAN) with the apartheid regime's SWATF in the new Namibian army meant that these two 'dangerous' forces might now 'neutralize' each other. Such a statement says almost as much about the history of SWAPO in exile as does the sweetness of the movement's victory, and the fact that the South African colonial presence had at last been overcome.

Notes

1. Even by the end of the decade it seems that there may have been no more than 300 SWAPO members in exile. Thus Ben Amathila, presently Minister of Information and Broadcasting and one of the principal organizers of the Tanga Congress, describes the SWAPO office in Dar es Salaam as operating, at the time of that Congress (1969), 'as a SWAPO branch for the +/− 300 SWAPO members abroad' (personal communication to the authors).
2. Colin Leys and John S. Saul, 'Liberation without democracy? The SWAPO crisis of 1976', paper presented to the Inaugural Research Seminar of the Canadian Research Consortium on Southern Africa, Montreal, 6 November 1992 and published in revised form but under the same title in the *Journal of Southern African Studies*, 20, 1 (March, 1994), pp. 123–47.
3. Andreas Shipanga's account in his *In Search of Freedom* ('As told to Sue Armstrong'; Gilbraltar: Ashanti Publishing, 1989), Chapters 16–20, of his life as an 'ambassador for SWAPO' – notably in Cairo – during this period is instructive.
4. The probable impact of the Cape Town–based Yu Chi Chen club (and, in particular, of Dr Kenneth Abrahams, an early SWAPO member) bears noting in this regard.
5. Some of our more sceptical informants, close to SWAPO at the time, have even suggested that this kind of jockeying for preeminence *vis-à-vis* the potential claims of other Namibian political movements was often at least as central to the preoccupations of the SWAPO leadership as was the task of finding the proper course to follow in confronting the South African regime.
6. Much of this early training took place elsewhere in Africa, although SWAPO had also received a lift when, in 1964, it began to obtain Soviet military support.
7. Abrahams paid for his expressed disagreement on this and other matters by being suspended by Nujoma from the movement's National Executive Committee while in Kenya on a SWAPO mission — a straw in the wind regarding future modes of settling differences within SWAPO.
8. Relations between the OPO and such an important non–Ovambo organization as the Herero Chiefs' Council were, in any case, very good at this time; it must have seemed a particularly good moment for the OPO to seek a national projection.
9. Thus, one of our informants, seeking the basis of the 'undemocratic bent of SWAPO', mentioned a specific 'cultural factor', referring to 'how things used to be decided in Ovamboland, where I think it had always been up to the Headman whether or not they consulted the people they ruled over': 'There were good Headmen and bad ones, popular ones and hated ones.... I don't think it inaccurate to think of Nujoma as a Headman of SWAPO, especially in the way he and the veterans around him reacted to the demands of the younger generation, from the "China-men" onwards, who got their ideas outside the "traditional Namibian ways"'

(private communication). Another informant also speculating on 'not only how Nujoma reached "the top" but how and why he managed to stay there' suggested two points: that 'various sections of Ovambo society (the Churches not least) see their interests taken care of in the affairs of the country by SWAPO' and that Nujoma 'the scion of a minor tribe [within the Ovambo], had proved his usefulness as a skillful (?) balancer of the claims for preponderance of the favourite sons around him – the trusted nucleus of power brokers from among the more powerful of the Ovambo tribes....'(private communication, question mark in the original). As noted (see Chapter 1), these are extremely difficult matters to penetrate from outside, even if they may be important; they must await their historian.

10. Peter Katjavivi, interview with the authors, 23 September 1992. Katjavivi was elected SWAPO Secretary for Economics and Justice at the 1969–70 Tanga Congress and later served as SWAPO Representative in London.

11. 'Castro' was eventually handed over to the Tanzanians and spent 17 years in prison there, also without trial.

12. Sam T. Ndeikwila, interview with the authors, 27 June 1991.

13. 'The Statement of our Resignation', dated 13 November 1968 and signed by A. Angunga Kamati, Merodak A. Ya Mnakapa [Zen Mnakapa], Nambali Msati, Haimbodi Ya Nambinga, Sam T. Ndeikwila, E. Petrus Njambali, and Leonard Taapopi (document in the authors' possession). One of the original seven returnees, Paul Kanyemba, was active with the group but, at the last minute, apparently backed away; however, as noted, Sam Ndeikwila had also linked himself to the group of 'China–men', so that their number levelled off, ultimately, at seven. It might be asked in what way, if any, resonances from the Sino–Soviet split played into this confrontation within SWAPO. It is interesting that it was not a factor emphasized by any of our informants.

14. It is worth noting that both Dimo Hamaambo, who become SWAPO army commander (and Commander of the Namibian Defence Force at independence), and Solomon Hawala (combat name 'Jesus'), later SWAPO head of Security, were amongst those in authority at this time.

15. Taapopi states that they found at Ndabaro others from Kongwa, the latter camp now closed in part because of tensions caused by other combatants demanding release of the 'China-men' (personal communication). For a list of others detained, in his view equally arbitrarily, both before and after the incarceration of the 'China-men', see the paper by one of that group, Zen Mnakapa, entitled '1986: The Tenth Anniversary of Death' (mimeo, n.d., in the authors' possession).

16. Strikingly, no mention seems to have been made during the Tanga Congress of the 'China-men' or indeed of any other of the detainees and/or 'defectors' to Kenya , an early case of the 'out of sight, out of mind' mentality regarding the casualties of SWAPO's internal struggles that was to become all too readily the *modus operandi* of even the best SWAPO cadres.

17. Katjavivi, 'The rise of nationalism in Namibia and its international dimensions', PhD thesis, Oxford University, 1986.

18. The Hon. Ben Amathila, interview with the authors, 6 July 1992.

19. For example, as we will see below, when youth leaders, duly elected by a large and impressively active SWAPO Youth League inside Namibia, came out to Zambia as part of the 1974 exodus, they were loath to accept uncritically the credentials of the 'Director of Youth' (Homateni Kaluenja), elected, as they saw it, merely by a very small group of exile delegates at Tanga.

20. Intended as a charitable explanation by a SWAPO loyalist, this is, in itself, a revealing formulation.

21. Andreas Shipanga, interview with the authors, 23 June 1992.

22. See 'John Ya Otto Commission of Inquiry into the Circumstances which Led to the Revolt of the SWAPO Cadres between June, 1974 and April, 1976' (hereinafter referred to as the 'Ya Otto Report'), p. 17. A copy of this report is in the authors' possession; some sections of it are also produced as an appendix in Katjavivi, 'The rise of nationalism in Namibia' (*op. cit.*), pp. 396–401.

23. Lucas Pohamba, present Minister of Home Affairs, interview with the authors, 1 July 1992. Erastus Shameena, one-time SWAPO representative in Romania, believes that the total number of SWAPO combatants in the camps on the 'western front' in Zambia when he arrived with the first wave of the exodus from inside the country in 1974 was only about 40 or 50, with just a few in each base (interview with Leys, 2 July 1991).

24. For example, Dr Libertine Appolus-Amathila was shocked by the primitive standards of medical practice she found in place at Old Farm when she returned to Zambia in 1975 – although she and others were soon to set about improving them (interview with the authors, 9 July 1992).

25. For further discussion of this congress see the following chapter.
26. James Barber and John Barratt, *South Africa's Foreign Policy: The Search for Status and Security 1945–1988* (Cambridge: Cambridge University Press, 1990), p. 182.
27. Paul Trewhela, for his part, infers that SWAPO leaders may even have embraced, up to a point, the detente–related initiatives of Vorster and Kaunda, perhaps seeing some potential pay-off there for their UN-centred approach to resolving the Namibian question internationally; this became all the more true, he argues, as Henry Kissinger, the US Secretary of State, began to take a more active role in detente. Trewhela's approach is suggestive but overstated, we feel; here as elsewhere in his innovative articles, Trewhela tends to extrapolate too quickly from the 'logic' of external events to an explanation of developments internal to SWAPO. See Trewhela, 'The Kissinger/Vorster/Kaunda Detente: The Genesis of the SWAPO "Spy-Drama" ', Parts I and II, *Searchlight South Africa*, nos 5 and 6 (1990–1).
28. Kaunda characterized the Soviet Union's role in the region, and more specifically in Angola, as that of 'a plundering tiger and its cubs', stating (in April 1975), for example, that he was 'anxious to remove what he considered to be a tide sweeping MPLA to victory' (Barber and Barratt, *op. cit.*, p. 188).
29. Shipanga, *op. cit.*, p. 116.
30. For a much more detailed account of this crisis than is possible to present in the following paragraphs see the present authors' 'Liberation without democracy? The SWAPO crisis of 1976', cited in footnote 1, above. One other existing account that makes a serious, if highly partisan, contribution to an understanding of these events is Erica Thiro–Beukes, Attie Beukes and Hewat Beukes, *A Struggle Betrayed* (Rehoboth: Akasia Drukkery, 1990), but it has had a very restricted circulation.
31. As soon as the coup took place in Angola, UNITA was engaged in a political struggle with the MPLA and the cooperation previously established between the small PLAN units and UNITA units became increasingly problematic. Soldiers returning to bases in south-west Zambia in mid-1975 reported appalling experiences of conflicting loyalties, of finding the UNITA units they were attached to engaging in battles with FAPLA units, and finally doing so in collaboration with the South Africans. At the same time the detente policy being pursued by Kaunda led to an embargo on arms for SWAPO, while UNITA was favoured with arms supplies – allegedly including some destined for PLAN – for its fight with the MPLA.
32. Suspicion that funds were being misused was common; in April 1976, the 'Anti–corruption fighters' also issued a statement that focussed heavily on 'the running of private businesses in Lusaka and the surroundings and in some other Zambian cities' (from 'The Virus that Caused the Disease', 28 April 1976, a document in the collection of Hewat and Erica Beukes). The most common allegation was that Nujoma, Nanyemba and Mueshihange owned two night–clubs in Lusaka and that Nanyemba sold drugs and blankets supplied by foreign aid donors. However, Ole Gjerstad, who was in Lusaka and close to the SWAPO leadership during this period (while helping John Ya–Otto write his autobiography, *Battlefront Namibia*), states that SWAPO leaders actually lived extremely modestly (interview with the authors, Montreal, 16 May 1992). A very different problem, but one cited later by many dissidents, was the attitude of many SWAPO leaders towards young women who came in the exodus and who were liable to be appropriated by leaders and PLAN commanders who should have protected them.
33. Statement from the 'SWAPO Military Wing Western Province' addressed 'To the President of SWAPO' dated 23 March 1975 (Beukes collection, *op. cit.*).
34. Not all prominent Youth Leaguers leaving the country agreed with the political tack being taken by Keshii, Shangula and others. But both Ben Ulenga and Ndali (Thomas) Kamati believed the Oniipa Congress had been a 'good' one – in spite of the fact that they were destined in exile to go into Angola to fight under Dimo Hamaambo, separating physically and politically from their former colleagues in the Youth League (interviews with the authors, 24 June and 7 July 1992, respectively).
35. For example, at one meeting at Old Farm at which both Nujoma and Keshii spoke, Nujoma was allegedly moved to say, 'If I were in Namibia I would order my soldiers to crush you small flies.' According to this 'dissident' account, such was the crowd's response that he was eventually obliged to deny that this was meant as a threat to Keshii's life (Reuben Shangula, interview with the authors, 7 July 1992).
36. Thus, a comprehensive SYL memorandum of February 1975 sought a response from the SWAPO leadership on such questions as (1) the tendency of SWAPO officials to treat all questions as treasonous; (2) the constitutional position of SWAPO and its ideology; and (3) problems of administrative and financial efficiency and control.
37. For further documentation see Leys and Saul, 'Liberation without Democracy?' *op. cit.*; see also Peter Katjavivi, 'The rise of nationalism', *op. cit.*, pp. 289 and 291.

38. After a first critical letter to Nujoma, Keshii and Shangula were posted to assignments in London and elsewhere. They decided to refuse to go until a congress was held.

39. For instance, the statement by SWAPO Military Wing, Western Province, *op. cit.*, asked (as the 20th out of 22 questions): 'Why is the President using the PLAN as his private force to blackmail the Namibians e.g. when the SYL was demanding the National Congress, they were threatened that force would be commanded against [them] in order to crush them?'

40. About this time, a group of Executive Committee members and overseas representatives of SWAPO also sent a memorandum to the Executive Committee in Lusaka calling for a congress; see Katjavivi, 'The rise of nationalism', *op. cit.*, p. 291, note 3. It is worth noting that as early as June 1975 an article in the UNIP (United National Independence Party) newspaper expressed the hope that the SWAPO leadership would not put off its overdue congress out of fear on the part of the incumbent leaders that a congress would make some changes (see Shipanga, *op. cit.*, p. 104); Shipanga believes such an article could not have been written without Kaunda's approval.

41. Statement from the 'SWAPO Military Wing Western Province', *op. cit.* Amongst other things, the document asked 'Why does the President as the leader of the Namibians limit people when bringing their problems forth?' But it also confirmed 'our loyalty and confidence in you as our President', stating that 'we are asking you, our President, to come and negotiate with the fighters confirming the arrangements of temporary commanders ... during the transitional period to the Congress when the permanent commanders will eventually be nominated by the new Central Committee'. In the event, it was the Zambian army, not the President, who was to arrive at the bases.

42. 'We Demand The Party Congress To Be Held As Soon As Possible Without Delay Or Deceiving Manoeuvres With The Following Conditions: [etc]', document in the possession of Onesimus Handjaba; Handjaba was one of the fifteen who first went to Lusaka and later one of the 48 commanders arrested in late April on a second visit there (see below). Interviewed by the authors, 20 June 1991.

43. Recounting these events fifteen years later, several of the anti-corruption fighters and the former Youth League leaders insist that their idea was to put in trustworthy new leaders alongside the old ones, not to replace them. But the evidence suggests that even if this had been made clear, it would have been wholly unacceptable to Nujoma, Nanyemba (a particular target of the soldiers in any event) and others. Given the treatment of all those who had put forward searching criticisms in the past, the leadership's response was wholly predictable, as the more experienced combatants – for many of whom the events at Kongwa in the 1960s was common knowledge – understood. 'Older commanders said, "We have experience of this: if you persist, the leaders are going to kill you"' (Onesimus Handjaba, interview with the authors, *op. cit.*).

44. Many of the soldiers' appeals were addressed to the existing Central Committee which, as the SWAPO Youth Leaguers had already established from their own meetings with the leaders, had never met (see Leys and Saul, 'Liberation without Democracy?', *op. cit.*). It is a measure of the dissidents' ultimate impotence that throughout these events they constantly appealed to the leadership to act on the basis of a constitution which they knew was being honoured largely in the breach.

45. Ironically (in the light of his subsequent falling out with the rest of the SWAPO leadership), Muyongo seems to have been a particularly important player throughout the period of the crackdown, tough enough to stand firm (many of the other senior leaders merely absented themselves, as one senior SWAPO leader told us) and well enough connected, in ethnic and other terms, to the Zambian military to interface effectively with it.

46. It was also during this period that Nujoma was reported in the *Times of Zambia* as saying that all the dissidents would be tried and could be put before a firing squad.

47. The distance from Mboroma to Dar es Salaam is over 800 miles. Shikondombolo and Elago walked much of this, without money or supplies. In Dar es Salaam they eventually found assistance to get to Nairobi, where they could safely make public the story of the detainees, including those in Tanzania.

48. 'Appeal for the Release of over 1,000 Namibians in Detentions in Zambia and in Tanzania', issued in Kenya on 27 April 1977 (copy provided by Hizipo Shikondombolo when interviewed by the authors, 17 June 1991).

49. The extent to which SWAPO came to exercise virtually exclusive control of the social and political space open to Namibians in exile was discussed in our introduction. In consequence of this reality, it was extremely difficult for the detainees to conceive their futures, political or practical, outside SWAPO. Thus an earlier proposal – by the new committee elected by the detainees in Mboroma – that everyone should resign from SWAPO had been rejected by the

majority, saying 'What are we going to do to survive [if we resign]?' (Onesimus Handjaba, interview with the authors, *op. cit.*) There is evidence to suggest that the nature of the rehabilitation process at Mboroma had something of the flavour of a witch-hunt about it (see the 'Appeal for the Release of over 1,000 Namibians in Detentions in Zambia and in Tanzania', cited above, which alludes to an early version of such attempted rehabilitation); further investigation may demonstrate that, in this, 'rehabilitation' foreshadowed the style of interrogation that was to become part and parcel of the 'spy-drama' in Angola a few years later (see below).

50. The evidence for this also needs to be investigated. At present it is largely hearsay and from dissident sources, but it cannot be easily dismissed.

51. Ndali (Thomas) Kamati, a Youth League activist contemporary with Keshii and Shangula inside Namibia but one who, in exile, associated himself closely with the established SWAPO leadership, has nonetheless argued that the situation 'could have been defused' had the leaders been more willing to talk to their critics, to share information and to stay informed of the combatants' demands. In this connection, Kamati also made reference to a booklet prepared in Angola by none other than Homuteni Kaluenja, the Tanga-elected 'Director of Youth', that he says presented a quite critical assessment of the leadership's political approach during the run-up to the crisis; unfortunately, we have been unable to locate a copy of this booklet. Yet Kamati is not inclined to absolve Keshii, Shangula, Nangutuwala 'and a few others' of their own share of responsibility for escalation of the crisis since, in his opinion, they were 'unnecessarily hard-headed' (interview with the authors, 7 July 1992).

52. Of course, the 'democratic demands' of the 'dissidents' were at once instrumental and principled. They were instrumental in the sense that an opening of the movement to democratic scrutiny (through the holding of a congress) was seen as crucial to exposing weaknesses in its activities and helping to overcome them; only then, they felt, might the struggle against the South Africans (the dissidents' main preoccupation) be advanced more effectively. But it is difficult to read the various documents produced during this period without being impressed by the more general import – reflecting a concern for democratic first principles (and, in this way, reminiscent of debates that had occurred several centuries earlier, at Putney, within another, very different citizen army) – of what was being demanded. For more on this point see Leys and Saul, 'Liberation without Democracy?', *op. cit.*

53. 'PLAN Fighters', statement of 23 April, 1976 (*op. cit.*). See also the document 'Oh World Hear Our Cries' (7 August, 1976), which states, inter alia, that 'we would like the whole world to know that what is currently taking place in SWAPO is an ideological struggle between the nationalist bourgeoisie comprised of the ruling clique ... and the anti-corruption fighters ... who [are] Marxist, socialist oriented guerillas....We want to make it categorically clear that under no circumstances will we ... fight a bourgeois revolution.... What we want is radical change' (quoted in Lauren Dobell, 'New lamps for old? The evolution of SWAPO's philosophy of development, 1960–1991', M.A. thesis, Queen's University, November, 1992).

54. The direct page references in the following three paragraphs are to the Ya-Otto Report (*op. cit.*).

55. Certainly, they were assisted in this task by the international press, quick to structure headlines around recognizable personalities and the gossipy nuance of factional intrigue. Shipanga was, after all, the person of highest profile amongst those arrested and the able efforts of his wife, Esme, to publicize his plight also helped place him, after the event, in the limelight.

56. Thus, the Commission's criticism that the SYL 'rose' at a time 'when most of the leadership of the mother body were either exiled, imprisoned, detained or restricted' and that this had 'created an illusion among some Youth leaders that SYL is a body unto itself' was particularly odious. As discussed in the following chapter the internal leaders in the early 1970s, of whom Meroro, the National Chairman, was the most senior, had been content to have the Youth League pay the price of providing the militancy and the organisation during those years; nothing had stopped them from doing it themselves.

57. Riundja Ali (Othniel) Kaakunga, Deputy Acting Administrative Secretary of internal SWAPO at the time and chief convener of the Walvis Bay Congress, felt the outcome was important in further strengthening the claim of the Nujoma leadership to Kaunda's military support during the crisis and recalls that when he arrived in Lusaka immediately after the congress parties were being held by SWAPO officials to celebrate the congress's endorsement of the leadership in exile. Kaakunga, himself a future victim of the Angola torture camps, was later to express regret that the congress's organizers did not take more seriously the charges of the dissenters, although it was not clear to him how, under the circumstances, the outcome could have been different (interview with Saul, 16 March 1992).

58. Katjavivi, writing in his thesis of 'SWAPO's 1976 Indabas' (Walvis Bay and Nampundwe), notes, without apparent irony, that Nampundwe was 'near where Shipanga and the other ten

dissidents had been held'. 'The Rise of Nationalism in Namibia', *op. cit.*, p. 302.

59. So long as they did not go too far – as they may momentarily have done in their unsuccessful attempt, alluded to earlier, to displace one particularly ineffectual member of the old guard. Katjavivi uses the cited, rather jejune phrase to epitomize the spirit of the proceedings in his *A History of Resistance in Namibia*, (London, Paris and Addis Ababa: James Currey, UNESCO and the OAU, 1988), p. 108.

60. Hidipo Hamutenya (now Minister of Information in the Namibian government), interview with Saul, 26 June 1991. Hamutenya is widely acknowledged to have been one of the principal drafters of the Programme.

61. Quoted in Katjavivi, *ibid.*, pp. 108–9.

62. Kaakunga, interview with Saul, *op. cit.*

63. SWAPO Documentation, *Laws Governing the Namibian People's Revolution* (adopted by the Central Committee of SWAPO on 24 September 1977, and signed by the SWAPO President Sam Nujoma) (Luanda: SWAPO Department of Information and Publicity, n. d.). One specific example from the decrees may suggest something of their flavour: 'Any propaganda using publications, leaflets, written and oral presentations or any other means to incite to struggle against the SWAPO movement and/or creation and survival of the Namibian state; disruption of unity of the Namibian people; introduction of inequality among ethnic groups; and resistance to decisions of the SWAPO movement and/or agencies of the new Namibian State shall constitute a felony' (p. 12). Perhaps by this means too the leadership sought to close a loophole revealed during the successful Habeas corpus appeal to a Zambian court by the eleven prisoners (including Shipanga). At the time, SWAPO could only whisk the eleven appellants off to prisons in Tanzania where Habeas corpus would not be applicable to them. But at least one of the eleven recalls a judge saying, during the Zambian proceedings, that had SWAPO had its own set of quasi-legal regulations their case might have gone quite differently.

64. This was the period, to take merely one of the most notorious examples, during which the South African agent, Craig Williamson, had great success in manipulating, from within, the prestigious Geneva–based International University Exchange Fund (IUEF) and passing back to Pretoria information obtained at the highest level from liberation movement leaders visiting Geneva.

65. It seems likely, nonetheless, that the grim presence of the SWAPO security apparatus continued to be felt beyond Angola. Certainly this was the opinion of many of those 200–300 'dissidents' who survived Mboroma yet chose not to be 'rehabilitated' by SWAPO. They sought, instead, protection from the UNHCR as 'refugees' and most spent the next decade eking out a marginal existence in Zambia. Unfortunately, they found it extremely difficult to escape the stain of their Mboroma days, many feeling that the Zambian government, perhaps instigated by SWAPO, set up obstacles to their accepting overseas scholarships and other opportunities outside Zambia. For one of them, Callistus Shafooli (identified, somewhat offhandedly, as a South African agent in the Ya–Otto Report), there was an even more grisly fate in store. In 1988, on the eve of Namibian independence and fully twelve years after the crisis itself, Shafooli was murdered outside a transit centre where he was awaiting a visa to Canada – murdered, his fellow refugees feel, by SWAPO. Indeed, they claim the existence of a list of Namibians living in Zambia who were to be eliminated, as 'unfinished business' from 1976, before SWAPO returned home. In response some 200 Namibian refugees then signed a petition to the Zambian government drawing its attention to this threat, at which point, they believe, the government requested SWAPO to back off.

66. The decision was that all the leadership should move to Luanda; but Mishake Muyongo, the former leader of CANU (which, as we have seen, merged with SWAPO in 1964) and by now SWAPO Vice-President, was reluctant to leave Lusaka, where his ethnic and personal connections were strong, for Angola, where he sensed that his significance for the struggle would inevitably become marginal. Some other members of the leadership were also reluctant to give up the Lusaka base, from which connections with the Western world were so much easier than from Luanda. Between 1978 and 1980 a Lusaka–based faction under Muyongo frequently questioned and even occasionally countermanded postings and other orders issued from Luanda. In 1980 Muyongo left SWAPO and reformed CANU. Some Caprivians active within SWAPO have described a pattern of victimization of Caprivians within the movement at this time (at UNIN, for example) and also suggest that a number of those first consigned to SWAPO dungeons in the 'spy drama' of the 1980s were Caprivians (Benjamin Mabuku, interview with Saul, 6 July 1992).

67. By that date, Cassinga had also become a reception and transit camp for the continuing flow of exiles.

68. Kwanza Sul was a big operation, but the numbers in the settlement were invariably

exaggerated. At independence a total of just over 50,000 Namibians returned from abroad, compared with a figure of 103,000 exiles cited in some UN–sponsored reports in the 1980s. The figure of 35,000 at Kwanza Sul is still higher than the best estimate of several sympathetic but objective observers who spent some time there in the 1980s, although the official figure given at the time was 40,000. The 35,000 estimate is more or less compatible with the figure of 50,000 returnees, another 9,000 or so being PLAN combatants and the remaining 6,000 or so coming from Nyango, Ntalandando, and education and training abroad.

69. The range of these achievements in Angola was underscored for the authors by, amongst others, two then senior SWAPO officials, Libertine Appolus-Amathila in the health field and Nahas Angula in education, who were later to become, respectively, Ministers of Local Government and of Education in SWAPO's post–liberation government (interviews with the authors, 9 July and 6 July 1992).

70. See, for example, Tony Dodds and John Mbango. 'The Namibian education and health centres in the Republic of Zambia and the Namibian Extension Unit, Lusaka, Zambia' (UNHCR TSS paper, TSS ZMB/EDU 4 (D)), p. 5: 'A camp council comprising members from all sections of the camp sets rules and regulations of each camp. Women's section, the clinic, the youth, the school, the elders' section, are all represented on the council. The camp council is therefore the supreme organ of the camp.' Enquiry among former residents at Nyango and Kwanza Sul does not suggest that this is how things were in practice, whatever the theory may have been.

71. Nanyemba had little more than a primary school education. He was, however, a 'military fanatic' who read a lot and whose military knowledge impressed his Russian advisers, according to a former member of his staff (Hans Peters, interview with the authors, 26 June 1991).

72. It should be pointed out that this antagonism was not all 'ethnic'. A significant number of 'southerners' were Oshivambo–speaking *mbuiti*, i.e. brought up outside Ovamboland, usually in towns like Windhoek or Walvis Bay.

73. Nanyemba was first replaced by Richard Kapelwa (as Acting Secretary of Defence) and ultimately by Peter Mueshihange (as Secretary of Defence), but the latter, in particular, was widely perceived as being ineffectual. This paragraph is heavily indebted to our interview with Hans Peters (*op. cit.*) , who was on the staff at Defence Headquarters from 1980 to 1983, when he was detained.

74. With the result that many of them went straight into the hands of SWAPO security. A letter of 16 August 1989 from Soldaat Ignatius Murorua, who was in detention from 1986 to 1989, to Siegfried Groth of the World Lutheran Federation makes the following observation: 'I'm not saying that Ovambos were not arrested, but comparatively speaking, out of +/– 2,000 non–Ovambos in exile, roughly 1,000 of them were in SWAPO prisons' (letter kindly supplied by Siegfried Groth). The specific figures suggested by Murorua are dubious, but as the perception of the situation by a southerner the statement has some significance.

75. Details are given in various publications produced during the independence election campaign, most of which are collected in Nico Basson (who subsequently disclosed that he was a paid South African propagandist) and Ben Motinga, *Call Them Spies* (African Communication Projects, Windhoek/Johannesburg, 1989). The UN Mission on Detainees (for the text of this 'Clark Report' see Basson and Motinga, pp. 140–4) compiled a list of about 1,100 people allegedly detained, of whom about 110 were found to be duplicated entries, 52 could not be identified owing to insufficient information, and 71 were reportedly not detained. The mission concluded that 484 people had been detained and released, 115 were dead, and 315 required further investigation. This implied a possible total of about 800 detainees. Critics challenged the Clark report in detail and in general, alleging that up to 1,400 other detainees remained unaccounted for. A reasonable conclusion seems to be that at least 900 people were detained at some point in the 1980s and that a third of these may have died – from physical abuse, poor food, lack of medical attention or natural causes.

76. Hamutenya was SWAPO Secretary for Information and Publicity, Mueshihange was Secretary for Foreign Affairs and later for Defence, and Garoeb was SWAPO's Administrative Secretary.

77. This extraordinary episode is so widely attested to that it must be considered *prima facie* established. It is not suggested that Mrs Nujoma was physically abused. What the security organization's motive for so detaining her could have been is hard to understand unless it was to weaken the president's authority. It is in this sort of context that the theme of the rivalry between the Kwanyama-speaking group and other smaller Ovambo clans, to one of which Nujoma belongs, is constantly raised.

78. The 'interrogations' to which those taken to Lubango were subjected seem to have been largely if not completely irrelevant to any serious concern with military security. If anyone had indeed been a spy, they had no need to confess the truth but only to 'confess' to fantastic

crimes acceptable to their interrogators. Indeed so opposite to the enhancing of SWAPO's security were the actual effects of the 'spy drama' that it has occurred to many people that if South Africa had wanted to subvert SWAPO they could not have done better than pay someone in SWAPO's highest ranks to engineer the creation of the SWAPO Security Organization.

79. Many witnesses state that the interrogators constantly suggested that they should implicate certain senior SWAPO leaders, such as Hage Geingob and Mose Tjitendero, some stating, as well, that Geingob was represented to them forcefully as being the 'master spy'.

80. According to Peters (interview, *op. cit.*) a majority of Nanyemba's DHQ staff were arrested between 1984 and 1986. Several then senior SWAPO officials have attested to serious ravages in other SWAPO departments in Luanda; in addition, a growing proportion of students returning from studies abroad were sent directly to Lubango and disappeared without ever taking up a post in the organization.

81. Students were recalled to Luanda from all over the world and, as noted, despatched to Lubango. In the Eastern bloc countries they were put on planes by the security services of those countries, acting as SWAPO's security agents just as the Tanzanian and Zambian governments had done in the 1960s and 1970s. Students recalled from Western countries mostly went back anyway, thinking they could easily clear their names, and fearing that refusal to go would be taken as admission of guilt. Moreover, most of them had grown up strongly identified with the liberation struggle, and the idea of leaving SWAPO and being obliged, eventually, to return to Namibia on the South Africans' terms was extremely difficult for them to swallow.

82. Some did run for cover, of course, the career of Hiskia Uanivi providing a particularly wry example. Uanivi (also known as Rirua Karihangana), who had initially been appointed SWAPO's first representative to Luanda in 1977, was able to turn himself, overnight, into the self–proclaimed leader of Namibia's (otherwise non–existent) Communist Party and thereby survive, for the best part of a decade, as a protected ward of the Angolan state (interview with the authors, 26 June 1991).

83. Reflecting on these matters more recently, Geingob (now Prime Minister of an independent Namibia) was inclined to assign responsibility for the events in Angola to, in his words, 'young cadres' who 'got carried away' and who 'went too far'. Stating that it would be inappropriate to open a formal enquiry into these events (since it could 'unravel endlessly'), he nonetheless promised that SWAPO would seek to identify accurately those who did die, apologize to their families and 'help them to grieve' (interview with the authors, 21 June 1991).

84. The term, 'the horrors', was used by now SWAPO Foreign Minister, Theo-Ben Gurirab, to evoke for us the events within SWAPO in the 1980s. Interestingly, Gurirab also was more inclined than many other senior SWAPO leaders whom we interviewed to concede that some 'small seeds' (his phrase) of these horrors may have been sewn by the manner of resolution of the mid-1970s crisis. More important to the explanation for him, however, were 'commanders [who were] out of control' and 'a political leadership [that] left too much room for manoeuvre to the Military Command' (interview with the authors, 24 June 1991).

85. A charge cited in 'The Youth's Request to the Authority to be Well Informed About Matters of Pertinent Importance for the Existence of its Persistent Dedication in the Struggle' issued by SWAPO Youth League Regional Headquarters (Lusaka), 26 February 1975 (Beukes collection, *op. cit.*).

86. Not surprisingly, those who have borne the brunt of the actual practices spawned by SWAPO's evolving political culture continue to regard the movement with particular scepticism on such matters. Perhaps their outlook was best summarized for us by one such informant, Hizipo Shikondombolo – he of the heroic 'long march' from Mboroma to Dar es Salaam, and thence to Nairobi – when we interviewed him in 1991 in Oshakati, in northern Namibia. Asked the significance of SWAPO's failure to win a two-thirds majority he replied: 'We would not be having the present conversation.... I would either be dead or living in another country.' Interview with the authors, *op. cit.*

87. A kind of neo–colonial 'pragmatism' tends now to be offered by senior SWAPO leaders as the sole 'sensible' alternative to Stalinoid socialism, with little space seen to exist for defining an alternative that might be more progressive than either of these extremes; this was, quite explicitly, the thrust of remarks by Namibian Minister of Foreign Affairs, Theo-Ben Gurirab when interviewed by the authors (24 June 1991) but it was also a refrain we were to hear often during the course of our research in Namibia. For a further exploration of this and related issues, see Chapter 10, below.

88. Not least in the office of the Prime Minister, in the person of Hage Geingob, former director of UNIN.

4
SWAPO Inside Namibia

COLIN LEYS & JOHN S. SAUL

Unlike the ANC in South Africa, SWAPO was never banned: it was illegal to support or advocate the armed struggle conducted by SWAPO in exile, but not to belong to SWAPO as an organization. There were at least two advantages for the South Africans in this arrangement. SWAPO's internal activities could be watched more easily if they were above ground; and South Africa could pretend internationally that it was SWAPO, and not South Africa, that was committed to the use of violence.

The reality, however, was that the South Africans harassed SWAPO with sweeping police powers and routine illegal and arbitrary use of force, to the point where any serious internal mobilization was regularly met with the arrest, beating, torture and jailing of as many militants in the leadership as did not escape into exile. Yet in spite of the repression, resistance was constantly renewed by succeeding waves of new activists; and this resistance was crucially important, in that it prevented South Africa from legitimating any of its own successive 'internal' settlements, based on installing coalitions of ethnically based leaders willing to collaborate with Pretoria in a form of pseudo-independence. This chapter, however, focusses less on the major confrontations the internal resistance produced (such as the 1971–2 general strike or the 1973 Ovamboland elections boycott), which have been well chronicled by Katjavivi and others, than on the distinctive kind of politics it involved: the political traditions and practices it bequeathed to the country at independence. What kind of politics was learned by the successive political generations of Namibians who were politicized by SWAPO, listening to its speakers, reading its pamphlets, becoming members, attending meetings, conferences and rallies – and paying the price, if they became activists, of losing their jobs, being arrested and beaten, tortured or even killed?

First, there was the logic of repression itself. With the escalation of the war the north of the country became a war zone in which all open political activity became impossible. Even in the 'police zone' south of Oshivelo, public political activity was increasingly restricted, especially after 1981 when public meetings were effectively prohibited for SWAPO under AG 22, as they had been in the north since 1972 under Proclamation R 17.[1] Public rallies gave way to 'house meetings' in the townships, or were 'seminars' or 'conferences' of party members or delegates, and after 1974 few if any of these were held in Ovamboland.[2]

Further, from at least 1970 the police Special Branch developed an extensive system of informers who reported on what took place at all meetings.[3] This severely limited what the internal SWAPO leaders felt they could say even in 'house meetings', unless these were confined to small groups of wholly trusted colleagues. Their mail was opened and their phones were tapped; and this meant that all sensitive information from abroad – concerning the course of the war, plans, internal differences, money, dealings with friendly states or organizations, etc. – could only be received by word of mouth from couriers, especially visiting church representatives who enjoyed the external leadership's confidence, or the few members of the national executive at home – typically also prominent churchmen such as the Revs Witbooi and Kameeta – who were allowed to travel abroad.

The repression of the internal movement, itself exacerbated by the exile movement's initial military successes, led to a further dynamic in which the internal leadership gradually came to cede all authority to the leadership abroad. Initially the fiction was maintained that apart from the SWAPO president and vice-president, the leaders in exile were acting on behalf of the leaders inside the country.[4] In reality, however, the gradually accumulating financial and diplomatic resources of the external leaders, coupled with the persecution of the internal movement and the constant haemorrhage of militant internal leaders into prison or exile, meant that policy was determined by the exile leadership, above all by SWAPO president Sam Nujoma and those closest to him. From the mid-1970s onwards most of the internal leaders understood this, and attached primary importance to presenting a united front under an internationally recognized individual leader. For this reason they also discouraged activists from publicly raising 'ideological' issues, especially Marxist themes, which were prominent in the resistance in South Africa and which they saw as potentially divisive in Namibia. They favoured 'mobilization' politics alone: rallying people to demonstrate their support for the single goal of ending South African rule.

The external leadership were also apprehensive about new internal leaders emerging with widespread internal support. They could not be sure, especially after the challenge posed by the SYL leaders who came from Namibia to Lusaka in 1974–6, described in Chapter 3 above, that such leaders would subordinate themselves to the authority of those outside. On the other hand they needed as much evidence as possible of continuing domestic resistance. So they encouraged the young activists inside the country, but supported the internal national executive against them when the activists demanded a greater share in decision making.

This logic reinforced some more deep-seated factors affecting internal SWAPO's political culture. Almost none of the models of politics to which SWAPO activists were exposed were democratic, or even liberal. The colonial state was frankly authoritarian. Down to the end of the 1970s judges rarely displayed much objectivity or excessive concern for the rule of law when it came to dealing with SWAPO activists; lawyers often refused to represent them, doctors declined to give evidence on the injuries inflicted on them by the police, head teachers expelled students for SWAPO activities. This changed significantly during the 1980s, but the damage had been done. Even the Christian churches, to which the vast majority of the people belonged, and which became rallying points for popular resistance, were not internally democratic (on this see also Chapter 5 below). Traditional political life does not seem to have been democratic, either. Even before chiefs were made into instruments of South African control there seems to have been no equivalent, at least among the Ovambo, of the Ashanti institution of 'destooling' unpopular chiefs, and no tradition of collective debate on issues of public interest.[5]

The one exception to all these non-democratic models was the development of popular organs of mass resistance in the townships of South Africa in the 1970s, which had a strong influence on those Namibians, mainly students at South African colleges and universities, who were exposed to them. And by the mid-1970s the number of well-educated activists who had been in South Africa was rising. In SWAPO's early years Nujoma, with primary education and some years of night school, counted as relatively well-educated, and Shipanga, with ten years of schooling and a teacher's certificate, as highly educated. By the end of the 1970s, however, young activists with high-school education were becoming relatively common, and a growing minority were university-educated. They wanted a say in SWAPO decision making and did not accept that seniority should confer authority unless backed by militancy and efficiency. The old guard tended to see them as inexperienced, impatient, potentially a threat to the movement's delicate diplomatic balancing act, and arrogant. There was, in addition, the fundamental problem, already alluded to in Chapter 1, that with open political activity made impossible in the 'war zone', where the majority of the population lived, internal activism would necessarily be primarily a southern, and almost wholly non-Ovambo, affair.

It must also be remembered that the adult population south of the war zone was not much more than 300,000 people (and considerably fewer if only the urban areas are counted). For both good and ill, politics in such conditions was necessarily the work of a small group with close personal connections, and this was often reinforced by people having been together at a very small number of secondary schools, such as Augustineum (the only full secondary school for black Namibians until 1967), St. Mary's Odibo, and Martin Luther High School.

These, then, were some of the main determinants of SWAPO politics inside the country. Before we look at the main phases of the internal struggle, however, it is necessary to examine briefly the movement's formal constitutional framework – which had and still has considerable significance for SWAPO members, however far theory and practice may have sometimes diverged – and the organizational structure it produced on the ground.

SWAPO's Constitution and Internal Organization

The original constitution of SWAPO was inherited from the Ovamboland People's Organization.[6] It provided for annual national conferences. No founding conference was held. According to Soggot a 'national conference' held in Windhoek in 1961 'reviewed progress on the political and diplomatic fronts'.[7] Putz and Von Egidy, however, say that 'In 1961 SWAPO activists inside the Territory secretly organized its first Congress in Rehoboth where the notion of armed struggle was first mooted, while the first Congress in exile happened in Dar es Salaam a year later.'[8]

The truth probably is that various meetings were held, none fully corresponding to any written constitution, and of very mixed representativeness. The 'Consultative Congress' held at Tanga in Tanzania in December–January 1969–70 was attended by about 30 people, comprising most of the senior leadership in exile, and was not attended by any delegates from inside Namibia. The only significant congress styling itself as such inside the country before independence was a five-day meeting of between 100 and 200 SWAPO members held at Walvis Bay in May 1976. The following March (1977) there was a weekend national conference in Katutura; and there was a further conference, the so-called 'bush meeting' at Dobra in 1982.[9] These seem to have been the only properly constituted national gatherings of SWAPO inside Namibia before the post-independence congress of December 1991, although as we shall see, several would-be 'national' conferences were called by either the Southern Region executive or the SWAPO Youth League executive between 1978 and 1982, in an effort to overcome the movement's internal problems. In other words, during the liberation struggle national SWAPO conferences or congresses were not where policy was set.

Inside Namibia the movement was run by an executive, originally called the 'National Committee'. The original members of this body went into exile in the early 1960s. The 1969–70 Tanga Consultative Congress, which extensively revised the constitution, replaced the National Committee with a National Executive (comprising the organization's office-bearers – Secretaries for Education, Health, Defence, etc.) and a larger Central Committee. Both of these existed in exile. Inside the country, a 'National Executive at Home' (NEH) was formed, corresponding to the National Executive abroad, but no Central Committee.[10] Six years later, in 1976, the internal organization's Walvis Bay Congress (discussed below) acknowledged that real power now rested with the leadership abroad by resolving that members of the NEH would automatically cease to hold their positions if they left Namibia permanently.[11]

Officially, after 1976 most members of the NEH, like the members of the National Executive in exile, had 'portfolios' (National Organizing Secretary, Secretary for

Education and Culture, etc.) but these were mostly quite nominal, given the internal organization's precarious existence and acute lack of resources. Places on the NEH were filled by co-option: the constant need to replace NEH members going into exile made this unavoidable. Apart from the 1976 Walvis Bay Congress and the 1977 Windhoek (Katutura) Conference, however, no systematic attempt seems to have been made to have the co-options ratified by the membership. This contrasted with the practice in most branches and at the regional level in at least some regions, and in the SWAPO Youth League. Probably the contrast would not have been questioned much had the NEH been seen as bold and energetic: but it became inactive, so that its non-elected and non-accountable character became a highly contentious issue, as we shall see.

SWAPO had members, but for security reasons membership lists were not kept: also, while people cherished their SWAPO cards like war medals, it was risky to keep one.[12] By the late 1970s the Windhoek branch had developed a system of groups of houses (in Katutura) called 'sections', as sub-units of the branch, testifying to an extensive membership. Members of the branch were from all ethnic groups, with an Ovambo majority. 'House meetings' were held fortnightly in some sections, while branch meetings were held every three to four weeks in active branches. The activity level varied considerably over time, according to the energy of local activists and with periodic interruptions due to arrests or people going into exile. It also varied by area. In the long run the Windhoek branch, based in Katutura, was clearly the most important, but initially Walvis Bay was the main SWAPO base in the south, based on the fishing industry, which also offered seasonal employment to students from all areas during the school holidays (or when expelled from school for political activities). Later, with the 1976 decision of the main Nama chiefs to support SWAPO, the Southern Region, with its headquarters at Gibeon, and a very militant branch in Rehoboth, became very active, tending to overshadow the branches of even major towns like Tsumeb and Grootfontein (cut off in the 'operational area'), or the inaccessible company town of Oranjemund (not to mention Oshakati, Ondangua or Rundu, in the war zone itself).

Activists knew who was a SWAPO member, who was a supporter and who was 'pro-South African' (although even an activist's loyalty could always be doubted, a fact on which the security police relied heavily for sowing suspicion). The price of being a well-known activist included frequent house searches and arrests, the likelihood of beatings or worse, and the loss of employment, while the cost to the South Africans of bribing people to be informers or agents provocateurs was low. The combination of an ill-defined membership, the inevitable presence of informers, and the risk of disruption by the police also made it hard to hold representative inner-party meetings. However, some were held, with reasonably wide representation, so these reasons alone do not fully explain why national conferences (to which the NEH was formally accountable) were not held more regularly, as provided for in the constitution.[13]

This, then, was the organizational constitutional framework within which SWAPO conducted the internal struggle, which unfolded in six broad stages.

1960-6: From the Old Location Massacre to Omgulumbashe: Proselytizing the Contract Workers

Following his central role in the resistance to the destruction of the Old Location in Windhoek, and the removal of its inhabitants to the distant new apartheid township of Katutura, Nujoma fled into exile in March 1960. At that point he was president of the Ovamboland People's Organization; in New York in April 1960, however, he and Mburumba Kerina renamed it SWAPO. Most of the OPO/SWAPO leaders followed Nujoma into exile and no arrangements had been made to replace them inside Namibia. The main remaining leaders were Andimba Toivo ya Toivo, who was restricted to Ondangua in Ovamboland, and Nathaniel Maxuilili, who was restricted to Walvis Bay. The focus remained strongly on the contract labour system, which affected only northerners, and above all the Ovambo.[14]

Ya-Otto has painted a picture of SWAPO's internal life in these years. Based in Windhoek, he went about one weekend a month with other Ovambo teachers (who were free to travel because they were not contract workers) to address meetings in Walvis Bay, Luderitz, Tsumeb, Okahandja and 'a dozen other places large enough to turn out a crowd for a public meeting'.[15] There were branches in seven towns including Windhoek, according to Ya-Otto, mainly places with concentrations of contract workers.[16] Toivo was officially Regional Organizer for Ovamboland, working with returning contract workers out of his shop in Ondangua. Ya-Otto himself became 'Acting Secretary General' in 1961. Such appointments were made at this time by the leading activists meeting together and assigning each other positions.[17]

The period may be summed up as one of proselytization, mainly among Ovambo contract workers. Branches existed, but consisted essentially of small groups of activists. Money was raised in subscriptions. According to Ndadi, 800 pounds was raised in this way in Walvis Bay alone in 1959, more than enough to maintain Nujoma as a full-time organizer and meet other expenses.[18] Later, funds were raised primarily from *braais* (barbecues) at which food and drinks were sold. In the early 1960s public meetings could still be held.[19] They were mostly devoted to denouncing South African oppression, demanding independence and explaining the situation at the United Nations.

1966–71: From the Treason Trial to the International Court of Justice Decision and the Bishops' Letter: the Reconstruction of 'Internal SWAPO'

In August 1966 SWAPO's barely established first military base at Omgulumbashe was discovered and destroyed by the South African Police. More than 200 SWAPO activists, including most of the internal leadership, were arrested or fled abroad. Internal activity largely stopped during the period of the treason trial in Pretoria which sent Toivo and 30 others to Robben Island for long terms. Only Maxuilili, Mutumbulua and Ya-Otto received relatively short sentences. On their release in 1968 Maxuilili and Ya-Otto were restricted to Walvis Bay and Ondangua respectively, but gradually re-established these as SWAPO centres for the south and north respectively, while Mutumbulua worked in the Katutura township of Windhoek with David Meroro. The scale of activity remained modest, however, being at first largely confined to house meetings. Neville Cupido, who practised medicine in Walvis Bay from 1968 to 1970, recalls regular meetings of 12–14 people at Maxuilili's house. In 1970, when Cupido moved to Windhoek, he found 50–60 people meeting about once a month in the house of a Mrs Namalambo, whose home became a regular SWAPO meeting place for many years (her husband had gone into exile after repeated jail terms for his SWAPO activities).

This was a transitional period in several ways. The Odendaal Report of 1964 had recommended the creation of bantustans but these were not yet being set up. SWAPO's military threat was limited by the small numbers of people it could recruit for PLAN and the difficulty of access to Namibia for combatants from bases in Zambia. The Omgulambashe affair did, however, give rise to a severe tightening of security, which came into play with full force in the South Africans' response to the 1971 contract workers' strike; it was also a factor prompting the major church leaders to come out against the colonial regime in the bishops' open letter of 1971 to the South African Prime Minister, Vorster, thus inaugurating an 18-year period of increasingly close identification between the churches and SWAPO. This cooperation afforded the internal SWAPO leadership valuable protection. For example, many members of the

NEH later found employment with the churches, and especially with the Council of Churches in Namibia (CCN), when it was denied to them elsewhere; after 1976 some were prominent church leaders.[20]

1971–5: From the General Strike to the Exodus: the Years of the SWAPO Youth League

The next four years are the heroic period of the internal struggle, and as far as SWAPO is concerned, they belong very largely to the SWAPO Youth League. Formal provision for the formation of a Youth League had been made at the 1969–70 Tanga Congress. The participants at that congress could hardly have foreseen the consequences, however. A new generation of black students, inspired by the struggles of South African students against Bantu Education, constituted themselves as the SYL and in effect occupied the vacuum created by the post-Omgulumbashe suppression of what had remained of the old SWAPO National Committee inside Namibia.

Of the remaining leaders who were not in jail, Maxuilili and Ya-Otto were in effect under a form of house arrest. Axel Johannes, a man of legendary courage, was now officially 'Acting Administrative Secretary', but was constantly being detained. Of the original national leadership only David Meroro, the National Chairman, remained free (most of the time) down to 1975. More recent recruits to the internal leadership, to replace the departed ex-OPO leaders, were drawn heavily from school teachers and did not have the same standing with the membership as those who had led the early mobilization of the contract workforce. And so in the early 1970s the internal leadership attempted no mass mobilization of the population around the burning issues of the time, especially the homelands policy, which the South African Prime Minister Vorster now determined to press ahead with, or even the still functioning and hated contract labour system. Instead, Meroro, the National Chairman, represented SWAPO in the National Convention (NC).

The NC was a grouping of anti-colonial parties chaired by Clemens Kapuuo of the Herero traditionalist party, NUDO. Its aim was to agitate around the International Court of Justice's ruling that South Africa's occupation of Namibia was illegal, and to produce a constitution for a united independent Namibia, as opposed to the Odendaal Plan for ethnic homelands. The NC's demand was that the UN should assume responsibility for administering Namibia in preparation for independence. National Convention meetings did afford Meroro an opportunity to address public meetings for which the police were expected to refuse permission had they been purely SWAPO rallies, but given the NC's nature and goals its meetings were moderate and constitutionalist in tone.[21]

A new generation of young activists, most of them students in the slowly expanding black secondary schools, became impatient with this.[22] They began by confronting their school authorities over the right to political expression, demands for Student Representative Councils, and other school-related issues, often getting themselves expelled in the process. Many of them migrated to Walvis Bay, where jobs were most easily to be had in the fish-processing plants. Thanks to the presence there (enforced by a state-imposed restriction order) of Nathaniel Maxuilili, SWAPO's Acting President, Walvis Bay 'was always the stronghold of SWAPO' at that time, and here a formidable group of young militants accumulated: Jerry Ekandjo, Dickson Namholo, Ndali (then Thomas) Kamati, Kandi Nehova and others.[23] They formed the SWAPO Youth League (SYL) that the Tanga Congress had envisaged, and Ekandjo became its national leader with the title of Chairman.

The Youth Leaguers began organizing meetings in Walvis Bay, and gradually spread to Windhoek and other centres. In April 1973 they were emboldened by a joint statement by Dr Alfred Escher (the UN Secretary General's Special Representative for

Namibia), and the South African Prime Minister (Vorster) in Pretoria, which seemed to say that parties in Namibia were now free to operate. The SYL called the first public rally to be held in Walvis Bay since 1966. This was followed by regular public meetings, also organized by the SYL, in Walvis Bay, and then by meetings in Oshakati-Ondangua, and finally, on 12 August 1973, by a big meeting in Katutura, which ended with a march to the migrant workers' compound and a major confrontation with the police.

Meanwhile, however, a parallel development of immense significance had occurred in the shape of the contract workers' general strike of 1971–2, in which some of the future Youth Leaguers also played significant roles. The strike, which had been brewing for some time, was precipitated by the arrogant statement of Jannie de Wet, the Bantu Commissioner, to Bishop Auala in November 1971, that contract workers accepted their contracts 'voluntarily'.[24] The strike began in December 1971 and lasted almost two months, paralysing the economy and shaking the regime. Between a quarter and a half of the total contract workforce stopped work, making this action perhaps the single most important blow ever struck by Namibians for their own liberation, and demonstrating the impossibility of permanently governing the country on terms unacceptable to the majority of the population. Its immediate result (besides some reforms that were initially cosmetic, but which eventually led to the dismantling of the contract labour system in 1978) was the transfer of the internal struggle to the north, with the return home of thousands of the striking workers, together with some of the leading SYL activists.

Here the two most potent elements of the internal movement – the wage-workers and the youth – dramatically converged in a confrontation with the Ovambo chiefs (appointed by and dependent on the South African authorities) in the context of the impending implementation of the Odendaal 'homelands' plan. In 1972 the chiefs, seeing that their 'tribal police' were completely insufficient to overawe the returned workers and the young SYL agitators, called for help. The South African Police, based in the 'police zone' south of Oshivelo and already stretched by the military threat in Caprivi, could not respond, and so the South African army (the South African Defence Force or SADF) were called in. Elections were due to be held for the legislature of the planned Ovambo homeland in 1973. A boycott campaign, coordinated largely by the Youth League and DEMCOP (a party organized by the contract workers' leader Johannes Nangutuuala), succeeded beyond the organizers' greatest hopes with a turnout of only 2.5 per cent at the poll on 1–2 August 1973.

The repression which followed plumbed new depths of barbarity, with the police arresting SYL activists and handing them over to the chiefs in small batches to be publicly flogged after brief travesties of traditional 'court' hearings. This was not the nadir of South African brutality – that was to be reached in the 1980s as the border war escalated – but it was a moment of truth about the moral bankruptcy of the system from which, in the long run, it would never recover. The floggings unambiguously exposed both the cynical racism of the South Africans, subjecting young men and women to barbarous punishment in the name of a traditional system of justice that the South Africans themselves had subverted;[25] and the complicity of the chiefs and their *omakakunya* or 'scavengers', the tribal police. Moreover this truth – and the real power of the people when mobilized and concentrated, for which the floggings were a retribution – had been finally exposed by the reckless courage and militancy of the Youth Leaguers.

The SYL was not just a network of articulate and militant young activists, convinced that the tide of world affairs was running in favour of liberation everywhere, and that with the help of world opinion Namibians could throw off the South African yoke by 1974.[26] There were also Youth League branches with elected office bearers, and a nominally national SYL Executive Committee chaired by Ekandjo. By 13 August, however, he was under arrest along with Martin Kapewasha and David Shikomba, and destined to be sentenced to Robben Island where he would remain until 1981; many others were also under arrest, destined to be flogged and then confined to their birthplaces in the north.[27] Replacements were urgently needed. Accordingly Reuben Shangula, who had recently returned from active involvement in the parallel struggles of the South African youth while at Fort Hare, and Keshii Pelao Nathanael (the younger brother of Nathaniel Maxuilili), decided to call a SYL Congress.

This congress took place at the Ovambo Lutheran centre at Oniipa, probably in May 1974, and was attended by 40–50 people.[28] Representation was imperfect (no one came from Caprivi, for instance), and there were personal conflicts that led to some people leaving before the Congress was over, but it seems to have commanded general approval among Youth Leaguers nonetheless.[29] Keshii was elected President, Shangula Secretary General, and an acting Chairman was chosen to fill Ekandjo's place while he was in South African hands.[30]

The SYL thus showed that an internal leadership could be elected, rather than always co-opted, even in times of acute political crisis and repression. Later, when Keshii and Shangula were in conflict with the exile SWAPO leaders in Lusaka, the Oniipa Congress would be criticized as having been unrepresentative. But it is not obvious that it was any less representative than the Tanga Congress, which essentially represented and elected to office those attending it.[31]

As so often happened, the dynamics of the conflict in southern Africa intervened to prevent the issue of inner-party democracy posed by the Youth League being put to the test in 'internal SWAPO'. In March the coup in Portugal threw open the border to Angola, and on 1 April the SADF formally took over responsibility for security in the north from the police and redefined it as a theatre of war, pushing any possibility of further civil political activity back to the south. The final shape of the internal struggle was emerging.

Shangula, Keshii, Nukwaawo, Nehova, Kamati and most of the other SYL activists who were not still detained or jailed left Namibia for Zambia in June or July 1974, soon after the Oniipa Congress. By 1978 a new generation of Youth Leaguers would emerge to take up their legacy, but this time they would be confined, effectively, to the south, and have to deal with the very different conditions produced by the results of the 1974 exodus, the 1976 crisis in exile, and the development of the 'border war'.

1974–8: From the Turnhalle Initiative to Resolution 435: the Walvis Bay Congress and the New National Executive at Home

In the immediate aftermath of the exodus, SWAPO inside Namibia was extremely weak. The SYL had effectively disappeared; of the senior NEH members, Ya-Otto fled in 1974 and Meroro in 1975, when the murder of the Ovambo Chief Elifas (who had been responsible for most of the worst floggings) led to a new wave of arrests, and Jason Mutumbulua had left politics. New elections were held for the Ovamboland Assembly in January 1974, with draconian penalties for abstention, and SWAPO was unable to repeat the boycott success of 1973: the turnout in Ovamboland this time was 70 per cent. Kavango and Caprivi were also made 'self-governing' in 1976. Neither had the exodus yet produced that literal 'return of the repressed' in the shape of an expanded offensive by PLAN from directly across the border. The National Convention had finally collapsed in February 1975 over Kapuuo's efforts to use it to challenge, in effect, the UN's 1973 declaration that SWAPO was 'the authentic representative of the Namibian people';[32] and on 1 September 1975 South Africa had initiated a conference in the Turnhalle in Windhoek between the all-white Legislative Assembly and representatives of the country's non-white 'ethnic groups', with the aim of working out a constitution for independence organized on ethnic lines, and without the involvement of either SWAPO or the UN. It was imperative for SWAPO to respond, but there was a glaring absence of effective internal leadership. The external organization produced, for example, a very shrewd *Discussion Paper on the Future of Namibia* to counter the homelands' strategy, which was quite widely circulated; but it was not made the focus of any widespread SWAPO campaign.

A number of younger and more highly educated activists had, however, been co-opted onto the 'National Executive' over the years since the Tanga Congress. They included Riundja Ali (Othniel) Kaakunga, who had been active with Maxuilili, Meroro, Johannes and Ya-Otto before 1974; and Aaron Muchimba, Jason Angula, Pejavi Elifas Munyaro, Festus Naholo and Hiskia Ndjoze-Uanivi, who were co-opted soon after the exodus. Kaakunga recalls that both he and these latest members were regarded by Meroro as 'not full members', even though Kaakunga, for example, was made Acting Secretary General while Axel Johannes was in jail.[33] Yet it was on the initiative of these young men that a party congress was held in Walvis Bay on 29–31 May 1976. One aim was to reassert the organization's vitality inside Namibia, and in particular, to confirm the internal party's identification with the external leadership, which South African propaganda was representing as having broken down; to elect a new internal leadership; and to reassert Namibia's claim to Walvis Bay by holding a congress there.

At the same time there was growing concern about the crisis of legitimacy of the leadership in Zambia, described in Chapter 3 above. Indeed, by the time the congress was held the crisis of SWAPO in Zambia had come to a head with the arrest of Shipanga, Keshii, Shangula, and eight others in Lusaka on 21 April, and the further arrest of 48 leaders of the 'anti-corruption fighters' among the PLAN troops recruited from the 1974–5 exodus.[34] The South African press and radio stepped up their claims that the organization was in decay and that the authority of the leadership, and especially Nujoma's, was hanging in the balance in the face of a widespread loss of confidence on the part of the recently arrived exiles.[35] The congress thus took place in the shadow of an acute external problem, in which some of the most prominent young internal leaders who had recently gone into exile were in conflict with Nujoma and most of his senior colleagues.[36]

Opinions differ as to how far the calling of the conference reflected a wish on the part of the internal leaders to intervene independently in the external crisis, or whether they were acting on explicit instructions from the external leadership. On the one hand there is some evidence that the external leaders were concerned that they might be criticized or even removed by the Walvis Bay Congress. On the other hand several participants remember the congress as having been called in response to a specific request from the exile leadership for an expression of confidence in them from inside the country.[37]

In fact, the conveners of the meeting were were well aware of the limitations under which they were operating. Their information about events in Zambia came largely from South African-oriented media and was therefore suspect. Some evidence from sources close to the dissidents in Zambia did reach Namibia, such as letters brought by friends from those who had recently gone into exile, or documents produced by the SYL and army dissidents in Zambia and smuggled back into Namibia by Mrs Hermanus Beukes, but even this evidence tended to be discounted: the polarization of politics was already so deep that one could easily be labelled a South African 'spy' just for voicing any criticism of the SWAPO leadership.[38] As one SWAPO activist of the period wryly put it, when asked about the reaction to the conflicting reports coming from Zambia, 'it was very difficult for our little minds to process this information'.[39]

On the basis of the fragmentary information they had, then, the conveners were not going to risk a catastrophic crisis in SWAPO, one that would be represented by the South Africans as evidence that the movement was collapsing and that the war strategy had failed. The existing members of the National Committee/National Executive proposed that the 100–200 delegates (recollections differ considerably as to the numbers) who filled the Lutheran church hall in Walvis Bay should re-elect only three leaders – Nujoma as President, Muyongo as Vice-President, and Meroro as Chairman – and then call on them to make the necessary appointments of the rest of the outside leadership: an invitation to which they responded, at an 'enlarged' Central Committee meeting held at Nampundwe, near Lusaka, in July, by confirming all the existing external Executive and Central Committee members in their positions.

Meanwhile, as regards the domestic agenda, resolutions were passed to appoint a new 'National Executive at Home' (including a number of intellectuals who were seen as valuable for enhancing SWAPO's status in the country), and to broaden the organization's social base by recruiting whites.[40] This led to the inclusion on the NEH of Tauno Hatuikilipi as National Treasurer, Milner Mokganedi Tlhabanello as Secretary for the Interior and Daniel Tjongarero as Secretary for Information and Publicity, even though all three were recently returned graduates from South Africa who had joined SWAPO only the previous year (Tjongarero in order to represent it on the executive of the new Namibia National Convention on which, as a church employee, he was helping the Rev. Kameeta, the NNC's chairman).[41]

Tjongarero was a key choice, as in 1978 he became Deputy National Chairman, effectively replacing the National Chairman David Meroro, who had gone into exile in 1975, as the main leader of SWAPO inside Namibia.[42] Unlike Meroro, who had popular support, despite his seeming lack of militancy, as a member of the SWAPO 'old guard', Tjongarero did not have a long history of involvement in the movement. He owed his position partly to having arrived back in Namibia, with his very considerable talents and energy, at a moment when the internal leadership roles were once again vacant; but also to what now emerged as a policy of making internal activity wholly subordinate to the military-diplomatic strategy of the leadership in exile, through installing an internal leadership endorsed by them rather than by activists inside Namibia. Later co-options onto the NEH increasingly reflected this policy, and converted it from a body drawn mainly from young militants (and having, through them, a popular base among SWAPO activists), into a committee of intellectuals or professionals, and leaders of particular ethnic groups, several of them with church connections.

Notable among these were the Rev. Hendrik Witbooi, Chief of the Gibeon Nama, who in 1977 became Acting Vice-President after having brought most of the Nama into SWAPO in November 1976; the Rev. Zephania Kameeta, already mentioned above, a prominent liberation theologian who had organized the Namibia National Convention (1974–6), co-opted as SWAPO Secretary for Health and Social Welfare; the Rev. Bartholemeus Karuaera, leader of the Association for the Preservation of the Royal House of Tjamuaha/Maharero in the NNC, who brought the support of the Association to SWAPO when he joined the National Executive in 1977; the Rev. Erwin Tjrimuje, an adviser to Karuaera, who also joined the executive in 1977 and was later made Secretary for Finance; Alexander Gaomab, the former chairman of NAPDO, a Damara grouping in the National Convention; Martha Ford of the former Volkspartei, a Rehoboth grouping; Joshua Hoebeb, a former principal of Martin Luther High School and subsequently director of the CCN-financed Literacy Campaign, who was brought in as Secretary for Education; and Nico Bessinger, an architect, co-opted for a short time as Secretary for Finance in 1978 and later, after returning from further studies in the USA in 1982, as Secretary for Foreign Affairs.[43] Except for Martha Ford, none of these people subsequently found it necessary to go into exile, and all of them were still on the NEH down to 1989: whereas none of the activists co-opted before the Walvis Bay Congress (Kaakunga, Muchimba, Angula, Munyaro, Naholo, Uanivi and Hatuikilipi) survived as NEH members.[44]

As has already been noted, the Walvis Bay Congress also changed the formal relationship between the NEH and the leadership abroad by declaring that when NEH members left Namibia they would cease to be leaders: it would be up to the leadership abroad to determine their subsequent role. In other words, the NEH was now to be considered as a 'caretaker' body, acting for the Executive Committee (or Politburo as it became known after 1978) abroad, the reverse of the position formally declared at the Tanga Congress. The leadership abroad reciprocated by co-opting the next group of

NEH members who survived the flight into exile onto the Central Committee (not the Executive Committee/Politburo): Kaakunga, Mushimba, Uanivi, Hatuikilipi and Ford.

Further changes were made to the NEH at a 'national conference' of SWAPO held in Katutura on 24–25 March 1977. K. A. S. Katamila, who had gone abroad (to Botswana, but not into exile), was replaced as Vice-Chairman by Mokganedi Tlhabanello, and room was made for the previously mentioned leaders of the various southern peoples who had joined SWAPO in late 1976.[45] The co-option of these southern leaders was, as Katjavivi puts it, the 'context' for the UN General Assembly's decision in December 1976 to declare SWAPO now not merely the 'authentic' representative of the Namibian people (a status already conferred in 1973), but the *sole and* authentic' representative – representing, that is, the peoples of the south as well as those of the north.[46]

While the NEH was thus being transformed, a very different tendency was, however, at work at the grassroots level in Windhoek and the south. With the adhesion of most of the Nama to SWAPO, Gibeon soon developed into an important SWAPO centre, with an office built by a group of young people;[47] Windhoek and Rehoboth developed active branches; more generally, another new political generation of activists was revitalizing the organization at its base. Most were southerners, and many were returning from further studies in South Africa. Susan Brown, arriving from South Africa towards the end of 1978, was struck by the number and vitality of SWAPO's southern branches:

> There were a number in and around Windhoek.... But every tin-shanty dorp in the South seemed to have its branch: Mariental, Maltahohe, Rehoboth (several), Gibeon, Hoachanas, Beerseba, Vaalgras, Koes, even Bethanien, though this was known to be pretty hostile territory and its existence was tenuous. In each area there was a more or less strong countervailing DTA branch, usually built around an opposing traditional leader and ethnic group, and building on the fact that opposing clans sharing the same districts and villages were naturally ready to come out on opposite sides in the first place.[48]

This activity had its limitations. One was that it was largely confined to the south. Brown recalls the chairperson of the Women's League at Gibeon, who had gone to Oshakati earlier in 1978 to show solidarity at a SWAPO rally that had been broken up by the police, speaking of the north 'as if it was a foreign country'. Another limitation was that it was 'mobilization politics'. No decisions were taken at the rallies, no campaigns were initiated. Meetings consisted above all of inspirational speeches (translated passage by passage into several languages) by party notables. No one seemed to demand more.

One important reason for this was that at this time people thought a transition to independence was imminent. Between 1976 and 1978, under pressure from the Carter administration in the USA and with major concessions on the part of the SWAPO leadership in exile, negotiations had led to the adoption in September 1978 of Security Council Resolution 435, which South Africa purported to accept. Although by the end of 1978 it was growing clear that South Africa was not about to implement the Resolution, it took some time for people to realize this. Even after Carter's defeat by Reagan in the US presidential election of November 1979, people did not immediately realize that the new administration's doctrine of 'constructive engagement' would in effect give South Africa a free hand to seek a military solution to the SWAPO threat for most of the next decade. In spite of Cassinga, in spite of the new wave of repression following the assassination of Chief Clemens Kapuuo in March 1978, and in spite of South Africa's decision to go ahead with elections to a national assembly without SWAPO participation or UN supervision in December 1978, people still felt for some time that independence was not far off. They were encouraged by the invitation to NEH members to attend the 'proximity talks' in New York in March 1979 (which also afforded the new NEH an unprecedented opportunity for extended consultations with the leadership in Luanda on their way home).[49]

1978–82: From Rehoboth to Dobra. The Struggle about the Struggle: Inner-Party Democracy and Accountability

In retrospect the years from 1978 to 1982 seem as decisive in determining the kind of political culture that SWAPO inside Namibia would bequeath to the nation at independence, as the years 1974–6 were for the political culture bequeathed to it from exile. Between 1978 and 1982 persistent efforts were made to induce the NEH to submit to election, or at least to some form of open accountability for its performance, because it was seen as being inactive. What is extraordinary about these efforts is not that they failed, but that they failed in spite of the fact that from December 1979 until at least some time in 1982 the NEH officially declared itself to be 'dissolved'; and in spite of the fact that the national office of SWAPO, which was also closed in 1979, stayed closed until 1987 or 1988. What has to be explained is how, in spite of this seeming abdication, the activists' efforts to get some action at the centre were repulsed, with the result that many of them, while remaining SWAPO members, transferred their activism into community-based organization of various kinds.

To understand this strange turn of events the increasingly complex context has to be borne in mind. On the military front, by 1979 SWAPO in exile had largely completed its move from Zambia to Angola. The party headquarters were in Luanda; the Kwanza Sul settlement was being developed to replace Cassinga; PLAN, dramatically expanded by the 'exodus' intake, was installed in its new bases near Lubango and was beginning to operate directly across the border into Ovamboland, where the great majority of the combatants were on their own terrain. Guerillas were infiltrating individually as far as Windhoek and beyond, and small units were reaching the settler area in the Otavi triangle.

The South Africans responded with a sharp increase in security measures, including the banning of public meetings in the north in 1979 and in the south in 1981; the establishment of Koevoet in 1978; and a very large build-up of military strength from Grootfontein to Ruacana, culminating in the occupation of a large part of southern Angola in 1981. As Susan Brown shows in Chapter 2, by 1982 PLAN's ability to threaten the settled areas had been virtually neutralized, although popular distrust of South African propaganda (and willingness to believe in SWAPO's) meant that people continued well into the 1980s to cherish the belief that they would soon be 'liberated' by PLAN.[50] Meanwhile, however, although SWAPO remained a legal organization, the costs of any SWAPO political activity, even in the south, continued to rise. Militants like Axel Johannes were arrested and tortured repeatedly, and death at the hands of state-encouraged vigilantes became a real possibility.

A new dimension of internal politics was also created by the fact that South Africa's formal acceptance of Resolution 435 in 1978 included an offer of amnesty for all exiles who returned to Namibia, provided that they renounced the use of force. This led to the return of a number of prominent exiles opposed to South Africa but outside SWAPO, including people who had left or been expelled from SWAPO in exile.[51] Some of these returnees, including Andreas Shipanga, president of the newly-formed 'SWAPO-Democrats' (later, SWAPO-D), would eventually take part in the last South African-sponsored attempt to achieve an independence settlement without UN control, the so-called Transitional Government of National Unity, formed in June 1985. Others, however, such as Kenneth and Ottilie Abrahams (also founding members of SWAPO-D, but who left it in 1980), and SWANU activists Vekuii Rukoro and Norah Chase (who dissolved SWANU's 'external council' and returned to Namibia in 1977), sought to mobilize popular support against the regime around issues such as resistance to military conscription (into the newly formed SWATF), introduced in 1980. South Africa, for its part, also began trying to complement its military strategy with civilian policies (a strategy called, apparently without any intended irony, 'Winning Hearts and Minds', or 'WHAM'). The Mixed Marriages and Immorality Acts were repealed, the non-white cadres of the civil service were enlarged, and various state-sponsored social service and cultural organizations were formed or encouraged, from Etango to the Boy Scouts.[52] In face of all these initiatives, it became increasingly difficult for SWAPO militants to remain inactive, especially when the drought that afflicted the whole region in the early 1980s began to drive people from the rural areas of the south into the towns, where overcrowding, poverty, malnutrition and sickness became chronic.

There was also the example of South Africa. There, in the 1970s, a generation of Namibian university students was exposed to a wave of student activism, epitomized by the Black Consciousness movement and the 1976 student uprising in Soweto. While the Namibian student activists rejected the exclusion of whites from their political struggles, they were nonetheless also inspired by 'BC'. They took from it a freshly reinforced sense of their identity as human beings endowed with rights, including the right to be more than passive agents of the SWAPO leadership in exile, let alone of a co-opted, secretive and inactive National Executive at Home. And then in the 1980s they were further inspired by the startling growth of grassroots popular activism that swept workplaces and townships alike under the auspices of organizations like the Congress of South African Trade Unions (COSATU) and the United Democratic Front (UDF).

These, then, are some of the elements of the situation in which the final evolution of 'internal SWAPO' occurred. Already in 1978 the key relationships between the activists and the NEH were becoming clear. Following the collapse of the NNC in 1976, some younger militants had reconstituted the SYL at a Congress in Rehoboth; some of the same people were also responsible for founding a dynamic SWAPO branch at Rehoboth, and another in Khomasdal, and restoring the Gibeon branch to the level of activity it had enjoyed under the leadership of its founding chairman, Eric Biwa, who was now in exile. They also played active roles in sustaining a region-wide Southern Region Executive, which from 1978 was chaired by Paul Vleermuis. Broadly speaking, in the years from 1976 to 1982 the Southern Region and the SYL were the main sources of the effort to do something about the NEH.

On 20 May 1978 there was a would-be 'national conference' of SWAPO at the Evangelical Lutheran Church in Windhoek, largely organized by the SYL, under the leadership of its President, Bernardus ('Bennie') Petrus.[53] As the former Youth Leaguers remember it, Petrus went to see Tjongarero, who had recently become SWAPO Deputy Chairman, and said a conference was needed to work out strategies, including a policy of resistance to the introduction of identity cards, the threatened introduction of conscription, and other issues. The National Executive being unwilling, the SYL decided to call a conference, inviting all SWAPO branches with which the SYL executive had contacts, and the National Executive members. Tjongarero's attitude, according to the same sources, was, 'I don't care, you can do it.' In fact, the SYL had no authority to call a National Conference of SWAPO. Nonetheless, between 100 and 200 people came, and one of the new NEH members, the former NAPDO leader Alexander Gaomab, took the chair. Other NEH members present included Karuaera, Tjrimuje, Jason Angula and Lucia Hamutenya. Tjongarero is remembered as having come, but not stayed.

The conference debated the issue of the need for activism, and the related issue of election versus co-option onto the NEH. People complained that SWAPO was 'falling apart', that co-option to the NEH had produced 'learned people' based in Windhoek and out of touch with the membership in the regions. Karuaera is remembered as having stated that once someone was elected to a position, he had a mandate to act without any obligation to report back. Security was also strongly appealed to as a reason for not throwing the executive open to election, as South African agents might get elected. Lucia Hamutenya is said to have stated that between sessions she had had a phone conversation with the movement's president, Sam Nujoma, and that he had told her that 'the youth should know that it was sometimes necessary to co-opt people you could trust'.[54] In the end, although the mood of the meeting appeared to be in favour of electing the NEH, the vote went against it, allegedly as a result of a procedural misunderstanding which Gaomab refused to rectify by a fresh vote.[55]

From this time on, although many further meetings were called by the activists in a continuing effort to get something done, the issue of election versus co-option seems to have been regarded as settled. This meant that the formal legitimacy of the existing NEH was accepted, and consequently that the critics could not constitutionally initiate any discussion capable of binding the organization – even when the NEH declared itself dissolved.

The dissolution occurred in June 1979, when Tjongarero returned from a conference abroad. As he recalls it, he found the party headquarters, which had already been firebombed, locked for non-payment of rent arrears, and a civil suit pending against him as the Deputy Chairman. Also, there had been a new wave of arrests and detentions; of the sixteen current members of the executive, only he and one other were still at large.[56] He therefore announced the dissolution of the National Executive, and the closing of the office, partly to avoid SWAPO being declared bankrupt and partly to ease the pressure that the leaders felt themselves to be under. Recollections differ quite widely about these circumstances and about the precise nature of the declarations made at the time. What seems fairly clear is that Tjongarero's object was to make the NEH formally disappear, even though its surviving members would continue to meet informally, which they did quite frequently.

Mixed messages were received from the SWAPO leaders in exile about this development. Moses Garoeb, the Administrative Secretary, publicly criticized the move and 'suspended' Tjongarero as Deputy Chairman, while Nujoma sent him a sympathetic letter, thanking him for his work and expressing support. Evidently the exile leadership had mixed feelings. On the one hand they needed an internal movement that appeared solid and active, to justify SWAPO's status (since 1976) as the 'sole and authentic representative of the Namibian people'. But they were also anxious to have an internal leadership that fully accepted the supremacy of the leadership in exile.

Several considerations were at work here. There was, to begin with, the fact that activism was only possible outside the war zone, in the 'south', and that any strong internal movement would therefore be based on a mainly non-Ovambo population, in contrast to the exile movement with its heavy preponderance of Ovambo. There was also the likelihood that a strong internal movement would tend to develop an independent political agenda that would not be wholly subordinate to the needs of the diplomatic and military strategy defined by the external leadership; and there was the certainty that South Africa would do its best to take advantage of any differences of view between the internal and external leaderships. Finally, there was the fact that the leaders of a militant internal movement would acquire popular support which would make them potential rivals with the external leaders at independence.

The National Executive at home, for their part, saw their critics as having leadership ambitions, and as being variously naïve and/or untrustworthy. They thought that the information they continued to receive from the leadership abroad could only be shared with fellow executive members selected by themselves, as opposed to anyone whom elections might throw up. They were also very conscious of the weight of the repressive apparatus ranged against them and saw no virtue in a policy of militant defiance that could, in their thinking, lead to the final destruction of the internal organization.

Many activists inside Namibia, however, took a different view. They suspected some of the motives of the external leadership mentioned above, and they also thought that the NEH were afraid to take risks, while being unwilling to make way for other people who were not afraid.[57]

Regardless of the motives of the various actors, what was objectively at stake was the fundamental question of whether SWAPO would encourage or stifle the development of a popular, mass-based political struggle in those parts of the country where it was possible. In the end the external leaders would lean in the latter direction, but in the short run they exhibited some contradictory reactions. For example, not long after the 'dissolution' of the NEH the Windhoek branch was asked by Moses Garoeb to take over the 'coordination' of SWAPO activities inside Namibia, and from 1980 to 1982 it did so, to the best of its abilities.[58] In practice this primarily meant asking the other branches, and the executives of the party's 'wings' (the SYL, the SWAPO Women's Council and the Elders' Council) to report to the Windhoek branch executive; and sending speakers from Windhoek to address meetings in the regions.

Such a role should also have involved keeping the regions and wings informed of developments outside Namibia: yet here again the external leadership showed its ambivalence: rather than sending information to Marco Hausiku, the Windhoek Branch chairman, or his colleagues, it went on sending it to the members of the 'dissolved' NEH.[59] The Windhoek branch's 'coordination' was thus necessarily limited; and it was also resented by some of the other branches, who only had the Windhoek Branch leaders' word for it that they had indeed been assigned this role.

As a result, between 1979 and 1982 the NEH's dissolution, endorsed however inconsistently by the external leadership, was an acute source of weakness and resentment in the internal movement, and it was repeatedly debated at meetings of various kinds. Three of these stand out in people's recollections: two conferences organized by the Southern Region Executive in Rehoboth in April and December 1981, and the so-called 'bush meeting' held at Dobra some time in 1982.

The April 1981 conference seems to have been attended by representatives from most of the branches in Namibia; the only NEH member present, however, was Jason Angula. An eight-person committee was struck to take the conference's demands to the National Executive in Windhoek: demands for 'proper' national conferences to be held, for a programme of political action, and for the leadership to account to the membership for their activities. The committee's views were heard, according to the NEH's critics, with disdain; and later Tjongarero and two other NEH members called a meeting of the Nama chiefs (one of whom, Chief Stephanus, had been on the committee sent by the conference) to warn them against collaborating with the activists.

Similar warnings were given to the veteran SYL leaders Jerry Ekandjo and Martin Kapewasha when they were released from Robben Island later that year, so that they did not attend a further conference organized by the Southern Region executive on the same theme in December 1981. This meeting was attended by delegates from thirteen branches and from the Windhoek branch of the SYL. Once again, Jason Angula alone came from the NEH. Some people wanted to replace the inactive NEH leadership; others stressed the risks of doing so. There was also some fear, according to some who were present, that those who would be removed from office would retaliate, and 'even go to the South Africans' – the same accusation that NEH members were inclined to level against some of their critics, questioning their 'loyalty' to SWAPO.

The last major confrontation over the national leadership issue occurred at the so-called 'bush meeting' held in the open air near the Catholic mission at Dobra, outside Windhoek, some time in 1982.[60] Here about 50 representatives of the branches, led on this occasion by those from Windhoek, finally confronted the members of the executive, most of whom were also present.[61] There was a lot of plain speaking. Tjongarero, in an emotional speech, offered to resign; the Windhoek delegates, however, are said to have demanded that the NEH fulfil its responsibilities. As for the outcome, some think it was agreed that the NEH would resume its functions, others that nothing was decided. In practice, things seem to have continued much as before, and the movement remained without a national office until the late 1980s, when one was opened in the old migrant workers' compound in Katutura. All accounts agree that

SWAPO activity remained at a low ebb until the late 1980s.

Before we examine the rest of the decade, however, three questions need to be asked about the demands of the NEH's critics in the years 1978–82: how democratic were they, how widely were they supported, and how far were they realistic?

In the first place, the demand seems to have been primarily for a more active, effective, aggressive kind of leadership. Listening to the retrospective accounts even of the critics, one gets the feeling that many of them demanded elections because they wanted action, and despaired of ever getting it from the sitting NEH members, rather than for the sake of elections as such. And unlike the 1976 'dissidents' in Zambia, the internal critics of 1978–82 do not seem to have produced any written declarations that have survived, so it is even harder to be sure of the nature of their democratic commitment. On the other hand there is no good reason to doubt the sincerity of their call for elections and accountability.

Secondly, it was not the case, as some NEH members claimed, that the demand for inner party democracy was confined to a small clique. The evidence shows that in 1978 this demand was widely supported in the branches, and not only by 'the youth'; after the dissolution of the NEH in 1979 it was even more general. As the Windhoek Branch chairman Marco Hausiku put it, 'Frustration was widespread everywhere, as well as [among] us [the Windhoek branch leadership].'[62]

The question of the realism of the demand is the most difficult to answer, and perhaps the most important. It seems that the Youth League, the Southern Region, and many branches (including the Windhoek and Rehoboth branches), held periodic elections for their executives.[63] The question why this could not also be done at the national level cannot really be disposed of by reference to security considerations, which were made so much of. It was argued that at the branch level the security risks were less, because at that level people knew each other so well that 'spies' were well known and would not be elected. Yet under any system of elections national office-bearers would obviously have been elected from among candidates who were equally well known at lower levels in at least some part of the country. It must also be asked why no effort was ever made to work out a system for vetting candidates, as is widely done for various reasons by parties even in democratic political systems, or to create any internal party intelligence system. It could even be argued plausibly that co-option involved greater security risks than elections. Moreover, the arguments against elections do not apply to the demands for action and accountability.

In sum, it is hard to avoid the conclusion that these were not the real reasons why the NEH, backed by the leadership abroad, resisted the extension of any aspect of inner-party democracy to the place where it seemed most needed – at the top.

1983–9: From the 'Bush Meeting' to the Independence Election: Community-Based Activism and SWAPO Inactivity

With the failure of 'the three conferences' (the phrase by which some remember them) to produce any significant change in the performance of the leadership, many of the younger activists increasingly transferred their energies to other organizations. They organized Bricks (originally a Katutura community newspaper, founded in 1983, which later expanded into a cluster of urban development projects); the Namibia Women's Voice (NWV); the YWCA; the Namibian National Students' Organization (NANSO); a transformed and effective National Union of Namibian Workers (NUNW); and many more local and sectoral, but nonetheless mobilizing and empowering, associations, cooperatives, and other agencies.

The main reasons for this have already been mentioned: the new politics of the returning SWAPO dissidents, the South African hearts and minds campaign, the drought, the example of mass-based, virtually insurrectionary activism in the South

Africa of the 1980s. There was also a perception that people were becoming tired of 'mobilization' politics: endless speeches about Resolution 435 were losing their appeal in face of hunger, the apparent failure of SWAPO's military effort, and the mounting costs of South African intransigence (now backed by the US administration under Reagan). As one activist recalls the period, people were beginning to say,

'You can explain to us what scientific socialism is in relation to SWAPO's constitution: nice, fine! I mean, we understand!' (There were even people who could recite the constitution, or parts of it.) 'But ... we are hungry!' In the south, people were actually dying. People came into Windhoek in their thousands, and it was just exploding....[64]

'Bread and butter issues' thus forced themselves onto the agenda and, as the NEH would not take them up, rank and file activists did. The apparent attitude of SWAPO's external leaders was that 'development' work was a diversion from the main struggle, liable to obscure the root cause of people's problems, namely South Africa's racist social and economic policies. At first the Council of Churches, under SWAPO influence, also refused to get involved in 'development' activities. The CCN was eventually forced to change tack, however, as the need mounted and as external agencies offered more and more funds for the purpose; eventually, as the following chapter explains, SWAPO was moved to change its attitude too, deciding to approve the new initiatives provided it had the power to veto them, which it got by making the CCN (which was thoroughly under its influence) the only approved channel for external aid.

Thus by the mid-1980s there was a dramatic expansion of grassroots or 'community-based' activism, which SWAPO as an organization accepted, but did not really encourage. In an article published in 1986 André Strauss listed 29 organizations, some of which were responsible for multiple development projects. By independence the count had risen to 54.[65] The 1986 listing included the CCN itself, with its departments of education and development (the latter having been an important component of its work from its inception in 1978); the trade union movement; and community-based organizations, from Bricks to the National Literacy Programme and the People's Crêche. Some were very modest and local. Others were major national movements, including the Namibian National Students' Organization (NANSO) (described by Sipho Maseko in Chapter 6 below), and the NWV.

The Women's Voice was a particularly potent phenomenon. Namibian women suffer from multiple forms of disadvantage – educational, economic, social and psychological, compounded by every aspect of apartheid, migrant labour, and the war – and in the early 1980s donor agencies were also pressing for women's needs to be addressed. The result was a sudden expansion of women's consciousness and the beginnings of a significant political mobilization. The Women's Voice appealed to women mostly through the churches, via the CCN connection, on issues that particularly affected women such as conscription (which affected all southern mothers with sons of military age). Its leaders were members of the SWAPO Women's Council (SWC) but, in accord with SWAPO's general stance, the SWC had not been mobilizing women around such issues. As recalled by one of the main NWV leaders, Lindi Kazombaue:

The bulk of women were not mobilized by *any* political party – they were available to any organization that would reach them in their homes. SWAPO was directed to SWAPO members, mostly in Ovambo areas. Most women were not reached, and were worried about practical issues that were caused by the political situation.... We were just sick and tired of the rhetoric, which didn't touch the real issues affecting people.... I was a social worker, I saw homeless, beaten people, hungry people: and SWAPO said, don't do anything, it will make them less revolutionary. But people who are hungry don't worry about politics. We were accused both of being *non*-political (by SWAPO) and *political* (by South Africa – women were not coming to work because of Women's Voice). Both sides wanted to own, to control, the organization. It was the first women's organization not under a political party, not under *men's* supervision.[66]

According to Kazombaue, when they visited Lusaka in April 1988 the Women's Voice leaders were encouraged by Pendukeni Ithana, the Secretary for Women on the Politburo abroad, but later she and her colleagues were called back to Lusaka and told that all Women's Voice projects should from now on come under the control of the SWC. By then, however, this was impossible, even if the NWV had been willing to accept it, because the internal leadership of the SWC was so bitterly opposed to the Women's Voice. Faced with the threat that, if they did not agree, SWAPO would campaign against the NWV, Kazombaue and her colleagues returned to Windhoek and recommended to their members that the NWV should dissolve – a blow from which the women's movement had not recovered three years after independence.[67]

There was also a dramatic mobilization of workers into trade unions from 1986 to 1989. Once again, this was organized by SWAPO activists and under the banner of the National Union of Namibian Workers, the name for an umbrella labour organization already adopted by previous SWAPO activists such as Arthur Pickering, Henry Boonzaaier and Jason Angula when they were organizing workers in 1977–8.[68] This earlier effort had been crushed relatively easily, putting an end to effective unionism for Africans for the next eight years – the years of SWAPO's own immobilization inside Namibia. In 1986, however, the mounting pressures inside South Africa and abroad, the emerging need of some employers – most notably, the Rossing Uranium Mine – for a permanent (non-migrant) workforce, and the increasingly desperate pursuit by the colonial authorities of an 'internal settlement', all combined to create space for a renewed effort at unionization. As it happened, a trio of seasoned SWAPO activists recently released from Robben Island – Ben Ulenga, John Pandeni and Petrus Iilonga – were on hand to seize the opportunity, while most workers were very willing to accept SWAPO's symbolic leadership and enthusiastically readopted the NUNW label.[69]

This time, however, the emphasis was somewhat different. In the 1970s, any serious prospect of improved working conditions still seemed to depend absolutely on first ending South African rule, and the distinction between industrial and political agitation remained hazy, as it had been for the Ovamboland People's Organization twenty years earlier still. Now, however, the influence of the latest South African model of working-class organization – democratically based unions focussing on concrete shop-floor demands – was undoubtedly powerful. In any case, the workers soon had the bit between their teeth. This was particularly true in the mining sector, where the newly emergent Mineworkers' Union of Namibia (MUN), which first took shape in 1985–6 at Consolidated Diamond Mines and at Rossing Uranium Mine, soon became a powerful, well organized hub for the whole trade union initiative of this period.[70] Despite considerable state harassment, actions like the dramatic 1987 strike (and the related consumer boycott) at the copper mine at Tsumeb were soon being mounted and recognition agreements were being extracted from management.

Trade union organizing and action also spread to other sectors: meatworkers at several meat-processing plants (under the banner of NAFAU, the National Food and Allied Union), chemical workers in Luderitz, construction workers in Windhoek. Striking roots in practical workers' struggles actually gave the new unions greater capacity to mobilize for broader goals as well: a dramatic case in point was the June 1988 stay-away of between 40,000 and 70,000 workers (60–75 per cent of the entire employed workforce in Namibia) in support of the school boycott of that year against the presence of SADF military bases in the northern part of the country.[71] In April 1989, with the run-up to national independence already under way, trade unions spear-headed impressive demonstrations against the selling off of state resources by the outgoing colonial regime.[72]

Yet in spite of the fact that this mobilization was led by SWAPO veterans and under the aegis of the NUNW, the external SWAPO leadership was uneasy about it. There was, of course, a union dimension to SWAPO undertakings in exile: a Labour Department, with John Ya-Otto as Secretary, and a training school, the Nduuvu Nangolo Trade Union Centre, in Angola. Such initiatives were geared mainly to working the circuits of the international labour movement, however, and could do little directly to advance working-class struggles at home.[73] When faced with militancy on the ground at home, SWAPO leaders tended to qualify their support, arguing that any improvement of conditions that the unions might win would tend to weaken the broader struggle for liberation; and out of the already mentioned anxiety about the emergence of autonomous centres of political power inside Namibia and political initiatives surfacing outside their immediate control. Thus, in the midst of an important union action at Rossing mine in 1988, the MUN leader Ben Ulenga was summoned to Europe, where he was told by the SWAPO president, Nujoma, that it was not up to him (let alone the workers) to determine when a strike should take place: he would receive instructions. And in 1989, when mass action was planned against the government's plans to privatize state and parastatal pension schemes, the union leadership attending a meeting in Zimbabwe were rather peremptorily ordered to do nothing that would jeopardize the implementation of Resolution 435.[74]

It is obviously impossible in this chapter to offer even a bare overview of the popular political activity represented by all these organizations in the 1980s. What is relevant here is simply that the opportunity, and the need, to engage in multiple forms of popular mobilization were so great that it occurred on an ever-expanding scale, in spite of SWAPO's initial opposition and continuing attempts to control it. Moreover, the energy and organizational talent that went into this mobilization was to a great extent that which SWAPO had stifled in its own organization.

Then, in 1984, the 'spy drama' broke. In May of that year representatives of all the internal parties, including SWAPO, were invited to a meeting in Lusaka on constitutional change, chaired jointly by President Kaunda and the South African Administrator General for Namibia, van Niekerk. The talks were abortive, but between the sessions delegates mixed with people from the SWAPO camps in Zambia and Angola and for the first time came to know of the scale and character of the arrests, which were just then reaching their peak. They realized then that it was above all the educated 'southerners' who were its main victims.[75] The full scale of the arrests, the torture, the forced confessions and the deaths in the pits would not be revealed until the first ex-detainees returned to Namibia in July 1989. But in late 1984 a Committee of Parents was formed by a group of detainees' relatives to demand an enquiry, and a year later (in late 1985), after receiving no response from either the SWAPO leadership or the churches (whether inside Namibia or abroad), they went public.

Most SWAPO activists, in spite of their suspicions and fears, refused to associate themselves with the Parents' Committee, seeing it as anti-SWAPO, but the issue greatly raised the 'loyalty' stakes, so that any criticism of the leadership was now even more apt to be denounced as collaborationism. As Steenkamp shows in the following chapter, church leaders in Namibia turned a deaf ear to the pleas for an enquiry, and the CCN denounced the Parents' Committee and punished those of its own employees who were active in it, even though they had been reliably informed (in private communications) about the situation in Lubango by Pastor Siegfried Groth and others. Even well after independence, when the Parents' Committee's demand for an investigation had been shown to be only too justified, those who had supported the Committee were still seen as renegades by party loyalists.

Conclusion

Namibia straddles the historic frontier between settler and tropical Africa, and the political history of internal SWAPO reflects this. The difference between the political culture of nationalist politics in the north, and that of the south, was exacerbated by the transformation of the north into a war zone from the mid-1970s onwards. SWAPO's internal activists were, from necessity, increasingly drawn from the 'south' (both non-Ovambo and *mbuiti*, or Oshivambo-speakers raised outside Ovamboland). These 'southerners' brought to their politics a more individualistic general culture; they were also more urbanized, more highly educated, and more exposed to South African politics through study, work and travel in the Republic. The militants among them put in question the politics of the 1960s generation of SWAPO leaders who had gone into exile, and the acceptance of those politics by the professionals' and notables who succeeded to the internal leadership at the end of the 1970s. The commitment of the militants to the values of democracy – to open debate, elections, and accountability – conflicted with those of hierarchy, precedence, age and personal authority. Riundja Ali Kaakunga, an NEH member and Acting Administrative Secretary inside Namibia in the early 1970s who later played an important role in the exile leadership in Angola, summed it up in retrospect in the following terms:

> The tradition is always not to contradict the person who takes the first line. Instead the meeting will be postponed, and a new decision made. If something is brought to a meeting, it means one or two powerful people have already made up their minds. There was never any debate. We were naïve, thinking we could influence decisions via debate. If you want to change something you should go through the President. If he makes up his mind, it is going to be endorsed. That has always been my experience of SWAPO – on the Central Committee, the Politburo [in Luanda], and already inside the country. It could have something to do with tradition. The whole question is one of consensus.[76]

Especially after 1978, the NEH acted as an effective barrier to the pressure from the younger activists for a serious domestic political strategy and for inner party democracy. This was made possible by a combination of factors.

First, there was the appeal to 'security'. Open political activity carried high risks, and the desire to exclude informers and provocateurs from the party's inner councils by not holding elections sounded reasonable, even though it also served to protect those already in the inner councils from challenge.

Second, the people who came to dominate the NEH by the end of the 1970s – university-educated professionals, holding relatively secure jobs – had quite a lot to lose, as some of them in retrospect acknowledge, relative to unemployed and often unmarried young militants who were prepared to devote themselves full-time to 'all-out' struggle and face the consequences.

A third crucial determinant was the constant loss of capable leaders, already drawn from a small pool, through jailing and exile, especially as the war and the repression intensified after 1974. SWAPO was perpetually being decapitated. Indeed, if there had been elections to the NEH and any of the militants had been elected to it, it is a fair guess that most if not all of them would also soon have disappeared into jail or exile.

Yet, fourthly, it was not only the NEH members who resisted the demands of the militants. Other factors also divided the militants from people whose support they would have needed in order to bring about a change. The Windhoek Branch leadership, in particular, never supported the demand for elections to the NEH, and at the Dobra bush meeting they acquiesced in a purely nominal 'restoration' of the NEH, rather than insisting on real changes. Part of the reason may be that many of the leading advocates of elections and accountability were from Rehoboth and Gibeon, not Windhoek; there was some anxiety in the Windhoek Branch that, if elections were held, leadership positions would be captured by these people, and they were not all seen as 'mature', or even trustworthy. Some of them were socialists and 'radicals', rather than simply nationalists; and perhaps they did not accord the deference that both the NEH and the Windhoek Branch leadership felt was due to them.

We feared new leaders might give us an *excess* of what we had been lacking. We suspected that among the organizers [of one of the meetings held to discuss elections to the NEH], though [they were] members, they wanted to replace the leaders. We had to tell our members, please be careful.[77]

Even some people who respected the militancy of the Youth League, and were critical of the NEH's passivity, also saw it as a contest between impatience and experience, and declined to back the youth in a struggle that could only benefit the South Africans. A member of the NEH in those years, Immanuel Ngatjizeko, spoke for many when he said: 'It was a difficult task to keep the body together. The one thing that kept us together was the South Africans.'[78] In the end this was, of course, the ultimately determining factor. Almost anything seemed better than an internal fight that would help the enemy.

And last but not least, by the mid-1970s there was a widespread acceptance of the idea that success in the Namibian struggle ultimately depended on what was achieved abroad, which placed a special premium on unity. Marco Hausiku, the Windhoek Branch chairman throughout the 1980s, was not only well aware of the diplomatic significance of the fact that leaders of key southern ethnic groups had been co-opted onto the NEH: he also grasped the significance of the external leadership's continued support for the NEH: 'We knew the weakness of the politburo [in this case the reference is to the NEH]. But ... they were well-known figures inside the country....And we saw the politburo [NEH] as the responsibility of the leadership abroad....'[79] And the leadership abroad preferred the status quo, with a passive NEH and a compliant CCN, to the risks of a wider mobilization.[80] So the NEH could do almost nothing and yet remain immune.

The ultimate result inside Namibia of SWAPO's adoption of a military-diplomatic strategy was thus a real demobilization. The /Ai //Gams Conference, initiated by the Secretary General of the CCN in 1986 to concert opposition to the 'Transitional Government of National Unity', received at most half-hearted support from SWAPO, and collapsed. Even some of SWAPO's most loyal internal activists, members of the Windhoek Branch executive, agree that SWAPO inside Namibia became 'weak'. After the dissolution of the National Executive the party was allowed to fall into 'a pathetic situation', which the efforts of the Windhoek Branch could not compensate for.[81] 'Active branches were a matter of a few individuals.... Some branches were active – Walvis Bay, Swakop, Tsumeb, Gibeon – but a small area.'[82] Even Mariental, which had been one of the stronger branches in the hey-day of the late 1970s, was completely dormant by the late 1980s.[83]

None of this alters the fact that it was SWAPO, rather than some combination of groupings less uncompromising in their resistance to South Africa, that succeeded to power at independence. It is also undeniable that the people of Namibia – above all in the north, but also in the south – were mobilized, and in a fundamental sense, too, empowered, by SWAPO's overall conduct of the liberation struggle. The SWAPO leadership's ability to win international recognition and to maintain an army in the field, however outnumbered and outgunned, gave people hope and the courage to go on defying the contempt and brutality meted out to them by the colonial regime. At the same time it must be acknowledged that SWAPO's succession to power did not primarily depend on its organizational achievements inside the country, and that it did not empower its members as individuals within the organization inside Namibia. Democratic ideas did develop inside the movement, but almost as much in opposition to the SWAPO leadership as with their encouragement and support. It remained to be seen if the party would find room after independence for the people who had voiced these ideas, and how far it would foster inner-party democracy once the need for unity in face of the South African enemy was no longer paramount.

Notes

1. For the force of these legal instruments see David Soggot, *Namibia: The Violent Heritage* (London: Rex Collings, 1986), pp. 50 and 297.
2. SWAPO rallies were held in Caprivi after 1974, but were increasingly apt to be broken up by DTA thugs with police connivance. In 1986 a court ruling held that existing legislation did not give the authorities power to ban meetings, but when a group of the internal leaders tested this by attempting to organize a rally in Oshakati they were quickly disillusioned by the army, who broke it up with a massive show of force. ('For the first time we realized the might and intensity of the security forces. They broke up the meeting and beat the hell out of us': Joshua Hoebeb, interview with the authors, 7 July 1992). The difference between the north and the south is also illustrated by the fact that in the same year the SYL was allowed to hold SWAPO's first public rally in Windhoek since 1981, which is said to have been attended by 3,000 people. The general idea between 1974 and 1986, however, was that any persistent activist could expect constant arrest and brutality (such as notoriously was meted out to Axel Johannes, SWAPO's Secretary-General, until he finally went into exile in 1979), or even assassination. Joshua Hoebeb, a national executive member, narrowly escaped assassination at the hands of DTA vigilantes who fired at his car in 1986. Many other cases could be cited.
3. According to the Rev. Joseph Avia, a Lutheran pastor who was working in Ovamboland at the time, this was evident to everyone from 1970 onwards. Interview with Leys, 18 June 1991.
4. This was formally decided at the Consultative Congress at Tanga in 1969–70, and in effect formally ended at the Walvis Bay Congress in 1976, discussed below.
5. Some of the evidence on this point is reviewed in G. Tötemeyer, *Namibia Old and New: Traditional and Modern Leaders in Ovamboland* (London: Christopher Hurst, 1978), pp. 5–9. Tötemeyer relies heavily on the work of H. Vedder, in *Das Alte Sudwestafrika* (Berlin: Warneck, 1934), which has been criticized as racist. However other sources, including F. N. Williams, *Precolonial Communites of Southwestern Africa: A History of Owambo Kingdoms* (Windhoek: National Archives of Namibia, 1991), take a similar view of this matter.
6. We have yet to see a copy of it, although copies are said to exist. According to Zen Asser Mnakapa, the OPO constitution provided for a congress every five years, at which the president would be elected, for a 35-member central committee and a 12-member executive committee. The Hon. Ben Amathila, however, who was one of the organizers of the 1969–70 Tanga Congress, states that before Tanga SWAPO's constitution provided only for annual conferences, not quinquennial congresses. Peter Katjavivi's thesis, 'The rise of nationalism in Namibia and its international dimensions', Oxford University 1986, cites the SWAPO constitution as providing for seven officers (president, vice-president, chairman, secretary-general, assistant secretary general, national treasurer, and organizing and publicity secretary), and says that 'the Annual Conference laid down broad policy and its decisions were implemented by the National Executive Committee, consisting of the officials and five additional members elected by the Conference' (i.e., to a total of 12). (*Ibid.*, p. 136). On page 137 he refers to '22 National Committee members', giving the names of fourteen. These were actually the original OPO leadership. On p. 162 Katjavivi states that inside Namibia in 1962 Maxuilili was Acting President (i.e. acting for Nujoma), with an executive committee based in Windhoek consisting of a Chairman, a Secretary for External Affairs (not provided for in the constitution), an Acting Secretary General (acting for Kuhangua), an Assistant Secretary General, a Treasurer, a Secretary for Propaganda and Publicity, and three other members (i.e., without national portfolios), to a total of ten. These were the first true SWAPO internal executive members, and were mainly teachers. The term 'national committee', Katjavivi believes, was originally adopted by Mburumba Kerina in New York to designate the leadership inside Namibia as opposed to those abroad. Interview with the authors in Toronto, 23 September 1992.
7. Soggot, *op. cit.*, p. 29.
8. J. Putz and H. Von Egidy, *Namibia Handbook and Political Who's Who* (Windhoek: The Magus Company, Post-Election Edition, 1990), p. 254.
9. The status of the Dobra meeting is not entirely clear, as it is not clear that it was formally convened by the National Executive, as provided for in the constitution. Further, although the Walvis Bay Congress was described as such at the time, subsequent SWAPO documents produced in exile call it a national conference rather than a congress, indicating that a real congress needed to represent all members, i.e. both those in exile and those inside Namibia.
10. According to Katjavivi, it was decided by the exile leadership at or after Tanga that the internal organization should as far as possible continue to work within the old constitution

(interview with the authors in Toronto, 23 September 1992). Not having a Central Committee inside the country created one less target for the South African Police; it also meant that there was no larger body inside the country to compete for legitimacy with the external Central Committee. The exile leaders were aware that the 30–40 participants at the Tanga 'Congress' had at best a doubtful right to make constitutional changes, but concluded that circumstances compelled it to assume this responsibility (Katjavivi, *A History*, p. 194, and the Hon. Ben Amathila, interview with the authors, 6 July 1992). After the SWAPO headquarters were moved to Luanda in 1978, the National Executive abroad was re-styled the 'Politburo', but this name never caught on for the 'National Executive at Home', which continued to be known to most people as 'the national executive'.

11. Sam Nujoma was President. Nelengani was Vice-President from 1961 to 1969, when he was expelled for giving state evidence against Toivo and the others accused in the 1967 treason trial. He was formally replaced as SWAPO Vice-President by Bredan Simbwaye, the Caprivi African National Congress (CANU) president, but as he was missing in South African hands he was in turn replaced by Mishake Muyongo as Acting Vice-President. Ya-Otto, after his release in 1968, became Acting Secretary General for Kuhangua in Dar es Salaam, to be replaced by Axel Johannes when Ya-Otto in turn fled into exile in 1974. Meantime, at the Tanga Congress in 1969–70, the post of Secretary General was abolished and replaced by that of Administrative Secretary, so Axel Johannes became Acting Administrative Secretary. Between Ya-Otto's departure in 1974 and 1976, however, Johannes was mostly in jail; Riundja Ali ('Othie') Kaakunga acted for him, and then officially became Deputy Acting Administrative Secretary at the Walvis Bay Congress. When Kaakunga himself left later in 1976 he became deputy to Moses Garoeb, the Administrative Secretary. The post of National Chairman was held by David Meroro; when he went into exile in 1975 he was eventually replaced in 1978 by Daniel Tjongarero as Deputy rather than as Acting Chairman, presumably to signify that this post was more than a fill-in for someone abroad. Significantly, the position of National Treasurer was never treated as an acting position, since it too was a real job. All other NEH 'portfolios' were also held substantively, not by people 'acting' for the parallel holders of the same positions abroad. The NEH did not, however, include a Secretary for Defence, to avoid identifying internal SWAPO formally with the illegal armed struggle.

12. Dr Neville Cupido, who was Khomasdal Branch chairman from the early 1980s, recalls keeping cards for several people because as a doctor he was relatively immune to police searches.

13. In 'The rise of nationalism', *op. cit.*, Peter Katjavivi states (p. 302) that 'SWAPO's internal organisation has held congresses on a regular basis according to the constitution'; the evidence of internal activists' recollections makes this seem doubtful.

14. Out of a total of 18 members of the original OPO/SWAPO executive whose names are given by Katjavivi and by Putz and von Egidy, only six were non-Ovambo. These were Kenneth Abrahams, Emil Appolus, Paul Helmuth, Mburumba Kerina, Hans Beukes and V. Eixab. They had all ceased to be leaders by the end of the 1960s, and then or later ceased to be SWAPO members.

15. John Ya-Otto, *Battlefront Namibia* (London: Heinemann 1982), p. 64.

16. Walvis Bay, Tsumeb, Luderitz, Oranjemund, Gobabis and Otjiwarongo: Ya-Otto, *op. cit.*, p. 69. Katjavivi says (cautiously) that ten branches were listed on SWAPO's letterhead at this time. Besides those mentioned by Ya-Otto he mentions Okahandja, Ovamboland, Kaokoveld, Swakopmund and Usakos. *A History, op. cit.*, p. 46.

17. Kenneth Abrahams, interview with Leys, 14 June 1990. According to various informants, Nujoma's title to the presidency arose even more informally. Originally there were five contenders, including some besides Nujoma who styled themselves president: Mattheo Nghikupulwa, who was rejected because he came from Angola; Jackson Kashikuka, favoured by some, but who declined because he did not speak English; and Louis Nelengani and Nathaniel Maxuilili. Nelengani agreed to take second place as Vice-President and Maxuilili declined to leave Namibia, becoming Acting President.

18. Vinnia Ndadi, *Breaking Contract: the Story of Vinnia Ndadi*, (Richmond, B.C.: LSM Press, 1976), pp. 65–7. This testifies to quite an extensive membership. As late as 1975 the joining fee was only 2.50 rand and the subscription one rand a year (50 cents in rural areas).

19. Nico Bessinger, who was Treasurer of the Windhoek branch in the late 1970s, recalls regularly raising 700-800 rand in a weekend in Katutura by this method.

20. According to H. Uanivi, the SWAPO leadership in exile, acting through Peter Katjavivi, actively fostered (and partly financed) this marriage between SWAPO and the churches, starting with the Ecumenical Centre in 1971 (personal communication to the authors: Uanivi was involved at that time while still a student at Paulineum Theological Seminary).

21. Some activists, including a number of SWAPO militants of the time, saw in the National Convention possibilities for the formation of a single national party with a radical project of popular mobilization. They blame its failure on the UN General Assembly's decision in 1973 to recognize SWAPO as the 'authentic representative of the Namibian people'; while the SWAPO leadership blame SWANU and NUDO for having sought to use the Convention to recoup, at SWAPO's expense, political ground that they had lost through their own shortcomings.

22. According to Jerry Ekandjo, the founding Chairman of the SWAPO Youth League, the SYL was motivated partly by a feeling among the youth that the NC was tending to eclipse SWAPO. They thought that SWAPO could have organized meetings independently of the NC, and eventually they took the initiative in organizing an independent SWAPO rally (in August 1973) partly as a reaction to a rumoured proposal that the NC should have its own flag, displacing 'SWAPO's colours' (interview with the authors, 26 June 1992).

23. Ekandjo, *ibid.*

24. De Wet's official title was Commissioner General for the Indigenous People of South West Africa, but it as as the Bantu Commissioner that he is still, understandably, remembered by Namibians.

25. Soggot, who researched this question when acting for the victims in an effort to get the floggings halted by the courts, established with the help of Robert Gordon, a Namibian anthropologist, that corporal punishment had been introduced in Ovamboland by a South African native commissioner, Hahn, who had a notorious taste for the sjambok. See Soggot, *Namibia*, p. 73.

26. Soggot asserts that an almost messianic belief in 1974 as the year of liberation was widespread among the Youth Leaguers in 1972-3 (*Namibia*, p. 77). Ekandjo and others recall this as being more like a target they set for themselves at this time.

27. Others detained and/or jailed included SYL leaders Nashilongo Taapopi, Ndali (Thomas) Kamati and Joseph Kashea; the SWAPO Acting Administrative Secretary Axel Johannes; the National Chairman David Meroro, and executive members Jacob Ngidinua, and Eliakim Andreas.

28. Recollections of the date of the Congress are hazy. As the exodus began in June, May seems likely.

29. As noted in note 32 of Chapter 3 above, even some SYL leaders who were not on the side of Keshii and Shangula over the 1976 crisis thought the Oniipa congress was a 'good' one.

30. In 1976 Keshii and Shangula were prominent among those detained by the SWAPO leadership in exile for their role in criticizing the leadership and articulating the demand for a party congress (see Chapter 3 above). This needs to be borne in mind when assessing Ekandjo's later criticism (in an interview with the authors) of Keshii's election as President, replacing him as the senior leader. The criticism is interesting for what it reveals about the political culture of the movement at this time, including the SYL. Keshii was the recognized successor to Ekandjo, who was *hors de combat*. He could have replaced Ekandjo as Chairman, but the practice had already been established in the 'mother body' (as SWAPO was called, in relation to its 'wings') of replacing prominent leaders arrested by the South Africans with acting office-bearers, out of respect, and perhaps out of a desire to show that the South Africans could not determine, just by making arrests, who the real leaders of the movement were. But an acting leader does not have the same weight as a real leader. The Oniipa Congress may therefore have made Keshii President, and appointed a lesser figure as acting Chairman, partly for this reason: though a desire to parallel the offices of the 'mother body', or vanity, could also have been involved.

31. The SYL leaders did have a good opinion of their own claims to status: in retrospect more than one has acknowledged that 'we were arrogant' (Jerry Ekandjo, interview with the authors, 26 June 1992). But their status as representatives looks quite reasonable in relation to that of many of their critics in the SWAPO leadership.

32. The SWAPO-led Namibia National Convention which succeeded it also collapsed in 1976 over conflict with SWANU on essentially the same issue. It was only in November 1976 that the UN General Assembly added the words 'sole and' to 'authentic representative', but this was already the meaning that the label conveyed to most people, and that Kapuuo was resisting.

33. Strictly speaking, he was Acting Administrative Secretary, this post having in effect replaced that of Secretary General at the Tanga Congress, but the name change did not register widely inside the country.

34. See Chapter 3, above, pp. 46–53; and also Leys and Saul, 'Liberation Without Democracy?', *op. cit.*, for the role of the SYL leaders and other details of these events.

35. This was also the view of independent observers in Lusaka: see, e.g., Proinsas Macaonghusa, a senior aide of the former UN Commissioner for Namibia, Sean MacBride, writing retrospectively in the *Sunday Press* and reported in the *Windhoek Advertiser*, 14 May 1977.
36. As noted in Chapter 3 above (note 54), when Kaakunga arrived in Lusaka immediately after the congress the leadership there seemed very relieved at the outcome.
37. Thus former NEH member H. Uanivi (interview with Leys, 9 July 1992) recalls the congress as having been called in response to urgent requests from the leadership abroad communicated by Peter Katjavivi in London. But Katjavivi himself (interview with the authors, 23 September 1992) remembers having only sought to find out about the congress organizers' plans, and this is also how it is remembered by Kaakunga who as Acting Administrative Secretary convened the Walvis Bay meeting, and Festus Naholo (see L. Dobell, 'New Lamps For Old? ...', unpublished MA thesis, Queen's University, Kingston, p. 51).
38. This may well have been an element in the failure to take seriously the materials brought back by Mrs Beukes, the wife of one of the most inveterate opponents of South African rule and head of a large family of political activists in Rehoboth. Her son Hans was a founder member of the SWAPO 'National Committee' who, after training as a teacher in Norway, rejoined the exile movement in Lusaka, where his mother was visiting him when the crisis broke. His sympathies were strongly with the dissidents and he narrowly avoided being detained himself in May 1976. Fortunately for him his Norwegian wife was serving as a diplomat in Lusaka and was able to secure his return to Norway. But before he left he gave his mother a collection of the dissidents' statements to deliver to the internal party on her return to Namibia. Her younger son Hewat, an uncompromising militant and critic of any and all authority, had already shown his independence of view and he was himself victimized by being dubbed a 'spy' and ostracized by fellow-detainees in Gobabis prison later in 1976.
39. Eric Biwa, interview with the authors, 23 June 1992.
40. This initiative, which was hotly debated before it passed, led to the early recruitment of Peter Manning, who later became SWAPO Information Officer in London, and Henning Melber: later white recruits included Anton Lubowski and Hartmut Ruppel. Lubowski was assassinated shortly before the independence elections, apparently by South African agents, for reasons that in late 1992 had still not been explained. Ruppel became Attorney General at independence.
41. Tauno Hatuikilipi had been a DEMCOP representative within the National Convention which came to an end in 1974. According to Hewat Beukes, Hatuikilipi, who was then working for the Lutheran church, attended a church conference in Senegal in early 1976 where he met some of the senior SWAPO leaders in exile. Beukes remembers him as coming back and asking him for suggestions for 'good people' to put on the NEH. In 1975 Tjongarero was helping the Rev. Zephania Kameeta to organize the Namibia National Convention (the successor to the National Convention). The senior SWAPO leaders wanted to have a voice on the NNC executive: 'so Tjongarero became a SWAPO member and Secretary General of the NNC on the same day [in 1975]'. (Othniel Kaakunga, interview with Leys, 14 July 1992).
42. As Vice-President Chief Witbooi was formally senior, but as Chairman of the NEH Tjongarero's was theoretically the more powerful role.
43. Some of these co-optees were dispensed with after independence, when their political utility was over: Karuaere and Tjirimuje, (along with Frans Kambangula, elected Secretary for Transport at the Walvis Bay Congress, and still in that position down to April 1989 after a brief spell as acting Treasurer), were the only members of the NEH whose names were not included in the list of Central Committee members nominated by the Politburo for re-election at the 1991 SWAPO Congress.
44. Hatuikilipi, Tlhabanello, Mushimba, Kaakunga, Munyaro, Naholo and Uanivi went into exile, as did Martha Ford. Tlhabanello resigned from SWAPO in 1979 and went to study in the USA, dying of an illness after his return to Namibia in the mid-1980s. Hatuikilipi, Mushimba, Kaakunga and Munyaro ended up in the dungeons in Angola, where Hatuikilipi and Munyaro died. Uanivi escaped a similar fate by forming the Communist Party of Namibia with himself as its President (and sole member) and placing himself under the protection of the MPLA government in Luanda, having established close personal ties with President Agostinho Neto. Martha Ford also left SWAPO and did not return from Angola at independence. Angula and Naholo were still in the middle ranks of the SWAPO leadership after independence.
45. It is noteworthy that the decisions of the Katutura Conference, and notably all the elections to offices, were reported in full detail in the *Windhoek Advertiser* on 23 March 1977 as a reshuffle that would merely be ratified at the Conference to be held that coming weekend: 'appointments for new portfolios have already been made by the National Executive but it is

the task of the Conference this weekend to sanction the various appointments'. After the weekend, no report of these parts of the proceedings was given. The *pro forma* nature of the Conference's elective role was perfectly clear.

46. Katjavivi, 'The Rise of Nationalism', *op. cit.*, p. 255.

47. The decision of Witbooi and the other Nama chiefs to throw in their lot with SWAPO also owed a great deal to the efforts of young militants like Eric Biwa and Martha Ford.

48. Susan Brown, personal communication. The impression of several branches existing in Windhoek and Rehoboth probably reflects the growth of the 'sections' system, which were effectively sub-branches covering different sections of a township.

49. The 'proximity talks' were so called because the South Africans agreed to take part in talks involving all parties about implementing Resolution 435, but without talking directly with SWAPO.

50. 'We had faith in the armed struggle. When people realized they couldn't mobilize inside the country, young people left, and we had this hope'. Immanuel Ngatjizeko, former NEH member, interview with the authors, 24 June 1992.

51. The latter category included Emil Appolus, Paul Helmuth, Kenneth and Ottilie Abrahams, and Andreas Shipanga.

52. Etango, Ezuva and Namvi were state-sponsored 'cultural' organizations designed for the Ovambo, Kavango and Caprivians respectively. Their military origins, fundamentalist Christian links and vaguely fascist ideologies are described in Denis Herbstein and John Evenson, *The Devils Are Among Us* (London: Zed Books, 1989), pp. 112–15.

53. Petrus replaced Nashilongo Taapopi as SYL president in 1978 when Taapopi went into exile. Taapopi died in the South African attack on Cassinga. Petrus went into exile later and died in the dungeons at Lubango. Biwa, the first Southern Region chairman, survived torture and imprisonment at Lubango to return in 1989 and become a leader of the ex-detainees' Patriotic Unity Movement. The PUM joined the United Democratic Front in the pre-independence election and Biwa was returned as a UDF member of the Constituent (later National) Assembly.

54. Erica Beukes, interview with the authors, 1 July 1992.

55. This account has been checked against the recollections of several people who were present, but this meeting stands in particular need of further research.

56. A new complicating issue at this time was the arrival in the south of PLAN combatants seeking help. To be caught giving them any assistance was punishable with the severest penalities under the Terrorism Act yet the PLAN command seems not to have made any effort either to make these guerillas independent or to assist the internal movement to identify and help them while reducing the risk of being caught. The NEH members took the view that as they were constantly watched, any contact between them and the guerillas meant certain discovery for both, so the burden fell on others, many of whom felt an absolute moral obligation to help, even though they could never be sure they were not dealing with a South African agent provocateur.

57. Tjongarero had previously appeared to display a lack of toughness when suddenly and crudely confronted with South African brutality. In December 1977, having been arrested on his way back from a seminar in Ovamboland, he issued a statement (which he retracted immediately afterwards) renouncing violence and SWAPO after being interrogated to the point of mental disorientation and then forced to handle the mutilated victims of a land-mine explosion (Soggot, *op. cit.*, pp. 217–8). Typical of many activists was the (not entirely unsympathetic) remark made to us by one of them that Tjongarero and his main colleagues were 'these soft guys'. Yet for a sensitive man to have sustained the role of Deputy National Chairman at all during the dark days of the 1980s did call for courage nonetheless.

58. According to the Windhoek Branch chairman of the time, Marco Hausiku, two members of the Windhoek Branch executive were called to Botswana where either Moses Garoeb or someone acting for him asked the Branch to coordinate the organization's activities nationally. Later, critics questioned whether, given the importance of the issue, such authority could have been given without an official letter, which was never produced, and in some versions later enquires abroad cast doubt on whether any such request had been made. In practice, however, an informal verbal request, seen as having the force of an instruction, seems quite likely in the circumstances.

59. 'The party outside communicated only via the Politburo [the NEH] members: we couldn't risk touching it [the NEH]' (the Hon. Marco Hausiku, interview with the authors, 25 June 1992). (Hausiku was one of the few internal leaders we interviewed who applied to the National Executive at home the term 'Politburo' which had replaced it in exile.)

60. The venue was chosen to avoid police detection. Delegates are said to have been driven in at

the last minute, only a handful of organizers knowing of the site in advance. Perhaps partly for this reason recollections of this meeting are unusually conflicting. Out of six respondents who were present, none could precisely recall the date and there were even differences of opinion as to the year. 1982 seems most likely.

61. Recollections differ more about this meeting than most others of this period. Some meetings are recalled in great detail, down to the date and day of the week. As noted above, in the case of the bush meeting, not even the year is agreed on. Some participants remember about 70 people, others less than 50.

62. Hausiku interview, *op. cit.*

63. Interviews with Marco Hausiku, Hewat Beukes, Paul Vleermuis and others.

64. André Strauss, interview with Leys, July 1990.

65. A. Strauss, 'Community development: community organisations in Namibia', in G. Tötemeyer, V. Kandetu and W. Werner (eds), *Namibia in Perspective* (Windhoek: Council of Churches in Namibia, 1987), pp. 184–95; and interview with Leys, 5 July 1990.

66. Interview with Leys, 4 July 1991.

67. For a cautious account of this story see Tessa Cleaver and Marion Wallace, *Namibia Women in War* (London: Zed Press, 1990), pp. 93–5. There seem to have been several distinct aspects to the problem, difficult to disentangle. One was that by staying non-affiliated to SWAPO, NWV could try to represent women regardless of party affiliation, including members of other parties; it also dealt directly with donors, instead of going through SWAPO, and was thus able to raise funds from various external sources that would not give money to the SWAPO Women's Council, the wing of a political party. Ethnic and class elements also entered in, the NWV top leaders being primarily southern and highly educated, relative to the primarily northern leadership of the SWC. And there was, finally, the question of whether women should be free to have their own organization, independent of men. In 1991 the last of several post-independence attempts to found a new independent women's organization came to nothing.

68. For this and much other valuable information on the Namibian labour movement see Pekka Peltola, 'The role of the National Union of Namibian Workers in the struggle for independence', an edited version of a paper presented at a seminar at NISER, University of Namibia, on 29 July 1992.

69. There was also a growth of regime-approved house unions at this time, as well as some union initiatives that distanced themselves from SWAPO – whether to the left or to the right is disputed – such as the National Building Workers' Union under Aloysius Yon.

70. See Brian Wood, 'The battle for trade unions in Namibia', *South Africa Labour Bulletin (SALB)*, 12, 6 (May–June 1987). The various updates compiled by Wolfgang Werner on the emergent Namibian trade union movement in later issues of *SALB* are also useful.

71. See Richard Pakleppa, '40,000 workers stayaway in Namibia', *SALB*, 13, 6 (September 1988).

72. Harald Harvey and Alana Dave, 'Namibian workers and national independence', *SALB* 14/1, April 1989.

73. Brian Wood describes SWAPO's Labour Department as being 'much like an embryonic 'Ministry of Labour''('The battle for trade unions', *op. cit.*).

74. The line taken by the external leadership here may well have been realistic. The still-remembered anger felt by the members of the trade union delegation, however, was not because their views were not accepted, but because they were not even listened to. They only dared express their resentment to each other informally, outside their sessions with Festus Naholo and other SWAPO leaders, feeling cowed by the high-handed style they encountered.

75. 'Southerners' in this context include Oshivambo speakers who had been born, or at least brought up, south of Ovamboland. On the 'spy drama' see Chapter 3, pp. 54–7.

76. Interview with Leys, 14 July 1992. As noted in Chapter 3 (p. 62, n. 57), Kaakunga was later a victim of the 'spy drama' and detained at Lubango.

77. The Hon. Marco Hausiku, interview with the authors, 25 June 1992. Hausiku's colleague on the Windhoek Branch executive at that time added: 'In the struggle you get radical people who, faced with a crisis, want to do radical things – replace the leadership.... Some comrades who were very radical ended up not loyal to the party.' (Jeremiah Nambinga, interview with the authors, 3 July 1992). The last reference is probably to people who were later active in the Parents' Committee.

78. He added: 'The Youth League is the militant arm of the party. In all our active challenges to the government the Youth League would normally be the people in the forefront. In the National Executive you had grey-haired people....' I. Ngatjizeko, interview with the authors, 24 June 1992. Joshua Hoebeb, another NEH member from about 1977 until 1989 (and later SWAPO Chief Whip in the National Assembly), also paid tribute to the youth: 'The young

ones were fearless, challenging, and the victory is to a large extent due to them. We felt ashamed to run [away] when they were not running.' Interview with the authors, 7 July 1992.

79. The Hon. Marco Hausiku, interview with the authors, 25 June 1992.
80. As one senior member of the former exile leadership acknowledged to us, 'as we came nearer independence, people were bound to speculate as to who would have power'.
81. The Hon. Marco Hausiku, interview with the authors, 25 June 1992.
82. Jeremiah Nambinga, SWAPO Secretary for Labour, interview with the authors, 3 July 1992.
83. Petronella Coetzee, returning from studies at the University of the Western Cape in 1987, became Secretary of the Mariental Branch in 1988 because 'there was nothing going on in Mariental – nothing whatsover, there was no branch, nothing. So I started one ... I initiated the process and somebody came from Windhoek' (interview with Leys, July 1990).

5
The Churches

PHILIP STEENKAMP

The role of the church in Namibia, the most Christian of African countries, was shaped by, and in turn shaped the nature of that country's liberation struggle.[1] It provides a classic illustration of liberation struggle as a 'two-edged sword'. The struggle was a noble endeavour, but it had costs. While all Namibians suffered the effects of South Africa's brutal military occupation and its divisive neo-colonial strategies, some also suffered at the hands of the SWAPO leadership. The church's role in this complex history, and the consequences for both the church and post-independence politics, are the subject of this chapter.

From 1970 on, the churches increasingly confronted the state and identified with the struggle for liberation. This role was not uncontested, leading to bitter struggle within and among the churches. But by the early 1980s the Council of Churches in Namibia, representing over 80 per cent of the total population, was closely identified with SWAPO, serving, in some respects, as an alternative internal wing of the organization. It accepted SWAPO's policies and actions, helping to reinforce SWAPO's monopoly of resistance politics. It was not democratized by this experience. It spoke and acted for people, rather than empowering them to speak and act for themselves. This paternalism, while partly necessitated by the exigencies of repression and war, also reflected the pre-existing authority structure of the churches, as well as that of the liberation movement generally.

The Radical Church

BREAKING THE SILENCE

There was a long tradition of submission to secular authority in Namibia: church leaders preferred to keep a low profile and to avoid confrontation with the South Africans. It took a number of developments, political and theological, to break the 'chrysalis of ecclesiastical silence'.[2] South Africa's attempt to implement apartheid in Namibia, as outlined in the report of the Odendaal Commission, shocked the churches into action. In 1964 and 1967 the two largest Namibian churches, the Evangelical Lutheran Ovambo-Kavango Church (ELOC) and the Evangelical Lutheran Church in South West Africa (ELC), reflecting the misgivings of the black community, drew up memoranda warning the government that its plans for separation would lead to chaos. Although these representations can hardly be described as either confrontational or challenging – they were not made public and were couched in polite, almost deferential, terms, and the legitimacy of the state was not questioned – they did indicate the emergence of a 'listening' church.

Other factors contributing to the breaking of silence included the rejection in Lutheran churches worldwide of the spiritualistic interpretation of the doctrine of the Two Kingdoms, which forbade church involvement in politics, and the reaffirmation of a theological principle authorizing and even commanding opposition to apartheid, which was described as a scourge of human experience. At the same time, pressing material conditions – the grinding poverty and brutal exploitation sufferered by their congregations – and the creation of new political parties, which offered an alternative framework for mobilization and political action, obliged them to take action or face oblivion.

On 30 June 1971, Bishop Auala of ELOC and Moderator Gowaseb of the ELC responded to an advisory opinion of the International Court of Justice, confirming the illegality of South Africa's occupation of Namibia, by issuing an Open Letter to South African Prime Minister B. J. Vorster. The letter began with the accusation that South Africa had failed 'to take cognizance of Human Rights as declared by [the] UNO in the year 1948 with respect to the non-white population'.[3] It listed a number of the injustices suffered by Namibians – restrictions on movement and settlement, the lack of freedom of expression, the denial of basic political rights, especially the franchise, the policy of job reservation and the migrant labour system, which resulted in low wages and the destruction of family life – and concluded with a call for justice and independence:

> Our urgent wish is that in terms of the declarations of the World Court in co-operation with the United Nations, of which South Africa is a member, your Government will seek a peaceful solution to the problems of the land, and will see to it that human rights be put into operation and that South West Africa may become a self-sufficient and independent State.[4]

The letter was strongly supported by the Anglican Bishop, Colin Winter, who wrote, 'The Christian Church, as the conscience of this nation, must speak out with clarity and without fear. Apartheid must be denounced as unacceptable before God;'[5] and by his counterpart in the Catholic church. While the churches had registered their opposition to certain colonial impositions before this date, the Open Letter represents a watershed. From this time on, these four churches – representing 75 per cent of the total population[6] – increasingly identified with and participated in the struggle for national liberation.

The Open Letter sent shock waves through the white community. The government was forced to recognize church leaders as major players in Namibian politics, and a meeting was arranged between Prime Minister Vorster and delegations from ELOC and ELC in Windhoek on 18 August 1971. It was a confrontation between two irreconcilable viewpoints: Vorster defended the policy of separate development, while the eight churchmen condemned it as 'the mother of all problems'.[7] The most important consequence of the Open Letter, however, was the political conscientization of the general black population. Among the people it encouraged a growing awareness of their oppression and an insistent demand for justice; while among church workers an indigenous political theology emerged which sought to reconcile spiritual commitment with political involvement.

SUPPORTING THE STRUGGLE

There were three distinct facets of the church's role in opposition to the authoritarian regime: institutional – providing a framework within which a culture of resistance could take root and grow; ideological – articulating the interests of oppressed Namibians; and operational – offering them protection and support, albeit in the role of a shepherd looking after a flock.[8]

In the aftermath of the colonial conquest, the church acted as 'the oxygen tent for comatose Africans'.[9] From the 1960s onwards, however, it was drawn into the growing political vacuum created by the repression of black opposition and the absence of a liberal white lobby, and found itself at the forefront of internal resistance to the state. The authorities responded with a campaign of harassment, but as the self-proclaimed defenders of Western civilization and Christianity, they could hardly ban the church.

With the other institutions of civil society under tight control, the churches were left to do battle alone. This prospect forced them into ever closer cooperation with one another. In 1972 ELOC and ELC joined together in a confederation – the United Evangelical Lutheran Church of South West Africa (UELCSWA); in 1974 the Christian Centre was set up as a forum for informal cooperation among the churches; and by 1978 a fully-fledged ecumenical body, the Council of Churches in Namibia, was established. This ecumenical drive, though it also had spiritual inspiration, should be seen primarily as an attempt to thwart South Africa's divide-and-rule tactics and to combine church resources in the struggle for liberation. It also challenged Pretoria's plans to balkanize Namibia and provided the institutional framework for the development of a new consciousness of 'One Namibia – One Nation'. The struggle was deepened and broadened through the strengthening of old and the establishment of new regional and international ties with bodies such as the South African Council of Churches (SACC), the Southern African Catholic Bishops' Conference (SACBC), the World Council of Churches (WCC), and the Lutheran World Federation (LWF).

The churches now provided practically the only solid institutional structures of opposition to the state. Church buildings offered physical sanctuary; church services, meetings of church men's, women's and youth groups, and church-established professional societies of teachers and nurses constituted the main fora for the formulation of an ideology and a praxis of liberation. This message was spread, to the country and the world beyond, through regular church newsletters such as *Immanuel* (ELC), *Omukwetu* (ELOC), and *Angelus* and *Omukuni* (both Catholic), and was reiterated in the letters and statements issued by church leaders in response to specific crises.

The church also acted as 'the voice of the voiceless'. It exposed the state's repression and formulated a liberation theology rooted in local experience. The church also played an active, if relatively low-level, political or operational role, aptly referred to as 'an ambulance service for the victims of apartheid' – initiating political actions, providing assistance (especially legal assistance) to the state's political opponents, and fostering the social and economic development of black communities.

As strife between SWAPO and South Africa escalated, church assistance to opponents of the state, including legal aid, support for dependants and the financing of prison visits, became central to its role in the struggle. For example, Bishop Colin Winter of the Anglican Church arranged for the defence of thirteen prisoners charged with inciting workers to strike during the 1971–2 general strike; the LWF raised legal costs of $120,000 for the 1976 trial of six people accused of assassinating the hated Chief Elifas, head of the South African-backed Ovamboland administration.

Churchmen also protested against torture. Bishop Auala and Praeses Lukas de Vries, the newly appointed head of the ELC, met with Vorster in April 1973 to protest at the torture and public floggings of members of SWAPO and other progressive organizations arrested for their opposition to the August 1973 Ovamboland election.[10] In November 1973 Bishop Auala, Suffragan Bishop Richard Wood of the Anglican church, and Thomas Kamati, a member of SWAPO's Youth League and a victim of the floggings, jointly applied to the Supreme Court of Windhoek to have the floggings halted. Although this application was rejected, the Court of Appeal in Bloemfontein ruled in their favour in February 1975. The boldest intervention came in May 1977, with the church leaders issuing an extraordinary document, *Statement on Torture*, which not only testified to the facts of repression, but also offered practical advice to victims. The document was quickly banned.

The growing involvement of the church in political matters naturally made it a target for attack. The movement of church workers within the country was increasingly restricted (permits to visit Ovamboland, for instance, were refused), visas were denied to foreign church personnel, and many resident churchmen who were not citizens were deported. The most dramatic physical attack on the church was the explosion which destroyed the ELOC printing press at Oniipa in the early hours of 11 May 1973.

The church's efforts to expose repression and assist the victims of apartheid were accompanied by a direct involvement in the fight for a political settlement. In numerous representations it called for an end to South African rule and for 'real' independence. The first combined political intervention of the four main churches was a dramatic and powerful letter, sent to Dr Kissinger, the US Secretary of State, in June 1976. The church leaders said they were writing to give him 'and the world at large a picture of the present situation in our country', and 'to suggest some ways out of the present dangerous impasse'. They feared that South African intransigence was 'dragging us all steadily into a vortex of increasing violence which threatens to destroy the whole community' and that 'this country could easily become an international battle-ground'. In conclusion, they urged Kissinger to persuade Mr Vorster to end South Africa's occupation and allow democratic elections under UN supervision.[11] The document received wide publicity in the international media as the fullest expression yet of the political aspirations of the majority. It stood, too, as a prophetic warning against the dangers of a non-representative internal settlement.

When the UN Security Council adopted Resolution 435 (UNSCR 435) on 29 September 1978, making provision for internationally supervised elections, the churches concentrated their attention on highlighting the weaknesses of, and the impediments to, the plans for independence. When, on 20 September, South Africa rejected the plans for independence as a violation of an earlier agreement, the churches warned the new South African Prime Minister P. W. Botha that this decision would lead to an 'escalation of an avoidable, terrible and tragic war in this country'.[12] Undaunted, South Africa continued with its plans for an internal settlement, announcing its intention to hold elections for a Constituent Assembly in December.

The repression of opposition intensified, and this forced the churches into ever-closer cooperation, culminating in the establishment of the CCN in October 1978 – the high point of ecumenical cooperation. There were six corporate members, ELOC, ELC, the Anglican Church, the African Methodist Episcopal Church (AME), the German Evangelical Lutheran Church (GELC), and the Congregational Church, and two observers, the Catholic Church and the Evangelical Reformed Church in Africa.[13] The objectives of the council were the facilitation, coordination and promotion of the various ecclesiastical and social services offered by the churches. Yet it was at this very moment that the struggles within and among the churches intensified, gravely threatening their newly forged unity.

THE STRUGGLES WITHIN

To understand what determined divisions among and within churches, one needs to take many factors into account. Among the most important of these are: the racial and ethnic composition of various congregations (which often coincided with class interests); the characters of church leaders; the history, tradition, teachings (theology), structure, and resources of different churches; and the policies and actions of the state and SWAPO. While the struggle within the churches over involvement in liberation was there from the beginning (1971), it reached fever pitch in 1979.

The church least affected by divisions, ELOC, was predominantly Ovambo, with a small Kavango minority. Its leaders and the vast majority of its members strongly identified with and participated in the liberation struggle. Bishop Auala's commitment to an almost fundamentalist theology did not translate into an apolitical approach to secular matters. In Africa, unlike Europe, an evangelical tradition did not preclude political involvement; on the contrary, it was most often accompanied by an emphatic insistence on social justice. In a context of oppression, political neutrality was tantamount to heresy, and an engagement in temporal affairs was viewed as a Christian obligation.

In contrast, ELC, with members drawn from a number of ethnic groups – Baster, Damara, Herero, Nama, and Ovambo – suffered considerable internal strain. The clear correspondence between ethnic diversity and dissimilar experiences of oppression, on the one hand, and different socio-economic opportunities and political expectations on the other, inevitably produced very different attitudes, and hence tensions, within the church. These centred on the issues of discriminatory practices within the church, identification with SWAPO, responses to the state's constitutional initiatives, and the personality and changing positions of its leader, Dr de Vries. In the early 1970s, de Vries was perhaps the most outspoken critic of the regime and was closely identified with the struggle for liberation, but as the decade wore on, he redefined his position as one of mediator between the warring parties. While some supported this universalist position, others felt that it was a fatal compromise in the battle against evil. A third faction, while not directly supportive of the *status quo*, opposed any church involvement in politics. As the struggle intensified, so did these tensions within the church.

The Anglican church was racially mixed, but the vast majority of its members were Ovambo. Though led by white bishops until 1978, it offered the most outspoken opposition to South African rule. Especially for Bishops Winter (1968–72) and Wood (1972–5), theological and political positions derived from a tradition of radical liberalism. The state responded to the church's activism by expelling four of its leaders – Bishops Mize (expelled 1968), Winter, and Wood, and Vicar-General Morrow (1975–8) – and by fostering disunity and dissent within the church. The small white membership attempted several times to have their leaders removed, deploring the church's close identification with SWAPO.

The Catholic church, like the Anglican, was predominantly black with a small but powerful white minority. Unlike the Anglicans, however, the almost exclusively white clergy, especially the senior leadership, were generally reluctant to become involved politically and were pushed along by a minority of radical priests and the majority of black Catholic laymen. Bishop Koppman (1957–79) was theologically conservative and his political views were coloured by Cold War concerns. While he was influenced by Vatican II's emphasis on social justice, he pursued a policy of 'gentle' diplomacy – really a cover for silence or neutrality – rooted in a concern to protect the church's institutions.

The relationship with SWAPO was highly contentious. Of particular concern was the supposedly Marxist character of SWAPO and its designation as 'the sole and authentic representative of the Namibian people.'[14] While SWAPO was a predominantly Christian organization, there were some in its ranks who were hostile to the church. The fact that SWAPO received most of its aid from Eastern bloc countries, and that many of its members received their training and education there, inevitably produced a fairly doctrinaire critique of religion on the part of some cadres. SWAPO's publication in 1976 of a Political Programme based on the principles of 'scientific socialism' led many to fear that it was moving towards a more anti-church position. SWAPO's designation as the 'sole and authentic representative of the Namibian people' was also bound to cause difficulties with the churches, as they had members of all political affiliations. The ELC, with its diverse constituency, was sharply divided over the issue of identification with SWAPO. SWAPO, for its part, made it clear that it would brook no rivals to its leadership: SWAPO was the only organization capable of leading the struggle. Other groups, including the churches, were welcome to join, but only in a supportive capacity.

The most dramatic split in the ELC came with the defection of its leader, Dr de Vries, to join the South African-controlled administration, and the breakaway in 1979 of its conservative Rehoboth congregation to form an independent church, the Rheinisch Evangelical Lutheran Church (RELC). While both actions were inspired by dissatisfaction with the church's ties with SWAPO, they were also a response to changes in state policies and actions.

In the absence of SWAPO, the South African-managed December 1978 election was won by the Democratic Turnhalle Alliance (DTA), a loose grouping of ethnically based parties. Although the UN, citing widespread intimidation and fraud, declared the election null and void, the DTA-dominated Constituent Assembly was transformed on 21 May 1979 into a National Assembly with limited legislative powers. In accordance with its election promises, the DTA passed, in July, 'The Abolition of Racial Discrimination (Urban Residential Areas and Public Amenities) Act No. 3 of 1979'. This act provided for the eradication of apartheid practices in residential areas and public amenities. In July 1980, the National Assembly was granted executive powers with the conversion of the Administrator-General's Advisory Council to a Council of Ministers, effectively a cabinet, and the creation of government departments which constituted an independent civil service.

De Vries's 'defection' to the enemy – he accepted a post on the Administrator-General's newly established Wage Board – has to be viewed against this background of constitutional reform. He justified his decision in these terms:

> I believe that the need for the Church to play the role of the spokesman for the voiceless and the voteless has diminished because the right of every Namibian to vote has now been conceded. The people of the country is [*sic*] no longer voiceless and voteless and political parties and their leaders can now to a much greater extent than before speak for their people.[15]

While de Vries had been won over to the regime, the majority of Namibian Christians in the four main churches remained implacably opposed to the 'internal settlement' and were determined to continue the fight for genuine independence.

The events of 1979 illustrate that the church's struggle against racist tyranny, which began as a simple Christian duty, became much more confused and controversial as the violence escalated, and as SWAPO switched from a predominantly nationalist to a more Marxist ideology, and South Africa from a strategy of naked colonial aggression to a form of neo-colonialism. The specific contours of the struggles within the churches over these issues were shaped by the idiosyncratic responses of different leaders, and the distinctive social composition of each church. ELOC and the Anglican church were relatively immune to the stresses associated with these changes, though the latter body had to endure continual sniping from its white constituency. ELC, in contrast, suffered greatly. The conflict over its role in the struggle was finally settled through the ousting of de Vries, and the schism of a dissident conservative faction. In the Catholic church, the contradiction between the conservatism of the hierarchy and the liberatory aspirations of the laity was resolved by the retirement of Bishop Koppman and his replacement by a Namibian, Bonifatius Haushiku. Under Haushiku, the cautious institutional church of old was transformed into an outspoken church of the people.

THE BATTLE REJOINED

Despite the divisions of 1979 the prophetic church held together and resumed its role in the struggle for liberation. During the 1980s, the efforts of the churches were increasingly coordinated by the CCN. At first the council was concerned to heal the rifts of 1979 and restore the unity of the church. However, it was soon clear that the CCN was a highly political, and partisan, institution. As South African repression intensified, it emerged as the most powerful political force in the internal opposition. Moreover, the party-political affiliations of many of its office-bearers, and the way in which it conducted its business, suggested very close links with SWAPO. Indeed, it would not be unfair to characterize the CCN, as so many of its critics did, as the internal religious wing of SWAPO.

At an ideological level, the pattern of protesting injustices and calling for independence continued. An increasingly important voice was that of foreign churchmen who visited the country to investigate conditions. These delegations produced a number of reports, the most influential of which was that by the Southern African Catholics Bishops' Conference (SACBC).

The bishops reported that the local population's name for the whole complex of security forces in the operational area – army units, police, security police, special constables and homeguards, black, white or brown – was *omakakunya*, an Ovambo word meaning bloodsuckers or bonepickers. They also had no doubt that 'support for SWAPO is massive and that it would be easily victorious in any free and fair election under United Nations supervision'.[16] As to South African propaganda claims that the organization was Marxist, they were told time and time again that this was untrue: SWAPO was 'essentially a national liberation movement'. The report was widely circulated and its findings were summarized in many major international newspapers. Clearly, it was an ideological challenge to South Africa. It called into question the regime's political authority: if the majority of the population neither sought nor desired South Africa's 'protection', then the justification for its presence fell away. Recognizing the dangers of such conclusions, the South Africans banned the report in January 1983. The banning was probably the most flagrant violation of the freedoms of religion and expression at the hands of an increasingly authoritarian state.

International negotiations for a settlement continued, but in 1981 there appeared a new and formidable obstacle to Namibian independence: the US administration, now under Reagan, introduced the issue of 'linking' the implementation of UNSCR 435 to the withdrawal of Cuban troops from Angola. In 1982, South Africa embraced the concept of 'linkage', announcing that it would not consider the implementation of UNSCR 435 until Cuban troops had been withdrawn; while SWAPO rejected 'linkage' out of hand. The CCN, in open letters to P. W. Botha and the Western Contact Group, was vigorous in its denunciation of the policy.

South Africa abolished the National Assembly on 18 January 1983 and all executive power reverted to the Administrator General: direct rule had been reestablished. In September 1983, a number of internal parties of the former National Assembly regrouped to form a Multi-Party Conference (MPC). In March 1984, the MPC leaders published a Bill of Fundamental Rights and Objectives, and called for the scrapping of ethnic governments, for integrated health and educational facilities, for the release of detainees, and for the easing of security measures. In 1985, the MPC agreed on a formula for the creation of an interim government and called on South Africa to create a Transitional Government of National Unity (TGNU). The TGNU was installed on 17 June 1985 with wide legislative and executive powers (only security, defence and foreign affairs remained in South African hands), although it was, at all times, subject to the State President's authority. While the MPC's Bill of Fundamental Rights and Objectives was enshrined in the constitution (this was the centrepiece in its propaganda campaign for international recognition), provision was made for the retention of the entire complex of security legislation.

These developments presented both challenges and opportunities to the state's opponents. On the one hand, the new constitutional strategy might win international support for an internal settlement, thus excluding SWAPO and other progressive forces and pre-empting the genuine independence promised by Resolution 435, or at the very least further delaying that independence. On the other hand, the social and political reforms accompanying these changes, which were necessary for their legitimation, created a significant political 'space' which could be used to mobilize a more effective opposition.

The churches were quick to respond: they constantly called the legitimacy of the new regime into question, challenged its authority at every turn, and kept Resolution 435 at the top of the political agenda. In the face of the entrenchment of the TGNU and South Africa's continued intransigence, the CCN felt obliged to support the call for the imposition of mandatory economic sanctions against South Africa. The Council saw this 'as the only relatively non-violent recourse left open to us,' and warned that 'the alternative of a genocidal civil war is all too real and spurs us to underline the urgency and importance of bringing about the end of South Africa's illegal occupation of Namibia'. It would prefer 'to live through the comparatively short discomfort of sanctions in hope, rather than endure one more day of dehumanization and degradation under the South African racist government or its surrogates'.[17]

At an organizational level, the CCN continued to initiate political actions – of special note were campaigns against conscription and against the curfew – and to offer assistance to the victims of repression. The legal action taken by the bishops to end the dusk-to-dawn curfew, which had been in force in northern Namibia since 1978, was a good illustration of the church's effective use of the political space opened up by reforms. Their application, brought in September 1986, argued that the curfew conflicted with the TGNU's Bill of Rights, specifically the freedom of movement and residence, freedom of religion, freedom of association and freedom of peaceful assembly. While the court dismissed the bishops' application with costs, in a sense it was a victory. It had demolished the liberal posturing of the state. The TGNU, which had introduced the Bill of Rights as part of a campaign to enhance its legitimacy and win recognition at home and abroad, was dealt a severe blow.

In addition to these political actions, the churches were involved in assisting the poor and oppressed through relief and development programmes. Part of the CCN's mandate was 'to assist indigent ... persons in need and to promote self-help projects'.[18] In the absence of a representative government, the CCN was playing both the roles of parallel government – taking care of health, welfare, education, and economic development – and opposition party. By 1985 the CCN was organized into five departments: communications, diaconal (social welfare and legal aid), education, development, and theology. These offered protection to the victims of state terror, alternative services for the marginalized, and forums for the articulation of opposition. The theology department was the most politically engaged. It had been set up to mobilize and unite people around identities or issues to oppose the government and fight for justice and liberation. In 1985 its work led to the establishment of the Namibian National Students' Organization (NANSO) and the Namibia Women's Voice (NWV).

The CCN executive's efforts to foster democratic, grassroots organizations were not self-generated, nor did they reflect a concern with democracy. While they had some local origins, reflecting the concerns of some CCN workers and impulses from its constituency, they were primarily a response to the pressure of its liberal donors for a more inclusive and participatory policy. This is clearly illustrated in the CCN's dealings with women. Following calls by donors for greater participation of women in Council programmes, CCN head Dr Abisai Shejavali proposed the establishment of a women's desk,[19] which was then welcomed by donors as a good idea.

The CCN was amenable to these pressures because it was heavily dependent on external aid. In 1985 only 2.2 per cent of the total budget of R2.2 million (US$1.7 million) was raised from local sources; the rest was provided by foreign donors via the WCC. In 1987, the local contribution was 3.3 per cent out of a total of R5 million ($US2.3 million), and in 1989 2.6 per cent of R8.6 million ($US4.3 million).[20] The CCN, while aware of its dependence, did little to rectify the situation. Entrepreneurial initiatives were never seriously pursued, largely because foreign donors were so forthcoming with pledges.

The increasingly repressive response of the state bears witness to the fact that the church remained the most important anti-colonial voice. Church buildings were the targets of attack. Incidents included the firebombing of the CCN's offices, a further two attacks on the ELOC church press at Oniipa, and the destruction of other church property, including the Anglican seminary at Odibo and the Catholic church at Omulukila. In the north, church services were frequently broken up and congregants abused by soldiers. On one such occasion, a service conducted by Bishop Dumeni at

Elombe was disrupted when troops surrounded the church. Dumeni pleaded with the commander to leave them in peace:

> The commander's answer was: 'We are following the footprints of SWAPO. Why are the people afraid? We are at war, and we are fighting for you. I have seven comrades killed by SWAPO.' He spoke angrily and ordered me to shut up immediately. I answered: 'You are representing a government which claims to be a subscriber to the principles of the freedom of religion, therefore it will be better if you can let us continue with our service in peace.' He then retorted: 'Go into the church right now. *Ek moer jou, jou kak*' [I'll kill you, you shit]. I can shoot all these people dead. It is the Ovambo government which has given me the order to do that.'[21]

The worshippers were then forced out of the church, the men taken aside and interrogated and beaten:

> The soldiers then ordered the men to move further behind the walls of the church ... where they were beaten and kicked with boots. All these things were done before our very eyes. All lasted for about an hour. After they [had] finished beating up the people, the soldiers left. Even though some were obliged to go home on account of injuries, most of the people were fortunately able and ready to continue with our worship service.[22]

Daily the church received reports of detention, torture and murder. Among those killed were prominent businessmen, like David Sheehama and Mateus Elago, suspected of pro-SWAPO activities. The holding of religious office provided little protection: a number of clerics were brutally treated in detention and others, including Pastor Mika Iilonga, dean of the western diocese of ELOC, and Pastor Gabriel Amupolo, died in what were believed to be South African-engineered land-mine explosions and ambushes. Bishop Dumeni himself was said to be on a deathlist, and he was once confronted by, but managed to deter, a would-be assassin.

Undeterred, the church continued in its mission to publicize atrocities and assist the victims of the war. Church personnel arranged for legal counsel and assisted in the collection of evidence for the prosecution of cases brought against the police and soldiery. At great risk, the staff at church missions throughout the north extended a helping hand, and often medical treatment, to SWAPO guerillas in need. Under these conditions, the mere fufilment of routine pastoral duties was an act of courage and a source of comfort to a beleagured population. The story of Reverend Philip Shilongo, who with his wife and a handful of the faithful kept the Anglican mission of St. Mary's Odibo open throughout the war, despite continual harassment, is one story among many that capture what Namibian artist John Muafangejo, in a poignant understatement, described as a spirit of 'hope and optimism in spite of the present difficulties'.[23]

While black priests were at the mercy of the security forces, the few white priests in the north enjoyed a certain immunity, and a number were able to intervene in ways not possible for their black counterparts. Father Franz Houben, a white Catholic priest stationed at Okatana and Anamulenge in Ovamboland, exploited this privilege to the full. He would visit police offices and the bases of the notorious counter-insurgency unit Koevoet to inquire after people reported detained or missing. While never allowed to speak with the prisoners, he was sometimes allowed to drop off food and clothing and almost always a bible stamped with the seal of the Okatana mission and inscribed with the message, 'You [detainee's name] are in our thoughts.'[24] This courageous gesture helped to verify the location of detainees (bibles would not be accepted if the subject was not at that location), and would be followed up by the publication of the names and locations of detainees in the national and international media. The giving of bibles also reassured prisoners that people outside knew they were there, making it less likely that they would 'disappear'. Houben remembers: 'I would say just to drop off the bible was for [the detainees] a very positive sign that they knew that [they were] not totally lost.' While many reported that their treatment improved following the receipt of bibles, the security forces were not always warned off, and many of their victims were killed or disappeared after being taken into custody.

By the mid-1980s, the depravity of the security forces had reached new lows: among other barbarities, there were reports that they were roasting their victims over open fires. Treated as little more than sentient meat by the South Africans and their agents, and faced with concerted counter-insurgency and what many felt was an inexorable move to a Rhodesian style UDI, many Christians in Namibia felt that the church's Kairos, or moment of truth, had arrived. The church was now obliged to move beyond protest and take decisive action to end oppression. It was essential to unite the progressive forces to formulate a plan of action to oppose the TGNU and reject its neo-colonial implications. The result was a CCN-sponsored meeting of churches, opposition political parties and ethnic councils, and student and women's groups, held on 29–30 April 1986 and involving some 60 delegates, which issued the now-famous /Ai-//Gams Declaration calling for independence. The declaration reaffirmed the inalienable right of the people to self-determination, the inviolability of the territorial integrity of the country and the obligations of the international community, and declared 'that UNSCR 435 is the only peaceful and democratic way of achieving internationally recognized independence for Namibia'. The declaration committed its signatories to 'mobilize and conscientize the Namibian masses' in a campaign to fight conscription, abolish the TGNU, and implement UNSCR 435.

The /Ai-//Gams meeting redefined the political landscape in Namibia. Henceforth, parties were described as belonging to the /Ai-//Gams grouping or to the DTA. It also illustrated how important the church had become in the political arena in the 15 years since the Open Letter – it was the only institution capable of bringing the opposition groupings together to form a united front against the South Africans and their client regime.[25]

Unfortunately /Ai-//Gams did not live up to its promise: attendance at public meetings was disappointing, a signature campaign calling for the implementation of UNSCR 435 fizzled out, and attempts at mass mobilization for civil disobedience were unsuccessful. Like other progressive alliances before it, the /Ai-//Gams grouping was bedevilled by personality clashes, ethnic differences and the individual ambitions of its constituent elements. Its action campaign was largely pre-empted after the Windhoek Supreme Court ruled on 3 July 1986 that, under the terms of the Notification and Prohibition of Meetings Act of 1981,[26] it was not illegal for SWAPO to hold public meetings. SWAPO, no longer obliged to organize under the /Ai-//Gams umbrella, struck out on its own, drawing 13,000 people to its first legal rally in years in Katutura. With the biggest opposition party free to act in the open, the momentum for alliance politics faltered. While the churches were successful in disseminating the message of /Ai-//Gams at an international level, by early 1987 the anti-government newspaper, the *Namibian*, declared the /Ai-//Gams grouping in Namibia 'all but dead and buried'.[27]

The Conservative Church

The CCN's role in the struggle was by no means outside or above the crises that afflicted SWAPO. SWAPO was interested in broadening, deepening and consolidating its power. Within Namibia it was interested in controlling all activities of the resistance, and the church was a critical ally in this process.

The CCN supported SWAPO's hegemony in two principal ways: first, legitimating and sacralizing SWAPO's dominance; and second, delegitimating and desacralizing any individuals or groups who challenged that dominance. In particular, the church did not provide cover for, voice the interests of, or extend protection and support to the victims of SWAPO's repression.

In addition to the substantial overlap in personnel at the leadership level, the links between the CCN and SWAPO were also forged through patronage agreements. The church received privileges and material benefits in exchange for its support of SWAPO's status as the sole and authentic representative of the Namibian people. This generated a feeling of indebtedness toward, and support for, SWAPO and the system which bestowed such rewards. The CCN's role in supporting SWAPO's hegemony was all the more efficacious because it was largely unconscious.

THE DETAINEES CRISIS

Since at least 1976, there had been a cycle of arrests, torture, imprisonment and executions of SWAPO members-in-exile on the orders of the leadership. The first major revolt within SWAPO, the anti-corruption rebellion or 'Shipanga affair', led some churchmen, notably Bishop Winter, to put pressure on SWAPO leaders to release the detainees, but the affair was never discussed in public and did not jeopardize church support for SWAPO. Even Winter, dismissing allegations that SWAPO was a dictatorship, held up the Shipanga affair as proof 'that they [the SWAPO leaders] must have the freedom to make mistakes [because] this is how they learn to govern'.[28]

In the early 1980s, rumours began to circulate of a new purge. A letter of 30 March 1984 to Bishop Frederick from Micha Ngapure, an ex-SWAPO member in Zambia, claimed that the internal SWAPO leaders were well aware of the crisis in the refugee settlements: 'They know exactly about these kidnappings, starvation, hauntings, prostitution, corruption, murders and killings within this organization that calls itself SWAPO, but they close their eyes to all those evils.' He called on the church to take action: 'Beware holy servants of God, beware. There's no difference between South Africa and SWAPO.... South Africa is a racist and fascist Government – SWAPO is a racist and fascist organization.... I'm [an] individual and have [to] inform you as The Shepherds of Us to do something....'[29]

At the Lusaka Conference in May 1984, SWAPO delegates from Namibia learnt of the terrors abroad: mass incarcerations, and strong rumours of torture and killings. They heard that Tauno Hatuikilipi, a former director of the Christian Centre who had fled Namibia and joined the PLAN high command, was believed to have been executed, along with sixteen others, in January 1984; hundreds of others accused of being South African spies were said to be languishing in 'mud holes' (primitive dungeon prisons).

On their return to Namibia, a number of the delegates, including CCN employees Attie and Erica Beukes, together with others who believed their relatives to be in danger, petitioned the internal SWAPO leadership, the International Red Cross, and church leaders to intervene to end this crisis. The Beukeses met with Bishop Frederick of ELC and passed on the information they had received; he expressed sympathy, but could not suggest a course of action. Shortly thereafter a group of concerned relatives of refugees, mainly mothers, met at Erica Beukes's house and decided to form a Committee of Parents. The committee was initiated to ascertain the whereabouts and establish contact with family members in SWAPO camps in Angola and Zambia, and to put pressure on the church and SWAPO leaders to investigate conditions at these camps. Attie Beukes urged his boss, the CCN Secretary General Dr Shejavali, to convene a meeting of church leaders to discuss the detainees issue and formulate a plan of action. There was no immediate response. On 2 June the committee delivered a memorandum to the church leadership detailing the critical conditions in the camps and reminding the church leaders of their responsibilities: 'This situation requires church leaders to take on their Christian responsibilities to our people and call the SWAPO leaders to order.'[30]

From outside the country, Pastor Siegfried Groth also urged the Namibian church leaders to take action. Groth, adviser on South African affairs to the Vereinigte Evangelische Mission (VEM) in Wuppertal since 1961 (and banned from Namibia since 1971), had been the pastor for exiled Namibians in Zambia and Botswana since the early 1970s. During a visit to Zambia in March and April of 1985, he discovered 'a very dangerous situation among the Namibians in exile'. Groth described this visit as 'the most difficult part of my work in decades',[31] and he suffered a nervous breakdown shortly after his departure from Zambia. On his return to Germany he raised the issue with Reverend Kameeta (15 May), Bishop Frederick (14 June) and Bishop Dumeni.

A meeting between the church leaders and the Committee of Parents was finally convened on 9 September 1985, some six months after the original request. On behalf of the church leaders, Bishop Dumeni stressed the sensitivity of the issue, and reminded the committee that 'it was a war situation and that the same atrocities that raised our concern also happened within Namibia.'[32] The meeting ended without a definite commitment from the church authorities, although they did promise to meet separately to discuss the matter.

This bland response convinced disillusioned parents and relatives that they would have to take matters into their own hands. Having kept their concerns out of the public spotlight for a year and a half, they launched a public campaign to halt the mal-treatment and secure the release of SWAPO's detainees. On 20 September letters were dispatched to Sam Nujoma (SWAPO president), the presidents of Angola, Zambia and Cuba, and the UN Secretary General. These were followed by letters to SWAPO support groups in Europe (Namibia Support Committee, Namibia Association) and international church bodies (WCC, LWF, VEM, the British Council of Churches, the Swedish Free Church, and the United Church of Canada).

Church leaders were agitated by the 'harm' done by the committee, and their sub-sequent deliberations seem to have been aimed less at finding solutions than at deciding on ways to defuse the issue. From this time on, according to the account of events given by the Committee of Parents, the battle-lines were drawn: 'From time to time, bishops, pastors, and priests would disappear to deliberate with the SWAPO leadership apparently to chart the course of counter action.' The committee members were con-vinced that the church leaders had entered into a conspiracy with the internal SWAPO leadership, the LWF, the WCC, and other support groups and donors to sabotage their campaign. They were stung by this betrayal: 'They found that in exercising their trust in the institutions which for generations they had considered their friends, they had instead created violent enemies. Priest and pastor slandered them, called them agents and destroyers and accused them of spreading malicious rumour.'[33] The wary replies of overseas church bodies to the letters detailing SWAPO's abuses seemed to confirm the Committee's suspicions of a tacit conspiracy to defuse or suppress their campaign.

In a letter sent to Ninan Koshy, an official with the WCC, in December 1985, and copied to other recipients of letters from the Committee of Parents, Shejavali launched a counter-attack. He dismissed the Committee's charges as 'allegations … not facts', and accused it of exaggerating and fabricating its evidence: 'I do not believe that there are 'hundreds of Namibian families and relatives' who 'have received letters' as was indicated in the documents of the Parents' Committee.' He also argued that South Africa's strategy to destroy SWAPO must include the use of agents, and he therefore defended the organization's 'right to protect her people from those who are collaborating with the enemy'. In conclusion, Shejavali promised that the church leaders would try to meet with SWAPO leaders to discuss the issue, and he requested 'that those who have been supporting SWAPO financially and otherwise should continue to do so, which is, in my opinion, a valuable contribution toward the exiled and suppressed.'[34] They were asked, in effect, to continue giving uncritical support to the CCN–SWAPO alliance. Most acceded to this request.

On 16 February 1986 two SWAPO leaders, Theo-Ben Gurirab, Foreign Relations Secretary, and Hidipo Hamutenya, Secretary of Information, announced to a press conference in London that SWAPO was holding at least one hundred of its members in prison as South African spies. The statement was a response to the 'rumours and allegations' that SWAPO was involved in fascist activities against Namibian refugees.

Other estimates, however, placed the number of detainees at 2,000; and subsequent evidence makes it clear that the overwhelming majority were not spies, but simply critics of the leadership, or just people believed liable to be such critics.

In early March Shejavali went to Europe where, according to the Committee of Parents, he conferred with SWAPO leaders. On 13 March Erica Beukes and Attie Beukes were dismissed from their jobs at the CCN. Shejavali's letter to Erica Beukes laid out the reasons: 'The decision to terminate your employment with the Council of Churches in Namibia was reached only after careful consideration of your leading role in the "committee of parents" and the various statements issued and published on behalf of that committee "care of the Council of Churches in Namibia". The Council is most perturbed about the way you have chosen to represent the serious allegations made by that committee. It regards the attack on the credibility of 'local pastors and priests' in a very serious light, unwarranted and uncalled for. The statement issued on behalf of that committee, coming, as it is, from an employee of the Council of Churches in Namibia, contains very serious allegations, *inter alia*, in regard to the role of the Churches and its commitment to upholding basic human rights.'[35]

Anton Lubowski, a leading SWAPO member in Namibia, dismissed the parents' allegations as 'the kind of false propaganda that is being spread by puppets, collaborators and spies'.[36] International church bodies accepted this interpretation. The LWF called the accusations 'part of the ongoing SA propaganda war aimed at discrediting the liberation movement', while a report of the World Council of Churches effectively endorsed the reign of terror with this statement: 'The illegal occupation of Namibia has been facilitated by Namibians who have collaborated with South Africa and have been traitors to the cause of a free Namibia. Yet SWAPO is willing to accommodate these people in a free Namibia and forgive their misguided behaviour.'[37]

Just when things seemed hopeless, the parents received a critical boost from an unimpeachable source. Amnesty International's *International Report for 1987* referred to human rights abuses in the SWAPO camps in Angola. This vindicated their efforts and dealt a blow to their critics. UN Chief Perez de Cuellar, who had ignored the parents' pleas for years, was finally moved to discuss the matter with Nujoma, and with Presidents Dos Santos of Angola and Kaunda of Zambia. He urged them to give the United Nations High Commission for Refugees and the Red Cross access to the SWAPO camps. And then in December 1988 wider changes in world politics finally led to the Geneva Peace Accord which paved the way for the ceasefire and the start of the transition to independence in April 1989. In this context, on 19 April 1989, SWAPO was obliged to release over 200 of the 'misguided' from its prisons in Lubango, Angola. A group of journalists, including John Liebenberg of the *Namibian*, flew up to interview the detainees in late May. Liebenberg's report, acknowledging that 'many detainees held by SWAPO for alleged spying were apparently subjected to severe beatings, rape, mental torture and extreme deprivation', and appearing as it did in a pro-SWAPO newspaper, sent shock-waves through church circles in Namibia and abroad. The detainees were eventually repatriated to Namibia.[38] The first group to return, numbering 153, told a press conference in Khomasdal, Windhoek on 6 July 1989 of their 'horrifying experience', and many disrobed to show their scars from torture. Their story was carried widely in the local and foreign press.

Among the churches, the first public response came in a press release from the Catholic church's Commission of Justice and Peace on 12 July 1989: 'With great pain and deep disappointment we have to listen to reports of former detainees about their sufferings in the camps in Angola.' The CCN executive met with a group of detainees on 23 August and with SWAPO leaders the next day. On 28 August it issued a statement noting that 'many of the victims of this vicious cycle of wars were innocent', and that the time 'has now come for us all to unite to bring about national healing, reconciliation and unity'. The concluding statement emphasized forgiveness: 'We welcome the willingness to show forgiveness, and we are convinced that, on the basis of this, we will be able to build a new and active nation.' The CCN's attempt to assume the role of mediator was rejected by many detainees who could not forgive its indifference to their suffering. One detainee, formerly a devout Christian, declared: 'The churches are against us. They are pro-SWAPO.'[39] While the ELOC and ELC leaders condemned the abuses suffered by detainees, they were equivocal in their criticism of SWAPO, blaming apartheid for spreading 'suspicion and distrust' and destroying 'the unity of the oppressed', and they failed to acknowledge their own failure to respond earlier.[40]

It may seem difficult to understand why the churches and other bodies appeared so indifferent to these horrors. In interviews, Namibian churchmen cited the lack of reliable information from war-torn southern Angola, and their inability to distinguish between the all-pervasive South African propaganda and fact, as important reasons for their inaction. The explanation is, however, unsatisfactory, because they had no reason to doubt the representations of Pastor Groth, their own appointee in the camps. Those who admitted knowledge of conditions in the camps often justified their inaction by stressing spiritual responsibilities over worldly ones. This retreat into the spiritual was indicative of the double standards of many religious bodies: while their opposition to apartheid was public and political, SWAPO's abuses were treated, if at all, as a private matter for spiritual resolution. The confessing churches that courageously confronted the evils of apartheid were thus non-confessing and timid in their dealings with SWAPO. In responding to the spy drama, they preferred, to use Paul Trewhela's words, the '"cheap grace" of conventional left-nationalist liberation theology to the "costly grace" of active commitment to their own professed principles.'[41] Solidarity organizations, driven by liberal guilt, were similarly ineffectual: their fixation on the evil of apartheid blinded them to the terror within SWAPO.

Some church leaders, while aware of SWAPO's abuses, believed that only SWAPO was capable of bringing peace, and that any public action by them on the detainees issue would have weakened the movement fatally, leaving the DTA, backed and financed by South Africa, to win any UN-sponsored elections. They were not prepared to allow this to happen for the sake of exposing a few 'bad apples' in SWAPO.[42] Their conviction that SWAPO and liberation were inseparable led them to sacrifice their religious principles on the altar of political expediency. Others believed that the church, the people and SWAPO were one – 'the "people" are SWAPO and the "people" are the church'[43] – and that a public attack on the movement would be an unthinkable act of self-destruction. There was no room for dissent within this 'unity of the oppressed'.

In the final analysis, it must be remembered that the moral authority and material interests of many organizations and individuals were closely intertwined with SWAPO's image. This ensured their silence, and even drove some to participate in efforts to conceal the movement's crimes.

Development and Dissent

That the CCN was locked into an attitude not to question SWAPO policy, directives or actions, is clearly revealed in its practice of development and its dealings with community activists.

Initially, SWAPO argued that there could be no development before liberation. It called for sanctions to cripple the government, destroy the economy and radicalize the population. It feared that development activities would divert energy and resources away from the political struggle for independence. It wished, secondly, to avoid an 'ambulance' ministry which, by offering relief, would obscure the roots of oppression and poverty, encourage reformism and diminish revolutionary fervour. Third, SWAPO opposed development in the hopes of painting a picture of total South African repression: SWAPO was keen to create the image that the South Africans would not allow Namibians to be assisted in any way and made it impossible to channel aid into the country.[44] Fourth, SWAPO leaders felt that development would strengthen other institutions and organizations *vis-à-vis* their movement, thus loosening its control and perhaps challenging its status as sole and authentic representative of the Namibian people. SWAPO justified its opposition to development with the short-hand explanation that it would 'confuse the people'. SWAPO remained rhetorically opposed to development virtually until independence; in practice, however, it allowed the disbursement of funds from the early 1980s.

A number of factors were responsible for this change in attitude. Within Namibia there was considerable pressure from internal SWAPO to agree to the provision of external aid, while the churches and other agencies concerned drew attention to the suffering of Namibians, especially after the onset of the drought in the early 1980s. Dr Kameeta, reflecting on SWAPO's opposition to development, was critical of his counterparts in the external wing of the organization on this issue: 'I think there was a very ... stupid understanding from the side of [external] SWAPO. I don't know whether it was SWAPO policy or some individuals who had the fear that if you started with a development project the people would forget the struggle for liberation.'[45] There was also external pressure from foreign churches, NGOs, and governments whose aim was to strengthen the churches as an alternative to the apartheid administration. Many of these bodies, while unwilling to give direct support to a political movement such as SWAPO, were eager to support the struggle for liberation with money for church-run development projects. SWAPO may also have been convinced of the need to support development as a counter to South Africa's WHAM (Winning Hearts and Minds) campaign, which had been quite successful in the south and the east of the country. Kaire Mbuende, a senior SWAPO leader, recalls their thinking: 'We saw that with the emergence of this new class of collaborators our strategy would now have to be different because we would have to compete ... and one aspect of that was competition to provide social services....'[46] Finally, the organization realized that development projects would probably have gone ahead without its approval, and so support for the principle of development was necessary in order to shape and control it.

While SWAPO agreed to the provision of development assistance, it imposed stringent conditions: all aid had to be channelled through the CCN and the emphasis was to be on educational, that is ideological, rather than socio-economic projects. By administering scholarships for study abroad and directing funds to selected community schools offering alternative education, the CCN became the conduit for SWAPO patronage. Some monies were spent on socio-economic projects, and for these SWAPO based its endorsements on CCN advice. The CCN's endorsement was critical for organizations seeking external funding.

The CCN also refused to accept funds for projects if it could not have complete control over finances. A case in point is its dealings with a German donor, the Otto Benicke Stiftung (OBS), which proposed to set up a Vocational Training Centre in Windhoek with monies received from the West German government. While the CCN wanted complete control of the project, the OBS was obliged by the conditions of the grant to remain in charge of the finances. Dr Shejavali demanded 'that the OBS offer the Churches full control of the *Budget*, and of the programmes.'[47] As the OBS was unable to agree to this condition, 'it is the Executive's view that we will not ... be able to continue with this project and are therefore withdrawing from the whole process as far as the Vocational Training College is concerned.'[48] Without CCN endorsement, the project lacked legitimacy and was abandoned for several years.

The whole issue of the origins of aid was highly contentious. Kameeta argued that the church should not 'accept aid from those who are not concerned with justice and peace in Namibia', and a CCN conference resolved that 'the projects sponsored and initiated by the multi-national companies ... are not real development but rather a public relations exercise'.

In April 1985 the SWAPO Central Committee in exile drew up a set of directives formalizing its relationship with its 'allies': SWAPO's 'leading role as the vanguard' was confirmed, and to 'avoid unnecessary misunderstanding between SWAPO and its allies and not to give room for enemy manipulations', internal allies (including the CCN), were instructed not to act without SWAPO's consent and to conduct all communications through internal SWAPO leaders, specifically the Acting Vice-President Hendrik Witbooi. To the CCN's opponents this was proof positive of, at the very least, a tacit alliance. Dr Lukas de Vries, former head of the ELC and then DTA member and Deputy Minister of Local Government, characterized the CCN as 'the financial front of SWAPO', and charged that it used aid 'not for humanitarian purposes but propaganda purposes for SWAPO'.[49]

The CCN's practice of development did have some tendency to perpetuate dependency. Development was from the top down, run from Windhoek with a strong bureaucratic flavour. The CCN rendered a service, assisting people rather than involving them in determining the nature of the service or the policy guiding the service. Moreover, the services offered by the social welfare desk, such as drought relief assistance, were little more than charity relief, and were commonly seen as the distribution of SWAPO patronage. The CCN's provision of food aid in Kaokoland and the DTA stronghold of Hereroland was especially contentious. In Otjokavare, headman Muzuma refused outright to allow the CCN to deliver food aid to the local school 'because they as the Herero Administration had proofs that said aid was received from SWAPO and was channelled under cover to buy off people for said organization.'[50] He said 'that even if his people nearly died of hunger, he would not allow the CCN to bring food to the people of the area since it was supplied by SWAPO and his community was "at war" with them.'[51] In the Aminuis district of east Hereroland recipients of CCN food aid were fined up to one head of cattle each by local authorities of the Herero Administration for 'accepting SWAPO bribes'.

The CCN's handling of scholarships also drew complaints about nepotism and its support for community schools which offered an alternative education also involved an extension of SWAPO patronage. Pastor Hendrik Witbooi's community especially benefited from their connection to SWAPO and the CCN. Of the CCN's 1985 budget of R2 million, R246,720 (over 12 per cent of the total) was spent on the AME school at Gibeon.[52]

Foreign assistance thus reinforced the CCN's paternalistic tendencies. External donors didn't really object to the inefficient use or even the misuse of their money – they gave out of a sense of solidarity, as a gesture of support, not in the expectation of results. Failures were apt to be blamed on sabotage by the South Africans and their surrogates.

The CCN's involvement in setting up and supporting organizations such as NANSO and NWV and other community-based groups was, by contrast, a contradictory process. The intention was to mobilize and unite progressive forces in opposition to the state and in support of political liberation and of SWAPO, the sole and authentic representative of the Namibian people. Instead, mobilization often led to the emergence of independent-minded individuals and organizations, and to challenges to the authority of the CCN and SWAPO, their conjoint monopoly of resistance politics, and their philosophy of development.

A number of activists, including some who worked with the CCN and who were members of SWAPO, were critical of the council's approach to development and called for democratization of the process. They rejected the CCN's paternalistic and welfarist approach to development, emphasizing instead popular participation and self-reliance: for them community development meant 'people's organisation for empowerment and self-sufficiency on a grassroots level'.[53] They dismissed the notion that there was a contradiction between this kind of development and political resistance.

The conflict revolved around the control and orientation of urban grassroots communities. The CCN's efforts to impose an ideological stance and organizational practice consonant with the official position were vigorously contested, not only by independent community groups but also by church-sponsored groups which had escaped the limitations of the official model to formulate alternative expressions of their interests.[54] While the CCN focussed on political issues, national independence and the international context, community groups were concerned with socio-economic issues, self-liberation, and the local context. They argued that SWAPO was preoccupied with distant and abstract political issues, ignoring day-to-day or 'bread and butter' issues, such as housing, transport, education, health and food, which were the concern of the vast majority of people. The CCN's emphasis on central authority, hierarchy and unity clashed with the critics' stress on egalitarianism, local autonomy and critical solidarity. For the church hierarchy the struggle was driven by authoritative doctrine (such as UNSCR 435); community groups, by contrast, worked from sociological analysis (or shared experience), without the mediation of an authoritative doctrine. For the latter, whether they were conscious of it or not, the cutting edge of the struggle was class: but the redefinition of the struggle as a class struggle threatened élite control of the nationalist resistance and, most critically, their control of funds.[55] The leaders responded with alarm, claiming that these activities would confuse the people and detract from the political struggle, and they tried to rein in independent initiatives, reaffirm hierarchy and stress the unity of the oppressed. Their critics were often labelled spies or collaborators: if you challenged the CCN or SWAPO, you had to be working for the enemy. In 1985 a number of activists were suspended from SWAPO for their involvement in community development. They were told that their suspension would be lifted if they ceased their community activity. The CCN, for its part, refused to fund new projects and cut off the existing funding of old projects, no matter how promising or successful, in which these activists were involved. Projects initiated by Attie and Erica Beukes suffered a similar fate following their expulsion from the CCN.

Community activists and organizations outside the CCN's control were also excluded from political initiatives such as the /Ai-//Gams meeting. Foreign sponsors obediently followed this lead. Paul Vleermuis's request to Oxfam-UK for funds to set up a non-party community organization was met with the reply that he should first secure the endorsement of SWAPO and the CCN. Oxfam also stopped funding a community educational project – the Science and Mathematics Programme – run by Erica Beukes's husband, Hewat. To quote Vleermuis, without SWAPO or the CCN, 'you [were] a zero'.[56]

While SWAPO was antagonistic towards independent-minded initiatives (including some of those set up by the CCN and individual churches), they could not suppress them all. Grassroots mobilization had built up such a momentum by the mid-1980s that many progressive individuals and organizations were able to continue operating despite SWAPO-CCN control. After initial opposition SWAPO was therefore obliged to recognize and support increasingly popular movements like the trade unions and NANSO in the hope of controlling them. Alongside the new strategy of co-option, the old strategy of suppression persisted, claiming, among its victims, even the CCN's showpiece, the Namibia Women's Voice.

As the Voice welcomed, as members, women from a great variety of political parties, it was distinct from, and its political position more ambiguous than, other less diverse progressive organizations. This led critics to question its loyalty to the struggle and charge that it had been infiltrated by collaborators and spies. As far as SWAPO was concerned, there was no room for ambiguity in the struggle – if you were not with SWAPO, or did not submit to its political direction, then you were against the struggle. Another important reason for opposition to NWV stemmed from the fact that it was in direct competition with the SWAPO Women's Council (SWC). NWV undoubtedly drew members away from the SWC. The fact that it had no party-political affiliation and focussed on developmental rather than political issues also meant it was able to attract much greater funding than the SWC. By 1986 the Voice had thirteen branches, an office, three staff members and a vehicle. Its success was resented by the SWC which, as a political group, did not meet the criteria of many donors.

While NWV's focus on women's liberation at the expense of the struggle for political liberation, and its success *vis-à-vis* the SWC, were important reasons for SWAPO's opposition, the critical factor was perhaps the challenge that the Voice represented to male authority in the churches and in SWAPO. While the supporters of the Voice were adamant that in theory there should be no contradiction between the struggle for women's liberation and that for national liberation, in practice, with an authoritarian and male-dominated movement leading the struggle, the contradiction was acute. NWV challenged not only the state, but also the *status quo* within the resistance movement. It was no surprise, then, when the organization was disbanded in March 1989 'for the sake of maintaining peace and good relations' and 'in order to unify resources for preparation for the election.'[57] With unity at a premium, diversity could not be tolerated.[58]

While the absence (or defeat) of a robust civil society was partly a result of state repression, it was thus also the result of the effective repression of independent initiatives by SWAPO, with the CCN's assistance. The CCN remained remote from the grassroots: its paternalistic approach to development meant that it acted as an instrument of domination rather than of liberation. It used development as welfare and patronage to win support and ensure control, not to empower people. In the political space created by state reform, the church then reinforced SWAPO's monopoly and stifled the emergence of a democratic, grassroots opposition.

While there was no concerted movement for democratization within the CCN, there was, by the late 1980s, a growing acceptance of independent development initiatives. In a significant shift in policy, a CCN conference in 1988 recognized 'the importance of community based volunteer work in the building of structures and strategies for national liberation and nation building', and called upon the CCN and member churches 'to facilitate and encourage such involvement'. Kameeta, in a speech to the conference, attempted to reconcile the competing definitions of community activists and those of the SWAPO-CCN alliance by redefining development as 'a revolutionary act of liberation'.[59] The CCN also declared its intention to 'move in its ministry towards the poor and oppressed'.[60]

These changes were forced on the council. By 1988 the internal resistance movement was not only threatening state control and military rule, but also threatening to break free of the bonds of church and SWAPO protection. As a nationwide schools' boycott sparked off a popular revolt, the church and SWAPO had their work cut out maintaining their authority over the opposition to colonial rule. In a sense, for them, independence came just in time.

THE CHALLENGES OF PEACE

During the transition phase, the CCN shifted its focus from liberation to a strategy of facilitating repatriation, resettlement and reconstruction. After independence, though, it all but collapsed. With the disappearance of a common enemy and the installation of a democratically elected government, the individual churches tended to pursue their own interests, and the centrality of the CCN in political and socio-economic organization and action faded. A great many people who had been driven into church structures during a time of political closure now left the church to fulfil their social agendas in new secular structures, and many of the groups that remained in the CCN fold emerged from the struggle with postures of independence and theological perspectives that threatened hierarchical control. Moreover, many of the functions of the CCN – popular education, health, economic development – were also assumed by the new government and the NGOs. The subsequent massive redirection of donor aid forced the organization to retrench much of its staff and lease out some of its office space. The CCN, a product of war, was a major casualty of the peace.

While the churches did not suffer the precipitous decline of the CCN – although church attendance dropped off drastically after independence, by as much as 75 per cent in some cases – they did face major new challenges from their base communities. The necessary decentralization of the church in recent years, primarily a response to the physical dangers of the war, precipitated demands for a new, more democratic institution opposed to the traditional hierarchical model. During the war, lower-level clergy and lay persons, preoccupied with combating repression and ameliorating its effects, did not have the time or energy to articulate or press this new agenda with the bishops. With the war over, however, these issues came to the fore, and there were soon indications of dissident rumblings within the church. Among groups like the Catholic Justice and Peace Commission the discourse of justice and equality was employed to interrogate the institutions of the church and the structures of the post-colonial state. A spokesperson for the commission pointed out that despite the hierarchy's rhetorical commitment to pastoral principles, there was little popular participation in decision making. In fact, for many of the faithful, especially female orders and parishioners, participation meant little more than performing unpaid or underpaid domestic labour such as cleaning church premises or making the beds and cooking the meals of priests and pastors.

The Justice and Peace Commission, and other self-designated representatives of the 'proletarian' church committed to addressing class issues, were determined to fight against oppression and for democratization in the church as well as in the broader society. The bishops, satisfied that democracy was won with national liberation, stressed reconciliation and unity, and urged close cooperation with the new government. A serious clash between the hierarchy and the base, the focus of struggles in the Latin American church,[61] also seemed possible in the Namibian church.

The struggle had not democratized the church – in fact, it may have delayed changes in the church – but it had necessitated a decentralization of the church, with potentially radical implications. More importantly, while most congregants accepted their subordinate position in the interests of unity during the struggle, the church's challenge to the South African regime threw into question *all* messages about hierarchy and deference to established authority. In this sense, the church's opposition to South African rule was truly a two-edged sword.

Notes

1. This chapter is particularly indebted to the Rev. John Evenson for valuable advice and access to the important documents collection of the Namibia Communications Centre. The estimates of the Christian faithful in Namibia range from 80 per cent to 97 per cent of the total population.
2. David Soggot, *Namibia: The Violent Heritage* (London: Rex Collings, 1986), p. 34.
3. Siegfried Groth, 'The condemnation of Apartheid by the churches in South West Africa – an historic occasion for the church and ecumenism,' *International Review of Mission*, 61, 242 (April 1972), pp. 192–3.
4. *Ibid.*
5. Colin Winter, *Namibia. Story of a Bishop in Exile* (London: Lutterworth Press, 1977), p. 116.
6. In 1989, ELOC had 360,000 members, ELC 193,000, the Catholic Church 195,000, and the Anglican Church 120,000. Peter Katjavivi, Per Forstin, and Kaire Mbuende (eds), *Church and Liberation in Namibia* (London: Pluto Press, 1989), pp. 5–6.
7. Carl-J. Hellberg, *A Voice of the Voiceless* (Lund: Verbum, 1979), p. 180.
8. These categories are suggested by Heinz Hunke, 'The role of European missionaries in Namibia,' in Brian Wood (ed.), *Namibia, 1894–1984* (London: Namibia Support Committee, 1988), p. 632.
9. *Ibid.*, p. 110.
10. The SWAPO-led boycott of the August elections was successful, resulting in a turnout of only 2.5 per cent. In the aftermath of this fiasco, the South Africans gave the newly 'elected' tribal authorities, Chief Elifas and his Ovamboland Independent Party, a free hand to punish their

political opponents. Many people, including respected members of the community, were rounded up, stripped and publicly flogged, up to 28 times, by Ovambo headmen.

11. Katjavivi, *et al.*, *op. cit.*, pp. 139-42.
12. Hunke, *op. cit.*, p. 106.
13. The Catholics joined as full members in 1982. GELC withdrew in 1987.
14. A UN General Assembly declaration (Resolution 31/146), December 1976.
15. *Windhoek Observer,*13 October 1979.
16. Oblates of Mary Immaculate, *The Green and the Dry Wood: The Roman Catholic Church (Vicariate of Windhoek) and the Namibian Socio-Political Situation* (Newcastle, South Africa: Zulu Publications, 1983), p. 232.
17. *Namibian*, 3 October 1986. Not the all progressive forces supported this call for sanctions; see *Namibian*, 4 April 1986.
18. CCN, *Constitution of the Council of Churches in Namibia*.
19. CCN, *General Secretary's Report: January 1984 to January 1985*, Appendix I.
20. See CCN, *Overall Budget for the Financial Year 1985*, and CCN, *Overall Budget Summary 1987*.
21. Denis Herbstein and John Evenson, *The Devils Are Among Us* (London: Zed Books, 1989), pp. 55-6.
22. *Ibid.*
23. This is the title of one of Muafangejo's famous prints.
24. Interview with Fr. Franz Houben, 2 July 1991.
25. A powerful symbol of this unity was the joint celebration of Corpus Christi on 1 June, a world-wide Catholic holy day. The Catholic church invited the other churches and the /Ai-//Gams signatories to participate in a religious procession. The authorities, intimidated by this display of defiance, attempted to ban the march. The order signalled a new low in church–state relations – it was, perhaps, the first explicit attempt to outlaw a religious event in Namibia.
26. The act applied to a party which had, as its sole objective, the overthrow of the state. The court ruled that this was not SWAPO's sole objective.
27. *Namibian*, 30 January 1987.
28. *Observer*, 3 September 1978.
29. Nico Basson and Ben Motinga (eds), *Call Them Spies: A Documentary Account of the Namibian Spy Drama* (Windhoek and Johannesburg: African Communications Project, 1989), p. 40. While the compilation of this book was a covert exercise in South African electoral interference, the documents it contains are authentic. Like all historical documents, they should be treated with due care.
30. 'In the Supreme Court of South West Africa. In the application of: Attie Beukes (Applicant) and Council of Churches in Namibia (Respondent).' Appendix E: 'Memorandum: Junie 1985. Aan die Namibiaanse Kerkleiers.'
31. Basson and Motinga, *op. cit.*, p. 34.
32. 'In the Supreme Court…', p. 41.
33. Basson and Motinga, *op. cit.*, 'Extracts from a report by the Committee of Parents on SWAPO leadership abuses, April 1987.'
34. Letter from Dr Abisai Shejavali to Mr Ninan Koshy, 23 December 1985.
35. Beukes, *op. cit.*, p. 164. The Beukeses challenged their dismissals in court, but lost the case.
36. *Windhoek Observer*, 30 May 1987.
37. Katjavivi, *et al.*, *op. cit.*, p. 202.
38. The ex-detainees insisted that not a single member of the CCN, the organization given primary responsibility for repatriation, be allowed to participate in the management of their return.
39. Basson and Motinga, *op. cit.*, p. 38.
40. The responses of some foreign churches and solidarity groups to the detainees' revelations were refreshingly honest in comparison. Groth, too, broke his silence after the release of the detainees, publishing his testimony – *Menschenrechtsverletzengun in der Exil-Swapo* (Human Rights Violations in SWAPO in Exile) – in Germany on 18 September 1989.
41. Paul Trewhela, 'SWAPO and the churches: an international scandal,' *Searchlight South Africa*, 2, 3 (July 1991), pp. 82–3.
42. This phrase was used by a senior church official in an interview with the author, 2 July 1991.
43. Katjavivi, *et al.*, *op. cit.*, p. 189.
44. I am grateful to Dr Kenneth Abrahams for this point.
45. Interview with Dr Zephania Kameeta, 21 November 1991. Dr Kameeta, formerly Vice-Bishop of the ELC and SWAPO's Secretary of Health and Welfare, became Deputy Speaker in the National Assembly at independence.
46. Interview with Dr Kaire Mbuende, 29 August 1991.

47. Notes of a meeting between: Dr Wolfgang Beitz, (Otto Benicke Stiftung, West Germany), Mr Peter Borsutzky (Namibian OBS), Dr Abisai Shejavali (CCN), Rev. Jimmy Palos (CCN Executive), Fr. B. Henning (Catholic Church) on 30 March 1986 at Mr Borsutzky's home, Windhoek.
48. Shejavali to Beitz, 13 November 1986.
49. *Namibian*, 28 February 1986.
50. CCN, *Report: Kaoko Revisited*, 21 February 1986.
51. *Namibian*, 28 February 1986.
52. Compare this with the R240,000 spent on development projects and social welfare for the whole country.
53. A. Strauss, 'Community development: community organisations in Namibia', in Gerhard Totemeyer, Vezera Kandetu and Wolfgang Werner (eds), *Namibia In Perspective* (Windhoek: CCN, 1987), p. 184.
54. The conflict between the CCN and community groups was akin to the conflict between church hierarchy and ecclesial base communities or CEBs in Latin America. For information on this, see Daniel H. Levine, *Religion and Political Conflict in Latin America* (Chapel Hill: University of North Carolina Press, 1986).
55. To be fair, there was also an understandable paranoia about the penetration of spies and the manipulations of charlatans, and there were really no mechanisms to check whether people were genuine activists or not.
56. Interview with Paul Vleermuis, 28 August 1991.
57. These quotes, and parts of the analysis presented above, are taken from Tessa Cleaver and Marion Wallace, *Namibia: Women in War* (London: Zed Books, 1990), p. 94.
58. Outside the main urban areas, there were few challenges from below: relations between church hierarchy and the laity remained, for the most part, dependent and deferential, despite the delegation of many ecclesiastical responsibilities to lower level clergy and lay persons. The traditional church characterized by clerical dominance, episcopal unity and tight authority, a trickle-down model well-suited for an élitist and authoritarian social order – remained unchallenged. This is in sharp contrast with the situation in a number of Latin American countries where the pastoral practice of ecclesial base communities or CEBs has created a new vision of the church very different from the traditional model in style, composition and decision making. There is also little evidence to suggest that contact between peasant communities and guerillas in the north of the country hastened the democratization of the church. In contrast to Nicaragua, where a more or less simultaneous revolution in church and polity encouraged strong identification with and collaboration between the FSLN guerrillas and the CEBs in pursuit of revolutionary socialist goals, in Namibia the meeting of church and PLAN fighters on the ground made for a mutually reinforcing hierarchical and authoritarian politics in pursuit, simply, of a South African withdrawal. In any case, as the pervasive presence of the South African military severely restricted the potential for alternative governance by the resistance (i.e. the setting up of liberation zones), the *modus vivendi* established between PLAN and the populace (including the clergy at rural missions) was not concerned with the larger issue of future social models, but was rather limited to the mechanics of the armed struggle, namely the establishment of rudimentary support networks and codes of conduct for guerillas and peasants alike. The local level struggles within communities, focussing on gender, generation, lineage and class tensions, preoccupied peasants and often meshed with the guerilla war to produce civil war. The church's involvement in the struggle on the ground, and in the struggles within the struggle, awaits further investigation.
59. *Namibian*, 8 July 1988.
60. CCN, *Resolutions from the CCN Conference held at Dobra, 4–8 July 1988*.
61. The response of the church hierarchy to demands for a smaller, democratic, declericalized and sexually egalitarian institution has varied widely from country to country throughout Latin America. While the national hierarchies in some countries, notably Brazil, have supported the work of the CEBs and even spearheaded the emergence of the 'new' church, hierarchies, or segments of hierarchies, in other countries have fiercely resisted the work of the CEBs and its implications for their church. While a communitarian model of the church has taken root in Brazil, in other countries, like Colombia, conservative bishops, with strong backing from the Vatican, have successfully reinforced the old model rooted in hierarchy and discipline and retained tight control over popular expression.

II THE IMPACT: Three Studies

6

The Namibian Student Movement
Its Role & Effects

SIPHO S. MASEKO

Young people – 'the youth' – have played important parts in every liberation struggle, including Namibia's, and students, with their advantages of education and concentration in schools, colleges and universities, have always been particularly prominent. At the same time, students are not identical with the youth in general. Not only have young people with little or no formal schooling often played key roles in the Namibian struggle, above all as combatants in PLAN, but it was often as a result of being expelled from school, and thrown out of the educational system, that Namibian students came to play crucially important roles in the political arena. The role of Namibian youth within the liberation movement in all its aspects needs to be researched; but the present study is confined to the role of youth as students. As we will see, this was at times, and especially in the years leading up to liberation, a significant element in the struggle inside Namibia; it also bequeathed to the country at independence a student organization, NANSO, with traditions and structures of some consequence for post-independence development.

The liberation struggle, including the armed struggle, and intense political repression gave rise to a distinctive style of organizational activity, and a distinctive inner political life, in the Namibian student movement. The movement was also profoundly marked by its relationship to the existing organizations of the national liberation struggle, and especially to SWAPO. This also involved having to define the student movement's relation to SWAPO's political line, a major preoccupation in the years leading up to independence.

The movement underwent changes as the context altered. Two distinct periods are identified. The first runs from the 1950s to the mid-1970s. This stage was characterized by tight restrictions on the movement of blacks between town and country (or 'reserves'), and severe bottlenecks in the educational system for blacks.[1] These factors militated against the emergence of a strong urban-based student movement. When one did emerge in the 1950s and later, it was short-lived, and had limited impact.

In the second phase, from the mid-1970s onwards, political and economic reforms created conditions conducive to the emergence of a significant student movement. Although the expansion of education for Africans was still severely constricted, more schools were built, an institution for higher education (the Academy of Tertiary Education)[2] was established, and an increasing number of students were enrolled in secondary and tertiary education. During this period the national liberation movement consisted of a number of political organizations divided by differences of political opinion and methods of struggle. These organizations competed for the allegiance of students. In order to avoid division along party political lines the student movement needed to pursue policies which could overcome such divisions. The movement was also influenced by Paulo Freire's idea of 'education for liberation'. Addressing 'oppressed' students generally, the movement sought to address 'oppressed' students irrespective of their political persuasions. This led to a deliberately 'non-partisan' political line (as between the different anti-colonial movements). With the advent of independence, however, the logic of elections imposed itself and for a time the movement was explicitly affiliated to SWAPO.

These influences on the evolution of the Namibian student movement are the themes of this chapter. It also examines the political ideals that student leaders sought to reflect in their organizational practice in the 1980s and the tension between these ideals and the reality that was dictated by the actual conditions of the struggle. First however, a brief account of the Namibian student movement before the 1980s is required.

Students' Anti-Colonial Awakening, 1952–84

The first Namibian student organization, the South West Africa Student Body (SWASB), was formed in 1952 under the influence of political events in South Africa. In 1952 the liberation movement there had organized the 'Defiance Campaign' to protest against the racist laws and practices of the dominant white minority. The students who created the SWASB were studying in South African urban secondary schools and post-secondary institutions, as in Namibia secondary and tertiary education were not yet offered to blacks except at the Augustineum Teachers College in Okahandja, which enrolled students with Standard Six. The SWASB did not perceive its role as actively political, but as that of promoting different indigenous cultures. In the course of time, however, SWASB began to address political issues.

Shortly after the creation of the SWASB its General Secretary, Mburumba Kerina, went to study in the USA. He was also secretly instructed by the Herero Chief Hosea Kutako to assist the Reverend Michael Scott in his petitioning at the UN, as some members of the Chief's Council wished to have an indigenous Namibian involved in the task.[3] The SWASB did not know about Kerina's impending departure until he had already left Namibia. According to Kerina, Chief Kutako feared that the South African government might withdraw his passport if the plan of involving him in petitioning was known.[4] However the organization tried to take advantage of the situation when Kerina was in the US. Jariretundu Kozonguizi, the President of the SWASB, wrote letters to the UN authorizing Kerina to speak on the SWASB's behalf. In 1958 Kozonguizi also left for Europe to study, and was also seconded by the SWASB to work with Scott and Kerina. Before leaving for Europe Kozonguizi had been co-opted onto the Chief's Council, thus ensuring better coordination in petitioning between the student body and the Chief's Council.

The SWASB had major shortcomings, however, which led to its disappearance by 1958. One was its miniature support base, owing to the small number of black students at school. This meant that essentially the SWASB was based in South Africa. Moreover, when its activists returned home, usually for short school vacations, they were unable to go around the country raising the consciousness of students on the inferior quality of their education, and the broader situation of oppression and exploitation, because of the restrictions that still existed at that time on the movement of blacks. Another weakness was the difficulty the SWASB encountered in organizing and mobilizing students when they were outside school premises. This also inhibited the grooming of a new leadership to guarantee continuity when the older student activists and leaders moved on. Nevertheless, the SWASB was important as the forerunner of later Namibian political groups which cut across the tribal divide. In 1958 the South West Africa Progressive Association (SWAPA), a 'cultural body with a political flavour' composed of clerks and other professional people, was founded with the help of former SWASB activists. And in 1959, after SWAPA collapsed, some of these same ex-SWASB activists were instrumental in setting up the South West African National Union (SWANU), and Kozonguizi was elected SWANU's president *in absentia*.

The disappearance of the SWASB led to a lull in terms of organized student activism until the beginning of the 1970s. However, the 1960s were momentous in international and domestic politics. In 1961 South Africa was obliged to withdraw from the Commonwealth because of her apartheid policies as colonial regimes began to capitulate in many parts of Africa. In 1963 the OAU was formed, which later recognized SWAPO as the 'sole and authentic representative of the Namibian people'. In the mid-1960s the UN General Assembly revoked South Africa's mandate over Namibia, and the Security Council described its occupation as illegal. In Namibia the South African-sponsored Odendaal Commission of 1964 recommended the balkanization of Namibia into different bantustans. These recommendations were promulgated as the Development of Self-Government Act of 1968. In the meantime, in 1966, SWAPO's military wing, PLAN, fired its first shots at Omgulumbashe, marking the launch of the 'war of liberation'. In response, the South African government cracked down on PLAN fighters and passed draconian laws such as the Terrorism Act of 1966, aimed at crushing the liberation movement. Detained PLAN fighters and SWAPO leaders, among them Andimba Toivo Ja Toivo, were charged under the latter Act in 1967.

The implications of these events frequently featured in students' discussions within the debating societies and the Students' Christian Movement at various schools. There were also isolated student actions against conditions in the schools and racism in the system.

It was against this background that the 1971 boycott in the north of Namibia occurred. Students boycotted classes, demanding the release of their fellows who had been beaten and arrested during a demonstration against a statement made by Jannie de Wet (Commissioner General for the Indigenous People of SWA) rejecting the advisory ruling of the International Court of Justice (ICJ), in June 1971, that the South African occupation of Namibia was illegal. Another demand was for the unconditional reinstatement of students expelled from school after the demonstration. The South African authorities' condition for readmitting the expelled students was that they should give an undertaking to abstain from politics and any activities that would disrupt the orderly functioning of the schools. Students refused and the boycott lasted for the rest of that year. Many of the expelled students later became active in the 1971 workers' strike, and also joined the Swapo Youth League (SYL).[5]

The crucial role played by the SYL in the years 1971 to 1974 has been outlined in Chapter 4 above. Its impact on popular consciousness inside the country, and on the 1976 crisis inside SWAPO in exile (described in Chapter 3) was very great. To a large extent, the SYL of these years was the creation of the generation of Namibian student leaders who had come to political maturity in the late 1960s and had been ejected by the school system for their political activities. Their departure from the student ranks left a void that took some time to fill.

Following the boycott and the 1971 workers' strike, students, including many from the south, met at a Christian students' conference in Okahandja in 1972 and suggested the establishment of an organization that would 'promote [the] unity of all students' in Namibia.[6] At a follow-up Christian students' conference, a commission was established to draw up a constitution for the new student organization, which was launched the following year. Meanwhile, many students who were involved in the 1971 workers' strike and the 1973 boycott of the 'Ovamboland' elections had gone into exile in the 'exodus' of 1974.

The conference climaxed on 2 September 1975 with the formation of the Namibian Black Students' Organization (NABSO), which subscribed to the Black Consciousness (BC) ideas propagated by opposition groups in South Africa in the 1970s. Although initially consisting only of secondary school students in Namibia, NABSO passed a resolution at its inaugural conference in October 1976 to open the membership to all Namibian students in black South African universities as well. At this congress NABSO also rejected the Turnhalle Conference of September 1975 as a 'racist hoax created by SA', and aligned itself with the Namibian National Convention, an umbrella organization that had been formed to oppose the Turnhalle Conference. On education,

NABSO 'rejected the concept of divided education as it promot[ed] racism'.[7]

On 16 June 1976, secondary school students in South Africa, organized under the South African Student Movement, a BC organization, took to the streets to protest against 'Bantu Education' generally, and the use of Afrikaans as a medium of instruction at schools in particular. Their action was followed five months later by school boycotts supported by Namibian students to demand an end to Bantu Education in Namibian schools. The boycott did not affect all black high schools, but it was effective in some major urban and semi-urban centres including Katutura, Khomasdal and Dobra, in and near Windhoek; at Tses and Okakarara; in Uis and Khorixas in Damaraland; and in Omaruru. The boycott was not centrally organized. NABSO only came in later to 'speak on behalf' of 'all' protesting students; and in January 1977 the students returned to class without gaining their demands.[8] Subsequently, NABSO collapsed, largely because of internal differences, and to a lesser extent because of harassment by the South African security forces.[9]

The majority of Namibian coloured and white students did not adhere to the BC ideas which NABSO espoused, seeing them as 'exclusionist' and 'racist in reverse'. Contrary to the BC definition of black as including Africans, Indians and coloureds, the coloured and the Baster students in Namibia did not regard themselves as black. While many of them had participated in the South African student protest, they felt left out of the framework of BC. Some of them met in Okahandja on 18–19 December 1976 and decided to form a new Namibian Student Organization (NAMSO), with membership open to all 'racial groups' in secondary and post-secondary education. Though it never succeeded in recruiting African students, NAMSO aimed at uniting all Namibian students in one organization, pressing for equal and free education, and struggling to end racism and colonialism. NAMSO also rejected the proposed Turnhalle interim government as an attempt by South Africa 'to impose an ethnically based neo-colonialism in Namibia' and demanded the holding of free elections under United Nations supervision and control.[10]

Eight months later, however, NAMSO was still small, its members limited to 'coloured and white' students. It had branches only at the Universities of the Western Cape (UWC), Cape Town (UCT) and Stellenbosch, and in Rehoboth and Walvis Bay. This situation prompted its chairperson, André Strauss, to write a letter to the branches asking NAMSO members to choose: they could either 'affiliate' to SWAPO, or 'continue as an irrelevant students' organization and [make] a marginal contribution towards the struggle for freedom, or disband'. The letter identified three factors which caused NAMSO to remain small and impotent: the non-existence of tertiary institutions, leading NAMSO members to be 'divorced from the real situation here in Namibia' while studying in South African universities; 'financial difficulties'; and, most seriously, the lack of legitimacy among or acceptance by the majority of the oppressed people on whose behalf it sought to speak: 'we did not represent the mass of [the African] Namibian student population'. [11]

Given the privileges that NAMSO's non-African members enjoyed under apartheid, the 'genuineness and commitment' of its professed role in the struggle were questionable in the eyes of the African students. Their privileged social positions resulted, the NAMSO chairperson's letter continued, in NAMSO members being 'apathetic', 'complacent', 'passive', and 'unwilling' to 'contribute toward the Namibian struggle for freedom'. Therefore, he suggested, if NAMSO as an organization were to affiliate to SWAPO its membership would increase dramatically. But a decision on whether or not to affiliate to SWAPO was never taken; not all members supported the idea, and this paralysed the organization.

From 1978 until 1984 when it disbanded, NAMSO's role in Namibian politics became more and more irrelevant. By the beginning of the 1980s it had only one surviving branch at UWC, and a handful of inactive members at UCT. At UWC it operated as an on-campus 'registered organization' whose role was to 'welcome first year students from Namibia', organize social events and road trips, and hold a yearly 'Namibia Week' to highlight the political situation back home. It avoided taking a clear political stand because 'the organization has members from different walks of life and therefore different political parties.'[12]

The preceding account has identified two major factors which limited the vitality and impact of the Namibian student movement from 1952 to 1984: the separation between town and country which severely limited students' communication, and the shortcomings of the educational system. The paucity of schools pushed a handful of the most successful Namibian students to study in South Africa, causing such Namibian student bodies as did emerge not to be based in Namibia. NAMSO's particular problem, however, was that of legitimacy among African students.

The political and economic changes in the mid-1970s and early 1980s altered this situation. The student population increased, while reforms permitted the relatively free movement of blacks between different parts of the country, alleviating the difficulties of organization.

The Formation of NANSO, 1984

In 1982 Namibian students at the University of Fort Hare began to canvass the idea of forming a national student organization among Namibian university students studying in South Africa, and on 2 January 1983 fourteen students again met at Dobra near Windhoek.[13] The poor turn-out was attributed by the organizers to 'organizational lapses' and communication difficulties.[14] However, the chief reason, it seemed, was differences between students from the University of Zululand, the Medical University of South Africa (Medunsa) and Fort Hare University over the speakers to be invited, and, crucially, on whether or not white students should be included in this new venture.[15] Failure to resolve these issues in advance led to the boycott of the meeting by the University of Zululand students.[16] Nonetheless, the meeting went ahead and ended with the election of an *ad hoc* committee mandated to bring in more students, including those who had stayed away. At another meeting early in July 1983, also poorly attended, it was decided that the new organization would be launched in December 1983, using NAMSO, which was still operating at UWC, as a base.

The January 1983 meeting was criticized for its apparent collusion with the private sector, and for failing to invite 'credible' community figures with experience of the educational problems faced by black students.[17] In spite of the explanation that 'our involvement with the Private Sector can be explained in terms of students' handicapped financial position',[18] the footing on which the meeting began seems to have led to some scepticism about the whole initiative. The plans for launching a new organization in December were, in any case, dropped after the CCN convened a separate and more representative students' conference in July.

The CCN's student conference was also held in Dobra on 10–14 July 1983, in order to 'introduce' the CCN to Namibian students and to facilitate the creation of a student union outside the structures of the church. This was the birth of the Namibian National Student Organization (NANSO). The CCN hoped that this organization would function under the auspices of the church in the struggle for 'peace and justice'. This, however, did not materialize.[19] At its founding congress in July 1984, NANSO had to grapple with the same concerns that had caused strains among students at the January 1983 students' meeting.

The question of the inclusion or exclusion of white students, and of the organization's alignment with a particular political group, became contentious issues after the CCN conference. In order to achieve the objective of 'uniting all the students of Namibia', irrespective of their political persuasions, NANSO resolved, first, to espouse a formal policy of 'non-racialism'. However, it neither recruited nor established branches at white schools, and its few white members were sooner or later forced either to operate underground or flee into exile to escape the call-up for military service.

As for alignment with the national liberation movement, this was not an issue: NANSO saw itself as an integral part of the movement. What *was* an issue was whether or not NANSO should follow the line of any particular political organization. The position that initially prevailed favoured a 'non-partisan', 'independent' student organization, unaffiliated to any particular liberation organization. As noted above, NANSO espoused the Freirian idea of 'education for liberation', and this was taken to imply that NANSO should try to embrace all oppressed students regardless of their political persuasions.[20] The struggle over educational issues was seen as inseparable from the struggle for national liberation.

NANSO's Structure and Functioning

NANSO's constitution envisaged the branches and regional structures forming the backbone of the organization.[21] In practice, however, two factors caused NANSO to depart from these stipulations. The first was the repressive conditions that prevailed within and outside school premises. Most branches could not operate or hold meetings at state-run schools and colleges, owing to harassment by the authorities. Students belonging to or merely supporting NANSO were either expelled or forced to give up NANSO activities. Consequently, most NANSO activities were conducted outside school premises.

Initially the state security forces concentrated on denigrating NANSO, accusing it of being an extension of SWAPO, of 'recruiting' students to join PLAN, and therefore of being a terrorist organization. From 1988 onwards, however, the state began to use violent methods against NANSO activists and leaders, including detention, intimidation, and beatings. If state repression was meant to destroy NANSO, it did not succeed, but it did succeed in disrupting the normal functioning of the organization in areas such as administration and keeping records.

Furthermore, the South African security forces' doctrine of 'winning hearts and minds' was also carried out in the educational sphere. While restricting NANSO, the school authorities allowed so-called 'moderate', or pro-internal settlement student organizations, such as the Namibia Council of Students (NACOS), established in 1987, to operate without any interference.[22] At the Academy for Tertiary Education, a campus-based 'moderate', white and 'coloured' students' organization called the Academy Students' Organization (ASO) was also formed on 17 March 1988, specifically to oppose what it saw as NANSO's 'radicalism' on campus, and demanding the 'banning of NANSO', the 'expulsion' of 'radical' activists such as Ignatius Shihuameni, General Secretary of NANSO, and so on.[23]

The second reason why NANSO did not function in the manner which its constitution stipulated was its top-down leadership style. As with most student organizations combining tertiary with secondary level students, NANSO membership consisted largely of secondary school students, which meant that the branches and regions were not 'strong' or sophisticated in terms of political ideas, but mainly discussed the 'bread and butter' issues they faced under Bantu Education. Moreover, the NANSO 'leadership did not encourage discussion of [major] political policy issues at regional level' because it feared that 'these issues would not be correctly guided'.[24] They were usually discussed at the National Student Congresses (NSC) and consultative conferences, and later also at the General Student Congresses (GSC), where the national leaders dominated.

The 'advanced' activists comprising NANSO's leadership were primarily tertiary-level students, most of whom were, moreover, studying at South African universities. This leadership was responsible for policy shifts such as NANSO's involvement in politics; affiliation with and disaffiliation from SWAPO in 1988/9 and 1991 respectively; leading the organization in its relationships with the community and the labour movement; and issuing leaflets and press releases. A few secondary school students such as Uhuru Dempers, Owen Shameena, Victoria Doeses and others assumed leadership positions after the 1988 school boycott, but they were exceptions.

Another problematic area of NANSO's practice concerns its approach to women's issues. Like most of the liberation movements in Africa, NANSO's fundamental assumption was that colonial subjugation and capitalism were the main causes of women's oppression; therefore, the attainment of independence was needed before the emancipation of women from male domination could be addressed. The Namibian situation, like that of South Africa, was also complicated by the racial factor. NANSO argued also that women in Namibia were faced with a triple oppression, not only as women but also as workers and blacks.[25] The only way to attain women's emancipation was to struggle for the total political transformation of Namibian society.[26]

This approach served to justify the suppression of questions about the sexual division of labour and other women-specific concerns: 'when it came to the question of women and when you spoke about feminism the [male] comrades silenced you'.[27] Thus NANSO's mobilization of female students was effectively a strategy to broaden its support base. A handful of female students were elected to the higher positions in the organization: Alwina Swartbooi became Vice-President in 1990, for example, and Sima Luipert Secretary General in 1991. NANSO was and still is a male-dominated organization, however.

Financially, NANSO faced the problem that its members were very poor by the standards of 'first' or even 'second' world students. To meet its expenses, NANSO was bound to depend on other sources. From the CCN-sponsored student conference of July 1983 until mid-1988, NANSO's chief source of funding was the CCN itself. From the end of 1988, however, NANSO began to receive substantial amounts of money from overseas solidarity groups and other supporters abroad.[28] NANSO's international funding was secured after SWAPO began to acknowledge its activities publicly from mid-1988. From then on, NANSO received most of its 'foreign assistance from the same sources that supported SWAPO',[29] since the latter enjoyed the status of being the 'sole and authentic representative of the Namibian people'. This also implied, however, that from this time onwards NANSO became dependent on SWAPO for its foreign support.

The organizational growth of NANSO went through two stages. During the first, from 1984 to 1986, NANSO was little known by the students on whose behalf it sought to speak, mainly because, as with the previous Namibian student bodies, its leadership was largely based in South Africa. Furthermore it 'never had a programme of action'.[30] The second stage began in mid-1986 after NANSO organized its first public rally in Katutura in June 1986, which marked the beginning of a new era of resistance and challenge.

However, NANSO did not automatically become a mass organization with fully functional grassroots structures. Most of the NANSO branches and regions were either weak or non-existent. The small membership relied on the leadership, which from 1986 onwards was based in Namibia, to carry out most of the activities of the organization, which meant that the leadership was not accountable in many respects, including financial matters. Maria Nduva, a secondary school NANSO activist, commented on the question of financial accountability as follows:

> At congresses our leadership give their report. I do not know about the issue of finances because at the time figures were not given because of technical problems with reports. But I would say, we did not experience a leadership misuse of funds because we still get money from outside donors. The fact that we still get money from them shows that our financial reports were in order and very good.[31]

Thus NANSO was, unavoidably in the circumstances, controlled by a small élite and there was a significant gap between democratic rhetoric and actual practice. However, in the post-independence period there seems to have emerged within NANSO a strong grassroots voice capable of challenging the leadership. An example of this was the controversy at the 1991 congress about the decision (discussed below) to disaffiliate from SWAPO.

NANSO in Politics, 1985–8

The second South African-sponsored attempt at an 'internal settlement' in June 1985 accentuated differences among Namibians in the perception of educational issues as well as the prevailing socio-political impasse. Ottilie Abrahams, a teacher and leading member of the (now defunct) Namibia Independence Party, for example, insisted on the Freirian idea of 'education for liberation'. While aware of the limitations of the so-called Transitional Government of National Unity (TGNU) in redressing educational grievances, she saw the establishment of non-government structures, which the settlement might permit, as offering potential means of empowerment.[32] Andrew Matjila, the Minister of National Education in the TGNU, however, dismissed the involvement of students in politics of any kind: 'Politics was for adults only.'[33]

Within NANSO, however, the limitations of the 1985 'internal settlement' led to frustration and radicalization. NANSO's approach to the struggle changed: in a statement to the press its executive declared that 'Bantu education like apartheid could never be reformed but had to be changed radically.'[34] At the 1987 National Student Congress, Paul Kalenga in his presidential address urged students to 'transform' NANSO from 'a school organization' to an organization that would 'confront the forces of domination' in order to bring about 'progress and social change'.[35] NANSO now argued that 'without the independence of Namibia from colonialism, a genuine education system could not be realized'.[36] In short, NANSO now began to cast itself in the sort of role that the SWAPO Youth League had performed in the early 1970s, although its field of action remained the educational system.

NANSO pursued three strategies to enhance the struggle for independence. The first was to demand educational 'reforms'. This demand was a tactic to deepen the contradictions and crises in the educational arena, and heighten the level of mobilization and consciousness among students, expecting that solutions would not be forthcoming under the existing colonial order. The demands included the free distribution of text books, upgrading the training and qualifications of teachers, the introduction of English as a medium of instruction, and the creation of Students' Representative Councils (SRCs).

Some of these reforms could be and were accommodated by the TGNU, as was the use of English as the medium of instruction at some schools in the reforms of 1985. Other demands, such as the introduction of an SRC system, were not in the interest of the TGNU. For NANSO's definition of the SRC essentially suggested a political function: 'The SRC is there to coordinate all student activities at school and to represent the students wherever possible.... It should act as mediator between the students and the school authority, [and] the public community organizations.'[37] 'Public community organizations' included the likes of SWAPO, SWANU and the trade union movement, all vehemently opposed to the TGNU. The latter, in collaboration with the South African government, wanted to neutralize, if not to completely destroy all of them.

Another demand was for an end to militarism and military conscription. The militarization of Namibian society from the early 1970s onwards entailed detention, injury, death and fear for the community at large. Militarization also affected students in a specific way. Military bases near the schools in the 'war zone' threatened the physical safety of students. In 1987 three students at one of these schools were killed and others injured during exchanges of fire between South African security forces and SWAPO insurgents.[38] The South African military authorities justified the proximity of the bases to schools as 'protect[ing] the pupils' from 'abductions' by SWAPO insurgents,[39] an argument dismissed by the students. They regarded SWAPO as freedom fighters:[40] the real forces behind abductions, they believed, were members of Koevoet.[41]

Militarization also directly affected students as a result of the introduction in 1980 of military conscription for all young Namibian men, black and white (although only Namibians south of the 'war zone' were actually called up). The policy was part of a political strategy of 'internalizing' the conflict in Namibia, to pit Namibians against Namibians, and it was for this reason that NANSO rejected it. At its Annual Consultative Conference in Windhoek on 15–17 January 1988, it resolved to declare 1988 the year of 'Decisive Action Against Militarization' because 'when the young Namibians enlist themselves in the SADF and the SWATF they were prolonging the [colonization] of Namibia and also should know that they were committing a crime against the nation'.[42]

Finally, NANSO's new strategy of fighting for independence meant that it would openly participate in a political programme. In 1986 NANSO pledged to support and work with the /Ai-//Gams Conference, a constellation of groups who were opposed to the TGNU, and who demanded the unconditional implementation of the UNSC Resolution 435. However, the /Ai-//Gams conference remained impotent, due to mistrust and strains among its members. NANSO, too, became critical of some /Ai-//Gams participants such as the Damara Council – whose name, according to NANSO, suggested the promotion of 'ethnic division'.

The increasing radicalization of NANSO came to a climax in the national school boycott of March to mid-September 1988. The objectives of the boycott alternated between drawing attention to the predicament of students near the military bases in the 'war zone' and pursuing the idea contained in some of NANSO's public statements of launching 'an insurrectionary action' to achieve independence. In its final stages, indeed, it clearly did become an attempt, however unrealistic it may seem in retrospect, to 'overthrow' the colonial government.

The boycott began spontaneously on 17 March 1988 when students at the Ponhofi Secondary school in the 'war zone', and at Ogongo and Ombalantu high schools a few days later, refused to attend classes until the military bases adjacent to their schools were removed. Two months later other students in the Oshivambo-speaking region, estimated at between 20,000 and 25,000, in 18 primary schools, 18 secondary schools and five colleges, joined the boycott in solidarity with their fellow students. These boycotts were followed by others in 'Hereroland' and 'Damaraland' whose objectives were, however, different.

In July 1988, the NANSO leadership released its first press statement on the boycott, supporting only the students in the north, and reiterating its stand against militarization. The class boycotts in Hereroland and Damaraland, which were about increased school fees, ended without support from NANSO. The failure to support the latter protests indicated the NANSO leadership's inexperience and their unreadiness to coordinate a national crisis to the organization's advantage.

By the end of May and the beginning of June, the boycott had spread to other areas: to Otjikoto Secondary school in Tsumeb; to schools in Katutura, Khomasdal and Dobra, in or near Windhoek; to Martin Luther High school in Omaruru; and to schools in Swakopmund, Uis, Arandis, Gibeon, Keetmanshoop and Luderitz in the south. The South Africans responded with the deployment of police in the schools, the detention of students, and intimidation and harassment; in July 1988 they also passed the Protection of Fundamental Rights Act, which made it an offence, punishable with a fine of R20,000 or ten years' imprisonment or both, to encourage strikes or school boycotts. The intensification of state harassment led to a new mass exodus of students into exile, estimated at 5,000 by the end of October, and the collapse of many NANSO branches, particularly in the north.

NANSO's initial objectives in the boycott were not clear. Was the demand for the removal of the army bases a strategic short-term demand which would also highlight the broader problems in education, and strengthen the 'emerging mass movement'? Or was it a long-term objective whereby students would make an ultimate 'sacrifice of their studies' to achieve political independence? This confusion was evident during the boycott and especially in the later statements issued by NANSO.[43] By September, according to NANSO, the boycott had reached the proportions of 'a mass revolutionary upsurge'. At a consultative conference held in Otjiwarongo, on 23–26 September 1988, NANSO decided to go further and embark on a 'no exams campaign': 'we are moving towards scoring our final victory against racist South Africa, let us be strong in order to be able to hit hard and deliver a final blow'.[44] In the confusion that this drastic shift of perspective produced, students in some schools in the north returned to their classes.

Parents in the north supported the actions of the students, and refused to allow their children to go back to school until the military bases were removed. Support for the students also came from the trade union movement, the churches and the teachers association, which issued statements pledging solidarity with students in the north. In an unprecedented display of support the National Union of Namibian Workers (NUNW) called a two-day (20 and 21 June) stay-away, which was supported by 40,000 to 50,000 workers (75 per cent of the estimated Namibian workforce).[45] Elsewhere, however, not all parents understood the students' actions, because the war situation was experienced very differently in different parts of the country.

The links it forged between NANSO and other sectors of Namibian society were an important feature of the boycott. These began with a meeting of parents and community leaders convened by the / Ai-/ /Gams group in Katutura on 8 June 1988. At this meeting a 'Committee of Seven' was elected to meet with the Administrator General (AG), Louis Pienaar, to demand that the military bases near the schools be removed 'before the boycott could be called off'.[46] The AG, however, merely promised to 'build bomb shelters' at the affected schools, a notion summarily dismissed by the Committee and NANSO. Shortly afterwards tensions emerged between some members of the Committee and NANSO, leading to the demise of the Committee. The Committee was accused by NANSO of wanting to become a permanent structure that would coordinate other similar structures to be created around the country, and of harbouring 'ulterior motives'. A document entitled 'The National Education Crisis Committee Programme', drawn up in 1988 by some members of the Committee, revealed the 'motives' as including, among other things, the launching of 'alternative education projects'. The aims of this document were in themselves neither dangerous nor retrogressive. However, they essentially suggested shifting the control of the protest from NANSO, and entailed the readoption of the Freirian discourse jettisoned by NANSO in 1987.

In July 1988 NANSO suggested an informal alliance with the wider community. A gathering of parents, workers and students from various parts of Namibia met to discuss this on 9 July 1988 at Dobra, near Windhoek, and formed the National People's Assembly (NPA). Representatives of major political organizations were deliberately left out because 'NANSO wanted to go to the thing [the alliance] with total control of the [whole] process' and 'strengthen the students' demands on our own terms'.[47]

The NPA I (as the first meeting was later called) resolved to call off the boycott, to set up a National Schools Crisis Committee (NSCC) to coordinate the school crisis generally, to facilitate the formation of 'democratic parent–teacher–student associations at all schools', and to create a 'progressive' teachers' union (because the existing Namibia Teachers Association was seen as conservative).[48] The formation of the Namibia National Teachers Union (NANTU) in December 1988 was a product of this initiative.

Strains between students and the community began to surface, however, at the second NPA meeting (NPA II) held at Otjimbingwe-Paulineum on 13–14 August 1988. The burning and destruction of schools, the harassment and detention of students, and the deployment of Koevoet, the army and security police at school premises, meant that the prospects of students going back to school were becoming remote. Under these circumstances, in NANSO's view, mass action for the total overthrow of 'the colonial forces' was the only alternative. But the 'older' members of the NPA were not in favour of this.[49] A compromise was reached, to 'call upon all Namibians to embark upon positive defiance action for a period of four weeks'.[50]

Another cause of tension was NANSO's resentment of what it perceived as the community delegates' concern with their 'self-interests'. When the NPA III met in early September, unity between NANSO and 'the community' finally collapsed. It was in this context that a NANSO consultative conference held later in September decided on a 'no exam campaign' without consultation with the other groups. But the unrealism of its vision of 'overthrowing' the regime by student and community protest was by now all too obvious. By the beginning of January 1989 the students were defeated. Many NANSO activists and supporters who were not already in detention or in exile were expelled from school and 'blacklisted' by the Department of National Education (that is, they were not allowed to re-register at other schools controlled by the Department).

However, the spirit of resistance was still alive, at least among the students in the north who were most concerned about the continued threat of atrocities committed against students (and other members of society) by Koevoet and the South African security forces. After the official launch of the transition to independence on 1 April 1989, students in the far northern region again boycotted classes on this issue, especially after the mass killing of PLAN fighters by South African military forces early in April 1989. The boycott 'affected 168,000 pupils and students at nearly all 518 schools' in the north.[51]

The state responded by closing most of the schools and imposing the condition that students, accompanied by their parents or guardians, should give an undertaking not to take part in politics. Students, backed by their parents, refused to comply. Teachers suspected of being behind the class boycott were also dismissed from their jobs. Attempts to coordinate a solidarity boycott by students south of the 'war zone' were unsuccessful, however, in spite of the NANSO leadership's call for a 'national stay-away' on 11 April 1989.[52] The former President of NANSO, Paul Kalenga, noted the chief reason for the failure of solidarity action:

> People in the north have completely different experiences of repression/war than any persons in the south and central Namibia.... There was never war in these parts of the country. Even when you talk about things like Koevoet to be disbanded or whatever, to many people it does not make sense. It takes time to conscientize people about such things.[53]

The boycott in the north nonetheless escalated and culminated in a massive three-day stay-away (8–10 June) called and coordinated by the Namibian Public Workers' Union (NAPWU), NANTU, and NANSO regional structures. On 20 June 1989 the boycott came to an end after the education officials of the Ovambo administration, at a meeting with the NANSO leadership, dropped their insistence on the dismissed students undertaking not to engage in political activities. In return NANSO agreed to call off the boycott and merely called upon the 'colonial governor', AG Louis Pienaar, and the 'UN Security Council' to take 'positive' steps towards resolving the 'Koevoet problem'.[54]

The Transition to Independence, 1988–90

The transition to independence imposed a new logic on NANSO. Having officially maintained a 'non-partisan' policy in the struggle for national liberation, NANSO now decided to rescind it and affiliate to SWAPO.[55] The origins of this decision date back to 1987 when NANSO abandoned the Freirian approach in favour of radical mass confrontation. Meanwhile socialist ideas had begun to emerge within the NANSO leadership, although they were not at any point strong. As we have already noted, NANSO now defined its approach to the liberation struggle in a way that resembled the SYL tradition of the early 1970s, and there had always been an overlap of leadership, membership and activities between NANSO and the SYL. But NANSO was now the stronger force; and although most NANSO members supported SWAPO, the organization was initially suspect in the eyes of the SWAPO leadership, particularly those in exile.

Given SWAPO's tendency to be suspicious of even seemingly progressive community structures and organizations outside its control, such as the Namibia Women's Voice and the Bricks Community Project in Katutura, it is not clear why SWAPO tolerated NANSO. It may have been because by 1985 NANSO had become one of the few organizations, apart from the /Ai-//Gams conference, that directly challenged the regime, as demonstrated initially by a NANSO rally held in Katutura in June 1986, at a time when SWAPO inside Namibia was barely operational. This may also explain NANSO's inclusion in the delegation representing various groups in Namibia at the Consultative Conference sponsored by SWAPO in Harare, Zimbabwe, on 25–27 September 1987.

For its part, NANSO had retained its policy of 'non-partisanship' up to 1987, largely for security reasons. By 1988, however, the situation had altered. Firstly, SWAPO had now publicly acknowledged the pivotal role played by NANSO. Consequently, there were regular contacts between NANSO and the SWAPO leaders in exile. For example, a NANSO delegation participated in a SWAPO Consultative Conference held in Kabwe, Zambia, on 8–13 September 1988, and another took part in a SWAPO election seminar held in Lusaka on 22–29 May 1989. Between January and June 1989, SWAPO also endorsed NANSO speaking tours and participation in various forums in countries such as Britain, Norway, Denmark and Zimbabwe, and the relationship also enabled NANSO to raise funds from international sources with SWAPO's endorsement.[56] The commencement of the tripartite negotiations between the South African, Cuban and Angolan governments in the aftermath of the battle at Cuito Cuanevale finally encouraged NANSO to take the risk of talking openly about its allegiance to SWAPO.

NANSO's decision to align with SWAPO was, however, also precipitated by the need to prevent what the leadership saw as 'ultra-left theoretical politics' from 'confusing' students. This fear was caused by the interest shown by non-SWAPO left-wing political organizations in the students' actions during the boycott. Some high-profile leaders such as Ottilie Abrahams and Ayesha Rajah of the Namibia Independence Party (NIP) participated in the discussions about its objectives, and affiliating NANSO to SWAPO was seen as a way of protecting impressionable young students from these influences. One group, the Workers' Revolutionary Party (WRP), indeed wanted to infiltrate NANSO in order to displace NANSO's 'petit-bourgeois leadership'.[57] However, this rationale also reflected the NANSO leadership's rather paternalistic attitude towards its secondary school members, in particular.

From this time onwards, partly on the pretext of preventing the confusion that might be induced by 'ultra-left theoretical politics', and partly as a manifestation of SWAPO's claim to be the sole authentic representative of all Namibians, NANSO began to perceive all non-SWAPO constituents of the liberation movement, such as SWANU, as a liability in the struggle. It accused the Namibian Student Education Movement (NASEM) of being tribalist, reactionary and divisive.[58] NANSO's new intolerance cut across the political spectrum. For example, the NANSO-controlled SRC at the Academy also refused to allow the Academy Student Organization to operate on campus.

At the 1989 National Students Congress NANSO formally affiliated to SWAPO. The leadership had two main reasons. The first was to address the immediate problems of electoral politics, which included the threat that SWAPO might be denied victory in the liberation struggle at the last minute by anti-SWAPO parties funded and inspired by South Africa.[59] Moreover, NANSO's affiliation would 'boost the morale of the party', threatened by the detainee issue which had caused 'long-standing SWAPO members and other people to get disillusioned'.[60] The second reason focussed on political prospects in post-independence Namibia. The leadership of NANSO envisaged that if SWAPO captured a two-thirds majority in the elections, Namibia would become a one-party socialist state and 'we thought the way to move along with that idea [one-party state] was to affiliate with SWAPO'.[61] But SWAPO did not obtain a two-thirds majority in the November 1989 elections, and this is one of the reasons why NANSO disaffiliated from SWAPO again in 1991.

While NANSO took the affiliation to SWAPO seriously, SWAPO did not. For SWAPO, it was mainly symbolic. As seen by the then Minister of Information and Broadcasting, Hidipo Hamutenya, 'NANSO's affiliation was unsolicited by the Party. So long as they worked ... and supported SWAPO, it was fine.'[62] This attitude acknowledged the students' role in the struggle, but perhaps only in a rather opportunistic manner.

NANSO in Post-Independence Namibia, 1990

On 1–5 July 1991, at NANSO's first Extraordinary National Student Congress, an overwhelming majority (96.3 per cent) of the 490 delegates decided 'to repeal our [1989] 5th NSC resolution on affiliation and mandate [*sic*] the NEC to seek a non-affiliate working relation with SWAPO' because of 'the challenges facing our organization in the post-colonial era, and taking note of the need to preserve inner organizational democracy and autonomy in order to successfully meet the burning demands of our constituency'.[63]

The background was the 1989 elections, which SWAPO had won without obtaining a two-thirds majority, combined with the economic and political limitations that confronted the incoming SWAPO government; these constraints meant that the government would not be able to address immediately the legacy of racial imbalances, including those in the educational system. Paul Kalenga, now the NANSO National Coordinator, argued that in this situation repealing 'structural affiliation' with the ruling party, SWAPO, would give NANSO more influence to secure the adoption of policies which would 'safeguard and promote the rights' of students in secondary and higher education.[64] In the words of the NANSO President, Vincent Likoro, 'the decision to disaffiliate [was] a logical response to new political realities and contradictions; the strategic goal is the challenge for control of education by democratic structures to make [it respond] to the needs of Namibia and its people'.[65]

Another factor was the realization that affiliation to SWAPO had caused disunity among students, resulting in the formation of NASEM. NANSO was no longer able to attract students who were not SWAPO supporters. As Likoro saw it, NANSO's role in the new Namibia had to have a 'trade union' character, which would allow it to organize and 'defend the basic interests' of its membership irrespective of 'whether a member belongs to SWAPO, NNF or UDF'. The 'existence of competing mass [students'] organizations usually weakens the struggle, a case in point are women's [organizations] in Namibia'.[66]

Finally, it seems, NANSO disaffiliated to prevent outside control of its processes and structures. NANSO had reservations about the manner in which SWAPO, as ruling party, failed to consult NANSO about the departure (which it initiated) of the NANSO Secretary General Paul Kalenga to Czechoslovakia in 1989, to assume the NANSO seat at the International Union of Students, and of Ignatius Shihuameni, President of

NANSO in 1990–1, to pursue further studies in Cuba in 1990. These issues caused suspicion that SWAPO was attempting to weaken NANSO as an independent structure. Likoro may also have been correct when he explained these undemocratic decisions by SWAPO as being partly a product of 'exile' and 'war' conditions which 'placed a limit to the extent to which democracy was practised'.[67] Consequently, for reasons both of organizational autonomy and of internal democracy, NANSO severed its structural links with SWAPO.

After the decision to disaffiliate from SWAPO was taken, 29 of the 96 delegates from the far northern region walked out of the Congress, accusing the NANSO leadership, of 'selling out' their 'mother body', and of succumbing to threats by international donors that they would cut funds if NANSO remained affiliated to SWAPO. They also accused white and 'coloured' students of having been behind the decision to disaffiliate: 'They were never with us in the struggle. Why compromise with them, and say goodbye to our Father and Mother [SWAPO]?'[68]

On 23–25 August 1991 the dissatisfied students held a regional conference, attended by 200 students from different branches, at the Gabriel Taapopi Secondary School in Ongwediva, and resolved to stay affiliated to SWAPO because 'to disaffiliate from SWAPO at this stage will only create confusion'.[69] They also argued that disaffiliation will 'divide us while we do not yet have Walvis Bay'.[70] Besides confirming the decision to remain affiliated to SWAPO, the conference also passed a vote of no confidence in the Regional Executive Committee (REC) elected earlier in the year, charging it with being corrupt.[71] Subsequently, Abraham Ndumbu was elected as the new chairperson of the REC.

The response of the NANSO leadership was to send a delegation led by the President, Vincent Likoro, to try and meet with the dissident group and the branches in the region, in an attempt to explain the 'real' reasons for disaffiliation. However, the delegation only managed to speak to NANSO members at a few schools in Oluno, Ongwediva, Odibo and Oshakati, and the dissident group refused to meet it.[72] At a press conference later Likoro hinted at the involvement of 'non-students' as the 'masterminds' of the crisis, an apparent reference to SWAPO officials who were suspected of being involved.[73] While at the time of writing it was not clear whether or not SWAPO was involved in this crisis, some SWAPO leaders did repeat some of the allegations made by the 'dissident' group. According to Hidipo Hamutenya, the then Minister of Information and Communications, for example, 'It is a fact that a condition to offer them money was disaffiliation from SWAPO.'[74]

All these allegations were denied by the NANSO leadership, who pointed out that the region of the far north had not discussed the question of disaffiliation at their regional conference, which should have been held before the NSC. Other regions of NANSO such as the western region and the Western Cape in South Africa also denied the charges and publicly pledged their support for the leadership. Nor did students elsewhere in Namibia support reaffiliation to SWAPO.

Nonetheless, the split in the organization was extremely serious, casting doubt on the viability of the NANSO leader's view of the organization's role in post-independence Namibia as being a struggle, on trade union lines, for the 'democratization of the educational system'.[75] This entailed the removal of all impediments to equal access to education – removing age restrictions, for example, and dismantling the racial imbalances in the educational system inherited by the SWAPO government.[76] At both primary and secondary school levels there were still many poorly qualified and untrained teachers, crowded classrooms, high student–teacher ratios, and inadequate physical infrastructures (teaching under trees in some schools, in thatched classrooms or in corrugated iron shacks). There were also lavishly equipped schools, still mainly for whites.[77] The basic material interests of students in Namibia were also seen as including the concerns of female students within and outside the structures of NANSO, as shown by the resolutions of the 1991 congress.

NANSO's conception of the 'democratization' of education also meant the participation of teachers, parents, and students in the running of schools. This was clearly demonstrated by NANSO's participation in the drawing-up of the new government's Educational Code of Conduct for Namibian schools. The aim of this document was 'to motivate all concerned to establish an environment at schools and community conducive to positive learning, education and personal development'.[78] It was also demonstrated by NANSO's submissions to the Commission on Higher Education, set up to plan the creation of a national university in Namibia.[79]

Success in the aim of mobilizing students across the political divide would depend, however, on how NANSO related to rival students' organizations like NASEM, with whom it now sought a working relationship or perhaps a merger between NANSO and NASEM.

Conclusion

This chapter has demonstrated the significant role that can be played by a student movement in the liberation struggle. However the specific character of any student movement involved in national politics will depend on the circumstances that gave birth to it. The Namibian student movement emerged out of a determination to address the inferior education offered to blacks, which was also linked to the system of racial oppression, repression, militarism, and racist and ethnic government institutions created by South Africa's colonial administration.

The evolution of the Namibian student movement into a significant force, especially in the 1980s, owed much to the structural changes that took place in the political economy of Namibia from the mid-1970s. In its earlier stages, from the 1950s to the 1970s, the encounter of Namibian students with South African liberation politics had an enormous influence in shaping the outlook and conduct of the Namibian student movement. Although the South African influence could still be discerned in the shaping of NANSO, it declined from 1987 onwards when NANSO opted for a radical, confrontational approach.

The student movement made a number of distinctive contributions to the struggle for liberation in Namibia. In the 1950s it became the forerunner of national political organizations which cut across ethnic or tribal affiliations. In the early 1970s student political activity was the seedbed for the crucial role that was played by the SYL between 1971 and 1974. In the mid-1980s, the creation of NANSO contributed to a marked revival, led by students, of an internal resistance movement which at this point had become relatively moribund, and thus helped significantly to frustrate South Africa's hopes of forging a viable neo-colonial arrangement to pre-empt the implementation of Resolution 435.

The chapter has also tried to assess the extent to which the student movement, and NANSO in particular, upheld and practised the democratic, accountable political culture which they professed in their documents and public speeches. The evidence shows that NANSO – no doubt like many if not most student bodies of its kind – was controlled by a small group of students who also consistently demonstrated an unwillingness to accept any significant influence over 'student affairs' by non-students, including even SWAPO. It must be recognized, however, that severe repression and militarization also made it very difficult for NANSO to practise and maintain the democratic values it formally upheld.

NANSO's resistance to outside control of its processes in post-independence Namibia, on the other hand, indicates that its leaders understood the politics demanded by an autonomous 'civil society' after independence, when they sought to convert NANSO into a movement that would pursue students' interests on trade union lines. The decision to disaffiliate from SWAPO, however, led to the creation, in effect, of a separate 'northern' student organization, which in 1993 was even seeking recruits in the south. This cast grave doubt on the practicability of NANSO's new ideal in the conditions inherited from Namibia's distinctive liberation struggle, at least in the short run.

Notes

1. For example, in the 1950s Namibians only received a four-year primary education and most of the schools were based in the rural areas or reserves. Secondary schooling was not offered until the 1960s. In 1962 there were 47,088 African pupils (9,053 based in town and 38,035 in the rural areas and reserves), and 6,235 coloured pupils (the majority based in town). In 1970 only 24 black pupils graduated from high school, while 21 (18 male and 3 female) were studying in the South African universities.
2. In 1980 the Academy for Tertiary Education was established with a total enrolment of 3,000 students. Between 1983 and 1986 there were 4,687 African pupils and 2,032 coloured in secondary school (i.e., Standards Eight to Ten).
3. Interview with Jariretundu Kozonguizi, President of SWASB, August 1991. At first there were objections to having Kerina involved because of a statement attributed to him at the time of his departure to the effect that there was nothing wrong with the South African government, as it issued him a passport. Nonetheless, in 1957 Kerina began to work with Scott 'after he proved himself credible' (interview with Dr Zedekia Ngavirue, Acting General Secretary of the SWASB, August 1991).
4. Interview with Mburumba Kerina, September 1991.
5. Interview with Tuli Hivelua, student leader in 1971, September 1991. Hivelua read a prepared statement on behalf of the demonstrating students at the offices of the Commissioner. However, he told me that he knew neither who had prepared the statement nor the political affiliation of the person who gave it to him. Another student in the north at the time, Martin Kapewasha, who later became a leading SYL activist in 1971, explained in an interview (July 1991) that during the boycott the SYL did not have organized structures, and was not behind the students' protest. So, contrary to suggestions in some literature, there is no conclusive evidence supporting the assertion that the SYL organized the protest.
6. Minutes of the Seventh Students' Conference, held in Okahandja, 1–4 September 1972.
7. K.Z. Mujoro, President of NABSO, 'Press Statement on the NABSO Congress', October 1976.
8. See a leaflet issued by NABSO quoted in an editorial, 'Bantu education in crisis', *South African Labour Bulletin*, 4, 1 & 2, 1978, pp. 61–2.
9. Vekuii Rukoro was at the time the President of NABSO and Secretary-General of SWANU, which also adhered to BC, while other executive members were active in SWAPO and did not support the latter ideology.
10. NAMSO's newsletter, *NAMSO News*, 1 May 1977.
11. Confidential letter to branches, signed by the chairperson of NAMSO, 1977.
12. *Namibia News*, NAMSO 'semester newspaper', UWC, 1st semester, 1983. The quotation is translated from Afrikaans by this writer.
13. They came from Universities of Cape Town, Rhodes, Witwatersrand and Fort Hare; the Academy for Tertiary Education, Paulineum Seminary, and Martin Luther High School.
14. J. Diescho, 'Towards student unity in Namibia', unpublished paper, University of Fort Hare, 1983.
15. *Namibia News, op. cit.*, 1983.
16. J. Diescho, *op. cit.*, p. 3.
17. See H. Abrahams, 'A reply to Joseph Diescho', in *The Namibian Review* (1983), *op. cit.*, p. 27.
18. J. Diescho, 'Letter to the editor', *ibid.*, p. 24.
19. The reason why the CCN chose to foster a students' organization outside the structures of the church when there was an existing Christian Students' Movement in Namibia is a matter that requires further research.
20. *The Student Voice of Namibia*, (hereafter *SVN*), March 1985. This newspaper became the official organ of NANSO from July 1984 and is controlled by the National Executive Committee.
21. At the beginning of 1985 NANSO had eight branches mainly at colleges and church-run schools. In 1989 it claimed a membership of 47,000 from 107 branches throughout the country. The exact membership of NANSO before 1989 is not known because most of its documents were confiscated by state security forces, but it is believed to have been far lower than the figure claimed here. In 1991 there were ten regions 'demarcated on the basis of convenient

administrative geographical location'. Two of these were vacant, however.

22. NACOS was a Democratic Turnhalle Alliance (DTA) effort to neutralize NANSO's influence and dominance in schools. However, apart from press statements issued at long intervals, little is known about this organization.
23. See *Windhoek Advertiser*, 8 March 1988. By 1990 ASO had disappeared.
24. Interview, Hafeni Nghinamwaami, the former NANSO Vice-President and General Secretary, August 1991.
25. NANSO's Acting Organizer of Women, Victoria Doeses, cited in *SVN*, 5, 2 (January–February, 1989).
26. *SVN*, 4, 3, (July–August, 1988).
27. Interview with Sima Luipert, Secretary General of NANSO, July 1991.
28. For example, between January and June 1989, NANSO received contributions totalling R309,277 from overseas donors. Besides these donations, the modest sum of R308 was generated from the sale of publicity items such as T-shirts, stickers, buttons, etc., while R7,741 was raised from membership subscriptions. These figures were provided by the auditors, Price Waterhouse, in Windhoek, July 1989.
29. Hafeni Nghinamwaami, former Vice-President and General Secretary of NANSO, cited in *The Namibian*, August 1991.
30. Interview with Paul Kalenga, President of NANSO (1986–9), July 1991.
31. Interview, July 1991. See note 28 for evidence that gives some substance to Nduva's last comment.
32. Interview with Ottilie Abrahams, July 1991.
33. Cited in *SVN*, 10 June 1988.
34. *Namibian*, 4 September 1987.
35. *Namibian*, 11 July 1987.
36. *SVN*, 6, 4 (June–July 1990).
37. *SVN*, 4, 3 (July–August 1988).
38. *Windhoek Observer*, 25 June 1988.
39. *Namibian*, 10 May 1988.
40. *Namibian*, 29 September 1987.
41. *Namibian*, 22–29 June 1988. A parent wrote to *The Namibian* saying, 'Now the army can blame SWAPO guerillas, and say that the school needed military bases nearby in order to protect the children from this sort of thing.'
42. *Namibian*, 29 April 1988.
43. The late entry into the protest of the Academy of Tertiary Education illustrated this. Before pronouncing their solidarity, students at the Academy inspired by NANSO had been involved in class boycotts in 1987 and February 1988, demanding the implementation of English as a medium of instruction and the recognition of their NANSO branch by the administration.
44. *SVN*, 4, 4 (September–October 1988).
45. *Windhoek Advertiser*, 25 June 1988.
46. *Namibian*, 3–10 June 1988.
47. Interview with NANSO's Secretary of Information and Publicity, Steve Katjiuanjo, August 1991.
48. Resolutions of the NPA I, *Namibian*, 10 July 1988.
49. Interview with Reverend Nankamela, a church representative at NPA I and II, September 1991.
50. Resolutions of the NPA II, *Namibian*, 22 August 1988.
51. *The Times of Namibia*, 6 June 1991.
52. 'Students Call For a National Day of Solidarity', leaflet issued by NANSO Head Office, April 1989.
53. Interview, July 1991.
54. *The Times of Namibia*, 20 June 1989.
55. The 1988 NANSO NSC decision to align with SWAPO resulted in disenchanted non-SWAPO supporters leaving NANSO and forming a students' organization called the Namibia Student Educational Movement (NASEM) in 1990, which, however, has so far remained ineffectual.
56. NANSO Annual Organizational Report, 1988/9.
57. Interview with Erica and Hewat Beukes, Central Committee members of the WRP, July 1991.
58. *SVN*, 6, 4, (July–August 1990).
59. Interview with Nathanael Areseb, Acting President, July 1991.
60. SWAPO 'detainees', who had formed the Patriotic Unity Movement (PUM) to contest the elections against SWAPO, were relatively highly educated people. In July 1989 NANSO went

on to pass a resolution at the GSC condemning PUM for furthering 'counter-revolutionary activities controlled by Pretoria with the aim of confusing our people'. *SVN*, 5, 4 (July–August 1989).

61. Interview with Hafeni Nghinamwaami, former NANSO Vice-President, August 1991. The resolution of the 1989 NSC implicitly confirmed these assertions. See *SVN*, 5, 4 (July–August 1989).
62. Interview with Hidipo Hamutenya, former Minister of Information and Broadcasting (currently Minister of Trade and Industry), August 1991.
63. Resolutions of the 1st Extraordinary Congress of NANSO, held at A. Shipena School, 1–5 July 1991.
64. *SVN*, 7, 2 (Congress edition, July 1991).
65. Cited in *New Era*, 24–30 October 1991.
66. *Namibia Today*, 11–17 October 1991.
67. *New Era*, 24–30 October 1991.
68. Abraham Ndumbu, cited in *Namibian*, 29 August 1991.
69. *Namibia Today*, 28 August 1991. According to this newspaper (an official SWAPO publication) 'nearly all secondary and combined schools in the [far north] region sent their representatives ....' However, a student from Valambola Technical College present at this conference disputed this claim. He also noted that students and teachers (present here) who spoke in favour of disaffiliation were booed and told to keep quiet (interview with Pelo Nzibandi, NANSO member, September 1991). The same edition of *Namibia Today* also reported incidents of intimidation against those who tried to argue for disaffiliation.
70. Interview with Abraham Ndumbu, September 1991.
71. *Ibid*.
72. *Namibia Today*, 31 August 1991.
73. At the time there were unconfirmed rumours of SWAPO officials in the region and in Windhoek having materially helped the 'dissident' group, for example by providing governments cars to organize the regional conference. In an interview (September 1991) with the writer, Ndumbu denied any involvement of SWAPO whatsoever.
74. Interview with the Minister of Information and Broadcasting, Hidipo Hamutenya, August 1991.
75. NANSO Annual Organizational Report, 1989.
76. According to the old education system, students over the age of 21 years were not allowed to enrol in the normal day schools.
77. See *Pedagogy in Transition: The Imperatives of Educational Development in the Republic of Namibia*, submission by the Ministry of Education, Culture, Youth and Sport to the National Assembly, Budget Debate, 1991/2 (Windhoek: May 1991).
78. Ministry of Education, Culture, Youth and Sport, *Namibian Educational Code of Conduct for Schools* (December 1990).
79. See *Atomos*, April 1991 edition.

7

State & Civil Society
Policing in Transition

COLIN LEYS

Few things reveal the relationship between the state and civil society, and above all the balance between coercion and consent, so clearly as policing: and in few African countries has this been so well understood as in Namibia, where the state of the police, and the maintenance of law and order, was seldom off the front pages of the newspapers for the first two years after independence. This chapter examines policing in Namibia before and after the transition to independence, both for its own intrinsic interest and importance, and for the light it sheds on some of the general problems involved in overcoming the country's bitter inheritance of violence.

In approaching this issue it should be borne in mind that it is only in comparatively recent times that policing has come to be entrusted to a specialized police *force*. In Namibia north of the 'police zone' before the 1960s law and order were generally maintained without the intervention of the police, based south of the 'Red Line'; and it is often forgotten how relatively recently this was a universal expectation, even in today's advanced industrial countries. Conversely, police forces as they exist today throughout the world perform many functions other than law enforcement and crime prevention, from traffic regulation and other kinds of social control, to morality enforcement, dispute mediation, social work and political surveillance. These functions were once performed by other means, and mostly still could be today. There is considerable variation in the scope of activities carried out by the police forces of different countries, in the way they are organized, and in their relationships to the societies in which they operate; in other words, many possible models of policing are available. In practice, of course, policy makers almost invariably work with only one particular model in mind, rather than reviewing alternative options, or tailoring one to local needs on the basis of first principles. In post-independence Namibia, help was sought from Britain, the first industrial country and one of the first to develop a modern police force.

The British model was attractive partly because of Namibia's historic links with Britain, and partly because the British model of 'policing by consent' represented such a complete contrast to the repressive model of policing that Nambians had known before. In the nineteenth century Britain was a relatively homogeneous society, and from about 1850 onwards the prevailing level of inequality gradually came to be seen as more or less acceptable as a result of a long period of liberal representative government, and the gradual incorporation of the working class into the political system; this in turn permitted the emergence of what has come to be known as 'policing by consent', with its seven principles of bureaucratization, the rule of law, the use of minimal force, political non-partisanship, providing services to the public, emphasizing the prevention of crime rather than detection, and providing effective law enforcement for all classes.[1]

The contrast between this model and the military concept of policing typical of settler colonies could hardly be greater; and in Namibia under South African rule the military model of policing, in defence of white settlement and racial oppression, was developed to its absolute limits, if not beyond them, especially in the effort to suppress the independence movement from 1977 onwards under P. W. Botha's 'total strategy'. That strategy having failed, it was natural, and very positive, that the incoming SWAPO government should adopt the principle of policing by consent to replace it – but Namibia's ethnic and cultural diversity, uneven development, post-war social dislocation, acute poverty and inequality combined to present a social situation very different from that of nineteenth-century Britain. It was therefore unlikely that the ideal of policing by consent would be realized without some far-reaching variations on the British model.

The difficulties involved were aggravated by the immediate circumstances of the transition to independence. The new government was preoccupied with maintaining security during the transition from war to peace. The police force that it had inherited – SWAPOL, the South West Africa Police force – was close to disintegration and steeped in ignominy, but for both practical and political reasons (the policy of reconciliation) it could not simply be scrapped and replaced. It was understandable, therefore, that policy focussed almost exclusively on the reconstruction of SWAPOL into a new Namibia Police *Service* – the last word emphasized to indicate the adoption of the idea of 'policing by consent'. This primary focus on SWAPOL had costs, since if the key to policing is genuinely to enhance the sense of security of citizens, the police themselves are only one of the elements (an important one, no doubt) that make for such security. [2]

The nature of the society in question is crucial, and policing by consent means that the police must be, and be seen to be, a supplement to the community's ideas and practices about security and justice. For, contrary to the impression usually given by the media (and often promoted by the police), the police are not what stands between decent society and chaos. Wherever the matter has been studied systematically it is clear that the police at most reinforce the security that communities basically provide for themselves, a fact that Namibian history also confirms.[3] For instance, there is no evidence that crime levels fell during two weeks in August 1990 when, in response to a media-fanned panic about rising crime and police ineffectiveness, the Namibian army was sent in to patrol the streets of Windhoek, armed with semi-automatic weapons; nor, on the other hand, is there any evidence that crime levels rose in the former 'war zone' when SADF and SWATF were withdrawn in April 1989, and Koevoet was officially disbanded, even though the police presence in Ovamboland immediately following these changes was extremely limited and of very doubtful efficiency. This is not to say that no police were needed in either place; but the provision of public security in Namibia, as elsewhere, depended on the country's distinctive history and circumstances.[4]

The basic determinants of people's security, on which any viable system of policing by consent must rest, are thus to be sought in social conditions and social organization: but in the circumstances of Namibia in 1990–2 the attention of the policy makers was almost wholly focussed on the immediate future of the Namibia Police (NAMPOL), rather than on the context in which it would have to work. In fairness to these policy makers, who were working under extreme political pressure, it must be acknowledged that the wider dimensions of policing have not been studied much by historians or social scientists, either. As M. E. Brogden has commented, in an important review of the history of policing in South Africa, 'it is self-evident that policing structures did exist' in precolonial southern Africa, but 'there is no accessible account of native policing and law enforcement'.[5] The same is true of Namibia, and not just in precolonial times: no reliable account seems to exist of how security was or still is provided in any of the former 'communal areas' demarcated following the 1964 Odendaal Report. Nor does any study seem to have been made of the actual practice of policing in the urban townships, including the policing activities of the residents themselves; nothing like the structures of 'self-policing' that developed in the townships of the major South African cities (let alone the development for a brief period in the mid-1980s of so-called 'people's courts') has ever existed in Katutura or the African areas of other Namibian towns.[6] Yet given the well-justified fear and distrust of the police, townspeople were bound to look to other means for their security. A brief look at how security has been provided, or at least sought, in the 'communal areas' and townships of Namibia since independence is offered below (pages 142–6). It seems worth asking how far any of these structures and practices have been grounded in cherished and desirable features of these rural or urban communities, and how far national policing policy might support and supplement them, rather than seeking to delegitimize and eliminate them, as has always happened in South Africa in the past.[7]

The Legacy of Repression

Namibia was in effect part of South Africa from 1915 to 1990, and, as Brogden notes, 'South African policing, from the eighteenth century to the present day, had and still has an almost unique character as an army of occupation acting (mainly) on behalf of the white incomers and their descendants against the indigenous population....'[8] Both in the Cape and in the Boer republics, the first police forces tended to be strongly oriented to ensuring the security of isolated white farmers on the borders with black populations. Later, after the Anglo-Boer War, the traditions of the Irish Constabulary ('strangers policing strangers') were imported from the United Kingdom and merged with the Afrikaner commando tradition to impart a strongly military organization and ethos to the South African Police (SAP), only modestly offset by the alternative 'Metropolitan Police' model, also imported from London. Throughout its history the SAP was 'trained on military principles and ready to turn soldier when required'.[9]

With the onset of industrial capitalism following the discovery of gold on the Rand, the defence of Boer values and culture against those of new immigrants, white as well as black, had also become an important ideological component of Afrikaner policing, which was transmitted to the SAP when Afrikaners and Afrikaans became dominant in it from the 1930s onwards. The main target of the SAP's endemic racism, however, remained the black population, to whose repression its military ethos and organization had always been mainly directed.

Namibia's experience as the main cockpit of the struggle unleashed by P. W. Botha's 'total strategy' in 1977 was thus part of a long tradition of border areas subjected to South African policing.[10] The SAP, of course, was directly involved. Even after the creation of SWAPOL as a formally separate police force in 1980, 'SWAPOL was never an independent force.... During the war you had only to pick up the phone to get more police – a busload or a planeload would arrive. SAP ran SWAPOL and at no time was SWAPOL capable of being an independent force.'[11] Nor was the police force's mutation into a primarily political-intelligence and counter-insurgency agency, within a total strategy directed mainly by SADF commanders, an altogether radical change, either for its officers or for the black population of Namibia. What was distinctive was only the intensity of the military focus from 1978 onwards.

The militarization of Namibian society had one clear effect on policing: it finally ended any pretence that the police upheld the rule of law. Of course the rule of law is always upheld unevenly, even by the most consent-based police forces. There are always sections of society who are considered 'police property', people whom the dominant powers of society leave the police to deal with and 'turn a blind eye to the manner in which this is done'.[12] The 'inhibiting rules' which limit the very wide latitude given to the police by the law in their dealings with the rest of society essentially do not apply when dealing with 'police property'.[13] But whereas in developed capitalist societies 'police property' comprises powerless minorities such as 'vagrants, skid row alcoholics, the unemployed or casually employed residuum, youth adopting a deviant cultural style, gays, prostitutes and radical political organizations', in Namibia it covered most of the black population, making up some 83 per cent of the total. For the majority, the police became solely and exclusively an instrument of repression.

Although SWAPO was a legal organization, harassment and arrest of its activists became so standard that no normal political life was possible for anyone identified with it. Strikers and political protesters of any kind were routinely dispersed with teargas and violence. Moreover, in this situation officers were less likely to be promoted for sterling work in crime detection than for intelligence work in the Security Branch.[14] The force's interest in and capacity for providing security to the black population was minimal.

Most of the literature on the use of terror during the war emphasizes atrocities by the armed forces, and by Koevoet.[15] This emphasis overlooks the extent to which SWAPOL as a whole became a lawless repressive force. By 1987–8 69 per cent of SWAPOL's budget was allocated to 'special duties' – paramilitary or counter-insurgency activity, including Koevoet – compared with 23 per cent devoted to crime prevention.[16] Prisoners suspected of having knowledge of PLAN activities were routinely beaten or tortured (rooms fitted with torture equipment were evidently so normal a feature of the larger police stations that in some cases no one bothered to remove the evidence, and two of them were identified and photographed by lawyers with search warrants acting for the Legal Assistance Centre during the transition to independence).[17]

In the south – in areas with few Ovambo migrant workers, especially Nama areas before 1976, when the Nama chiefs aligned themselves with SWAPO, and especially at police stations under commanders with long service – police treatment of Africans could still be more or less correct, within the arbitrary and racist assumptions of apartheid. But in the rest of the country, where the vast majority of people lived, the police became very much a part of the apparatus of repression. This story needs to be told, because unless it is understood it is hardly possible to understand public attitudes towards the police in the post-independence era.

In the space available here all that can be done is to cite one incident that came to light almost by accident in the course of the work of the O'Linn Commission on the Prevention and Combating of Election Malpractices during the pre-independence elections.[18] On 6 June 1989 five policemen came to the room of a Mr Josiah Pineas in Katutura's Single Quarters and questioned another occupant of the room, Mr Paulus Ndume, about a radio he had bought from a man called Abson. Being satisfied that the radio he had was not the stolen radio they were looking for (Abson had come with them and confirmed this) the police nonetheless took it away and told Ndume and Pineas to come to the Windhoek charge office next day to collect it. At the station, instead of giving back the radio, the police bound and blindfolded the two men, and repeatedly tortured them.

> He [Pineas] was ordered to sit on the floor with his knees bent and with his arms on the outside of his knees. A rod of iron or a similar object was then pushed between his arms and his knees. He was lifted from the floor and suspended in the air in such a manner that he hung upside down with the whole weight of his body on his arms pressing down on this rod of iron or similar object. Water was then thrown onto his face, something was attached to one of his arms and he was then shocked and asked about the stolen radio.[19]

> This was repeated four times. 'The police also asked him about his affiliations with SWAPO. He denied any affiliation to SWAPO because he was afraid.'

> After the fourth 'session' he was released. A white policemen then hit him against his chest with a clenched fist as a result of which he fell to the floor. He was then made to lie on his back and this white policeman twice stepped on his chest saying something in Afrikaans which he could not understand.

Ndume was tortured in the same way. Doctors' evidence and the consistency of the victims' evidence convinced the Commission that they had been tortured as they described. The Commission felt unable to pursue the matter further because no contravention of the electoral law had been demonstrated; it could only request the Commissioner of SWAPOL to 'institute a proper investigation on an urgent basis to attempt to identify the policemen involved'. No charges were brought.

This case is interesting because it indicates the casual and seemingly routine use of brutality towards people whom there were no grounds to suspect of having committed any crime – but who were Ovambos. This was SWAPOL's chief legacy to the issue of policing after independence.[20]

In his closing remarks at the Commission's last hearing Mr O'Linn defined the problem of policing in Namibia as one of 'rotten apples' (albeit in rather large quantities): 'it is now overdue to separate the good or potentially good policemen from the others and to train sufficient policemen to be objective and competent investigators, with imagination, dedication and objectivity', something which had been neglected 'during the war years'. Such training was therefore 'one of the most urgent problems to be given attention to in any new scheme for a new police force on which the whole community can rely and of which the whole community can be proud'.[21] This was surely to expect too much of training. In any case, there was no disputing the fact that, although SWAPOL remained in control during the transition to independence, it could not survive into an independent Namibia. Many of its personnel, identified as they were with repressive violence (and in most cases being members of the SAP, only seconded to SWAPOL), left the country. There was a real rupture in policing. Innovation became not only possible but necessary. The question was, how far would it exploit the potential that existed for creative changes that would enhance security in the particular circumstances of Namibia?

The Transition, 1990–2

Accurate statistics are hard to come by, but the staffing situation inherited from SWAPOL at independence seems to have been approximately as follows.[22] The official complement was 6,000 police officers, a nominal figure representing the total which South Africa was permitted to have during the transition to independence, and which allowed, in effect, for large numbers of the paramilitary Koevoet to be 'integrated' into the regular police.[23] The actual number of trained policemen in SWAPOL had never been more than about 4,000, of whom a large proportion were still seconded from the SAP after SWAPOL became an independent force. Virtually all of the seconded officers, and large numbers of white (and some non-white) SWAPOL officers, left Namibia at independence. By April 1990 there were no more than 1,558 trained police officers, of whom only 751 were constables – a small and extremely 'top-heavy' trained force.[24] There were 302 Student Constables – people with a Standard Eight education who were either in basic training or temporarily attached to police stations, waiting to go for basic training. There were also 1,717 Special Constables who were daily-paid personnel, previously used for a wide variety of support functions, and having the authority of police officers while on duty, but not trained as police officers (and normally lacking the requisite education to be trained).

Even for Namibia's small population in less disturbed conditions, this force would probably have been inadequate, and yet the number of trained officers leaving the service continued at a high level:[25] the SAP appeared willing to accept police officers from Namibia at much higher salaries (or higher ranks) and even in mid-1991 NAMPOL was said to be losing about 20 officers a month.[26] Some relief was to be had by employing police officers trained by SWAPO in exile (mainly in Tanzania): by mid-1991 about 600 such officers, including about 100 above the rank of constable, had been recruited. New recruits, who were supposed to have a Standard Eight education or its equivalent, were also taken on and given a special programme of basic training that was designed and implemented with the assistance of a team of British police trainers, lasting only three months and without the military focus and style of the former six-month SWAPOL basic training courses.[27]

At the same time the new SWAPO government was under a lot of pressure to give employment to ex-combatants. Former PLAN fighters expected that SWAPO would provide them with jobs, while the danger presented by large numbers of unemployed ex-soldiers from the SWATF battalions and ex-members of Koevoet was also obvious.[28] Most of the ex-SWAPOL police officers in NAMPOL looked favourably on ex-SWATF and ex-Koevoet personnel as recruits, while the government and its northern supporters reasonably expected that the ex-PLAN combatants would be a major source for redressing the ethnic imbalance in the police force (at independence only 125 permanent members of SWAPOL, or 6 per cent of the total, were Ovambo, and only one of these was a commissioned officer). Moreover, following the disbandment of Koevoet in October 1989 the South Africans had undertaken a last-minute recruitment drive, with the evident hope of filling as many as possible of the vacancies thus created within the permitted establishment of SWAPOL with new people willing to work with them. This manoeuvre was eventually confronted by the UN, however, and converted into the first step towards integrating ex-combatants from both sides into the police: 68 former PLAN members and 90 former SWAPOL Special Constables were recruited for a four-week training course and then posted to Ovambo just before independence.[29]

After independence this model was adopted for further recruitment, but with the balance strongly the other way round. A hundred 'SWAPO members' were recruited and sent to Zambia for training soon after independence, and taken on as members of NAMPOL when they returned in October 1990; similarly a further 60 were sent after independence for training in Tanzania.[30] Large numbers of ex-PLAN combatants, most of them possessing equivalents, at best, to the Standard Eight entry qualification, were also included in the new intake of some 500 Student Constables recruited into the permanent force and given basic training in 1990–1; and new Presidential and Ministerial (or 'Home') Guard units were established to protect the President, ministers and public places, and recruited entirely from ex-PLAN combatants. In the case of the Presidential Guard the personnel concerned were former PLAN security personnel who had been doing the same work in exile.[31] A large additional recruitment of ex-PLAN personnel into the force of Special Constables also occurred – of the order of 1,000–1,500 men and a few women – and a further 1,500 men, consisting mainly of former PLAN fighters but also including ex-SWATF troops, were rapidly formed into a special force of Border Guards, to control the border between Caprivi and Angola until a new National Defence Force had been formed to take over the task of guarding Namibia's borders where serious security risks still existed.

The Border Guards, logistically under the command of the police, were intended to be, and eventually were, incorporated into the Namibian Defence Force (NDF) once it was in a position to take over responsibility for border defence. Before this could happen, however, they had become the focus of intense controversy. Lacking a clear command structure under NAMPOL, with indeterminate authority and using forceful methods learned in the war, they set themselves up as an occupying force in Kavango and Caprivi (the sector of the border facing the UNITA-controlled part of Angola), establishing roadblocks, conducting house searches for arms, and generally intimidating the civilian population, particularly anyone seen as anti-SWAPO.[32] Eventually, after a number of highly-publicized incidents affecting white residents and tourists, the Border Guards were withdrawn in September 1990, and later integrated into the NDF.

Adverse public reactions were probably also a factor in the transfer of the Presidential Guard from the police to the NDF. Its high-handed treatment of the public, especially in clearing the way for the presidential motorcade in its periodic transits through Windhoek and other centres, had likewise attracted a lot of adverse comment.[33] This left NAMPOL with a force composed as follows:[34]

Rank	July 1991	July 1992
Student Constables	219	141
Constables	1,070	1,143
Sergeants	518	458
Warrant Officers	238	238
Inspectors	129	117
Chief Inspectors	43	42
Senior officers[35]	30	27
Total	2,247	2,166

By July 1992 there were also roughly 2,300 Protection Officers (as the Special Constables had now been redesignated), down from 2,400 a year earlier. With 72 police stations to be staffed, and general administration and specialist services to be provided, it is obvious that a force of roughly 2,000 non-commissioned officers could not begin to provide adequate patrols, so that most of the Protection Officers (those not in the specialized Ministerial or Home Guard unit, or the Task Force) were in fact used for law enforcement duties, although most of them had not been trained for this work. In addition, significant numbers of the recently recruited constables, and some student constables, did not have the equivalent of Standard Eight (eight years of education). Some were not fully literate, and so could not perform the essential routine work of taking evidence and compiling 'dockets';[36] while many of those who could had received only three months' basic training and lacked experience, as did many of those trained in exile (some had police experience in Tanzania or elsewhere, but most had served, if at all, in SWAPO camps in Angola or Zambia, in conditions very different from those of normal police work).[37]

Thus, in terms of the scale and quality of its human resources alone, NAMPOL was faced with inevitable difficulties. An impression of what this meant to officers in charge of the police immediately after independence is given in the following comments by the (white) commander of a large police station in the north, made in August 1990:

> Only four policemen in the charge room are permanent members [of the police service, as opposed to untrained and daily-paid Special Constables]. There is one sergeant, one female inspector trained in Tanzania – 17 in all are permanent, out of a total complement of 140 – plus six policewomen trained in Tanzania, of whom two are literate. Perhaps 20 of the Special Constables are literate. One of the permanent members was trained in 1988 – he is very young, with not much experience. Then there are two Student Constables (pre-training). There are two women in the charge office who speak only Oshivambo. If you ask them to write something down they do it very, very slowly.... Some of the Special Constables are not educated but very bright, they can become good policemen.... Many Special Constables are not doing police work but are caretakers, maintenance [workers], etc. Seven sergeants share the work of being on patrol, supervising four patrols of four Special Constables in each of the four areas of my district. Their dealing with the public is OK. They speak Oshivambo and that helps. But the charge office work is a huge problem....[38]

The decision to convert all the special constables into a permanent body of Protection Officers (POs) constituting, in mid-1991, 51 per cent of the police service, was intended to meet several needs: to create an immediate *masse de manoeuvre* of people with at least some acquaintance with police practices, and some relevant skills;[39] to improve their morale by giving them security and pension rights; while clearly distinguishing them from trained police officers by their title. In effect, they became a sort of assistant police officer. Official policy was to upgrade those with the necessary educational qualifications (Standard Eight or its equivalent) by recruiting them for training as Student Constables; and to offer the others on-the-job training and classes in English, so that those with the necessary ability could in due course also be upgraded into Student Constables. For the rest, in the words of the Minister of Home Affairs, Hifikepunya Pohamba:

> We will not dismiss them. We will keep them. They will gradually get their pensions. We will not *replace* the Protection Officers either. We will appoint only people who can be trained as constables from now on. There are many difficulties. It *is* very difficult. But my aim is to leave this Ministry having created a fully professional service. After another four years.... I hope we will be well on the way to this. In fifteen years it should be completed.[40]

One of the biggest difficulties was the feeling on the part of many Protection Officers that they were being excluded unfairly from the ranks of police constables because they were ex-PLAN combatants (ex-PLAN personnel constituted the overwhelming majority of POs by 1991). They tended to see the Standard Eight qualification as a politically inspired barrier to becoming regular police officers, enforced by a still overwhelmingly white ex-SWAPOL cadre of senior officers who had spent their professional lives fighting them. According to Commissioner Eimbeck, some POs had refused to wear the distinctive red berets initially allocated to them, saying that these were badges of illiteracy. A similar problem, according to him, had also arisen with ex-PLAN combatants recruited into the Special Unit (the police paramilitary special duties and crowd control force), who had on one occasion refused to hand in their weapons when going off duty.

On the other side of the coin was the reluctance of many ex-SWAPOL officers to accept and respect ex-PLAN personnel, or many of the SWAPO-trained constables or, indeed, all former exiles who were now appointed as commissioned officers alongside – or even over – them.[41] Time and personal contact might overcome some of the resistance based on prejudice, and the continued departure of ex-SWAPOL personnel would remove many of the most prejudiced. The most serious problem was perhaps the disinclination of many ex-SWAPOL officers to throw themselves into serious on-the-job training by example. Many professed themselves alienated and frustrated. The unrealistic career expectations engendered by the war years were now replaced by the fear that further promotion for whites was impossible.[42] At some police stations commissioned officers declined to be concerned with the routine work of patrolling and Charge Office duties where the essential work of on-the-job training needed to be done.[43] On the other hand there were some ex-SWAPOL officers who were willing to accept the implications of creating a new kind of police force or service, including compromises with past standards, and the sacrifice of career expectations.

Only time would show how far the combination of personnel changes, training, management reforms and public education would overcome these problems, besides which most of the others appeared relatively unimportant, and often somewhat ambiguous. For instance there was a controversy about whether police should be armed. For about a year the policy was to insist on unarmed police patrolling, to symbolize the break with SWAPOL – but with large numbers of weapons, including automatics, circulating in post-war Namibia, and crimes involving firearms not uncommon, the government bowed to police pressure and in mid-1991 authorized NAMPOL members to carry side arms while on duty. No obvious negative reaction occurred.

Although former SWAPOL officers were often very critical of the quality of officers trained in exile, most had been trained in Tanzania, where the basic training programme was thought by the acting head of the Namibian Police Training College to be more demanding than that given in Namibia.[44] Undoubtedly the 'returnee' officers included some of limited quality, in that they lacked education or experience – including some who for political reasons had to be given relatively senior positions in NAMPOL at the outset. But it was not obvious that this was more true of them than of their ex-SWAPOL colleagues, and some of the senior returnees were talented officers of obvious leadership calibre.

Moreover, against their relative lack of experience had to be set the fact that nearly all of them spoke, or at least understood, Oshivambo, which after twenty years of policing the north was spoken by hardly any ex-SWAPOL officers, other than the handful of Ovambos in the force, in spite of the fact that it is the first language of the majority of the population. In addition, returnee officers typically spoke more fluent English, the newly proclaimed official language, than many ex-SWAPOL officers, whose working language had always been Afrikaans. And, finally, it was not among the returnee officers that police misdemeanours or corruption presented a serious problem in the immediate post-independence years.[45] Nor was it from them that the government had any fears about police complicity in treasonable activities.[46]

Quick solutions were not to be expected to the problems involved in integrating the diverse elements within NAMPOL;[47] in stabilizing its senior officer cadre; and in upgrading the technical competence of its members, from their proficiency in English and the preparation of 'dockets' capable of supporting prosecutions in the most straightforward of cases, to the development of investigative skills and sound management practices. Those responsible for trying to overcome the problems could be forgiven for oscillating between euphoria and pessimism, as tended to occur. For the foreseeable future NAMPOL was unlikely to be able to do more than deal with the most serious crimes, such as murder or treason; afford essential protection to Ministers; and maintain a somewhat patchy presence in support of the community's own efforts to combat all other crimes.

The progress made by mid-1991 should not be minimized, however. In the first place, people were less afraid of NAMPOL, and it was no longer automatically perceived as anti-social for an Oshivambo-speaker to join the police ranks, or for a crime victim to appeal for police help, as had been the case in the north, and in Katutura and most urban areas, under SWAPOL. People criticized NAMPOL more for incompetence than for brutality or arrogance. Cases of police violence were still occasionally reported, but the admittedly scanty evidence suggests that by mid-1991 the use of violence, which had been routine in SWAPOL, was not the rule in NAMPOL. A survey of Magistrates' Courts in December 1990 and January 1991, in which 37 defendants were explicitly asked about their treatment by the police, reported allegations of assault or the use of excessive force by the police by seven of the accused, and an alleged use of torture by an eighth.[48] The best judgement would seem to be that NAMPOL had substantially broken with its SWAPOL past in this respect, but that a serious and continuing effort would be required, by the Minister of Home Affairs, the Attorney General, senior police officers, the courts, the media and members of the public, before a reliable service committed to the use of minimum force, the rule of law, impartiality and other aspects of 'policing by consent' could be expected to emerge.

Policing and Personal Security: the Social Context

While the authorities grappled with the internal problems of the police, less attention was given to the wider determinants of security. This is not to say that everyone concerned was unaware of the significance of the social context, or of the limitations of policing as a means of making people secure. Commissioner Siggi Eimbeck, NAMPOL's official spokesperson and the senior officer responsible for relations with the public, expressed the reality well when he said: 'The police must be the *pivotal point* for all crime prevention activities', but 'the public must be the main preventers of crime'.[49]

His efforts in this direction included the establishment of a Police Public Relations Advisory Council (PPRAC), composed of representatives of various sectors of civic life, appointed by the Minister of Home Affairs and meeting monthly in Windhoek: and Police Public Relations Committees at the local level in the main urban areas elsewhere. By March 1991 the PPRAC consisted of 21 members of the public and the three NAMPOL Regional Commissioners, meeting monthly under Eimbeck's chairmanship. It was not a representative body either politically or socially, being strongly biased towards the official and still heavily white establishment;[50] the absence, until 1992, of elected local government bodies was a general problem for any policy of policing by consent. The PPR Committee for Katutura was probably more representative of its constituency and was functioning, but elsewhere the PPR Committee initiative seemed to have petered out.[51] The minutes of the PPRAC and the Katutura Committee show that they were effective communication channels, at least in letting a few senior police officers hear about the Windhoek public's perceptions and needs, and in giving a group of Windhoek opinion leaders better insight into the police's current policies and problems. It is less clear that in the first year of its operation the PPR structure had produced many tangible benefits, although it may have contributed to such improvements as did occur. Perhaps its chief value lay in its mere existence, in symbolizing NAMPOL's wish at least to be seen as being at the service of the public.

The main limitation of the PPRAC idea was that it was, in the end, a police initiative, aimed at fulfilling police objectives, legitimate though these were; and so it had two serious defects. First, it was not democratically structured, so that its civilian members had no mandate; and second, it did not include some other elements that are relevant to the creation of genuine security.

For instance, although there was a representative of Windhoek Municipality – responsible for street lighting, the absence of which was critical for security in large parts of Katutura – there was no one from the Post Office, which was responsible for telephones, the absence of which in the same parts of Katutura was equally critical. Similarly, there was no representative of the Ministry of Justice, with responsibility for the magistrates' courts, whose efficiency was crucial for crime control throughout the country; nor of the office of the Attorney General, who was responsible for the no less crucial efficiency of the state prosecutors. The absence of representatives of these units of the state meant that the true parameters of the security problem, of which the police can only ever be at best a 'pivotal point', could not be addressed adequately by the PPRAC. Its purely advisory status, moreover, and its unrepresentative nature, were bound in any case to limit its efficacy. A more representative body with a wider definition of the problem might have proved a source of innovative and creative thinking, through which genuine security might have been significantly enhanced, greatly altering the burden placed on the police.

For, speaking generally, it would not be a great exaggeration to say that for people living in the so-called communal areas of the countryside neither the traditional court system nor the system of magistrates' courts offered any reliable redress. The problem of the traditional courts is discussed again briefly below: the essential point about them was that they had become in most areas irredeemably partial, if not venal. The magistrates' courts, on the other hand, were usually very remote – for instance, before 1991 there was only one magistrate's court, at Ondangua, for the whole of Ovambo country – and the personal costs to complainants and other witnesses of attending these courts, frequently on numerous successive occasions when the case was repeatedly postponed, could be literally unbearable.[52] The Ministry of Justice, to its credit, pushed ahead after independence, in the face of considerable difficulty, with the appointment of large numbers of new magistrates – a total of 24 new magistrates was envisaged, an increase of 75 per cent – and the establishment of new courts; but no systematic enquiry seems to have been undertaken into possible ways of reducing the number of court appearances of witnesses and complainants so as to make the system more responsive to the real security interests of the rural public.[53]

Another problem was the lack of adequately trained prosecutors. The combination of inadequately prepared 'dockets' – police records of the evidence – and insufficiently trained prosecutors resulted in a high proportion of the delays, and frequently in failures to convict, even in cases where everyone concerned knew a conviction was justified. Of course the involvement of the Attorney General's office in a wider debate about security might not have enhanced the efficacy of the magistrates' courts much in the short run, but it might have led to new thinking about the trade-offs to be made between securing watertight convictions – the normal and proper concern of the Attorney General – and other means of helping to protect citizens against crime, for instance by the introduction of some form of plea bargaining, or by the use of specially selected police officers as prosecutors for minor offences, and so on.

A related issue concerns the relative roles of punishment and compensation in criminal cases. Provision exists under the criminal law for compensating the victims of crime, but it is rarely used; yet for many crimes (especially stock theft, but also others) it is often compensation more than punishment of the culprit that people want, and this was the second main reason usually given (besides accessibility and speed) why people in rural areas continued to turn to the unsatisfactory 'traditional' courts, where compensation was the standard result of a finding of guilt. In 1991 the Law Reform Commission did have the introduction of compensation on its agenda, but it was not clear if the potential gain which quick action on this issue might bring to many people's security, especially in rural areas, was widely appreciated.[54]

A broader perspective on policing would also need to look at the so-called traditional judicial system generally. In theory the precolonial justice systems in Namibia used to afford accessible, speedy justice, with the power to give remedies that enjoyed general approval within the community. In reality the system put in place by the South Africans was at best a colonial modification of the traditional justice systems, and by independence was far gone in decay. Although the rate of decline of this system varied from place to place, by 1991 for many people in many rural areas it could no longer be relied on. Part of the problem was the dubious legality of the so-called traditional system:[55] as people became more aware of their rights, the legitimacy of the traditional courts was brought increasingly into question.[56] More fundamentally, however, the politicization of the so-called traditional authorities by the South African colonial authorities resulted in a drastic loss of perceived impartiality. A SWAPO supporter would be very reluctant to have his or her case heard by a headman who was a DTA appointee (or vice versa).

More generally still, disputes about the claims of particular 'traditional' leaders, and their lack of a popular base, have eroded their legitimacy in an age of increasing emphasis on democracy. They also lack any formal training as judges, so that their capacity to follow any rules of evidence or due process is often limited, even when acting in councils. Political, financial and family influence have come to be widely seen as crucial assets in cases before traditional courts.

For all these reasons fewer and fewer people look to the traditional court system. In the south, even cases of stock theft are more and more taken to the police and the magistrates' courts, even though no useful compensation can be expected from this. One rural development worker with long experience in the south summed it up as follows:

> Today hardly anyone [in the Gibeon area] uses the traditional system. It is confused. The tendency is towards anarchy. People don't take theft cases anywhere. The police always say, you must bring the evidence. People go into a kraal, and seize back what they think is theirs. Women farmers especially feel vulnerable. People prefer the police to the traditional courts, but neither is popular.[57]

Thus the security of rural people is not really protected by either system. Most lawyers, especially those concerned with civil liberties, favour removing all criminal jurisdiction from the traditional courts. However, even an expanded magistrates' court system, and a gradually improving police service, cannot provide the sort of quick, locally knowledgeable justice which in theory could be provided by a 'lay' (if not necessarily 'traditional') system of popular local courts. Moreover, if the traditional courts lack impartiality and due process, can it be satisfactory to leave them still hearing civil cases?

It is not obvious why the rural majority should not have a system capable of providing them with reasonably effective and impartial justice at the local level: why, for instance, there could not be a local judicial structure of adjudicators or judges, distinct from the executive structure of chiefs and headmen, appointed and given a modicum of training by the state, assisted by lay assessors, and supervised by the magistrates' courts or some other body (just as the magistrates' courts are supervised by the High Court). The use of such a system by aggrieved persons in criminal matters could be voluntary, with the magistrates' courts as an alternative. The relation of the police service to such a system would need to be defined (this is needed, in any case, in relation to the existing traditional system); and undoubtedly any such development would pose problems. The question that needs to be answered, however, is whether the prevailing absence of any effective system of justice in rural areas has not been a worse problem, and one which has played a part in making the police appear largely irrelevant to the security needs of the majority of the population.

The situation in the urban areas is very different. There, the problems of policing are not essentially different from those of any other society at an early stage of capitalist development, with acute inequalities of wealth and incomes, great absolute poverty, high levels of unemployment, chronic overcrowding and homelessness, and so on, compounded by the effects of the war such as continual in-migration from depressed rural areas and a high incidence of women single parents, plus poor or non-existent social services, from sewerage to social security.[58]

Given the apartheid town planning of all Namibian urban areas, at least three quite different kinds of security situation arise in them. The white-owned central business district primarily presents a problem of petty offences by individuals such as shoplifting and bag-snatching, and the risk of more serious robbery or burglary of business premises by more professional criminals. The formerly white suburbs, now increasingly desegregated but retaining their class character, are chiefly vulnerable to housebreaking. Crimes against persons have been very rare in either of these areas. Crimes against property are generally supposed to have risen since independence – insurance companies increased their premiums and private security firms expanded – but the evidence on crime levels is weak and the safest guess would seem to be that a more or less 'normal' incidence of crime, for the kind of society Namibia had become, was rather quickly established.[59]

A quite different set of problems was presented by the non-white 'townships', especially Katutura, at an estimated 80,000 the largest and most complex urban concentration in the country.[60] Here the homeless, poor, orphaned and unemployed are concentrated, especially in certain districts such as the Single Quarters and Hakahana (one of the most remote and soulless districts, created as a receptacle for the men of the former single men's compound). In Katutura crimes against property are high, and crimes against persons are frequent, and in some areas endemic. There is perhaps nothing new in this situation, though it is generally felt to have become worse since independence. Whether this was true or not, the general ineffectiveness of the police, and the perceived unwillingness of most ex-SWAPOL officers to act as true protectors of the public in Katutura, became a critical issue.

'There is no security in Katutura': with these words Tyappa Namutewa, crime reporter for the *Namibian* and a Katutura resident, summed up the prevailing view:

Old SWAPOL [officers] should be posted elsewhere – you never trust those who abused their power in the past. Quite a few are left. These police [officers] won't do anything. Thieves can be arrested and be released next day. Some of the old police [officers] want to discredit the government. People think that, and I agree. They are all anti-SWAPO.[61]

Another constant complaint of Katutura residents was that the police offered them no protection against retaliation by criminals whom they identified. When criminals identified by members of the public were arrested, people felt, they were often almost immediately released again, placing those who had identified them at serious risk. This could be because the police were genuinely convinced of the innocence of those arrested, or because they saw no chance of proving their guilt (or lacked the resources to try to do so), or because they were incompetent, or even because they were friendly with the alleged culprits. Whatever the cause, it was seen as making collaboration with the police too risky.

In evaluating the question of security, the conditions of daily life of most residents of Katutura need to be kept in mind The average household size in 1990 was 7.8, most houses having at most two very small bedrooms. Most adults were tenants of others, usually sharing rooms, with little or no privacy. Consequently, criminal activities could rarely be concealed. 'Many people are aware that they have a criminal renting a room in their house, bringing stolen goods there. But they don't want to report them, maybe because of money (they may be paid off), [but also] from fear of being killed in retaliation – that's why people are afraid to give evidence.'[62] The existence of criminal groups or gangs aggravates the problem, so long as there is no effective police counter-force, as other gang members can take reprisals on informants if one of their colleagues is arrested.[63]

In response to Katutura's distinctive law and order problem the authorities stressed 'self-policing', and the Minister for Home Affairs called on citizens to form self-policing committees. However this revealed some basic differences. SWAPO organized a 'People's Police' in Katutura's Single Quarters: the government asked it to disband. Elsewhere in Katutura, and especially in Wanaheda and Soweto, committees were also formed, again mainly on the initiative of SWAPO activists, and once again the police viewed the result with considerable aversion: ostensibly because policing should be non-political, and these were more or less openly SWAPO groups, but also because of the antipathy that existed towards SWAPO on the part of the ex-SWAPOL police officers.

The result was that the police were not inclined to respond to calls from these groups, and eventually this led to people taking the law into their own hands and killing a number of alleged murderers by beating and stoning.[64] Commissioner Eimbeck issued a denunciation of these actions, which for their part none of the Wanaheda residents were pleased with, either.[65] The question was whether the police's attitude to the 'political' committees was defensible: the committees were based on localities, after all, and in Katutura every locality tends to have a party political character, thanks to the colonial regime's original policy of housing blacks in separate ethnic quarters. It remained unclear whether the allegation that two successive police officers had refused to act on the information given them, which was said to have led to frustration and eventually to two of the stonings, had been investigated. Most people in Katutura believed this allegation was true.

In contrast with its cold-shouldering of the committees, NAMPOL (in the person of Commissioner Eimbeck) fostered the establishment in the Single Quarters (a notoriously crime-ridden section of Katutura, consisting of desperately overcrowded single room accommodation) of a group of 86 Police Reservists, who were sworn in at a ceremony in June 1991.[66] These were volunteers, who undertook to do a minimum of eight hours per month of police duties under the supervision of a regular police officer, after receiving some training from existing Reservists at the Police Training College.

The hope was that they would feel confident enough, as a result of their numbers and their official membership of the police service, to stand up to the criminal elements. Commissioner Eimbeck expressed it thus:

> Most of them [the new Reservists in the Single Quarters] are shebeen owners. Many have a criminal record, but they are not habitual criminals. Now we have eighty, there is safety in numbers.... We must also identify the leaders, equip them with radios: and they live there, they are not intruders. Eventually they will be used to clean out the Single Quarters of all illegal activities – including shebeens! [67]

In effect, two different conceptions of the way policing should be grounded in the urban community were in conflict here, a conflict reflected in the somewhat contradictory roles played by SWAPO. On the one hand, as a party, it was responsible for the initiative that led to the emergence of the self-policing committees; on the other, as the government, it was now also responsible for NAMPOL and Commissioner Eimbeck's reservists. Each approach involved distinctive risks: in the case of the committees, the risk that they might become party-political vigilante organizations, tending to take the law into their own hands; in the case of the Reservists, the risk that they might become police-supported vigilantes, with the same tendency to abuse. The 'people's courts' that were established in many South African townships in 1984 illustrate the first of these risks, and the *Kitskonstabels* and police-backed vigilantes in the townships of South Africa generally illustrate the second.[68]

To an outside observer it was not obvious that the situation really called for either of these risks to be accepted. It seemed rather that some of the quite modest measures discussed above – to improve the amenities of Katutura and other townships, and to adopt a collaborative approach to the residents in setting and implementing policing policy – could significantly improve real security, and significantly improve the prospects of 'policing by consent'.

Notes

1. Reiner, *The Politics of the Police* (Sussex: Wheatsheaf Books, 1985), pp. 51–61.
2. On this point see also S. Spitzer, 'Security and control in capitalist societies: the fetishism of security and the secret thereof', in L. Lowman *et al.* (eds), *Transcarceration: Essays in the Sociology of Social Control* (Aldershot: Gower, 1987), pp. 43–58.
3. Reiner, *op. cit.* pp. 118 and 121. Reiner concludes soberly that 'the police [in Britain] were part of a process which made cities less violent, crime-ridden and disorderly during the course of the nineteenth century. The precise contribution of the police to this, compared with more general processes of social pacification, is hard to pinpoint exactly, but it is probable that they were a significant factor' (pp. 116–17).
4. In 1990 a former SWAPOL officer told a researcher in Ovamboland that before the period of armed struggle the work of the police (when they were called in there from the police zone to the south) had been very easy: 'in nine cases out of ten an officer called to the scene of a crime would find all the witnesses waiting to see him, together with the culprit' (personal communication from Chris Tapscott). From what has been said above, it can be appreciated that this is not a comment on the naïvety of the Ovambo, however it may have been intended, but a statement of the fundamental truth about policing by consent everywhere. The police's basic function is to act as agents for applying state sanctions to people the community wants dealt with.
5. M. E. Brogden, 'The origins of the South African Police – institutional versus structural approaches', in T. W. Bennett *et al.* (eds), *Acta Juridica* (Cape Town, 1985), p. 11.
6. See W. Scharf, 'Community policing in South Africa', in Bennett *et al.* (eds), *op. cit.*, pp. 206–33. Of course, the SAP only sought to delegitimize and eliminate community police agencies it did not control. *Kitskonstabels* and vigilantes were extensions of the SAP, not expressions of community self-policing.
7. Brogden, *op. cit.*, pp. 11–12.

8. *Ibid.*, p. 3.
9. R. F. Curry, cited in *ibid.*, p. 13.
10. For this period of South African policing see D. Hansson, 'Changes in counter-revolutionary state strategy in the decade 1979 to 1989', in D. Hansson and D. Van Zyl Smit, *Towards Justice? Crime and State Control in South Africa* (Cape Town: Oxford University Press, 1990), pp. 28–62; and A. Prior, 'The South African Police and the counter-revolution of 1985–87', in Bennett *et al.*, *op. cit.*, pp. 189–205.
11. Chief Inspector Derek Brune, interview, 17 August 1990.
12. Reiner, *op. cit.*, p. 95.
13. For the distinction between the police's 'working rules' (the actual guiding principles of police work), the externally imposed 'inhibiting rules' which they have to take into account, and the 'presentation rules' which are appealed to for public relations purposes, see Reiner, citing the Policy Studies Institute's research on the Metropolitan Police, *op. cit.*, p. 86.
14. Chief Inspector Brune, *op. cit.*
15. See for example, Barbara Konig, *Namibia: the Ravages of War* (London: International Defence and Aid Fund, 1982), Chapter 5. Elsewhere the police are mentioned – for example in *Namibia: the Facts* (London: IDAF 1980), Chapter 8 – but even in such sources it is the special counter-insurgency police units that are cited, and, of course, Koevoet. On Koevoet, see the very detailed report by M. Hinz and N. G. Leuven-Lachinski, *Koevoet versus Namibia: Report of a Human Rights Mission to Namibia on Behalf of the Working Group Kairos* (1990). (I am indebted to Inspector Joe Healy of the RCMP for this document.) Some details of South African Police and SWAPOL violence are also given in the careful documentation by David Soggot, *Namibia, the Violent Heritage* (London: Rex Collings, 1986), although here, too, the worst cases tend to involve SADF or SWATF.
16. SWAPOL *Annual Report*, 1987–8. The previous year the share taken by 'special duties' was 72 per cent. These reports, though generally as uninformative as possible, are also coloured by the desire to show achievements and win support. They strongly emphasize the counter-insurgency function and list the numbers of policemen killed, which rose as follows until 1986–7, after which the item was omitted: 1981–2 (the first SWAPOL *Annual Report*), 8: 1982–3, 9; 1983–4, 12; 1984–5, 35; 1985–6, 27; 1986–7, 26. From 1985–6 (when Koevoet was officially transferred to SWAPOL from SAP) onwards the numbers of 'terrorists' killed or 'eliminated' were also given as: 1985–6, 358; 1986–7, 498; 1987–8, 259.
17. Specially darkened rooms with torture equipment were found at the back of the Walvis Bay police complex on 25 August 1989 and also at the Katima Mulilo police station in Caprivi on 27 January 1990 (interview with Andrew Corbett of the Legal Assistance Centre, 1 July 1991). Corbett believed that similar premises still existed at other police stations in independent Namibia.
18. Some court cases were brought against the police for abuse of power during the war years, and a great deal of evidence from the mid-1980s onwards exists in the files of the Legal Assistance Centre in Windhoek. More than 200 complaints were made to the O'Linn Commission. Most of them were abandoned but several dozen received extensive investigation, and the most important of these were heard under the chairmanship of the forthright Mr (later Judge) O'Linn. Some of them tell a great deal about police practices and attitudes during the war years. Mr O'Linn remarked in his last finding (the Commission's mandate lapsed, with the successful outcome of the elections, on 17 November 1989) that 'there were still many policemen who continued with their duties in an exemplary manner, notwithstanding a shortage of manpower, extreme pressures, aggravation and provocation'; to the extent that was so, the cases the Commission heard were not typical of SWAPOL conduct. The dominant impression given by these hearings, however, is of a police force for whom law enforcement, crime prevention and crime detection, not to mention the protection of citizens' rights, were essentially irrelevant as far as the black population were concerned. Researching all this material and interviewing people who were policemen, lawyers, or affected members of the public during these years would be a significant contribution to Namibian history and to future policing policy.
19. Case No. K25/1989, pp. 2–4.
20. All the other cases investigated by the O'Linn Commission seem to have been political. In many of them the central role was played by former Koevoet officers who at independence were nominally 'integrated' into the regular police, until public outrage at their continued flagrant lawbreaking and political intervention eventually brought about their disbandment (as provided for in the Peace Accords governing the transition to independence) at the insistence of the UN Secretary General. The role of the UN Police Monitors, and especially those from the Netherlands who understood Afrikaans and who in many cases stood up

firmly to SWAPOL officers who often sided quite blatantly with the DTA against SWAPO, was very important in this process. For a particularly striking example, see the exemplary testimony of UN Police Monitor Major van der Weerd on the shooting, by the ex-Koevoet SWAPOL officer Sgt McMaster, of Petrus Joseph, a captured PLAN combatant who had been 'turned' to become a member of Koevoet, but who had resigned shortly before independence (O'Linn Commission, Case No. 207/89).

21. Case K 154/89 and K174/89, p. 19.

22. The following section makes no pretence to be a complete or systematic account of the transition, but pursues only certain themes addressed in previous sections. For an excellent overview down to the end of 1990, see L. Nathan, 'Marching to a Different Drum: a Description and Assessment of the Formation of the Namibian Police and Defence Force', Southern Africa Perspectives working paper series, No. 4, Centre for Southern African Studies, University of the Western Cape, February 1991. I am also indebted for helpful advice to Inspector J. Healy of the RCMP, who was closely involved in the provision of technical assistance for the reform of the Namibian police.

23. The figure of 6,000 was retained after independence as NAMPOL's official establishment, but the budgetary provision for 1991–2 was only for approximately 4,700 actually on strength, including 2,395 Protection Officers (former Special Constables), in mid-1991.

24. Data supplied by Inspector Ferreira, Police Training College, to the Middle Management Course, 4 June 1991.

25. As a ratio of police officers to population the country's figures were well above the African norm, but the peculiarly diverse and dispersed nature of Namibia's population would probably necessitate a relatively high ratio, even if social dislocations and tensions were greatly reduced.

26. According to Commissioner Eimbeck, NAMPOL's official spokesperson, SAP salaries were up to 70 per cent higher than those of NAMPOL.

27. The new training programme, which included three-week middle management courses for inspectors and warrant officers and five-week specialist courses for uniformed investigators and for CID work, was part of a comprehensive package of reforms broadly following a report made in early 1990 by Inspector Sampson of the British police and Chief Superintendant Pickover, commander of the Police Training College at Wakefield in Yorkshire.

28. In early November 1989 ex-Koevoet members demonstrated for three successive days at Rundu and in mid-December there was a similar manifestation by former Koevoet and 101 Battalion members at Oshakati, at which the crowd 'demanded their weapons back'. In August 1990 there were still large pockets of disaffected ex-Koevoet and ex-SWATF men in certain areas of Oshakati. The problem was gradually eased by, among other things, the organized transfer of large numbers of ex-Koevoet to South Africa, perhaps to form part of the 'special units' used to attack ANC supporters while disguised as Inkatha members, as appeared from the revelations in 'Inkathagate' in July 1991. An apparently well-informed unsigned article in the *Windhoek Observer* of 15 December 1990 stated that a group of ex-Koevoet members was 'leaving for Pretoria to join a 'special paramilitary unit of the SAP'. It also listed four other 'ex-security force groups seeking exile in other countries': ex-101 Battalion members in Namibia who claimed to be endangered by SWAPO and who had earlier been told by the South Africans that, if they chose, they should leave for South Africa as 'tourists' and would then be taken from Upington to a new base inside the Republic; the 4,000 men and their families of the former 201 Bushmen Battalion of SWATF, who had been moved wholesale to South Africa prior to independence; and two 500-strong groups, from the former 101 (Ovambo) and 201 (Kavango) Battalions of SWATF respectively, presently in Angola. The former had been mainly Angolan refugees, in any case, the article claimed, and had been recruited to serve with UNITA when the SWATF units were disbanded. The latter had fled into Angola when the Border Guards were harassing ex-SWATF members between April and September 1990. The *Namibian* reported on 23 November 1990 that a group estimated at 140 former Koevoet and 101 Battalion members had boarded a train for South Africa on 21 November.

29. *Windhoek Observer*, 17 February 1990 and *Namibian*, 13 March 1990. According to the latter report, the total graduating from the course was 163.

30. *Times of Namibia*, 4 October 1990.

31. Interview with Inspector Derek Brune, commander of the Special Unit including the Task Force (a special emergency and anti-riot unit) and the Presidential and Ministerial Guard units at that time, on 17 August 1990.

32. There were, inevitably, also severe tensions within the Border Guards between ex-PLAN and ex-SWATF members. For an example, see the complaints of 17 ex-SWATF 'Special Constables'

made to an internal police commission of inquiry and reported in the *Times of Namibia* on 10 September 1990.

33. The issue came to a head when members of the Guard fired shots at civilian cars which failed to obey their orders, in a series of incidents in Windhoek, Swakopmund and Henties Bay in December 1990 and January 1990 (see the *Windhoek Observer*, 12 January 1991), including one in which a civilian was wounded in the leg. In a court case arising from the last-mentioned incident the magistrate stated that the Presidential Guard had endangered lives and dismissed charges brought against the civilian driver. The subsequent behaviour of the Presidential Guard unit was generally felt to have been more effective and acceptable. See also the *Windhoek Observer* of 15 December 1990.

34. Statistics provided by Inspector A. S. Theron. Because of continual changes during the transition period, the figures should be taken as true only for the date given, and, especially as regards the numbers of Protection Officers, as approximate. Protection Officers, unlike Special Constables, became permanent members of NAMPOL, with pension and other benefits.

35. By July 1992 these comprised 12 Deputy Commanders (down from 17 in July 1991), 9 Commanders (up from 6), 2 Assistant Inspector Generals and 1 Deputy Inspector General. The Inspector General's job was vacant following the resignation of the first NAMPOL Inspector General, Piet Fouché, earlier in 1992.

36. In the third post-independence Basic Training Course at the Luipardsvallei Police Training College, in 1991, 28 out of the 145 Student Constables failed to reach 20 per cent in their final marks. The staff of the College recognized that some of these students were capable people who lacked either the necessary basic education or adequate English, or both: the fact remained that they were not able to do some of the things required of policemen. The Minister of Home Affairs decided, in the end, to allow them to pass.

37. SWAPO camps, especially in Angola, were typically situated a long way from any significant local population centre and had controlled boundaries. Permission had to be obtained to leave the camp. Policing, as opposed to political security work, was mainly concerned with preventing the theft of camp property and dealing with minor offences.

38. This officer's remarks testify to his perceptions and feelings, without necessarily being wholly objective (for instance, the Tanzanian police force would not, in theory, train illiterate people). They also display the tone of slightly condescending impatience that even the best of the remaining ex-SWAPOL officers tended to adopt, and their unconcealed preference for 'their' former Special Constables over police personnel recruited from former exiles.

39. Special Constables, being paid on a daily basis, had no obligation to be available for duty on a particular day. Their conversion into permanent members of the service made them into a fully deployable, and more accountable, resource.

40. Interview, 5 July 1991.

41. At the beginning of July 1991 the numbers of senior officers drawn from those trained in exile were: Inspectors, 24/129 (19 per cent), Chief Inspectors, 4/43 (9 per cent), Deputy Commissioners and above, 3/30 (10 per cent).

42. Whereas an officer in Britain or South Africa would normally expect to reach the rank of inspector, if at all, after 20 years of service, SWAPOL inspectors with only four or five years of service were not uncommon, and just prior to independence a large number of promotions were made, including some officers with even shorter periods of service. There was also the fact, already referred to, that in the war years the best talent tended to go into the security branch, the great majority of whose members left the country at independence.

43. One senior officer commented: '[a large urban police station] is chaos. As soon as experienced officers are promoted inspector they are given nine-to-five jobs, while a shift of 15–25 men is under a sergeant. All the work is falling on the shifts but the commander has not reassigned commissioned officers to shifts. I told the General [ex-General, later Assistant Inspector General Pool] he must do something. He agreed and said, 'You don't know half of what goes on.… There are old SWAPOL officers who want to be able to say "I told you so". It is completely negative.'

44. Chief Inspector N. A. Smith, interview, 3 June 1991.

45. According to Chief Inspector N. A. Smith, Acting Commandant of the Police Training College, only two of the returnee officers involved in the numerous complaints and departmental investigations for alleged assaults, thefts, etc., since independence had been former exiles (interview, 3 June 1991). It was generally said in Katutura's Single Quarters that criminals frequently hid in the adjacent police camp, and Commissioner Eimbeck accepted that this was true (in a lecture on 'The multi-agency approach to policing problems' given at the Police Training College, 4 June 1991). Trafficking in cars stolen in Windhoek and sold in Angola was also widely supposed to be impossible without the connivance of police officers. Whatever the

truth of these beliefs, any such links between the police and criminal elements were seen as predating the recruitment of the returnees. In this connection it is worth observing that Koevoet officers, who had been part of SWAPOL and had links with some personnel who were now in NAMPOL, had been extensively involved in dubious and illegal private enterprises of various kinds in northern Namibia. There were also a few well-publicized prosecutions of individual ex-SWAPOL policemen for corruption during the first year and a half of independence.

46. After independence a series of incidents indicated that some ex-SWAPOL police officers were involved with right-wing elements interested in destabilizing the SWAPO government. Joseph Kleynhans, an ex-SWAPOL member of NAMPOL's Task Force, testified in court that he had been involved in moving large quantities of arms and ammunition stolen from government arsenals in July 1990, and apparently intended for use in a coup attempt, although he stated that he had refused to take part in the planned coup. In spite of the fact that all those arrested were charged with treason and that two men who were thought to be the prime movers in the plot had evaded arrest and were believed to have fled the country, the court later granted bail to six of the accused, of whom three later jumped bail and left the country. Even after this, the remaining three were allowed to remain free on bail. In an earlier incident, five men in custody pending a trial for the bombing of an UNTAG office in Outjo in August 1989 were 'sprung' while being transported in a police vehicle, and were later also believed to have left the country undetected. None of these incidents implicated Namibian police officers other than Kleynhans, but there was an understandable feeling on the part of the public that ex-SWAPOL officers in NAMPOL might be less exercised about these cases than they had been about threats to the security of the South African regime prior to independence. It was noticeable, for example, that senior NAMPOL officers expressed stronger sentiments in criticizing the *Namibian* for reporting a leaked document concerning the planned coup than they later did in commenting on the coup plot that was subsequently discovered (see the *Namibian*, 3 August 1990).

47. Two examples may serve to illustrate the problems involved, with their inevitable political and ethnic overtones (bearing in mind that it is the perceptions and feelings expressed, and not the alleged facts, that are significant). A spokesman for 'about twelve' Special Constables posted to Luderitz from Ovambo in June 1990 wrote to The *Namibian*: 'We were welcomed in Luderitz by the local police who are headed by the station commander, Inspector Folscher. Then we were told to sleep in the vehicle garage and in a small room next to a toilet. After some days we asked for better accommodation, because we were sleeping on a concrete floor without mattresses. We were told there was no other place to sleep, but on the upper floor of the building there are some constables who sleep there. These constables had served the previous colonial government, and none of them are Oshivambo-speaking. It is these constables who call us stupid Vambos because we don't know how to read or write. In Luderitz we are not really regarded as proper police constables. We are called Special Constables, and even the public is told this. We are prohibited from sitting in the office, and we are only allowed in there when we are giving the report from the beat patrol. Why are we not police members? Are we treated like this because we are Ovambo?' (The *Namibian*, 10 August 1990). Conversely, the anti-SWAPO *Times of Namibia* carried the following story on 28 August 1990: 'Discontent is building up in the police force in Ovambo, with women constables claiming discrimination in favour of returnee recruits.... During June all women, new recruits from the ranks of the refugees as well as the women who previously held the rank of Special Constables, had to write exams for promotion to the rank of full constables.... The results came as a surprise to many, when all the returnee applicants passed. The *Times* was told that no formal entry qualification was demanded from them, with some being barely able to read and write. The women who previously served on a temporary basis in the police all had the minimum qualification of Standard Eight – with a fair share of matriculants among them. None of these applicants passed the exam.... The women who failed the exams went to an Inspector Du Toit with their complaints. The Inspector acknowledged that the new intake of permanent women constables could not cope, but warned the women not to complain, as 'you did not return from Angola'.... The permanent positions were reserved for returnees, he said.'

48. See A. Corbett, *An Assessment of the Functioning of the Magistrates' Courts in Post-Independence Namibia: A Report by the Legal Assistance Centre, September 1991*. The courts concerned were at Rundu, Ondangua, Windhoek (two courts) and Keetmanshoop. The observer at Rundu reported that most defendants were afraid to talk about their treatment by the police for fear of reprisals. The case of alleged torture was said to involve inflicting burns with a blowtorch. The regional distribution of the alleged cases of police violence was as follows: Windhoek (15

defendants), three alleged cases of assault, one of torture, and one of being teargassed inside a police vehicle while a prisoner; Ondangua (10 defendants), one assault; Keetmanshoop (12 defendants), none. More common complaints by defendants were that the police were partial and apt to jump to conclusions; that they failed to investigate, gave undue weight to the allegations of complainants and refused to listen to the accused's version; that they allowed complainants to abuse or even assault the accused while in custody; that they failed to provide adequate treatment for injuries; and that in one case they refused to allow the accused to lay charges. While all these were uncorroborated complaints they probably convey fairly accurately the view of the police held by many of those arrested by them, as being arbitrary or even partial, prone to treat you as guilty, and deferring to members of the public with status and power. How far this view is well founded, and how far it differs from the view of the police held by most people arrested in any other country, are open questions. It should be added that most of the 37 defendants interviewed stated that they had not been physically abused by the police.

49. Lecture on 'The Multi-Agency Approach to Policing Problems', 4 June 1991.
50. In May 1991 the 'public' side of the Council consisted of three black and one white church representatives: three black trade unionists and two NANSO representatives; a black representative of the Academy; six other non-black representatives of non-government organizations; and two black and three non-black representatives of state or municipal agencies (PPRAC press release, 20 May 1991).
51. Minute 12.1 of the PPRAC, 18 March 1991. Some parts of Katutura were also poorly represented in attendance at the Katutura PPRC, according to the Rev. Michael Yates (see minute 12.3 of the PPRAC of 18 March 1991).
52. On 1 July the *Namibian* reported that 212 prisoners in Oshakati prison had refused to appear in the Oshakati Magistrate's Court in protest against the delays - sometimes of several months - in getting their cases heard.
53. The planned expansion in the number of magistrates was announced by the Minister of Justice in the National Assembly on 25 July 1990.
54. H. Ruppel, interview, 24 June 1991.
55. According to one legal opinion, all criminal jurisdiction given by previous laws to traditional authorities has been invalid since 21 March 1990, with the introduction of the Bill of Rights; while the criminal jurisdiction actually assumed by traditional authorities, and many of their practices – including the power of arrest, especially by so-called 'tribal police' – had in any case often exceeded the powers actually conferred on them by previous legislation. See C. Kahanowitz, 'Memorandum on the Statutory Powers of Tribal Authorities, Chiefs and Headmen to Arrest, Detain and Try Namibian Citizens': evidence submitted to the Kozonguizi Commission, Legal Assistance Centre, Windhoek, December 1990, pp. 16–22.
56. Cases of the manifestly illegal use of corporate punishment by traditional courts have been reported from time to time. The practice was acknowledged and defended by Chief Constance Kgosimeng, MP, when a series of cases in his Tswana constituency came to light in June 1991 (see the *Namibian*, 1 July 1991). According to these reports, 'Aminuis headman Michael Simana adds that the powers are frequently abused, with people being held down and beaten in order to help them admit guilt.' Other reports from time to time record that the police have been called in to liberate people held in custody by traditional courts, pending the payment of the penalties imposed by them; typically these reports are of people chained to trees.
57. Interview with Paul Vleermuis, 10 June 1991. According to the Deputy Minister of Justice, Vekuii Rukoro, stock theft in the rural areas was reaching 'epidemic proportions': bad as it was in the ranching areas of Windhoek, Okahandja, and elsewhere, 'in the so-called homelands or reserves stock theft was much more acute due to the lack of law enforcement agencies' (the *Namibian*, 31 August 1990).
58. A 1991 survey of Katutura found that 38.1 per cent of the adult population were unemployed: see Wade Pendleton, *The 1991 Katutura Survey Report* (Windhoek: Namibian Institute of Social and Economic Research, University of Namibia, 1991). This brief report is an important source of quantitative data on many aspects of social conditions in Katutura after independence. See also C. von Garnier *et al.*, *Katutura Revisited 1986: Essays on a Black Namibian Apartheid Suburb* (Windhoek, 1986).
59. NAMPOL made a point of publishing monthly crime statistics, but given the parlous state of the charge offices in most police stations not too much weight can be placed on them. If anything they indicated a decline in the value of stolen goods since independence, since the reported current values stayed more or less constant, while inflation was running at 15 per cent or more, and this is hard to believe. (For a useful review of the police data, see Chris Coetzee, 'As thick as thieves', in the *Times of Namibia*, 31 May 1991. This article is typical of

most public discussion in its tone of crisis, which is contradicted by the data it provides, except for the evidence that insurance companies had greatly increased their premiums.) Perhaps some weight can be attached to the proportion of the value of stolen goods reported by the police as having been stolen in Windhoek: 73 per cent. The most important changes probably were the increased movement of non-whites into the white suburbs and the central business districts, and the removal of the omnipresent armed forces, and especially their control over movement between Windhoek and the north: all these factors shifted the geographical and social incidence of criminal activities, and much of the public discussion about crime is probably best understood as an adjustment to this shift. Discussion about the scale of the private security industry tends to have the same exaggerated character, and for the same reason (see note 7 above; and see also Gregory Fahrenfort, 'Fighting crime 24 hours a day', in the *Windhoek Observer*, 1 June 1991, for an example of the genre). The actual number of employees of the largest private security firm in 1991 proved to be half the number estimated by the police.

60. The security problems of Khomasdal, the former 'coloured' township, are neglected here. Like problems in many other spheres, they were neither as acute as those of Katutura, nor as modest as those of the white suburbs.

61. Interview, 25 June 1991. Another Katutura resident (a social worker) expressed the other side of the problem: 'In the past you wouldn't report someone to the police because the police were the enemy, and you were in danger of attack from others if you did. Even now, if you turn someone in and he goes to jail, he will be beaten in jail, and you don't want to do that to a fellow worker' (Lindi Kazombaue, interview, 6 June 1991).

62. Tyappa Namutewa, interview, 25 June 1991.

63. According to Frederick Gawaseb, 'Born to be wild', *Windhoek Observer*, 15 December 1990, gangs have been a feature of Katutura life since the mid-1960s. According to him the Red Eye Gang, which was formed in 1986, represents a new and more dangerous kind of gang because it has shown itself able to organise effective legal defence. Knowledgeable Katutura residents state that this particular gang was formed by the DTA from former Special Constables, and continues to enjoy a substantial measure of police connivance. In July 1991 members of the gang who had openly used firearms to break up two football matches in Windhoek in front of several thousand spectators in August 1990 had still not been put on trial. On the Red Eye Gang see 'Eye to eye: exclusive insight into the gang, as told to Chris Coetzee', the *Times of Namibia*, 22 August 1990. Another less publicized result of the relative impunity of gangs in Katutura, according to social worker Lindi Kazombaue, was the decline in 'bazaars', a traditional institution involving free music and dancing and the sale of food and other items to raise funds for the purchase of furniture, etc; gangsters would take the drink and break up the party.

64. These events occurred in May 1991. In the best-known case, two men were killed by a crowd of 50 or 60 people in Wanaheda. They were believed to have been responsible for the death by stabbing of a Wanaheda resident three days before, and were then seen attacking a 60-year-old man, whose eyes were gouged out in the struggle. According to one member of the Wanaheda committee, this was reported to two separate police officers in police vehicles, both of whom declined to act, saying they were off duty. The crowd then attacked and killed the two men.

65. See 'Press Statement on Advocated Lawlessness in Katutura', April 1991, commenting on a statement in 'a local daily paper' of 23 April that 'Katutura vowed that people's justice [a reference to one of the stonings] will stay, unless police can protect us.'

66. Minutes of PPRAC, 21 May 1991, and interview with Commissioner Eimbeck, 4 June 1991.

67. Lecture on 'The multi-agency approach to policing problems', Police Training College, 4 June 1991. The new reservists were not screened in advance of their appointment. Com. Eimbeck stated that if further investigation showed that any of them had a 'bad' record, 'their leaders must decide if they want to work with them ' - i.e. to be a criminal was not to be an automatic disqualification (interview, 4 June 1991).

68. See W. Scharff, 'Community policing in South Africa', in Bennett *et al.*, *op. cit.*, pp. 206–33.

8
War, Peace & Social Classes

CHRIS TAPSCOTT

The demands of the liberation struggle in Namibia served to differentiate Namibian society into those who opposed and those who collaborated with the apartheid regime, those who went into exile and those who remained, and those who attained rank and status within each of the opposing forces and those who did not. The policies of the apartheid era further served to reify racial and ethnic divisions throughout the society, to the extent that different communities were segregated geographically, economically and socially. The combined impacts of the war and of apartheid rule have thus inevitably shaped both the form of the state inherited at independence and the evolving patterns of social differentiation.

A review of the literature of decolonization in Africa suggests that despite its unique status as the last colony in Africa to attain independence, Namibia reflects many of the characteristic patterns of a neo-colonial state, including continued economic dependence on its former colonizers, accelerated social differentiation amongst the formerly subordinated population, and the emergence of a new élite, elsewhere described as an organizational or bureaucratic bourgeoisie.[1]

As in other developing societies, however, a degree of circumspection is called for in discussing class formation in Namibia, not least in that social and economic relations are not directly comparable to those in the economically developed societies on which much of class theory has been based. 'The class structure of post-colonial Africa', as Magubane emphasizes, is 'not just a matter of traditional division into bourgeoisie, proletariat and peasantry, but also a matter of relations between those classes that were inheritors of the colonial state and imperialism. Cutting across the traditional divisions was the link between those classes in the former colonies who benefited from imperialism and those who suffered from it.'[2]

Furthermore, as Wolpe has pointed out, the concept of class merely establishes the essential but limited nexus between capital and labour; beyond that it remains abstract.[3] In the economy itself classes exist in forms that are fragmented and fractured in numerous ways by politics, culture, ideology and, significantly, by racial and ethnic differentiation. Where classes are constituted as unified social forces, this occurs as a largely conjunctural phenomenon.

What is of particular interest in analysing emerging trends in the process of class formation in independent Namibia is the inflection given to this process by the country's dependent and subordinate status within the international economy, by apartheid rule and by the impact of more than twenty years of war. The structure of civil society, in particular, may be seen to have been shaped not only by the imperatives of colonial capitalism but also by the populism of the national liberation movements and by the counteractive strategies of the occupying South African forces. Of further interest in analysing trends in social differentiation and class contradiction in Namibia is an investigation of the potential that exists for the emergence of alternative political forces in the country. For analytical purposes, discussion of this process may be divided into three phases: (1) the formative period up to 1974; (2) the intensive war years from 1974 until the onset of independence in 1989; and (3) the post-independence era.

The Social Structure and Political Economy of Colonialism up to 1974

The dispossession and disempowerment of the indigenous African population in Namibia that began under German colonial rule in the 1880s was further systematized under South African domination after 1915, culminating in the implementation of the apartheid policies of the 1960s. Up to and including this period, Namibian society manifested the familiar characteristics of a colonial society: the hegemony of the metropole in Pretoria, economic domination by a handful of international corporations, a small settler society which administered the country on behalf of the metropole and which controlled both the economy and the polity, and a broad mass of indigenes, predominantly resident in the rural areas and dependent on subsistence agriculture and the remittances of migrant labour.

From the days of German colonization the structure of the then South West African economy was geared primarily to the demands of foreign capital, which controlled the lucrative mining industry, and secondarily to the needs of settler farmers.[4] Of central importance to the profitability of both sectors was the availability of abundant supplies of cheap labour. In that respect both the mines and the ranchers were interested in the indigenous population as unskilled labourers, not consumers. The economy was characterized by the extraction and exportation of primary resources (minerals, beef and karakul pelts), while the strategy of foreign owners was directed overwhelmingly at maximizing profits for repatriation to their home bases.[5] There was little if any local production and the importation of processed goods was oriented to the consumer patterns of the colonial élite; in that respect Namibia was no different from many other colonies in Africa at the time.

Until the uprisings of 1904–7, the Nama and Herero people had been the primary source of labour for the mines and farms of the German colonists in the centre and south of the country. Following the genocide of these people, the demand for labour at the copper mine in Tsumeb and the diamond mines in the southern Namib desert led to a concerted recruitment drive in the reserves to the north.

The establishment of a system of migrant contract labour in many respects set the pattern of development in northern Namibia (and hence for more than two-thirds of the national population) for much of the century. South African occupation did not noticeably change existing labour policies, and the northern territories continued to serve primarily as reservoirs of labour for commercial undertakings to the south of the country. Little infrastructural development took place and only rudimentary social services were provided. The migrant labour system effectively subsidized colonial capital by displacing the social costs of reproduction from the mining and commercial agricultural sectors to the African reserves.

As a consequence of the generally uneven pattern of development, and as a consequence of the discriminatory practices of white South African rule (which included the extension of most of its own laws to the colony), educational opportunities were limited among the black population and economic mobility was constrained by both a lack of training and a job colour bar. As in South Africa, the categories of race and class tended to coincide.

Following the findings of the Odendaal Commission of 1963, a programme of bantustanization was introduced from the late 1960s onwards. As in South Africa, this system consigned all African Namibians to one of ten designated ethnic 'homelands' where, it was intended, they would realize their political aspirations as distinct nations. The bantustan system was coupled with stringent influx control measures which restricted access to the 'white' areas, and limited the number of Africans with the right to reside permanently in the urban areas to those who had been born there or who had lived or worked continuously in the area for ten or more years. This legislation effectively constrained the process of urbanization and forestalled the growth of an urban population with an economic base independent of subsistence agriculture, and with class identities of its own.

Since the principles on which this system was founded were premised on the ethnic distinctiveness of the various African population groups, primacy was accorded to traditional authority structures. Under the apartheid system the power of traditional leaders was considerably strengthened while, at the same time, their legitimacy as traditional leaders was progressively subverted.[6] Although there was notable resistance to this process in various quarters (the Herero Chiefs' Council in particular) and among particular traditional leaders in all ethnic groups, the bantustan programme accelerated the co-option of chiefs and headmen to the service of the colonial state. As salaried officials of the state, they were expected to dissipate or control resistance in the rural areas, and increasingly served as surrogates for state control and repression.

In the years immediately following the Second World War, however, resistance to South African rule had come from the Herero Chiefs' Council under the leadership of Chief Hosea Kutako. The Herero Chiefs' Council continued to petition the UN on the injustices of South African rule throughout the 1950s, but the most significant political development of this decade was undoubtedly the emergence of the embryonic nationalist movements SWANU and OPO (the latter subsequently becoming SWAPO).

While the establishment of OPO and SWAPO has been portrayed in the official SWAPO literature as a joint project of Namibian intellectuals and contract workers,[7] reality suggests a more conventional nationalist path: that of a popular mobilization of workers and other class forces by a nascent intellectual élite.[8] It has, for example, been suggested that many of the Namibians living in Cape Town in the 1950s had effectively opted out of the contract labour system (with its strictly regulated permits and passes) and were living (albeit illegally) semi-permanently in the area.[9] The work which they undertook, moreover, although menial (for instance, as waiters, barbers, or wine stewards), was not of the arduous type to which contract workers were normally subjected. As a consequence, they experienced greater mobility and generally had more free time at their disposal, both of which facilitated the organization of political meetings and political discussion.

As in most other African countries at the time, the aspirations of intellectuals in Namibia were generally thwarted by the colonial administration, which restricted access to the commercial sector, while itself recruiting few indigenous intellectuals, and then only to minor ranks in the bureaucratic echelon. In consequence, many of the demands of these organizations, at least in their early stages, related to the disadvantaged position of their constituent members. Thus the Ovamboland People's Congress (OPC), the predecessor of OPO, while broadly campaigning for the abolition of the contract labour system, also embarked on a campaign to open up the commercial sector of Ovamboland to Africans. The establishment of the Ovamboland People's Advancement Society by the OPC, for example, was intended to raise funds for Africans to establish their own businesses.[10]

Differentiation within the Settler Society

The white community as a whole presented a united front to the challenge mounted by the black nationalists and to the low-intensity guerilla war launched in 1966. Nevertheless, within the settler community, too, social differentiation had always existed along both ethnic and class lines. Following the South African takeover in 1915 the influence of German settlers in the country diminished dramatically, although they still comprised the bulk of the white community until the late 1920s. After the Second World War, however, the number of German settlers rose again, thanks to a new immigration from Germany. Although they were still a minority among the whites, they re-established their social and economic position and controlled much of the commercial sector, while retaining some prominence in the commercial agricultural sector.

Afrikaans-speaking whites, in contrast, predominated at all levels of the state administration. However, through generous state subsidies (low-cost farm loans in particular) and through preferential access to state tenders, they gradually improved their economic standing and influence. During the 1920s and 1930s, moreover, following an extensive programme of state-sponsored settlement, thousands of Afrikaners from South Africa were settled on the central Namibian plateau.[11]

With the National Party's ascent to power in 1948, efforts were made to secure a greater share of Namibia's wealth for local South African (and especially Afrikaner) capitalists in sectors hitherto dominated by foreign capital. Thus, in the late 1940s and early 1950s a cartel of Afrikaner-owned companies, protected by government licences and quotas, established a modern fish processing industry at Walvis Bay. Similarly, in the 1960s and 1970s Afrikaner and state-owned companies had begun to make small inroads into the foreign mining sector through joint ventures with transnational companies.[12] The capitalist class as a whole, however, remained small and was for the most part rooted in South Africa.

Class differentiation within the Afrikaner population, moreover, was masked by a populist ideology which stressed the unity of the Afrikaner 'volk'. And while the economy thrived, in the late 1950s and 1960s in particular, class contradictions within the white population as a whole were generally subordinated to the collective pursuit of the material gains which the colonial programme afforded.

The Intensification of the War, 1974–89

The revolution in Portugal in April 1974 and the subsequent collapse of Portuguese colonial rule in Africa led to the illicit departure of several thousand young SWAPO supporters. Many of these underwent military training and began to escalate the armed struggle. The increase in guerilla attacks precipitated a further deployment of South African troops in the north of Namibia, numbering over 70,000 in the peak years of the early 1980s.[13]

Much of the colonial state's policy towards the black population during the 1970s and 1980s, thus, can be ascribed directly to the formative action of the South African military in its efforts to counteract the threats of SWAPO insurgency. The approach encapsulated in the notion of a 'total strategy' was intended to counter what was seen as a communist/Soviet-inspired onslaught on South Africa from without.

The Creation of a Black Middle Class

With the collapse of Portuguese rule, and under mounting international pressure to withdraw from Namibia, the South African government attempted to engineer its own internal solution to independence, which in 1978 culminated in the establishment of an interim Constituent Assembly under the leadership of the white dominated Democratic Turnhalle Alliance (DTA). The DTA administration and its successor, the Multi-Party Conference, were intended to appease the international community while retaining South African dominance in the region, but they also conformed to the broader objectives of the total strategy. The reformist policies pursued included efforts to defuse mass struggle by incorporating leading strata of the black population into an anti-SWAPO coalition.

As in South Africa at the time, the creation of a black middle class was intended to act as a hedge against the growing militancy of the masses and to counter their growing antipathy towards capitalism. Consequently, in 1977 a range of discriminatory laws, including those governing freedom of movement, residential settlement and inter-racial sex and marriage were repealed by the Administrator General. These liberalizations, although nominally improving conditions for all blacks, in practice benefited only those who could afford to take advantage of the new dispensation, the new collaborative élite. As Simon has pointed out in respect to the repeal of laws governing residential segregation, only those in senior public positions could afford to buy housing at the prevailing prices. In such a context, 'the operation of a capitalist land and property market ... replaced legislative *fiat* as the regulator of residential integration'.[14]

The new élite, referred to by some as the *Waserauta* (a corruption of the term 'sell-out'), comprised a range of politicians, civil servants and professionals (teachers and nurses) who earned salaries which were sometimes on a par with those of their white counterparts, and which were vastly higher than those of the average black worker.[15] Indicative of the success of the programme to create a black middle class, it was estimated in 1984 that this class then comprised some 30,000-40,000 households.[16]

The establishment from the late 1960s onwards of 11 second-tier ethnic administrations afforded further opportunities for high salaries and benefits for those wishing to collaborate. The considerable autonomy exercised by the ethnic governments and a general lack of accountability also presented opportunities for some individuals to enrich themselves through corruption. Evidence from the Van Eeden and Thirion commissions of enquiry, for example, provided evidence of widespread misappropriation of public funds among second-tier governments.[17] It is evident that corruption and inefficiency, while not endorsed, were nevertheless tolerated as necessary for retaining the support of the leadership of the second-tier authorities. As Dutkiewicz and Shenton have noted in other contexts, inefficiency and mismanagement of the state, far from preventing the reproduction of a ruling group, are often a prerequisite for it.[18]

Wage Workers

Although a significant proportion of the Namibian work force remained in the subsistence agricultural sector (an estimated 48 per cent of those potentially economically active in 1977),[19] increasing population pressures, shortages of land and declining productivity in this sector drove ever greater numbers of people to seek wage labour in the formal economy. Of these, the bulk found employment in the tertiary service sector in the urban areas (59 per cent of formal sector workers) and on white commercial farms (28 per cent).[20]

Although workers in the mining industry were known to be the best organized, their relative numbers (7 per cent of the work force in 1977) were small. In addition, following a series of successful strikes in the early 1970s, wages in this sector were improved as transnational corporations sought to stabilize their work forces. The mine workers, thus, although mobilizing around real workers' issues (as opposed to some workers' groups which mobilized largely along political lines) were a somewhat privileged group. Many of those with access to higher incomes, or to the profits of illicit dealings in diamonds, invested their gains in business ventures in the north and became petty traders.

The formal organization of the work force in Namibia, in general, was constrained by two factors: the small size of the population (in relation to the size of the country) and the extreme dualism of the economy. Namibia's economy was both heavily dependent on South Africa and narrowly based. The country's GDP in 1977 was largely accounted for by three sectors: mining and quarrying (42 per cent), distribution and services (30 per cent) and agriculture and fishing (16 per cent).[21] In the 1970s and 1980s a tendency to greater capital intensity in both the mining and commercial agricultural sectors increased the demand for skilled workers and, at the same time, limited the potential for mass employment generation.

The manufacturing sector (which is usually a significant generator of new jobs) was always extremely limited and in 1977 accounted for less than 3 per cent of total wage employment in Namibia. Major determinants of this state of affairs were Namibia's incorporation in the Southern African Customs Union (which historically tended to discourage local manufacture) and the limited domestic market. While the domestic market was limited by the size of the population, overall effective demand was also depressed by income inequality and the poverty of the majority. At the same time, the prospects for export-led manufacturing were limited by the low skill levels of the work force and the relatively high level of real wages in comparison to other economies at similar levels of *per capita* income (those in Asia in particular).

The organization of Namibian labour was also constrained by state repression which prohibited the establishment of trade unions for much of the colonial period. At the same time, however, it must also be noted that SWAPO's own attitude (particularly that of the exiled leadership) towards organized labour appears to have militated against the establishment of a more vigorous worker consciousness. As late as 1970, when the SWAPO Central Committee held its consultative conference in Tanga, Tanzania, and established structures for SWAPO Youth, SWAPO Women and SWAPO Elders, no consideration appears to have been given to supporting a trade union movement, although a department of labour was established.[22]

When SWAPO did become actively involved in the labour movement in the 1970s, its interest in organized labour appears to have been largely instrumental. That is to say, the political mobilization of workers in support of the liberation struggle was given precedence over workplace demands, including campaigns for higher wages and better conditions of service.[23]

This pattern can be traced back to the activities of both OPO and the early SWAPO which, although publicly espousing the interests of Namibian workers, were primarily nationalistic in orientation and focussed on campaigns to internationalize the liberation struggle rather than on the more immediate problems of contract workers themselves. This, according to Peltola, was due to the fact that much of the impetus for the establishment of labour organizations in Namibia had come from students and intellectuals, rather than the workers themselves, and that the ideas of the former generally held sway.[24] In 1971 SWAPO youth activists had, for example, played leading roles in mobilizing contract workers in the general strike. Further, it was SWAPO cadres inside Namibia who in 1977 had made a reality of the National Union of Namibian Workers.

However, while activists within Namibia were engaged in the mobilization of workers, their activities were not well coordinated with those of members outside the country. Training of trade unionists did take place in exile under the auspices of John Ya-Otto and Victor Nkandi, but there was little communication with the labour movement inside Namibia. The decision to affiliate the NUNW with the World Federation of Trade Unions, for example, appears to have taken place without any consultation with the internal membership.[25]

There is evidence that some of the SWAPO leadership were deeply suspicious of the trade union training conducted in the camps in exile. According to Peltola, himself active in these training programmes, the leadership feared that an independent trade union movement might, through industrial action, disrupt plans to transform the Namibian economy after independence.[26] In consequence, he maintains, every effort was made to keep a tight rein on the trade unions, and to control appointments to the top leadership. Perhaps reflecting the prevailing suspicions, a number of the most prominent trade union activists in exile were incarcerated by SWAPO during the so-called 'spy drama' of the mid-1980s.[27]

Petty Traders and the Northern War Economy

The repatriation of remittances and the invested savings of retiring migrant workers (those from the mines in particular) over the years provided a platform for the emergence of a sizeable class of black traders, particularly in Ovamboland, where there were estimated to be over 5,000 full- or part-time traders by the mid 1970s.[28] This number was boosted by the military occupation of northern Namibia which created its own network of patronage and clientelism.

Commencing with the formation of 201 Battalion (consisting of men classified as 'Bushmen') in 1974 and culminating with the establishment of the South West Africa Territorial Force (SWATF) in 1980, the SADF progressively attempted to indigenize its military effort in Namibia. In a context where wage employment was extremely scarce, the salaries offered by the military were very attractive to struggling subsistence agriculturalists. The SADF, in consequence, experienced few difficulties in recruiting local troops (even to the notorious counter-insurgency unit Koevoet) and by 1985 the strength of SWATF was estimated to be 21,000.[29] Although many of those in military service simply consumed their wages, others used their earnings to establish small businesses or to secure farms in the communal areas.

As is so often the case, the war economy in northern Namibia was a boon for many small traders who capitalized on the free spending of soldiers.[30] The liquor trade, in particular, flourished and for those business people who were compliant, the military occupation provided a captive market free of most trading constraints.[31] It is perhaps ironic that in the midst of the struggle for national liberation some of these traders expanded their businesses into multi-million rand ventures and emerged from the war as full-blooded capitalists.

The insecurity, violence and social dislocation caused by the war,[32] together with the employment opportunities generated by the occupying forces, also served to accelerate movement off the land in the north, and contributed to the rapid growth of towns in centres such as Oshakati, Ondangua, Rundu, and Katima Mulilo.[33] In the process, many of the rural areas of Namibia underwent a transformation as peasant farmers were propelled into petty commodity trading in the informal sector.

Peasants

Although the vast majority of black Namibians lived in the rural areas and relied to a greater or lesser extent on subsistence agriculture for their livelihood, peasant farmers, as in so many other countries, displayed little class consciousness. Where they were mobilized, it was under the banner of SWAPO nationalism, although it must be noted that this was severely constrained by the oppression of the colonial forces. In the north, community mobilization was further restricted by the repression of the traditional leaders who sometimes arrested and flogged those suspected of being SWAPO members.

At the same time, the South African occupation forces actively discouraged the establishment of independent community-based organizations, in the belief that they could be mobilized towards resistance by forces sympathetic to SWAPO. In their attempts to win the 'hearts and minds' of the local population, the SADF attempted to establish its own community-based structures, most notably Etango in Ovambo and Evuza in Kavango. However, such organizations, which were frequently connected to traditional authority structures and included a number of independent churches, attracted little popular support and their leaders were generally viewed as collaborators.

The influence of autocratic traditional authority structures (even those which did not overtly collaborate with the colonial administration) further militated against the establishment of peasant organizations. For many chiefs and headmen, autonomous and democratically elected community organizations posed a threat to their power and influence over local communities. The predominant rural churches in the north (Lutheran and Catholic) likewise, despite the importance of their role in providing a moral base to the liberation struggle, were not known for their democratic or participatory base. Finally, the dictates of the war of independence, and SWAPO's own penchant for authoritarianism, implied that the dominant political force in much of the north was, for much of the period leading up to independence, both military and hierarchical in orientation. Under these circumstances, it was not possible for a tradition of mass-based organization to develop in the rural areas of Namibia.

What was of significance during the 1980s, however, was the emergence from the ranks of the peasantry of a small group of black commercial farmers, who were allocated farms by the colonial administration or who themselves alienated communal land with the collusion of local traditional leaders.[34] These individuals, some of whom had started out as peasant farmers, developed as a powerful lobby group for the commercialization of communal land in Hereroland and, to a lesser extent, in Ovamboland.

Classes within the White Community

Due in large part to the structure of the political economy of Namibia and in particular to its heavy orientation towards South Africa, the development of an indigenous capitalist class was severely limited. Nevertheless, by the late 1970s and early 1980s a small number of white Namibian business people had developed significant interests in fishing, commercial agriculture, commerce, light industry and other assorted ventures. The lucrative mining sector, however, remained almost wholly foreign-owned.[35]

While the emergence of a capitalist class was constrained, colonial rule facilitated the development of a (proportionately) significant white middle class. Although the various interim governments had incorporated a limited number of blacks into the political power structures, the upper echelons of the administration remained dominated by whites. Over and above the lucrative salaries earned (commensurate with those earned in South Africa), politicians and senior civil servants received generous employment packages including low-cost housing subsidies, car allowances and the like.

Although apartheid policies had, in general, afforded material benefits to most whites, the military occupation also represented a boon for certain sectors of the white business community. To those who were prepared to risk the dangers of the war zone, the returns were significant. Tendering procedures were frequently waived and lucrative contracts were renewed by the military on a regular basis.[36] In the decade prior to independence considerable wealth was thus accumulated by certain strata of the white community. It is this economic élite, moreover, which appears to have ridden the period of transition most successfully and who became some of the most direct beneficiaries of the policy of national reconciliation.

Within the white settler community such class distinction as there was was expressed in occupational and residential differentiation.[37] In that respect, the political divide among whites in Namibia to a considerable extent mirrored that of South Africa at the time, and with the dissolution of the Afrikaner nationalist alliance much of the white society was divided into *verkramptes* (conservatives) and *verligtes* (reformers), each group having its own social base. The *verkrampte* group generally consisted of white workers, certain smaller and less successful farmers and small business people, while the *verligtes* consisted of Afrikaner capital and the emerging Afrikaner middle class. The lower strata of the white population, blue-collar workers and those who occupied protected jobs within the state administration, in contrast, were generally those who were most threatened by the liberalizations that followed the Turnhalle Conference, and in particular the repeal of laws governing the racial division of labour and subsequent changes in employment policy. To these social forces, the most direct beneficiaries of apartheid policy, the reforms threatened their economic and social privileges and advanced the prospect of direct competition with the black population. In the years immediately following the establishment of the interim government in 1978, therefore, there was a major exodus of whites from Namibia to South Africa and the white population decreased by some 25 per cent.[38] The exodus immediately prior to and after independence was considerably smaller, no doubt due to the collapse of apartheid rule and South Africa's deteriorating socio-political climate, and to the fact that many of the die-hard apartheid supporters had already left in the late 1970s.

Setting the Mould

South Africa's continuing illegal occupation of Namibia throughout the 1970s and the 1980s can be ascribed to a variety of factors, including the country's strategic importance and the value of its primary resources. Nevertheless, South Africa, playing to the conservatism of governments in the West (those of Reagan and Thatcher in particular), to a large extent justified its continued occupation of Namibia in terms of the need to stem the spreading tide of communism in Africa, and in this SWAPO was portrayed as the servant of Moscow.[39] This portrayal, moreover, was not entirely the fictive creation of total strategy theorists seeking to generate support for their notion of a 'total onslaught'. SWAPO had, in its 1976 Political Programme, committed itself to 'unite all Namibian people, particularly the working class, the peasantry and progressive intellectuals into a vanguard party capable of safeguarding national independence and of building a classless, non-exploitative society based on the ideals and principles of scientific socialism'.[40]

The extent to which SWAPO had committed itself to these aims is debatable, as Dobell shows in Chapter 9. It is likely, moreover, that a latent contradiction persisted between the aspirations of the incipient élite within SWAPO as a nationalist movement and the goals of scientific socialism. In that respect, it is noteworthy that many of the young people who went into exile were motivated as much by a desire for better education to improve their social standing as by the drive to take up arms in the struggle.

Certainly by 1982, following pressure from the Western Five Contact Group, SWAPO had abandoned many of the more radical tenets of its 1976 programme and was adopting an increasingly moderate and conciliatory line on such issues as nationalization, property rights and a free market economy.[41]

Thus the structure of the political economy in Namibia, the reformist policies of the South African-designed 'interim' administrations (the creation of a new élite in particular), together with the increasing squeeze on SWAPO by the Contact Group, and the movement's own nationalistic predispositions, in many respects cast the mould for a post-independence society and set the pattern for future social differentiation. Writing in 1982 of the implications of the establishment of a black élite, Abrahams presciently asserted:

> In the meantime an élite, 'the black middle class', has been created which can serve as the social force sponsoring neo-colonial control. UN-supervised elections, when they are eventually held, will accordingly mean that the winner will no longer 'take all'. He will not, in fact, be much better off than the loser. Everything will have been agreed to in advance and a certain system will be imposed regardless of the electoral result.[42]

Structural Inequality and the Emergence of New Élites

At independence the incoming SWAPO government inherited a society in which racial, ethnic and class differentiation were firmly entrenched, and in which political enmity and social distrust were endemic. As Chapter 9 also shows, in attempting to overcome these divisions the new government adopted a policy of national reconciliation as its lode star in its efforts to forge a new national identity. However, while the adoption of this policy was politically and economically expedient in the light of the experiences of Angola, Mozambique and Zimbabwe, national reconciliation also reinforced the *status quo* by protecting the pre-independence gains of the minority, by reproducing existing relations of production and by legitimizing patterns of social differentiation that had existed in the colonial era. The settler community, together with the tiny black élite which had emerged under the interim governments, made up just 5 per cent of the population, but in 1989 was estimated to generate 71 per cent of the GDP. The bottom 55 per cent of the population, in contrast, generated just 3 per cent of the GDP.[43] Access to primary resources and services, likewise, was heavily skewed towards the élite.

While it is not possible to determine class formation from a series of social indicators, there is evidence of a growing class stratification which in the post-independence period has begun to transcend previous racial and ethnic boundaries. This observation relates primarily to the emergence of a new élite (a combination of the previously existing élite with an expanded organizational élite of senior black administrators, politicians and business people) who inhabit an economic and social world largely divorced from that of the majority of the urban and rural poor. With the limited resources available to the country, it may be argued, sustaining the lifestyles of this élite must inevitably be at the expense of development projects for the poor.

While this trend is, as already noted, rather typical in newly independent countries in Africa, it is of particular interest in a country ruled by a political party that had been viewed by many Western governments as Marxist in orientation and which had demonstrated its own predilection for socialism. SWAPO, however, was first and foremost a nationalist movement, composed of a broad spectrum of social strata, mobilized for national liberation. As with many other nationalist movements its populism, packaged in the rhetoric of socialism, to a significant degree became a vehicle for the advancement of specific interest groups within the movement.[44] Although there is little evidence that individuals from among the (extremely small) indigenous élite joined SWAPO specifically to advance their own interests (this only occurred, to a limited extent, near the end of the liberation war),[45] it is evident that the struggle did create its own élite, both in exile and, to a lesser extent, amongst those who remained in Namibia.

Over and above the cadre of political and military leaders who emerged in the liberation struggle and who came to occupy leading positions in the new government, the primary determinant of social and economic standing in the post-independence era appears to have been education. Of the 40,000–50,000 Namibians who went into exile, a relatively small proportion underwent comprehensive post-secondary training.[46] The remainder were trained as soldiers or learnt rudimentary artisanal and agricultural skills in camps in Angola. Access to training, thus, would seem to have been a key determinant in the social differentiation of exiles, not least in the employment opportunities which it has afforded in the post-independence era, but also in the lifestyles to which it accustomed many repatriated exiles. Although educated individuals by no means lived lives of affluence in exile, their expectations of life after independence were clearly influenced by their years in Europe, the USA and elsewhere.

The post-independence era has also undoubtedly accentuated the latent divide between the different social strata (workers, subsistence farmers, business people, intellectuals, etc.) of which SWAPO was composed. In part due to the policy of national reconciliation and in part to a commonality of material interest, the new élite have reached a measure of accord with both the white settler community and the previously existing black élite.

The New Bureaucratic Bourgeoisie

Although the independence struggle was primarily a battle between the white settler minority and the black majority, both the exigencies of war and the practicalities of administering the interim governments and of forming a black middle class necessitated a degree of racial integration. Mixing of the leading strata of the white and black populations at independence thus was not as precipitous a step as it might have been even a decade earlier. As a consequence there is little to suggest that élite formation is proceeding primarily along ethnic lines, as many of SWAPO's opponents had predicted. A review of recent senior appointments to the civil service does not indicate any undue favouritism towards the Ovambo-speaking population who form the backbone of SWAPO and who comprise nearly 50 per cent of the total population.[47] Although race and ethnicity remain latent lines of stress, they do not, at present, appear to be a limiting factor in the development of a broader class identity.

Nevertheless, following pre-independence trends, racial integration in the post-apartheid era has tended to take place almost exclusively in the upper echelons of the social order. This was a process first set in motion by the establishment of a government of national unity, whereby a number of opposition leaders were brought into the cabinet and white Namibians (not all of whom were SWAPO members) were appointed to key portfolios in the Ministries of Finance, Agriculture, Justice and Transport.[48]

Following this the opportunities which higher incomes afford have ensured that most senior black politicians and civil servants have been able to purchase homes in the more affluent and formerly exclusively white suburbs of Windhoek. By the end of 1992 not a single cabinet minister, for instance, lived in Katutura, the African township that used to be the bastion of political activism in Namibia. Senior government officials, in part for language reasons, have also tended to send their children to formerly exclusively white schools, where the medium of instruction is English and where the standard of education is generally higher than in predominantly black (but less expensive) schools.

Reproduction of Relations of Production

While the demands of the liberation struggle may have served to differentiate SWAPO's members, the inherited political economy also reinforced tendencies towards élitism. The decision to opt for a 'mixed economy' – in practice a capitalist economy – although in large part dictated by circumstances (Namibia's dependent economic status, and the collapse of support from socialist countries in particular), set the parameters in which the new government must operate. SWAPO controlled the political arena but not the economy, which continued to be dominated by forces which varied in their support from indifference to open hostility.[49] Consequently, in its efforts to promote the confidence of the business sector (which retained the ultimate sanction of disinvestment from Namibia), the government moved extremely cautiously on issues of affirmative action and minimum wages which are fundamental to the redress of past inequities.

The hegemony of transnational capital and the country's extreme dependence on the South African economy will clearly not be easily diminished. Much of the inequity of the past dualistic system, in consequence, is simply being replicated in the new political order. While it must be recognized that the policy options open to the SWAPO government are limited, it is also questionable whether the emerging élites would wish to promote a radically different social order from that which existed at independence.

Given the prevailing geo-political climate, the new government's pursuit of a policy of national reconciliation was both politically and economically necessary. Not only did it forestall the flight of skills and capital, but it also minimized the potential for political destabilization by disaffected opponents. The policy of national reconciliation has nevertheless done much to reinforce the *status quo* and in so doing it has further strengthened trends towards élitism amongst the indigenous population. This is nowhere more evident than in state policy towards conditions of service in the public sector.

Article 141 (1) of the Constitution, in particular, has served to reinforce the *status quo*, by affirming that 'any person holding office under any law in force on the date of Independence shall continue to hold such office unless and until he or she resigns or is retired, transferred or removed from office in accordance with law'.[50] This clause has been interpreted to imply that individuals employed by the colonial government would lose none of their existing employment benefits including generous housing, pension, medical aid and car allowances. This presented the SWAPO government with something of a dilemma: whether to implement a differential system of benefits for existing and in-coming civil servants (many of whom were SWAPO members) or whether to equalize all employment packages. For both practical and political reasons the decision was taken to maintain the existing system of benefits. As a result Namibia is now reputed to have one of the highest civil service salary structures in sub-Saharan Africa.

A New Underclass

Whilst on one level this decision was understandable, at other levels it has done nothing to redress one of the most glaring inequities of the colonial system: that of the disproportionate expenditure of public funds on the towns, to service in the first instance a largely urban élite.[51] This factor, together with a progressive decline in the productivity of the traditional agricultural sector and the loss of military-related employment, has contributed to a massive influx of people into the capital in the post-independence era.[52] The township of Katutura, for example, is reputed to be growing at a rate of 12 per cent per annum or more.

As a consequence of a distorted economy and as a legacy of apartheid rule, there is both a critical shortage of skills (exacerbated by departing South Africans and only partially offset by returning exiles) and a severe problem of unemployment among the semi-skilled and unskilled. For those black Namibians with skills, demand generally exceeds supply and thus far there has been little competition for employment. The jobs which they fill, moreover, tend to be in the urban areas (in Windhoek in particular) where social services are relatively good and lifestyles are easier. The converse applies to those who have limited skills. Competition for employment is fierce, wages are low, and many are forced to eke out a subsistence in the rural areas where services are limited or non-existent.

In view of the shortage of formal wage opportunities, the majority of the new work seekers in the urban areas are compelled to seek employment in the informal sector. However, due to the absence of a strong productive base in Namibia, the informal sector is supported largely by the recycling of wages earned in the formal sector, and its capacity to absorb the influx of migrants is severely constrained. This implies that levels of urban unemployment are likely to increase rather than decrease in the years to come. The consequence of this expansion in the numbers of the urban unemployed is likely to be the consolidation of a new underclass. In the absence of the unifying goal of national liberation, the lumpen predisposition of these subaltern classes is likely to be reinforced. The steady rise in crime rates in Windhoek since independence is probably indicative of this trend.

Emerging Contradictions

The government's caution in effecting extensive changes within the political economy led to public charges that national reconciliation was a one-sided process that benefited the white settler community far more than the poor majority.[53] This bitterness was perhaps most strongly felt by the thousands of repatriated exiles who struggled, mostly with scant success, to re-enter the labour market and to reintegrate themselves fully into Namibian society. For these individuals, the widening economic gap between themselves and their former comrades-in-arms was most cruelly felt.[54]

Within the private sector there was a marked antipathy towards employing 'returnees', who were often seen by potential employers as representatives of the ruling party. Linked to this, the qualifications, experience and work ethic of individuals trained in the former socialist countries were also the subject of scepticism among prospective employers, and undoubtedly contributed to their reluctance to recruit repatriated exiles despite skill shortages in their firms.

Most exiles were welcomed back by their families and the community as returning heroes who had brought liberation to the country. Whilst this outpouring undoubtedly reflected the joy and pride of the community in their returned sons and daughters, it also reflected certain expectations about the future. In particular, many families believed that with the return of family members educated abroad, their own fortunes would improve, both through the salaries earned by the 'returnees' and through the new opportunities which they imagined would open up through their influential positions in society. The inability of returned exiles to acquire employment was therefore a source of considerable disappointment and embarrassment to themselves and to their families. The failure to live up to the expectations of their families was acutely felt, and aggravated by the fact that many of those who had remained in the country (among them many who, to a lesser or greater degree, were seen as having collaborated with the colonial regime) appeared to be better off than most 'returnees'.

The 'land question' in Namibia also remained highly problematic. Unequal access to productive land and to water is a central feature of Namibia's colonial inheritance. In a context where both resources are absolutely scarce, the private ownership of some 45 per cent of the total land area and 74 per cent of the potentially arable land by some 4,045 mainly white commercial farmers is a major source of the inequality of incomes and wealth. In attempting to redress these imbalances, however, the government once again confronts the paradox of matching increased production (or at least maintaining existing levels of production) with greater social equity, since much of Namibia is unsuitable for agriculture. Despite land shortages in the 'communal areas' and popular pressure for land redistribution, the extensive (and expensive) nature of farming in many commercial farming areas (15 hectares are required per livestock unit in certain areas) renders them unsuitable for small-scale farming activities.[55] Whilst a measure of consensus on the issue of redistribution was reached during the National Land Conference held in June 1991,[56] the land question remained far from resolved.

The issue of social equity, however, is not confined solely to imbalances in land ownership between white and black Namibians. In the post-independence era the most vocal and articulate claims for land redistribution came not from the land-scarce or landless poor but from wealthier black farmers seeking to increase their own access to land. These claims, moreover, were not confined to the commercial farming areas. In a number of the communal areas (in Ovambo, Kavango and Hereroland in particular) there was a growing trend among certain wealthier farmers (business people, former officials of the second-tier governments, senior civil servants and some politicians) to illegally fence rangelands, hitherto recognized as communal pasture, for private use.[57] For these individuals it was not the inequitable distribution of land in itself which was unsatisfactory, but rather their share of it. Although the government indicated that it will take action against illegal fencing, there appeared to be little urgency to do so and the process continued.

For many repatriated exiles, as well as many others who supported SWAPO during the liberation struggle, the distinction between party, government and state proved difficult to grasp. For those repatriated exiles who had been schooled in a Marxist tradition, the three entities were understood to be largely synonymous, or at least closely interactive. SWAPO was perceived as the party of the workers, of the students and of the dispossessed. And yet in a multi-party democracy and in pursuit of national reconciliation, the government portrayed itself as the government of all Namibians. Although three years after independence there were no signs of serious desertions from SWAPO, there was unquestionably growing disillusionment in many quarters, not least in the party's Ovambo heartland, however difficult it would be for an opposition party such as the DTA to capitalize on it.

Prospects for the Emergence of Alternative Political Movements

The prospects for the emergence of alternative mass-based political opposition, however, were limited by the fact that as a legacy of colonial rule relatively few community-based organizations existed in Namibia outside party political structures. Within the major urban centres, and within Windhoek in particular, community-based structures were relatively well established, but there were few such organizations in the populous rural areas of the north. The tradition of spontaneous mass mobilization is thus not well established – indeed, as Chapter 4 shows, it was not infrequently discouraged – and such public demonstrations as took place after independence were carefully orchestrated by one or other political party.

The extended family system that exists throughout the rural areas of Namibia is also likely to mitigate the effects of growing class contradictions in the short run. Charney, in other contexts, speaks of the role of 'lineage ideologies' in reinforcing the legitimacy of élites in societies where capitalist and domestic modes of production inter-penetrate.[58] Kinship obligations and clientelism, under such circumstances, serve to reduce tensions between the élite and subaltern classes by extending influence and, to a lesser extent, economic gains to subordinate groups. In Namibia, the reciprocities and obligations of the extended family system are such that the socio-economic standing of many rural households depends heavily on remittances from those in waged employment in the public sector. Undermining the jobs of those in positions of influence in the public sector thus could prove to be self-defeating.

The Prospects for Organized Labour

The prospects for the emergence of a coherent working-class movement also seemed limited, despite the fact that considerable dissatisfaction existed within the trade unions, particularly in respect to delays in the implementation of a labour code and the introduction of a policy on minimum wages. Thus the president of the SWAPO-affiliated National Union of Namibian Workers (NUNW), in addressing a May Day rally in Windhoek in 1991 and in the presence of cabinet ministers, accused the government of lacking commitment to the plight of Namibian workers. More pointedly, however, he raised the now familiar complaint about the one-sidedness of national reconciliation:

The working class of Namibia is experiencing a lot of problems in terms of employers who misinterpret reconciliation. If reconciliation is understood by the employers as a perpetuation of apartheid laws and equated with exploitation, then workers will no longer tolerate this. If reconciliation is a ticket for the employers to re-exploit us and to secure their jobs, while the blacks are getting more unemployed and roaming the streets, then reconciliation will no longer be accepted by the working class.[59]

The growing dissatisfaction of Namibian workers aside, the trade union movement as a whole was in disarray and in no position to mount a sustained challenge either to employers or, should it so wish, to the government. While this was in part due to the limitations of the economy and to the composition of the Namibian labour force, it was also, as already indicated, influenced by the role of the trade union movement in the national liberation movement and by its relationship to SWAPO. Until the advent of independence, the trade union movement was characterized more by its capacity to mobilize politically than by its ability to win concessions for its members.

Since independence the conventional line taken by SWAPO officials has been that of the unity of party and unions.[60] While this perception was still prevalent among some workers who remained fiercely loyal to SWAPO, it was clear that many among the leadership of the unions would have liked to disaffiliate from the party and steer a more independent line. The June 1992 edition of the NUNW News, for example, spoke of the need to view the current phase 'as a transition to disentangle political activities from trade union activities'.[61]

The emergence of a strongly independent union movement, however, was constrained by the fact that some of its most prominent leaders were still closely linked to SWAPO – the Secretary General of the NUNW federation, for example, was appointed to the SWAPO National Executive Committee at the 1991 Congress. Further, the leadership of the unions has been reduced by the appointment of a number of trade unionists to key positions within the government or to senior positions within the public sector.[62] In this context, and with the growing realization that the trade union movement and the party represented discrete interests, some union leaders were struggling to redefine the role of organized labour in Namibia.[63]

Conclusion

While it is perhaps too soon to make definitive pronouncements on the political economy of independent Namibia, discernible trends in the post-independence years indicated a drift towards a familiar neo-colonial pattern, and in particular the replication of the social and productive relations established under colonialism. Namibia remained heavily dependent on the South African economy both for the import of consumer goods and for the export of its primary commodities. At the same time, the Southern African Customs Union, the Southern African Regional Industrial Development Programme, and the Export Incentives Programme, all of which were controlled by Pretoria, severely hampered the development of Namibian industry and restricted much-needed programmes to diversify the economy and broaden the employment base.[64]

The policies of national reconciliation, the inherited (and increasingly entrenched) structural inequalities of the political economy and the emergence of a new organizational élite did not, taken together, augur well for the development of a significantly greater measure of equity in Namibia in the immediate future. Although SWAPO had not formally abandoned the ideals espoused in its independence election manifesto in November 1989,[65] with the passage of time the leadership seemed to be losing any sense of urgency with regard to many of these issues. Whether SWAPO's supporters would continue to remain quiescent under these circumstances remained to be seen.

Notes

1. I. L. Markowitz, *Power and Class in Africa* (New Jersey: Prentice Hall, 1977), p. 205.
2. B. Magubane, 'The evolution of class structure in Africa', in P. C. Gutkind and I. Wallerstein (eds), *The Political Economy of Contemporary Africa* (London: Sage Publications, 1976), p. 185. Magubane also cautions that the concept of élite should not be considered as a substitute for class, since the former 'refers to groups exercising power at a particular time and the latter to an economic relationship.... [I]n the present conditions in Africa', he maintains, 'an élite as a group which is not the owner of the means of production is a transitory formation whose hold on the state is extremely tenuous, as the recent military coups have demonstrated.' *Ibid.*, p. 194. However, to this must be added the observation that, given sufficient time, élites can and do reproduce themselves (coups notwithstanding) and are capable of developing into, or merging with, independent classes.
3. H. Wolpe, *Race, Class and the Apartheid State* (London: James Currey, 1988), p. 50.
4. A. Cooper, 'Namibia in the world economy', in B. Wood (ed.), *Namibia 1884–1984: Readings on Namibia's History and Society* (London: Namibia Support Committee, 1988).
5. R. Moorsom, 'In the grip of imperialism', in B. Wood (ed.), *op. cit.*, p. 303.
6. R. Gordon, *Vernacular Law and the Future of Human Rights in Namibia* (Windhoek: NISER Discussion Paper No. 11, 1991).
7. See SWAPO, *To Be Born a Nation, The Liberation Struggle for Namibia* (London: Zed Press, 1981), p. 172; and UNIN, *Namibia, Perspectives for National Reconstruction and Development* (Lusaka: UNIN, 1986), p. 44.
8. Intellectuals in this context are distinguished from a professional intelligentsia. See A. D. Smith, *The Ethnic Revival* (Cambridge: Cambridge University Press, 1981), pp. 108–12, for a discussion of this distinction. Although only some of the early nationalist leaders were, in fact, students or teachers (Toivo ya Toivo, Andreas Shipanga, Fanuel Kozonguizi, Mburumba Kerina, Emil Appolus and Kenneth Abrahams, for example), the majority were individuals with the drive and ambition to rise above the oppression and inertia of colonial rule. They were what Gramsci would have called 'organic intellectuals'. See Gramsci, *Selections from the Prison Notebooks* (London: Lawrence and Wishart, 1971), p. 6.
9. Interview with Dr Kenneth Abrahams, 20 September 1992, Windhoek. Abrahams, who was a founding member of SWAPO and part of the intellectual élite, recalls that some Namibians survived in Cape Town by passing themselves off as coloureds, thus obviating the need for contract labour passes.
10. A. Shipanga and S. Armstrong, *In Search of Freedom* (Gibraltar: Ashanti Publishing, 1989), p. 36. According to Shipanga, the first black-owned store, the Ondangwa Cash Store, was established by Toivo ya Toivo, following his expulsion from Cape Town in 1958.
11. SWAPO, *op. cit.*, p. 21.
12. *Ibid.*, p. 22.
13. G. Cawthra, *Brutal Force, The Apartheid War Machine* (London: IDAF, 1986), p. 183.
14. D. Simon, 'Windhoek: desegregation and change in the capital of South Africa's erstwhile colony', in A. Lemon (ed.), *Homes Apart: South Africa's Segregated Cities* (Cape Town, 1991), p. 187.
15. Abrahams, for example, states that while 86 per cent of black workers were earning incomes below a Household Subsistence Level of R261 per month, high school teachers and middle-level civil servants were earning salaries of R1,000 to R1,500 a month together with such perks as 100 per cent housing loans, car purchase schemes, entertainment allowances and a range of other benefits. K. Abrahams, 'The "Waserauta" phenomenon: additional notes on the Namibian élite', *The Namibian Review*, 25 (July/August 1982b), pp. 23–4.
16. R. Green, 'Namibia – notes on the political economy of transition: an applied planning and policy perspective', in B. Wood (ed.), *op. cit.*, p. 380.
17. W. Werner, 'Ethnicity and reformism in Namibia', in G. Totemeyer, V. Kandetu and W. Werner, *Namibia in Perspective* (Windhoek: Council of Churches in Namibia, 1987), p. 75.
18. P. Dutkiewicz and R. Shenton, 'Crisis in Africa: "Etatization" and the logic of diminished reproduction', *Review of African Political Economy*, 37 (1986), p. 111. According to the Van Eeden Commission, 'The primary concern (of the second-tier governments) is not administrative utility, or effectiveness *per se*. These matters are important of course, but the stability of communities in the same spirit, as determined by the division of functions already established between the Central Government and Representative Authorities, is of paramount importance' (cited in W. Werner, *op. cit.*).

19. SWAPO, *op. cit.*, p. 59.
20. *Ibid.*, p. 325.
21. *Ibid.*, p. 42.
22. P. Peltola, 'The role of the National Union of Namibian Workers in the struggle for indepen-dence', unpublished seminar paper, NISER, University of Namibia, July 1992.
23. This was in strong contrast to the situation which pertained in South Africa where organized labour, COSATU in particular, while committed to the overthrow of apartheid rule, insisted strongly on maintaining a clear distinction between the nationalist struggle and the workers' struggle. See E. Webster, 'New force on the shop floor', in SARS, *South African Review Two* (Braamfontein: Ravan Press, 1984), p. 84.
24. P. Peltola, *op. cit.*, p. 4. The importance of the role played by the SWAPO Youth League in mobilizing workers is also mentioned in the official SWAPO publication, *To Be Born a Nation*, *op. cit.*, p. 272.
25. P. Peltola, *ibid.*, p. 6.
26. Peltola cites the rise of Solidarity in Poland as the type of union which the leadership feared might disrupt SWAPO plans in an independent Namibia. *Ibid.*, p. 7.
27. These included Henry Boonzaaier, Fritz Spiegel, Theodor Thaniseb, Aron Seibeb, Pejavi Munyaro and Victor Nkandi, the latter two of whom died in detention. *Ibid.*, p. 7.
28. SWAPO, *op. cit.*, p. 41.
29. G. Cawthra, *op. cit.*, p. 262. At the close of the war an estimated 9,200 individuals in the four northern regions were directly dependent on the military for their income. See I. J. van der Merwe, *The Role of War in Regional Development in Namibia* (Institute for Cartography, University of Stellenbosch, 1990).
30. Of the 240 businesses identified in Oshakati and Ondangua in April 1990, 20 per cent were liquor related. C. Tapscott, 'The cuca shops of Owambo – social institution or social blight?', *Namibian*, 19 June 1990.
31. A businessman in the former Ovambo region reports that SWATF and SADF soldiers were instructed to boycott shops where the owners were known to be SWAPO sympathizers. Interview with Prins Shiimi, Ondangua, 18 August 1992.
32. This included forced removal from 'free fire zones' on the borders of Namibia and in areas known for high guerilla activity. See A. Weaver, 'The South African Defence Force in Namibia', in J. Cock and L. Nathan (eds), *War and Society – the Militarisation of South Africa* (Cape Town: David Philip, 1989), p. 98.
33. This process was exacerbated by a series of drought years in the early 1980s.
34. W. Werner, *op. cit.*, p. 77.
35. In the early 1980s, 17 foreign-based companies held major and usually complete ownership in the 18 significant mines in Namibia (SWAPO, *op. cit.*, p. 36).
36. A Windhoek businessman who supplied telecommunications equipment to the military confided that he had never had to submit a tender in more than nine years of business with the SWATF. Private interview, name withheld, Windhoek, 5 September 1992.
37. D. Simon, *op. cit.*, p. 179.
38. 1970 Population Census; 1981 Population Census; SWAPO, *op. cit.*, p. 322.
39. The 1979 White Paper on Defence, for example, speaks of 'the RSA's military responsibility in SWA where SWAPO is trying to intimidate and subjugate the population with terrorism with the help of its Soviet allies'. Republic of South Africa, *White Paper on Defence and Armaments Supply 1979*, (Pretoria: Government Printer, 1979), p. 2.
40. SWAPO, *Political Programme* (Lusaka: 1976), p. 6.
41. K. Abrahams, 'Namibian independence negotiations: approaching a neo-colonialist settlement', *The Namibian Review*, 25 (July/August 1982a), p. 11.
42. *Ibid.*, p. 7.
43. World Bank, *Namibia Poverty Alleviation with Sustainable Growth* (Washington, 1991), p. 3.
44. See for example A. D. Smith, *op. cit.*; E. Kedourie, *Nationalism in Asia and Africa* (London: Weidenfeld and Nicolson, 1971); H. J. Brenda, 'Non-Western intelligentsia as political élites', in H. Kautsky (ed.), *Political Change in Underdeveloped Countries* (New York: Wiley, 1962).
45. Perhaps the most controversial of these last-minute conversions was the announcement in the late 1980s by the millionaire businessman Frans Indonga that he was siding with SWAPO. Indonga had previously been a Minister of Finance in the second-tier Owambo 'government', and had built his fortune during the period of military occupation.
46. C. Tapscott and B. Mulongeni, *An Evaluation of the Welfare and Future Prospects of Repatriated Namibians in Northern Namibia* (Windhoek: NISER Research Report No. 3, 1990).
47. Public Service Commission, unpublished staff records (Windhoek, 1990).
48. These included Otto Herrigel as Minister of Finance (since resigned), Gert Hanekom as

Minister of Agriculture, Water and Rural Development (now Minister of Finance), Dr Zedekia Ngavirue as Director General of the National Planning Commission, Vekuui Rukoro (president of the NNF) as Deputy Minister of Justice, Reggie Diergaard (UDF) as Deputy Minister of Youth and Sports and Claus Dierks (SWAPO) as Deputy Minister of Transport and Telecommunications.

49. According to Bob Meiring, Chairman of the Board of the parastatal First National Development Corporation, many local business people have been 'sitting on their hands' since independence, withholding new investment in Namibia until the political scenario becomes clearer. This, inevitably, is having an effect on general investor confidence in the country. Personal communication, H. A. R. Meiring, Windhoek, 22 February 1992.

50. Republic of Namibia, *Constitution* (Windhoek: 1990), p. 70.

51. Department of Economic Affairs, *Manpower Survey 1988* (Windhoek: 1988), p. 13.

52. B. Frayne, *Urbanization in Post-Independence Windhoek* (Windhoek: NISER, 1992).

53. This is expressed in numerous letters to local newspapers, epitomized as follows: 'Our country has gone through a long struggle. The People have struggled together, workers and students have really sacrificed; our PLAN combatants have given up their education and lives to serve (for no salary) the motherland, but it seems our ministers have forgotten.... Our education system has to continue to support racists and autocrats who now pretend to have changed so as to retain their jobs, all for the sake of reconciliation. Is reconciliation the reason for these high salaries?', *Namibian*, 11 May 1990.

54. 'What about the people who were at the battlefront during the liberation of our country, and who are not educated? What are we going to do? Many of us are illiterate people who only know how to fight. Now we are being threatened by intellectuals who were lucky to be sent abroad by SWAPO to study for the benefit of the Namibian nation. Many of them are now proud and arrogant because they have been given jobs and driving luxurious cars.' Amaandjange, *Namibian*, 23 July 1990.

55. F. Adams. W. Werner and P. Vale, *The Land Issue in Namibia: An Enquiry* (Windhoek: NISER Research Report No. 1, 1990), pp. 81–2.

56. Republic of Namibia, *National Conference on Land Reform and the Land Question* (Windhoek: Office of the Prime Minister, 1991); S. Brown, 'Land reform in Namibia: rhetoric, reform or revolution', *Southern Africa Report*, 7, 2 (November 1991).

57. *New Era*, 7 May 1992; *The Namibian*, 3 June 1992. Many of those who have carried out this fencing (which is beyond the means of most peasant farmers) accrued their wealth under the colonial administration and are now consolidating their positions under the SWAPO government.

58. C. Charney, 'Political power and social class in neo-colonial African states', *Review of African Political Economy*, 38, April 1987, p. 52.

59. *Namibian Worker*, June 1991.

60. This view is consistently reinforced by SWAPO officials, as in pronouncements by Festus Naholo, SWAPO deputy head, that 'SWAPO and the NUNW (trade union) are one, and both fought for the liberation of Namibia.... SWAPO will make sure that workers' rights are achieved.' *Namibian Worker*, June 1991.

61. *NUNW News*, June 1992.

62. Most notable in that respect was the appointment of the militant mine workers' leader, Ben Ulenga, to the post of Deputy Minister of Wildlife, Conservation and Tourism.

63. The NUNW, in particular, embarked upon a series of seminars, workshops and training programmes in 1992 both to redefine their role and to train new leadership.

64. Republic of Namibia, *Draft Transitional Development Plan, 1991/2–1993/4*, (Windhoek: 1991); D. Simon, 'The ties that bind: decolonisation and neo-colonialism in Southern Africa', in C. Dixon and M. J. Hefferman (eds), *Colonialism and Development in the Contemporary World* (London: Mansell, 1991).

65. This stated that 'the goal of SWAPO's policy on economic reconstruction and development will ... be to bring change in ownership relations, bring about equitable distribution of national income, create rational linkages of sectors and diversify the economy', SWAPO, *Election Manifesto: Towards an Independent and Democratic Namibia: SWAPO's Policy Positions* (Windhoek: SWAPO Directorate of Elections, 1989), p. 8.

III THE LEGACY

9

SWAPO in Office[1]

LAUREN DOBELL

In the first 20 months following independence, the policies of the new SWAPO government astonished many observers, at home and abroad, with their emphasis on the pivotal role of the private sector in promoting economic growth, and the paramount importance of creating an 'enabling environment' for foreign investment. When and how, journalists, diplomats and academics wondered, had this erstwhile guerilla movement shed the 'scientific socialist' philosophy which had ostensibly guided its struggle for liberation, to adopt, with little apparent regret, the capitalist orthodoxies of the post-Cold War global economy? It will be argued here that this apparent metamorphosis was neither sudden nor surprising, nor was the relative ease with which a SWAPO government was able to market neo-colonial solutions to its constituents cause for dismay. Both, rather, were predictable consequences of the externally oriented diplomatic strategy pursued by SWAPO's leadership throughout its struggle to liberate Namibia from South African colonial rule.

The first part of this paper outlines briefly the origins of this strategy, and its consequences for the politics and practice of SWAPO as a liberation movement. The second part examines the early months of SWAPO's inaugural term in office as Namibia's first democratically elected government for clues as to the direction its programme of 'national reconstruction and development' would take.

The Origins and Consequences of SWAPO's Liberation Strategy

Owing to historically imposed circumstances, the most important of which were South West Africa/Namibia's unique status in international law, and the overwhelming military superiority of the South African regime, SWAPO's leadership in exile chose to pursue a diplomatic strategy with military underpinnings rather than one based primarily on internal struggle. SWAPO's consequent reliance on the financial, moral, material, organizational, institutional, and, most critically, diplomatic support offered by the international community would have crucial consequences, both for the nature of the struggle and for the outcome of the transition from authoritarian rule to independence under a SWAPO government.

In the first place it ensured that the direction of the struggle would come, by the early 1970s, to be guided almost entirely by SWAPO's leaders in exile, whose development thinking, at least in so far as this was expressed in official documents and statements, inevitably came to reflect more emphatically the preferences and expectations of its diverse foreign sponsors than the objective needs of its domestic constituency. The only constant in the documents and statements issued by SWAPO during the struggle was the demand for independence. All else was negotiable, it seemed, and the language employed depended mostly on the intended audience. This is not, of course, to exclude other influences, including the lack of contact, and the differences in approach, between the internal and exiled leaderships of SWAPO; a serious crisis in the movement (its second) in 1976, which forced the leadership to adopt, at least temporarily, the more militant rhetoric embodied in the oft-quoted 1976 Political Programme; and the not-inconsiderable involvement of foreign experts in the drafting of the SWAPO documents released during this period.[2] But it was the external orientation of SWAPO's strategy which underlay and overdetermined the rest.

Its focus on external allies was largely at the expense of the other two strands in SWAPO's approach: armed struggle, and the organization and mobilization of resistance at home, the latter in particular. SWAPO's support at home was usually, and understandably, taken for granted by its leaders. As the only movement perceived as capable of overthrowing the South African regime, SWAPO was guaranteed broad popular support inside Namibia. It had no need to engage in intensive political work to win the people from a regime that offered them nothing.[3]

Finally, and this is a central point, SWAPO's leadership, while it mastered the many 'languages' of foreign diplomacy necessary to survive within a constantly changing international environment – the African idiom, the Eastern bloc idiom, the Western idiom, the United Nations, Non-Aligned Movement (NAM) and Commonwealth idioms, even the solidarity idiom – did not develop a coherent vision of a radically transformed society in an independent Namibia consistent with its claim to be a national liberation movement with a scientific socialist programme. The frequent, almost Zelig-like, shifts in rhetoric over its three decades of struggle led SWAPO to be variously reviled or admired, at different times, and in different quarters, as a Soviet puppet, as a model of moderation, or, again, as the Marxist-Leninist vanguard of a genuine people's revolution. Of course, SWAPO was by no means a monolith – like any national front it spanned an array of classes and perspectives – but the absence of a single ideological outlook was primarily due to a deliberate pragmatism on the part of its leaders. SWAPO's pursuit of its one overriding objective, majority rule in an independent Namibia, never faltered, a quest only rarely described as bluntly as in this observation, attributed to a 'high-ranking UN official': 'To SWAPO ... labels of ideology have no meaning.... But one thing is important – nationalism. Nationalism is fact. The others are only labels.'[4]

INTERNATIONAL RESOURCES AND THE DIPLOMATIC CAMPAIGN
The sources and extent of its external support are critical to understanding why SWAPO was never able to move beyond a nationalist programme or vision, its claims and those of others notwithstanding. For almost two decades preceding Namibia's independence, SWAPO enjoyed material assistance which, calculated on a *per capita* basis, far exceeded that of any other Southern African liberation movement. The total bilateral aid received from Western governments,[5] as well as the considerable monies channelled through international church groups, solidarity movements, the United Nations Institute for Namibia (UNIN), the FAO, UNHCR and other UN special agencies was, relatively speaking, massive;[6] it was exceeded, however, by the contribution of Eastern bloc countries, which were estimated in 1984 to be providing 60 per cent of the total funding given to SWAPO, in addition to 90 per cent of its arms.[7] SWAPO's diplomatic corps consistently maintained that in its struggle for independence SWAPO would accept aid from any quarter, so long as it came with 'no strings attached'. In the sense that SWAPO was not held accountable to its external allies, while, at the same time, the resources these provided made SWAPO's leaders much less dependent on the support of their followers, this absence of strings had very real consequences.

The diversity of SWAPO's sponsors made it impolitic for the movement to align itself with any one source. Fortunately for SWAPO, it was also unnecessary. In the broadest terms, material support for SWAPO was of two kinds: what might be termed 'solidarity aid' and 'Cold War aid'. The solidarity aid encompassed that of the OAU, the NAM, the Commonwealth, Nordic governments, refugee support groups and human rights organizations, and was primarily a response to two factors: recognition of Namibia's claim to be an 'international responsibility', and of SWAPO's status as the 'authentic representative' of a people opposing South African apartheid-colonial rule. The requirements of this support were few. The very brutality of the South African regime was enough to guarantee continued backing from these sources, and, in the absence of any recognized alternative, SWAPO was the beneficiary.

The Cold War aid was of two kinds: arms and material assistance donated by Eastern bloc countries to SWAPO's military wing, and the financial and material assistance given by Western governments, and usually channelled through UNIN and the UN Nationhood Programme for Namibia. Here again, little was required of SWAPO, which was regarded by the donors as another pawn in the confrontation between the superpowers. SWAPO's policy documents, to the extent that they were taken seriously by the West as statements of intent, were measured primarily in terms of their impact on the balance of power in the region. Once it was acknowledged by the Western powers that no internal settlement in Namibia could succeed without SWAPO, they set about incorporating SWAPO into the solution. SWAPO's own programme for independent Namibia would, ultimately, be irrelevant to the outcome of the settlement initiated by the Western Contact Group.

Closely related to the other forms of support available to SWAPO were its moral resources, the most influential of which were the support of Namibia's churches and international abhorrence of the apartheid system. For present purposes it is necessary only to observe that the Namibian churches' staunch support of SWAPO (after 1971) provided it with a moral legitimacy enjoyed by few ostensibly Marxist-Leninist guerilla movements, and secured for it not only the powerful backing of international church bodies but widespread sympathy from generally conservative congregations around the world.[8] South Africa's intransigence was enough to frustrate even its would-be defenders in international fora, of which the Reagan administration was the most determined, while its brutality domestically, particularly in northern Namibia, rendered ineffective its successive attempts to 'win the hearts and minds' of sufficient Namibians for an internal settlement. To a considerable extent, the sheer odiousness of the enemy shielded SWAPO's policies and practice from the sort of critical scrutiny they might otherwise have been subjected to, both inside and outside Namibia.

SWAPO's greatest resources, however, were diplomatic. By the end of 1976, its position at the United Nations was entrenched, when General Assembly resolutions confirmed SWAPO's status as the 'sole and authentic' representative of the Namibian people, and granted the movement observer status.[9] The General Assembly also formally recognized the legitimacy of the armed struggle, and stipulated that SWAPO be present at talks with South Africa concerning the transfer of power to the Namibian people under the auspices of the United Nations. Membership or observer status in a number of UN special agencies soon followed. Though not a member of the Commonwealth, SWAPO was, after 1975, the beneficiary of a programme established by the Commonwealth for the training of Namibians. In 1978 SWAPO was invited to become a full member of the NAM. In addition, by the late 1970s, the movement was represented by quasi-diplomatic missions in numerous countries. By the time the Contact Group embarked on the negotiations designed to ensure a smooth, and, from its perspective, non-disruptive transition to independence in Namibia, SWAPO, not surprisingly, was confident that its position as the future government of Namibia was assured. It was a faith that would be tested severely in the long years that followed, but never shattered.

TRANSITION WITHOUT TRANSFORMATION
It took more than a decade following the adoption of UNSCR 435 to negotiate a settlement of the Namibian issue. During this time the attention of the SWAPO leader-

ship was focussed on interminable rounds of 'proximity talks' and pre-implementation meetings.[10] What lay beyond – the reconstruction and development of Namibia under a democratically elected government – was rarely, it seems, substantively discussed.

Space does not permit a detailed discussion of the three major documents, all produced during 1975 and 1976 (prior to the adoption of Resolution 435), that did purport to outline SWAPO's thinking with respect to the social, economic and political arrangements that would obtain in an independent Namibia, to wit: the 'Discussion Paper on the Constitution of Independent Namibia' (1975); the Political Programme (1976); and the National Programme, which was never officially released, but is thought to have been written in the latter part of 1976.

Of these, it is the 1976 Political Programme – the first and the last to be adopted by the movement in exile – which was, and is, widely regarded as marking a critical transition in the movement's thinking.[11] Yet the Programme did not represent a fundamental transformation in SWAPO's development thinking or political practice, as declared by its supporters and critics who painstakingly dissected it for evidence in support of various positions, but rather a calculated response to the challenges, both internal and external, then facing the movement.

These were threefold. First, within SWAPO itself, some recognition of the emerging radical discourse of the youth and PLAN fighters was needed, if only to prevent a recurrence of the so-called Shipanga crisis of 1974–6. Second, inside Namibia, arrangements for an internal settlement were proceeding apace, with the Turnhalle talks having by this time produced a Democratic Turnhalle Alliance (DTA), an alliance of ethnic groups prepared to establish an internal government. The Political Programme can be seen in part as an attempt to establish SWAPO's counter-claim to a cohesive national strategy for winning Namibian independence.

The third and main purpose of the Political Programme, however, was international. SWAPO had planned to use the 1976 OAU and NAM meetings as a springboard for gaining UN recognition as a government-in-waiting, but this plan had been scuttled by SWAPO's internal crisis and the resistance of the Western members of the UN Security Council. The movement therefore needed to step up its armed struggle in a bid for renewed diplomatic attention, and for this reason it had to move its headquarters from Zambia; this required that the leadership effect a reconciliation with the MPLA and its allies.[12] Since late 1975, when the tide had begun to turn in Angola and Kissinger's detente strategy for Southern Africa, in which SWAPO had been a minor but captive player, was unravelling, Nujoma had been hedging his bets, paying visits to Cuba, the Soviet Union, and finally Luanda. By the time 'detente' had been finally abandoned, the move to Angola was secured. The Political Programme must be understood primarily as the final touch to this strategic manoeuvring, and not as a statement of deeply held political beliefs of whatever stripe – whether 'communist-inspired', Marxist-Leninist, African or scientific socialist. As Hidipo Hamutenya, one of its main architects, subsequently observed:

> It was a period of a hardening of positions in Pretoria and elsewhere.... There was no prospect for an early settlement in Southern Africa. Things were bleak. There was no indication of any possibility of negotiation. [But with the collapse of the Portuguese regime, and the escalation of the war in Zimbabwe] the tar-baby strategy was discredited. The West realized they had made a mistake. Now they weren't in a position to influence events in Mozambique and Angola. These came to power and declared themselves Marxist-Leninists.... At this point what I'm trying to say is that it didn't take long between this [the release of SWAPO's Political Programme] and the resuscitation of the negotiations.[13]

Little has been written concerning the nature of the political education that took place in the SWAPO camps, usually led by political commissars trained on scholarships in China, the USSR, and in Eastern European countries. The evidence suggests, however, that rote learning rather than critical thinking was emphasized in such instruction, especially after the 1974–6 crisis.[14] That the National Programme, which hinted in places at a more sincere radical bent than the Political Programme, was never officially released, might indicate such an intolerance of independent expressions of political conviction.[15] In any case, all evidence points to official SWAPO documents being born primarily out of political expediency, and given shape by a small cadre of top SWAPO leaders assisted by some foreign academics, who after 1976 were mostly associated with UNIN.

ANTICIPATING INDEPENDENCE

Even had SWAPO been committed to a socialist vision, of course, it would have been under enormous, perhaps irresistible, pressure to abandon it. Having placed all their eggs in the diplomatic basket, SWAPO leaders may have perceived no option but to accede to the compromises demanded by the other parties to the negotiations brokered by the Western Contact Group (the USA, Canada, France, the UK and West Germany). There is little evidence, however, to suggest that SWAPO leaders made any effort to protect the movement's 1976 Political Programme for post-independence development from dilution. From the outset, the movement's nationalist ambitions were foremost, and its primary concern was to ensure that the conditions under which state power was transferred were those most favourable to an overwhelming SWAPO victory at the polls. The rest was negotiable, as Nujoma asserted unequivocally in a 1988 speech:

> For SWAPO all questions about Namibia's future can be discussed. The only issue over which there can be no negotiation is Namibia's right to independence and sovereign right to determine its own destiny.[16]

Of course, much had changed between the drafting of Resolution 435 and its long-awaited implementation ten years later.[17] The Cold War, at its height when the Western Contact Group was formed, had been replaced by a new era of superpower detente, the 'communist threat' had receded. Successive liberation movements had come to power in Southern Africa promising far-reaching socialist reforms, but had largely failed to surmount the daunting obstacles to their implementation. A negotiated settlement in Zimbabwe had demonstrated to South African policy makers how a satisfactory result could be achieved without military intervention; while similar constitutional safeguards (embodied in the 1982 Constitutional Principles drafted by the Contact Group)[18] and far more extensive economic ties had ensured that a SWAPO government would have even less room to manoeuvre when its turn came. A decade of successive multiracial 'internal solutions' had helped to foster a conservative political opposition in Namibia, at the same time doing much to reconcile right-wing whites to the idea of majority rule. By the time the transition process got formally under way, then, a neo-colonial outcome was perhaps inevitable. Those anticipating a fundamental transformation in Namibia along socialist lines were to be disappointed. SWAPO's response to the context in which the transition to independence took place clearly indicated its adjustment to the strict limitations that circumstances imposed.

The policy statements released by SWAPO during the transition period were notable for their businesslike tone and the relative absence of socialist rhetoric.[19] Intended mainly for an external audience, the documents expressed some token resistance to the abandonment, ostensibly temporary, of SWAPO's socialist ideals, but the emphasis was clear, as in these excerpts from its 1988 economic policy document, 'SWAPO's prospects brighten up':

> No wholesale nationalization of the mines, lands and other productive sectors is … envisaged for the foreseeable future. Instead … Namibia will stand ready to negotiate new and appropriate agreements with both existing foreign companies and new investors.… The central plank of SWAPO's policy on economic restructur-

ing and development is to achieve a necessary measure of national control of the country's resources and to bring about a balance between just economic returns to the Namibian people, on the one hand, and reasonable profits for foreign and local private investors on the other.[20]

SWAPO's ready acceptance of the results of the national election, in which it won a comfortable majority of 57.4 per cent, but failed to achieve the two-thirds majority required to unilaterally draft the new constitution, reflected both the absence of any alternative to acquiesence, and its recognition that, with or without a two-thirds majority, the broad outlines of the Namibian Constitution were predetermined. This was confirmed on the first day of the constitutional deliberations, when Nujoma opened the talks by proposing that, in the interests of making speedy progress, the newly elected Constituent Assembly adopt the 1982 Constitutional Principles as the basis for a new constitution. The unanimous approval of the proposal hastened the drafting process significantly, but at the price of circumventing debate on many fundamental issues.

As the constitutional talks progressed, it became increasingly clear that there were few areas of serious contention between the major parties, and on 9 February 1990, after a mere eighty days, the seven parties of the Assembly reached consensus on a model liberal democratic constitution, fulsomely praised by participants and observers as one of the best in the world. The essential similarity in outlook of most of the members of the Assembly undoubtedly facilitated the negotiation of inter-party 'pacts', which smoothed the drafting of the constitution, but simultaneously imposed crucial limitations on its potential to accommodate a fundamental restructuring of the nation. Amidst the general euphoria which marked the final stages of the transition to independence, however, only a few voices questioned the extent to which the constitution would permit, let alone actively assist, efforts to implement fundamental social and economic reform.

Declared socialists within SWAPO were quick to insist that the constitution left ample scope for socialist solutions. This position was succinctly expressed by Kaire Mbuende:

> There are sufficient provisions in the constitution to implement a radical policy.... [Y]ou don't blame the constitution for not pursuing a radical policy, you blame your political courage. The constitution is broad enough for different interpretations and different tendencies. There are sufficient provisions for a socialist approach.[21]

At the same time, however, Mbuende offered a new definition of socialism, one increasingly employed by SWAPO as they adapted the label to fit the liberal democratic model they sought to implement in practice:

> We have a market model at the same time that we are concerned about social justice.... We are not neutral about illiteracy, we are not neutral about disease, and that to me is what socialism is all about. The question of collective ownership of production is ... a controversial one.... There are other ways to redistribute wealth.[22]

This, then, was the SWAPO that came to power after three decades of nationalist struggle – a practical, pragmatic political party, espousing multi-party democracy, the rule of law, the separation of powers and the need for political stability to encourage productivity and prosperity. How it would balance its obligations to those who had supported it throughout the struggle, and had the most to gain from its success – workers, students, women, subsistence farmers, the unemployed – against the demands of local capital and powerful domestic interests, on the one hand, and of foreign investors and donors on the other, remained to be seen.

The Politics of Power

That the months immediately following independence witnessed a marked retreat, on the part of the government, from the socialist vision it had ostensibly embraced during the struggle should not, then, have been surprising to observers, in particular those familiar with SWAPO's political strategy as a national liberation movement. The politics of power had consistently come first for the SWAPO leadership in its bid for independence and majority rule in Namibia.[23] As it grappled with the realities of running a state and governing a nation – and in a dramatically changed world – it evinced the same pragmatism with respect to critical alliances, both local and international.

THE INTERNATIONAL DONORS' CONFERENCE
A top priority for the government was to parlay an international focus on Namibia into investment dollars while the iron was hot. Exactly three months after independence, on 21 June 1990, the new government of Namibia made its appeal for foreign aid and investment directly to the international community at a UN-sponsored Donors' Conference held in New York.

The documents submitted to the Donors' Conference provided a blueprint for at least the first phase of Namibia's development strategy, described as follows by the Director of Namibia's new National Planning Commission, Zedekia Ngavirue:

> We knew that we'd inherited a budget deficit and as there wasn't a lot of money to correct the imbalances, we needed outside help, and we also knew that the days when developing countries were spoiled were gone.... The pledges that were made [at the Donors' Conference] were for a three-year period, so we felt we should try to have a transitional development period while we are enjoying international support. I think a lot of the donors were aware that we really needed a period of high social spending and were willing to support us on that basis.[24]

Three documents comprised the core of the Namibian submission: 'The Reconstruction and Development of Namibia,' a 'Provisional Investment Programme,' and 'Policy Recommendations for Private Sector Development'. In addition to identifying the immediate requirements of the Namibian government, the General Policy Statement offered strong assurances to the donor and investment communities:

> The economic system will be based on the principles of a mixed market economy and social responsibility.... Foreign investments ... will be welcome.... While a strong and democratic state is necessary to initiate economic growth and development, foster social justice and establish security for the Namibian people, a dynamic private sector and well-functioning markets are, on the other hand, engines of income generation and safeguards against stagnation. It is of vital importance that the wealth creating sector is in appropriate balance with the wealth distributing sector.[25]

The 'Policy Recommendations for Private Sector Development', based on an overview of the Namibian economy by a World Bank team,[26] was emphatic on the dynamic role it foresaw for the private sector in Namibia, and the means for securing that role. Of particular importance in the creation of an 'enabling environment' for investment and enterprise development, the authors observed, would be (a) an Investment Code 'designed to attract economically viable and productive local and foreign investment', (b) a Labour Code, (c) 'growth-oriented incentives, especially for the export sector', and (d) a supportive financial regime, to include a National Development Bank and an Enterprise Development Corporation.

Finally, the 'Provisional Investment Programme' submitted at the Donors' Conference identified specific investment opportunities. The document was explicit regarding the role of the government in the Namibian economy:

> The role of the state in the economy will be limited to initiating reconstruction and development, securing basic needs to all Namibians, redistributing incomes in favour of the less fortunate, as well as safe-guarding the proper functioning of the markets....

> The Namibian government will ... make an environment conducive for private investments on issues such as taxation, foreign trade and capital regulations, capital markets and company legislation. Issues like political risks and Government participation will be approached in the spirit of good Government behaviour along the lines of international conventions.[27]

The programme for Namibia's reconstruction and development outlined in the three documents was well received by donor nations who felt that the general thrust of the proposed policies struck 'a healthy balance' between addressing 'the heightened expectations of the majority' for a rapid redistribution of wealth and services, and 'the need to attain sustainable and rapid growth in output and employment'. The government's proposed investment plan was approved as 'realistic', and Namibia's development prospects overall as 'promising'.[28]

Despite the warm reception, donor pledges, amounting to approximately $US200 million for 1990 and $US150 million for each of the two subsequent years, fell well short of the $US810 million over a three-year period sought by the Namibian government. This reflected perhaps both 'aid fatigue' on the part of donor countries, and traces of the West's former scepticism with respect to the genuine intentions of a SWAPO government.[29] At the same time, of course, there was considerable competition from Eastern European countries which were perceived by many potential investors as likely to produce more immediate and substantial returns.

Nonetheless, the Namibian government left little doubt during its mission's visit to New York about its desire to solidify its ties with the West. Nujoma paid a state visit to US President Bush, at which Namibia's intention to open an embassy in Washington was announced, and met separately with the World Bank president and the managing director of the IMF. A bilateral agreement with the Overseas Private Investment Corporation (OPIC), a US government agency, was also signed, a move which President Nujoma said he hoped would encourage American businesses to invest generously in Namibia's economic development.[30]

THE 1990 BUDGET

The free-market path to development outlined in the donors' package was confirmed in the SWAPO government's conservative first budget, tabled in July 1990 – a budget more likely to reassure still-cautious investors than to benefit ordinary Namibians, as the opposition *Times of Namibia* noted:

> The man who walks the streets of the country in his business suit might be relieved by the budget introduced by Minister of Finance Otto Herrigel ... with no rises in income tax and no increase in sales tax. But ... others, in particular blue collar workers, the army of the unemployed (estimated conservatively at 33 per cent of the workforce) and the embattled commercial farming sector could find little consolation in the ... budget.[31]

That Herrigel had accomplished a remarkable feat by reducing an anticipated budget deficit from R500 million to R210 million without raising taxes was widely acknowledged;[32] but opinions varied widely as to whether the costs of fiscal responsibility were acceptable. Herrigel's own preference for what was described as 'an evolutionary, instead of revolutionary approach to rectifying social ills' was clear, and Namibians were warned that short-term sacrifices would be needed for long-term gains.[33]

The response to the budget by opposition parties and various interest groups was a telling reflection of how far political lines, and perceptions of SWAPO, had shifted since independence. Speaking on behalf of the DTA, Dirk Mudge called it 'a *status quo* budget, almost a continuation of the colonial era.... [F]or all practical purposes the budget could have been presented by [former Administrator-General] Louis Pienaar.'[34]

Of especial concern to the DTA, Mudge continued, was the government's planned expenditure on the purchasing and staffing of embassies abroad. The government was spending R50 million to sell itself abroad when it should instead be selling itself 'to the people by building more houses for the poor'.[35] On the whole, though, the DTA seemed to find little else of substance to which to object, contenting itself with defending the record of previous interim administrations of which it had been a part.

The other opposition parties also found little to disagree with in the budget. Typical of their reactions was that of UDF leader Justus Garoeb, who called it 'a realistic attempt under the circumstances', while acknowledging that he sympathized with those who 'justifiably' felt the budget had not gone far enough in addressing urgent needs such as employment and housing. Overall, however, the UDF commended the government's approach to reconciling 'the burning needs of the masses and ... of the business community' on the one hand, and 'the requirements and capacity of the economy on the other', within the context of severe economic constraints.[36]

The budget's most enthusiastic endorsement came from the President of the Chamber of Commerce:

> We are very impressed with the budget. We feel the Minister attempted to identify problems and faults in a gradual manner. We think it is very correct not to increase taxes.... It is very encouraging that capital projects are focused particularly in the North and rural areas, where, of course, they are needed the most.[37]

While the opposition remarks underlined the essential similarity in outlook of the major parties represented in the National Assembly, there was clearly some uneasiness among members of the SWAPO caucus itself about the free-market course it was charting as a government. This ambivalence was reflected in the Prime Minister's statement regarding the budget.[38] Geingob noted that the budget had received 'wide acclaim':

> The Chamber of Commerce referred to it as a good and realistic budget. The BBC ran a favourable comment on the budget, and several high commissioners and ambassadors based here commended us on our good understanding of the realities prevailing in this country.[39]

At the same time, Geingob characterized the budget as 'transitional', and therefore 'cast very much in the same mould as the old'. It was not perfect, he acknowledged, and, surprisingly, admitted that some ministers had opposed it in Cabinet.

> We want to assure all Namibians ... that next year's budget will look completely different from this one. Cabinet has instructed the Finance Minister to radically overhaul our system of budgeting in favour of programme budgeting which yields to development programmes.... By next year the crystallisation of policies [will] have been completed and properly translated into programmes.... [T]his Government is not a transitional government.... When you have a transitional government you have to hurry to put some projects in place, for you are not sure what your mandate is. We are very much sure, we were elected democratically, we have a five year mandate and we know where we stand.[40]

TAKING STOCK

SWAPO's first year in office, then, was dedicated largely to establishing and consolidating relationships with Western financial institutions, foreign capital, white settlers, and local business. In this endeavour it was generally supported by opposition parties in the National Assembly, and by the press, both of which, though frequently critical of specific government actions or initiatives, did not take issue with the capitalist orientation of its overall development programme.[41] The business community, for its part, admitted to being pleasantly surprised by the government's 'realism' and 'good sense'.[42]

Negotiating the politics of power in a world capitalist economy, however, entails maintaining an equilibrium between accumulation and the social stability necessary to ensure its continuance. It was apparent, towards the end of SWAPO's inaugural year in government, that this equilibrium was threatened.

For much of this period, the Namibian masses had seemed content to wait patiently for the government's election promises to be realized. The very fact of the ending of the war and the removal of apartheid legislation gave the government a substantial period of grace, and not only among its own supporters. Trade unions, women's groups, community organizations and the main student organization, NANSO, were mostly supportive of the government's stated objectives, albeit occasionally expressing concern that the policy of national reconciliation was being deliberately misconstrued by white employers and others to justify continued discriminatory or exploitative practices.[43]

Towards the end of Namibia's first year of independence, however, there were signs of a growing restlessness and rising discontent with the lack of noticeable change, especially among the rural peasantry and the urban unemployed (whose ranks included thousands of civilian and ex-combatant 'returnees'). Demands for action crystallized around one issue in particular – that of land reform.

THE LAND CONFERENCE

No less than for other Southern African countries at independence, land reform in Namibia promised to be a vexing issue for the new government. The concentration of land in the hands of European settlers and the consequent dispossession and dis-location of the African majority had been fundamental to the system of white settler privilege, and was now the most important domestic issue facing the SWAPO government. To many Namibians, comprehensive land reform was central to any redistribution of wealth. How a SWAPO government dealt with the issue would be seen as the first major indication of how it intended to strike a balance between economic growth and social justice.[44]

The government's response to escalating demands for land reform was to convene a long-promised 'National Conference on Land Reform and the Land Question' between 25 June and 1 July 1991, at which it sought to reconcile the needs of a land hungry electorate with pressures for increasing agricultural productivity.[45]

More than 500 people attended the Land Conference, representing all parts of the country and a wide array of relationships to the land – from commercial to peasant subsistence farmers, from women's rights advocates to traditional leaders.[46] From the outset, the government made it clear that it considered the gathering a consultative conference, and its recommendations therefore not binding. It was, nonetheless, an exceptional display of openness and democratic practice on the part of a government grown out of a movement not previously noted for either. An impressive collection of background studies had been prepared, including comparative studies of land tenure systems in Botswana and Zimbabwe, as well as regional studies comparing agricultural practices, and attitudes to land settlement and distribution in different parts of Namibia. The diversity of the findings by region highlighted the many potential obstacles to constructing a national land policy in Namibia.[47]

Conference participants addressed themselves to the complex issues of land owner-ship and use from a variety of positions and perspectives. As the debate progressed, however, it became evident that it was not only the specific content of government policy with respect to land that was at issue, but the ideological underpinnings and direction of its entire programme of national reconstruction. Through the efforts of worker and youth delegates, a class analysis was introduced into a debate hitherto largely focussed on traditional alliances based on party, tribe, ethnic or racial affiliation.[48]

In his opening remarks to the conference, President Nujoma outlined the basis of the government's approach to the land question, stressing the need to redress historic injustices of land theft, to improve access while maintaining production, and to ensure the sustainable use of the land. In convening the Land Conference, Nujoma told participants, the government was seeking to achieve the greatest possible national consensus in tackling this critical issue, by providing 'the opportunity for all Namibians to come forward with their problems and to suggest solutions to the land question.'[49]

The suggestions contained in the position paper put forward by SWAPO as a party differed little from the government's guidelines,[50] though it is significant that the party submitted its recommendations separately – making a distinction between the two structures, whose positions would be seen to diverge more fundamentally over the following months. The paper noted that addressing the question of land tenure, 'arguably the single most important reason that led to the liberation war', was now 'the most expensive and the most explosive' issue facing the government. The lessons learned from other countries' experiences should help Namibia to avoid their pitfalls, and to adopt a 'relevant and sustainable' land reform policy, in which social justice would take precedence over economic growth.[51]

The system of mixed ownership, already embodied in the government's Investment Code (promulgated in December 1990),[52] was recommended as equally applicable to the management and ownership of land. The adoption of an activist role on the part of the government in the redistribution of land, in the promotion of community-based agricultural cooperatives, and in the provision of assistance to subsistence farmers, could result in a 'broadly-shared increase in production, income, and a reduction in unemployment', the SWAPO document asserted.[53]

In endeavouring to rectify existing imbalances, the government had a number of options, including a 'state leasehold system', whereby ultimate ownership of the land would rest with the state, but individuals and institutions could lease land for private use; and 'customary land tenure' administered by tribal authorities, whereby ownership of the land was vested in the community. Consistent with the contents of the SWAPO election manifesto, the party's position paper recommended that, when seeking to acquire land for redistribution, the government focus on land held by absentee landlords, underutilized land and landowners with excessively large or numerous properties.[54]

While the SWAPO position paper, with its moderately worded and relatively uncontroversial recommendations, fell broadly within the framework of government guidelines, a much more fundamental challenge to the new political dispensation was offered by the separate submissions of the National Union of Namibian Workers (NUNW) and the SWAPO Youth League (SYL).

The NUNW was unequivocal with regard to its demand for 'meaningful' land reform effected by means of state action:

> The organized labour movement in Namibia is fundamentally opposed to any attempt that regards the market as a mechanism for redistributing land from the privileged propertied minority to the landless majority. We are also convinced that the process of land redistribution and acquisition should not be confined to existing racial disparities alone, but should be done in the interest of social equity and justice....
>
> Workers feel very much bitter about the fact that the land that once was occupied by the Namibian people and seized violently from them cannot be expropriated

without full compensation.... If landlessness and the state of land hunger in our country can only be dealt with through ... market forces, or through expropriation with full compensation, then the land question will not be resolved but worsened.[55]

The SYL submission went even further, building on the implicit criticism of protection for property rights contained in the NUNW paper, with a direct attack on the constitutional foundations upon which a future land policy would be built, and even questioning the legitimacy of the constitutional process:

> In view [of] our present constitutional dispensation which makes property rights a cornerstone of independent Namibia, SYL finds it almost impossible for the ... aspirations and dreams of the majority of our people to be realized. It is the considered opinion of SYL that the founding fathers of the Namibian Constitution could have shown concern for the rights of those dispossessed by German and apartheid colonialism, besides upholding the rights of those who purport to have 'title deeds'....
>
> SYL would like to submit further that the majority of the Namibian people were not consulted during the drafting of the Constitution by the Constituent Assembly.... [N]ot enough public debate was accorded to this important document and ... in some major respects, the present Namibian Constitution is not a clear testimony or reflection of the aspirations of the majority of the Namibian people.... [T]he battle over the Constitution was and still is as vital for the Namibian people as the battle for independence was.... [56]

Though the ensuing discussion conflated race- and class-based inequities, it was clear that within SWAPO's traditional constituency new political battle lines were being drawn.

That the constitutional provisions regarding the protection of property would seriously limit options for land reform was underlined when the state leasehold option was rejected as equivalent to nationalization and hence unconstitutional, and in any case unworkable. The proposal was ultimately dropped from the final communique, and replaced with the more conservative recommendation that all Namibians have 'access' to the land, as opposed to collective ownership as a nation via a state leasehold system.[57]

Despite the lively nature of the debates, a spirit of cooperation and compromise prevailed throughout the conference, with Prime Minister Geingob reprising the role of chairperson for which he was widely admired during the drafting of the Constitution. Though he himself favoured the state leasehold option, Geingob acknowledged its defeat with good grace, observing that despite the non-binding nature of the conference resolutions, 'it would be foolhardy of those of us in positions of authority to disregard your views in the formulation of a national policy on land reform'.[58] In the end, the six days of intense discussion produced a 24-point Consensus of the Conference, which, while not pleasing anyone entirely, gave grounds for optimism to many. Women's rights to own, inherit, cultivate or bequeath land were recognized, as was their right to equal access to training programmes, loans and markets. The sweeping powers of traditional leaders over the allocation and administration of communal lands were severely curtailed, while even the large land-owners present appeared willing to concede the need for some redistribution of resources. There was broad agreement among conference participants that significant land reform was needed to redress serious existing inequities, that foreigners should be able to lease and develop land, but not own it, and that abandoned and underutilized land should be re-allocated for productive use; but these were the easy decisions. Much more difficult and divisive ones lay ahead, as the following months would demonstrate.[59]

THE ROAD TO THE SWAPO CONGRESS
The afterglow of hope following the closing of the land conference was short-lived.

Discontent at the lack of prompt action on the recommendations of the Conference was soon added to a growing list of grievances and disappointed expectations among unemployed ex-combatants, returnees, and Namibia's poor. Providing a focus for this anger in the months following the Conference were a number of 'hot' issues, among them the confusion surrounding demobilization payments to ex-PLAN combatants, widespread dissatisfaction with the government-sponsored Development Brigades, the proposed composition of the Namibian team to compete in the All-Africa Games in Cairo, the controversial disaffiliation of NANSO from SWAPO, and, most explosive, the trial of three white men charged with treason for allegedly plotting to overthrow the government. These in turn reflected broader concerns among Namibians regarding the administration of justice, the maintenance of law and order, the distribution of resources, and the representation of the nation abroad in the post-colonial dispensation. With each of these issues the contrast between the rhetoric and approach of those representing SWAPO the party, and those representing SWAPO the government, grew more pronounced, especially with respect to the policy of national reconciliation. The line between the two leaderships was far from absolute – as the opposition never tired of observing, there were 'hardliners' in government (favourite examples of the opposition press were the Minister of Information and Broadcasting Hidipo Hamutenya, and Minister of Youth and Sport Pendukeni Ithana), whose sympathies seemed to lie more clearly with the traditional party line than with their 'moderate' caucus colleagues. As used by SWAPO's critics, the terms had less to do with ideology than with idiom – but there was no question that the respective positions of government and party were diverging.

Although the party was mobilizing around issues of concern to SWAPO supporters, and was increasingly vocal in its criticisms of the costs to the majority of 'national reconciliation', it was not yet possible, 18 months after independence, to refer with confidence to the political or development programme of SWAPO as a party. In large measure it was to redefine SWAPO's programme and policy, in order to ensure the continued relevance of its vision for an independent Namibia (especially in the light of forthcoming regional elections for the National Council), that the first truly national SWAPO Congress was held on Namibian soil in December 1991.

THE SWAPO CONGRESS

The SWAPO Congress – the first genuine congress in the history of the movement[60] – was billed by the organizing committee[61] as marking the 'transformation from liberation movement to mass political party', and the launching of the second phase of the struggle: the struggle for economic liberation. The media and opposition parties predicted clashes and power struggles between 'hardliners' and 'moderates' in the SWAPO government, between government and party hierarchies, and between leaders of the erstwhile 'internal' and 'exile' wings of the movement. The one thousand delegates, selected from 13 regions,[62] came hoping for solutions to immediate 'bread and butter' concerns, while Moses Garoeb, party chief and congress coordinator, promised that 'the good, the bad, and the ugly' in SWAPO's history would be revealed during the course of the congress.[63] If, not surprisingly, none of these expectations was fully realized, the congress nevertheless was a watershed in SWAPO's evolution as a movement. Perhaps most importantly, it ushered in a new era for the party in which a more assertive rank and file membership would strive for a more active role in shaping party positions and, through these, to guide government policy in a direction that would reflect more clearly the aspirations of SWAPO's traditional constituencies among the workers, youth and peasantry.

The congress, then, was to serve a dual function. For the government leadership it provided an opportunity to explain their policies directly to the party membership, and to defend their record after 20 months in office. To the party membership it offered a forum in which to articulate their dissatisfaction with aspects of the government's programme of national reconstruction and development. Although at the end it was clear to participants that 'reasons of state' had taken precedence at this inaugural congress, notice was given to the leadership of both party and government that in future the support of the rank and file could no longer be assumed, but would have to be earned.

In the weeks leading up to the congress, it was clear that some government leaders were looking forward to the exchange. Pendukeni Ithana, Minister for Youth and Sport, was one of them:

> The majority of the people feel we need to look critically at the party now that it is no longer a liberation party. We must have a new vision of what we would like our party to be. This can only be arrived at through looking at different interests. Although people keep saying SWAPO is a communist or socialist party they fail to see that although we may strive for social justice, those in the leadership are not all looking at this goal from the same perspective....
>
> For us to be effective and fulfil our promises – I know we won't fulfil them all, but to keep them always in our minds – we must have a party strong enough to keep us on our toes.... Because of that, the opposition may think we are two camps. We are clashing, but that is because we are now serving two groups – SWAPO and the public – and they don't necessarily feel the same things.[64]

The Deputy Minister of Information and Broadcasting, Daniel Tjongarero, while anticipating 'a lot of hard talk', agreed that a congress was badly needed:

> When the congress comes we will have been in government twenty, twenty-one months. Obviously we will look at our performance – not only our performance in government, how efficient we are, but also our performance in addressing specific issues: unemployment, social welfare, housing and other crucial areas. The second thing is that we will obviously have to deal with the question of dissatisfaction among the rank and file on the whole issue of national reconciliation.... Obviously it is our responsibility to explain why we have done certain things, [otherwise] the opposition, if it doesn't find fault with what you are doing, it instigates your own supporters against you, saying 'Look, these people have done nothing to help your lot.' But once you start talking to people about the limitations you have, and also about their own responsibility to take control of their own lives, then I think it becomes much easier.'[65]

Among the leadership, however, insiders predicted, there would be those who would feel less comfortable with an open exchange of views regarding the government's mandate. A SWAPO backbencher, Danie Botha, predicted that

> some of the guys are in for a shock, because they are not used to people saying just what they like – and there is a lot of anger and a lot of frustration – and again the only way for these problems to be resolved is for the links to be strengthened between the leadership and their supporters. Because of our historical situation these are not as strong as they should be – but again the onus is on us to look critically at ourselves.... We are lucky here that the people are ... not so terribly critical [as they are in South Africa], but we must not misuse that openness and accepting kind of spirit.... I think some of the leadership is not really aware of how much more critical the membership has become just in the last two years. Some of them are aware, and when you speak to them you realize just how very much aware. But my feeling is sometimes ... that there is still a tendency to want to tell people to 'support us and don't be so negative'.[66]

The congress itself was a blend of symbolism and substance. The opening ceremonies, moved indoors at the last moment owing to torrential rain, were attended by the entire diplomatic community, old friends and new, but the event belonged to the former. The President, Sam Nujoma, the Prime Minister, Hage Geingob, SWAPO

Secretary-General Andimba Toivo ya Toivo, and SWAPO Chief Coordinator Moses Garoeb, sat resplendent in outfits of blue, green and red in front of a giant banner which read

FIRST SWAPO CONGRESS IN INDEPENDENT NAMIBIA: FROM NATIONAL LIBERATION MOVEMENT TO POLITICAL PARTY. SOLIDARITY, FREEDOM AND JUSTICE

with the word 'mass' squeezed in as an afterthought before 'political party'.

Tributes were made to North Korea, the USSR, Cuba, China, and the Frontline States, whose delegates responded with messages of solidarity – often shouting to be heard over the rain pounding on the tin roof – in what the *Namibian* described as a 'revolutionary aura'.[67] On the other hand, the list of those who donated funds for the occasion included the names of a number of large corporate sponsors.[68]

The content of the congress is perhaps best summarized in three parts: substantive, procedural, and sociological. The 60-page 'Report of the Central Committee', covering the events of three decades of struggle, and read by the President, contained no surprises. Rather than 'the good, the bad and the ugly' promised by Comrade Garoeb, it dutifully summarized the official history of SWAPO.[69] Here again old friends were saluted, with the Frontline States, the OAU, Cuba, the USSR, the former GDR and other former East European socialist states thanked for providing 'all-round disinterested support in our cause during the dark days of struggle', while, of the Western hemisphere, the Nordic countries, Italy and Holland were singled out for their 'invaluable solidarity support and humanitarian assistance'.[70]

If the 'Report of the Central Committee' echoed the rhetoric of the liberation struggle, both the new Political Programme and the new Party Constitution reflected the electoral perspectives and priorities of a ruling party in a post-Cold War world. The first part of the Political Programme recapitulated, for the benefit of younger cadres, the history of the struggle for independence. The narrative made no mention whatever of the socialist principles which had ostensibly guided SWAPO as a liberation movement from 1976 to 1989, and was startlingly candid in its evaluation of the guiding force behind its strategies in its triumphal concluding paragraph:

> This has been the celebrated life of SWAPO, a movement born and bred in the crucible of the struggle and steeled to be ever self-confident, achievement-oriented and optimistic. Also, SWAPO is an organisation that is capable of reading which way history is breaking and thus always alive to the need to adapt its policy and programme to suit new conditions; and guided by this battle-tested tradition of far-sightedness and realism, SWAPO is well-placed to blaze new trails in leading Namibia and its people to a bright future.[71]

In the second part of the Political Programme, the four main tasks of the party were outlined. The first was the institutionalization of democratic political processes in Namibian society through 'the political education of the masses', and their mobilization for 'participation in the affairs of the state and society'. The second was to define the role of the state in the country's socio-economic development:

> despite the broad consensus in the country to allow the private sector to play an important and unimpeded role in the economy, the people still expect the state to play a role ... especially with respect to the building of schools, hospitals and roads, the provision of employment and establishing credit for Namibian entrepreneurs and developing favourable market conditions for them abroad.... Therefore, the second main task [of the] Party is to work out ... sound economic guidelines for its government to implement.[72]

The third task was to 'bring about social justice' through progressive policies designed to bring about equality of opportunity and a balanced and fair allocation of resources; and the fourth was to weld together a nation by uniting the country 'around a common consensus of values, goals and objectives' through mass-based organization.

A more detailed 'guide to action' was contained in the final part of the Political Programme, which called for the pursuit of 'political empowerment', 'economic empowerment', 'social empowerment', and empowerment in the realms of education, health and housing. These exhorted the party, *inter alia*: 'to organize the people to demand accountability from their elected representatives', 'to inculcate in the masses … patriotic sentiments around which their creative and productive energies could be galvanized and channelled toward development', 'to promote full and active participation of the Namibian people, especially the colonially disadvantaged majority, in the process of economic reconstruction', 'to work for the acceleration of economic growth', 'to encourage the government to work out the best mechanisms of effective land reform', 'to promote family life … where the youth are taught … the norms and values of the community', 'to help combat the anti-social practices of crime, alcoholism, drug-abuse, etc.', 'to work for progressive labour relations and [improved] living and working conditions for workers', 'to advance the struggle for equal rights for women … in all fields', 'to join the government … in combating illiteracy', 'to press for the training of more health workers', and 'to work for the provision of adequate and affordable housing for all'. The document concluded as follows:

> the SWAPO political programme spells out the line for the Party to follow in order to play a leading role toward the building of a society that is materially and spiritually strong and productive, and whose people are secure from the anxiety of basic socio-economic needs. The implementation of the Programme will ensure that SWAPO fulfils its present and future tasks as a vital agent of development and a guarantor of democracy in our country.[73]

If the Political Programme represented an attempt by the party to differentiate its objectives and underlying philosophy from those of the government, it failed in this regard. There was little in the programme to indicate that the two structures diverged significantly in any area of their publicly stated aims, which is not surprising given that the document was drafted by a small committee whose members straddled the top ranks of both hierarchies.[74] More than anything, the document perhaps best reflected the perspectives of élites in both the party and the government, a bent which might not have been so pronounced had the party's rank and file members been more involved in the party's policy making.[75]

SWAPO's constitution was little changed from the one previously ratified in 1983.[76] SWAPO's objectives were amended to 'reflect independence and SWAPO's party status in a multi-party democracy', and were henceforth to be 'founded on the principles of democracy, solidarity, freedom, social justice and progress'. The party 'exist[ed] to arouse and mobilize Namibians for meaningful political participation and to translate their desires into policy', and the goal of political activity was to 'improve the quality of life of the people, especially the colonially disadvantaged majority'. The 'essential characteristics' distinguishing SWAPO from other political parties in Namibia, the constitution asserted, were:

> its roots in the militant struggle against foreign domination, its firm commitment to the ideals of solidarity, social justice and progress, through broad democratic reforms of the Namibian society, as well as its faith and confidence in the Namibian people's ability to accomplish the great tasks of socio-economic reconstruction and development.[77]

Following the adoption of the Political Programme and constitution, with few amendments, the congress heard from 12 policy sub-committees. The delegates' main concerns were clearly apparent from the time devoted to discussing each report. More esoteric subjects such as foreign relations, transportation, communications and information policy were dealt with relatively quickly. By contrast education, national defence, crime and the judicial system were each subjected to prolonged and intense discussion. The debate on education alone lasted nine hours, and the debate on defence and security even longer, with participants advocating a tough line on both. Delegates condemned corruption in the school system, alcohol abuse by teachers and students, sexual abuse of students by teachers, and absenteeism by both. A full-scale 'war on crime' was called for, and substantial increases in both the National Defence Force and police were recommended.

Delegates' many concerns regarding the overburdened legal system focussed on four issues: inefficiency in the courts, a perceived leniency with respect to serious crimes, the relationship between customary law and common law, and the need for affirmative action in the judicial system.

It was the government's policy of national reconciliation, however, that came under the fiercest fire from delegates, who perceived it as shoring up an unjust *status quo*. Reconciliation could not work – was too high a price to pay for stability, they insisted – if it continued to be seen to benefit the 'haves' at the expense of the 'have nots'. While the debates over other policy areas reflected primarily differences in detail, strategy or emphasis, the clash over the issue of national reconciliation highlighted an area of genuine ideological dissension within SWAPO.

The resolutions emanating from the discussions in each of the 12 areas were summarized in the closing remarks, again delivered by the President, who observed that the congress had been a 'practical demonstration of democracy in action', which

> builds on the firm foundations of a political culture which we want to nurture, develop and consolidate in our society. The seeds of this political culture were sown during the work of the historic Constituent Assembly which produced the much acclaimed model, democratic constitution of the independent Republic of Namibia. We continued with that same tradition during the Land Reform Conference, and this Congress [is] yet another milestone in the consolidation of that democratic culture.[78]

The President also briefly summarized the debates on economic and foreign policy, in a way which again echoed more closely the perceptions and preferences of the leadership than those of the rank and file:

> Congress identified pragmatic economic management, a viable democracy, the policy of national reconciliation, the creation of a competitively attractive domestic investment environment, a rationalised, professional and efficient public service, and a good infrastructure, as essential ingredients for harnessing the potential wealth offered by our natural resources, especially mineral and marine resources. But above all else, maintenance of peace and security is uppermost and to this end the Party and Government remain absolutely committed.[79]

As the first of its kind inside Namibia, it is not surprising that the congress was plagued by procedural glitches. For the most part both organizers and delegates accepted these with good humour and patience. After several consecutive 20-hour days, however, delegates began to question some of the more glaring problems with the organization of the congress. Their concerns stemmed primarily from the lack of consultation with the rank and file in the preparation of the congress agenda and documents (these were only presented to most delegates upon their arrival, and a number of government representatives complained that they had received theirs only two days prior to the congress), and a perceived lack of democratic procedure at times. Both flaws were especially apparent when the time came to hold elections for the new SWAPO Central Committee.

The election procedures were not only unwieldy but overtly exclusionary, rendering it very difficult for any but incumbents to fulfil the necessary conditions.[80] In the first popular revolt of the congress, the delegates insisted that these provisions be redrafted, and then redrafted again, before they finally allowed them to pass. Even so, the final version was confusing, and clearly weighted in favour of former Central Committee members. Among the technical biases which worked to skew the result in favour of the incumbents was the fact that, of the 100 eligible nominees listed on an eight-page ballot, from which delegates could select a maximum of 58 names, they occupied the first 45 slots.[81] In the end, the newly expanded Central Committee was remarkable mostly for its striking resemblance to the old. As expected, Sam Nujoma was acclaimed to the position of Party President. The Rev. Hendrik Witbooi was reacclaimed (following a last-minute withdrawal by Prime Minister Hage Geingob) to the post of Vice-President, and Moses Garoeb decisively defeated Andimba Toivo ya Toivo for the revised post of Secretary General.[82] Three seats were reserved, *ex officio*, for the elected heads of the SWAPO Elders' Council, the SWAPO Women's Council and the SWAPO Youth League, and an additional six for presidential appointments. Of the remaining 58 positions – elected by congress delegates from a list of 100 names by secret ballot – only eleven were not current members of the Cabinet, senior party functionaries, former Central Committee members, or all three. A total of seven women (three of them members of Cabinet) were elected. A few of the old guard were snubbed, and a little new blood was injected.[83]

But if the Central Committee remained, on the surface, largely unchanged, it was clear that the SWAPO Party Congress would never be quite the same. For the most fascinating aspect of the congress was the growing assertiveness of the rank and file delegates. At the beginning of the congress, one of the delegates privately expressed his frustration at the seemingly quiescent nature of Namibian political culture. South Africans, he said, would never permit a proposed agenda to pass without debate, would never allow background documents to be distributed at the last minute, and would never demonstrate such reluctance to challenge, question or criticize their leaders. And initially the delegates did appear to be surprisingly uncritical. But as the congress progressed, a dramatic transformation began to take place. The shyness was shed, and participants – the women in particular – became more outspoken about the issues that directly affected their lives. Time limits to debates on such issues as education were ignored. The proposed election procedures were rejected not once, but twice, and the election committee was sent back to redraft them. The delegates' new assertiveness meant that discussion often went on deep into the night, and that the congress itself ran almost two days overtime, but in the end the exhausted delegates seemed satisfied. At the closing of the congress, one of the younger, more radical members of the leadership, quietly delighted at the change that had taken place, summed up its significance:

> The congress was an important demythologizing experience. It wasn't always democratic – not so much intentionally, it's just what the leadership is used to – but that won't happen again. The delegates could see what was happening. They're inexperienced, but they're not stupid. Next time they will decide more things for themselves.[84]

Another pleased delegate added:

> I think we are in for some lively debates that are going to transform SWAPO into a very dynamic party.... [85]

LESSONS FROM THE CONGRESS

The preamble to the final resolutions, released following the congress, assessed its historic significance on three levels:

> It [was] not only the first Congress of the mighty SWAPO in an independent Namibia, but also the first 'conventional' Congress ever....

> The second importance of this congress [lay] in its representativity. For the first time

in the history of SWAPO, over 1,000 delegates and observers from all corners of Namibia and from all the wings and affiliated organisations gathered under the same roof to discuss the future of their organisation and country.

A third dimension to the importance of the Congress was added by the atmosphere of frankness and open debate that reigned. Everyone spoke his mind, and those who wished could be self-styled controversial delegates. In this sense the Congress was a triumph for democracy and put to rest, once and for all, all speculations about the problems of democracy in SWAPO.[86]

While it is true that the congress did indeed provide reason to believe that a traditionally hierarchical and authoritarian party was showing signs of opening somewhat, it would be a mistake to overestimate the extent to which the Congress represented a fundamental change in the way decisions were reached and policy formulated within SWAPO, or how quickly or willingly further democratization of party structures would follow.

Many of the more significant concessions to democratic practice on the part of the leadership, including the redrafting of the election guidelines, were conceded only in response to pressure from the delegates, and even then were minimal in their effects. Though time limits to discussions on various topics were ignored, this did not guarantee that all opinions were voiced, or all voices heard. The omission from the delegates' conference package of the SYL's 'memorandum' to the congress – a militant document fiercely critical of what the SYL saw as 'inherent flaws in the Namibian Constitution' and of the government's policy of national reconciliation, especially with regard to the appointment of non-SWAPO members to 'strategic positions' and the protection of civil servants left over from the colonial regime – was particularly striking.[87] And though the policy discussions were wide-ranging, and often highly charged, it is noteworthy that, in the end, the 42 pages of official congress resolutions (issued by SWAPO Party headquarters some months after the congress) contained very few recommendations at odds with the government's publicly stated strategies for socio-economic development.[88]

On a procedural level, the provisions enshrined in the new constitution also indicated that any further opening of party structures would be controlled and monitored tightly. Future congresses would be much smaller, would strongly favour urban élites, and would most likely act to reinforce rather than help to dismantle the hierarchical nature of the party. Delegates would include all members of the incumbent Central Committee, four representatives from each of the 13 regions, and two from each district's executive committee.[89] Four representatives from each of the party's wings would also be invited, as well as representatives from each affiliated organiza-tion. Finally, there would be 'thirty specially invited personalities who must have made an outstanding contribution to the work and development of SWAPO, but non-office bearing members of SWAPO'.[90] A congress would only be convened once every five years (earlier drafts had proposed first two, then four years); while the Central Committee would meet at least once annually, and the Politburo at least monthly, concentrating the power and authority to determine day-to-day party policy in very few hands.[91]

In short, although there were signs at the congress of a growing desire among delegates for fuller participation in party policy making, it seemed likely that further democratic reforms within the party would be conceded with reluctance. The difference in perspective highlighted by the congress was, in essence, not between representatives of the party and of the government, nor between those perceived as 'hardliners' and 'moderates' in each, but between SWAPO's élite members and its rank and file. The traditional insularity of SWAPO's leadership was not challenged fundamentally by the structures entrenched in the party's new constitution, nor were the 'bread and butter' concerns of SWAPO's grassroots membership paramount in shaping the content of its Political Programme and resolutions. At the same time, however, representatives of both the government and party were given notice that the consent of the people to its policies could no longer be taken for granted. As the party would henceforth depend on institutional and individual subscriptions for its funds (grants from foreign sources having largely been redirected to the state since independence), and the government would face regional elections within a year and national elections within four, both had a vested interest in finding the necessary equilibrium between the politics of support and the politics of power.

Conclusion

Throughout the struggle for independence, and into its first term in office, SWAPO deliberately left room for differing interpretations as to its genuine beliefs and intentions. The essential question of the transition from authoritarian rule to democracy in Namibia, however, was not the extent to which genuine conviction played a role in the values and policies publicly espoused by the government, but the extent to which, following independence, awakening elements within Namibian society would be able to press for the fulfilment of their expectations and to push for reforms beyond the institutionalization of democratic political structures dictated by the new constitution – to push, ultimately, for the radical redistribution of wealth and resources in a fundamentally transformed polity. Almost two years after independence, there were signs that the patience born of long suffering and a political culture of entrenched hierarchy was giving way at last to the stirrings of an autonomous 'civil society', and that Namibians were beginning to contest the limitations to transformation ostensibly imposed by the 'politics of power', and too readily incorporated into the policies of the SWAPO government. People's demands for a greater role in shaping the institutions that governed their lives may have met with very limited success during the first 20 months of SWAPO's term in office, but there were, nonetheless, strong indications at its 1991 party congress that popular forces would not be ignored indefinitely.

Notes

1. The following observations are drawn from my MA thesis, 'New lamps for old? The evolution of SWAPO's philosophy of development, 1960–1990', Queen's University, Kingston, November 1992; and a more detailed 'Report to the Canadian Bureau for International Education', submitted in September 1992. I am grateful to the CBIE for financing my research, and to the Namibian Institute for Social and Economic Research for its generous logistical support. Those who provided invaluable advice and assistance in locating materials, or carved time from busy schedules to answer my questions, are too numerous to list here, but I am indebted to them all.
2. The involvement of foreign experts in SWAPO policy formulation became particularly pronounced following the formal creation, in August 1976, of the United Nations Institute for Namibia (UNIN).
3. There was, of course, only very limited scope for internal political organization, especially from the early 1970s onward. See Colin Leys and John Saul, 'SWAPO inside Namibia', in this volume.
4. Quoted in the *Washington Post*, 5 May 1984.
5. In 1975 the Swedish government set a precedent of giving direct aid to SWAPO, with a grant amounting to approximately US$600,000. Other Nordic governments soon followed suit. See the *Rand Daily Mail*, 7 September 1976.
6. At a time when the Rand was worth more than the US dollar, a 1978 estimate put total Western aid to SWAPO over the previous five years at R69 million. In 1979 alone, aid channelled to SWAPO through the United Nations was estimated at US$15 million. See *Windhoek Advertiser*, 2 November 1978; 9 August 1979; 22 September 1981; 18 February 1981; and *Windhoek Observer*, 8 September 1982; 9 September 1983 for details of grants to SWAPO.

7. *Washington Post*, 5 May 1984.
8. See Philip Steenkamp, 'The Churches', in this volume.
9. UN General Assembly Resolution 3111 (12 December 1973) had recognized the movement as 'authentic'. 'Sole' was added with the adoption of Resolutions 31/147 and 31/152 (20 December 1976).
10. See 'Namibia – essential documents of the United Nations' independence plan 1976–1989', compiled in 1990 by the London-based Namibia Communications Centre, for a valuable record of the negotiations.
11. See André du Pisani, *SWA/Namibia: The Politics of Continuity and Change* (Johannesburg: Jonathan Ball, 1986); Gerhard Totemeyer, *Namibia Old and New* (London: Christopher Hurst, 1978), and *South West Africa/Namibia: Facts, Attitudes, Assessments and Prospects* (Randburg: Fokus Suid Publishers, 1977), Wolfgang Thomas, *Economic Development in Namibia* (Munich: Kaiser-Grunewald, 1978); Sue Cullinan, 'SWAPO and the future of Namibia,' in *South Africa International*, 15, 3 (January 1985); and O. J. Adebayo, 'Namibia: a study of the interests, attitudes and approaches of international parties to the conflict, 1960–1980,' MA thesis, Keele University, 1985, for discussions of these documents. None of these provides a date or a source for the National Programme.
12. For widely differing interpretations of SWAPO's motives and actions during this period, see, for example, Paul Trewhela, 'The Kissinger/Vorster/Kaunda detente: genesis of the SWAPO spy-drama', in *Searchlight South Africa*, 2, 2 and 2, 3 (1990); and J. H. P. Serfontein, *Namibia?* (London: Rex Collings, 1977). See also Leys and Saul in this volume, and Dobell, *op. cit.*, for a more detailed treatment of the arguments in this section.
13. Interview with the author, 15 November 1991.
14. See Somadoda Fikeni, 'Exile and return: the politics of Namibia's "returnees"', MA thesis (Queen's University, Kingston, Ontario, June 1992).
15. According to its cover page, the National Programme was drawn up by a 'drafting committee,' although only then Acting Organizing Secretary Homateni Kaluenja is acknowledged by name. Kaluenja was dropped from the executive shortly after the document was written.
16. Quoted in the 'Report on consultation between SWAPO and the representatives of the white community of Namibia', Stockholm, 19–21 June 1988.
17. The transition period is among the most thoroughly researched in Namibia's history. Among a number of valuable recent additions are Christopher Saunders, 'Transition in Namibia: and the South African case,' in *Transformation*, 17 (1992); Brian Wood, 'Preventing the vacuum: determinants of the Namibian settlement,' in *Journal of Southern African Studies*, 17, 4 (1991); and Pieter Esterhuysen, 'Countdown to independence', in *Namibia 1990: A Country Survey* (Pretoria: Africa Institute, 1991).
18. The 'Principles concerning the Constituent Assembly and the constitution for an independent Namibia' were contained in a letter dated 12 July 1982 from the Representatives of Canada, France, Germany, the United Kingdom and the USA to the Secretary General of the United Nations. They stipulated, *inter alia*, a three-branch system of government, regular elections, the safeguarding of fundamental rights and freedoms, due process and equality before the law. Two provisions in particular were intended to preempt any attempt to implement socialist policies: there would be no deprivation of property without just compensation, and 'fair administration of personnel policy' in the civil service (no dismissal of South African-appointed civil servants) would be assured.
19. Notable among these were the 'Report on consultation between SWAPO and the representatives of the white community of Namibia', Stockholm, 19–21 June 1988; 'Namibia's prospects brighten up', Luanda, 28 November 1988; 'SWAPO's goals and aspirations,' speech delivered to a meeting of Business International, London, 21 April 1989; and SWAPO's 'Election Manifesto: towards an independent and democratic Namibia – SWAPO's policy positions', released in July 1989.
20. SWAPO, 'Namibia's economic prospects brighten up,' pp. 5-6.
21. Kaire Mbuende, interview with the author, 13 November 1991.
22. *Ibid.*
23. In *The Conservative Nation* (London: Routledge and Kegan Paul, 1974), Andrew Gamble makes the useful distinction between the politics of power and the politics of support which informs the discussion in this section.
24. Interview with the author, 11 September 1991.
25. Government of the Republic of Namibia, 'The Reconstruction and Development of Namibia: A General Policy Statement', Windhoek, May 1990. Presented to the United Nations Donors' Pledging Conference, 21 June 1990, pp. 4–6.

26. IBRD, 'Namibia: Preliminary Economic Review', 18 May 1990.
27. Government of Namibia, 'Provisional Investment Programme,' May 1990, pp. 36, 39. Though presented as a government policy document, it was largely drafted by UNDP personnel in Windhoek.
28. The address of the Honourable Walter Maclean, Canada's Special Representative on Southern Africa and Commonwealth Affairs, to the Namibian Donors' Pledging Conference was representative of the reception by western donors to the Namibian proposals.
29. 'Glad tidings', *Windhoek Observer*, 30 June 1990; 'We are the poorest people in the world', *Windhoek Observer*, 30 June 1990; Da'oud Vries, 'Government to stimulate investment', *Namibian*, 21 June 1990; Africa News Service, 'Namibia seeks world help,' *Namibia Today*, 23 June 1990; 'Forging ahead with agriculture, fisheries and mining,' *Namibian*, 21 June 1990; Sapa, 'Nujoma asks for a billion', *Times of Namibia*, 22 June 1990.
30. Africa News Service, 'We like your democracy', *Namibia Today*, 23 June 1990; John Sedlins 'Money rolls in', *Times of Namibia*, 22 June 1990; Africa News Service, 'Nujoma signs business pact', *Namibia Today*, 23 June 1990.
31. Chris Coetzee, '"Painful cuts" for 1991', *Times of Namibia*, 9 July 1990.
32. This was accomplished in large measure by including R160 million in donor pledges already received in the calculation of national revenue. See, for details regarding deficit reduction, the financing of the 1990 budget, and the costs of servicing Namibia's R700 million total debt: 'Focus on the budget: deficit R210 million', *Namibian*, 9 July 1990.
33. *Ibid.* See also 'Bitter medicine budget, but it could be a cure', *Windhoek Observer*, 7 July 1980.
34. 'A *status quo* budget containing little new – Mudge', *Windhoek Observer*, 14 July 1990.
35. 'Mudge slates budget', *Namibian*, 11 July 1990.
36. '"Too little too late in the budget" – UDF', *Windhoek Observer*, 14 July 1990. See also the NPF's 'Comment on budget presented by Minister of Finance Dr Otto Herrigel', *Times of Namibia*, 9 July 1990.
37. 'Comment on budget,' *ibid.*
38. 'Next budget different', *Times of Namibia*, 16 July 1990; 'A responsible budget for all says Nujoma', *Namibian*, 17 July 1990; 'President hails historic budget', *Times of Namibia*, 17 July 1990; 'President defends the budget', *Windhoek Observer*, 21 July 1990.
39. Republic of Namibia, *Debates of the National Assembly*, 3 (12–23 July 1990), p. 91.
40. *Ibid.*, p. 92.
41. Dirk Mudge, Mishake Muyongo, Ben Africa, Barney Barnes, Eric Biwa, Fanuel Kozonguizi, interviews with the author.
42. Fanuel Tjingaete, interview with the author, 30 August 1991; see also press coverage of the Private Sector Investors' Conference convened in Windhoek by the Namibian government in February 1991.
43. See, for example, 'Trade union perspective', *Namibian*, 1 February 1991. Letters to the editors of Namibia's many newspapers are also a good indicator of the mood of the nation during this period.
44. In its election manifesto SWAPO had given few specifics regarding its intended land policy. It was 'committed to land reform in order to redress the [existing] imbalance', and thus to transferring 'some of the land from the few with too much of it to the landless majority'. This would be done through redistributing land belonging to foreign absentee landlords (which was estimated at as much as 48 per cent of the total number of farms) and of some of the land belonging to farmers with several farms. 'No full-scale nationalization of the land' was foreseen. A strategy of mixed ownership of land was intended as a means of both promoting 'the broad participation of the Namibian people' in agriculture, and increasing production. SWAPO, 'Election Manifesto', June 1990, pp. 9–10.
45. It was in fact Moses Katjiuongua, the sole elected representative of the National Patriotic Front, who introduced the idea of a land conference in a motion tabled shortly after independence. See the *Debates of the National Assembly*, 2 (1 June 1990), pp. 3–25.
46. The all-party Advisory Committee appointed by the Prime Minister to organize the Land Conference included, in addition to himself, the Ministers of Agriculture and of Lands, Resettlement and Housing, four SWAPO MPs, two DTA MPs, one member from each of the other parties represented in the National Assembly, fifteen regional representatives, two representatives of the Chamber of Commerce and Industry, and one each from the Council of Churches, the Namibian Agricultural Union, the Namibia Community Co-operative Alliance, the Namibia Development Trust, the Namibia National Chamber of Commerce and Industry, the Namibia National Students' Organization (NANSO) and the Women's Desk in the Office of the President. These were in turn responsible for entertaining applications from, and issuing invitations to, groups or individuals wishing to attend the conference. In the end, the

500 delegates selected were generally considered to be a reasonably representative cross-section of the population.

47. Background documentation for the conference included: NEPRU, 'Socio-economic questionnaire'; 'Methodology for the national sample survey on socio-economic conditions and attitudes to the land question'; 'Socio-economic conditions and attitudes to the land question: main results'; 'Attitudes to land issues: main conclusions'; 'Land-related issues in the communal areas: 1. Ovambo; 2. Kavango; 3. Caprivi; 4. Kaokoland, Damaraland, Namaland, Hereroland and Bushmanland (and Rehoboth); 'Water situation in the communal areas'; 'Degradation of agricultural land'; 'Subsidization, taxation and viability of the commercial agricultural sector'; 'Alternative approaches to the use and settlement of land'; 'Institutions for land reform'; 'Land reform experience in Zimbabwe'; 'Land tenure reform in Botswana'; 'Economic and financial analysis of land reform options: note on methodology'. UNICEF, 'Conceptual framework of the analysis'. Wolfgang Werner, 'A brief history of dispossession in Namibia'. Namibia, Ministry of Agriculture, 'The current land tenure system in the commercial districts of Namibia'. E. G. Segosebe, 'Land tenure reforms in Botswana: a case study with special reference to the tribal grazing land policy'. In addition, a local film-maker, Richard Pakleppa, commissioned by the government, produced a thought-provoking three-part documentary on the land issue in Namibia.

48. In debates over the land issue in Namibia, it had frequently been observed (mainly by non-Ovambo) that as the Ovambo had never in fact been dispossessed of their land, they could never fully identify with the 'land hunger' of the Herero and others who were conquered in battle with the colonial forces. An Ovambo-dominated government, it was argued, would not treat land reform with the urgency it deserved. Though to many minds long overdue, the holding of the land conference went a long way toward diffusing this criticism.

49. 'Statement by His Excellency Dr Sam Nujoma, President of the Republic, on the occasion of the official opening of the Land Reform Conference', Windhoek, 25 June 1991.

50. Government of Namibia, 'Namibian government policy on cooperative development', June 1991.

51. SWAPO, 'SWAPO's position paper on land reform and the land question', June 1991.

52. Government of Namibia, *Foreign Investment Act*, 4 December 1990.

53. SWAPO, 'SWAPO's position paper', *op. cit.*, p. 3.

54. *Ibid.*, pp. 8–9.

55. NUNW, 'Position paper', June 1991.

56. SYL, 'SWAPO Youth League's view point on the land question', June 1991.

57. See Susan Brown, 'Land in Namibia: rhetoric, reform or revolution?' *Southern Africa Report*, 7, 2 (1991).

58. Quoted in Bill Luckett, 'SWAPO's Gordian knot', *Windhoek Observer*, 7 July 1991.

59. More than a year after the Land Conference, the prospects for land reform seemed much bleaker. The constitutional clause prohibiting the expropriation of land without just compensation – criticized by the NUNW and SWAPO Youth League at the conference – has proved a tremendous obstacle to government purchases of foreign-owned or underutilized land. By mid-1992 only ten farms, totalling 123,000 acres, had been bought. The resettling of 3,000 landless peasants onto the new land proved unsuccessful, owing largely to their lack of farming experience. The technical committee appointed by the Land Conference to draft land reform legislation had still not submitted its report a year after the conference, and political insiders are sceptical that its recommendations, when they are finally tabled, will produce significant changes. See *Africa Report*, November/December 1992.

60. There was, of course, the Walvis Bay meeting held in May 1976, but it is usually referred to as a 'Conference' rather than a congress, as the exiled office-holders in SWAPO were naturally unable to attend.

61. The 27-member National Preparatory Committee for the congress was appointed at a July 1991 meeting of SWAPO's Central Committee and included SWAPO Chief Coordinator, Moses Garoeb as chairman, Minister of Information and Broadcasting Hidipo Hamutenya, Speaker of the National Assembly Mose Tjitendero, SWAPO MP Pashukeni Shoombe, Deputy Secretary of the SYL Martin Kapewasha, President of the NUNW Tjekero Tweya, and Minister of Wildlife, Tourism and the Environment Niko Bessinger, among others. SWAPO's thirteen regional offices were each represented by one member of the Committee, with all but three of the remaining fourteen members (including all those named above) based in Windhoek, giving the Committee an urban bias which strongly favoured the established party hierarchy. The perception that the composition of the committee favoured SWAPO 'militants' was reinforced when SWAPO leaders met with visiting leaders of the Italian, Japanese and French communist parties to 'discuss the future of socialism' in the week following the Central

Committee meeting. 'SWAPO congress taking shape', *Windhoek Observer*, 13 July 1991.
62. To what extent the delegates were democratically elected by their respective branches is a matter of some contention. New section, branch, district and regional boundaries were announced less than six months prior to the congress, following a meeting of the Central Committee on 5–7 July 1991, and party structures were far from organized. Compounding the problem was a scarcity of funds at all levels, the government having become, since independence, the recipient of much of the aid formerly channelled through the party. In the months preceding the congress, bitter struggles were waged in some branches over nominations of delegates to the congress, with accusations of patronage and corrupt practices exchanged by contending factions. (The Khomasdal branch, traditionally a political hotbed, witnessed one of the most heated battles, according to congress delegates). Charges that many delegates were 'handpicked' by the Organizing Committee for loyal service to the party were also widespread. A dictate issued by Party Headquarters in August that fully one-third of the delegates to the congress should be women may have helped to ensure that some newcomers were selected, but on the whole the disorder favoured the established party élite.
63. Interview with the author, 30 November. See also accounts in the *Namibian*, *Advertiser*, *Windhoek Observer*, and *New Era*, 4–13 December 1991.
64. Pendukeni Ithana, interview with the author, 2 October 1991.
65. Interview with the author, 5 September 1991.
66. Danie Botha, interview with the author, 7 December 1991.
67. *Namibian*, 7 December 1991.
68. See *Namibian*, 5 December 1991, for a partial list of corporate sponsors.
69. 'Report of the Central Committee to the First Congress of SWAPO, held in Windhoek on 6–10 December 1991.'
70. *Ibid.*, p. 7.
71. SWAPO, 'Political Programme', December 1991, p. 6.
72. *Ibid.*, p. 7.
73. *Ibid.*, p. 12.
74. Hidipo Hamutenya led the subcommittee responsible for the drafting of the Political Programme, which in turn was appointed by the congress's Preparatory (or Organizing) Committee.
75. Most delegates received their conference packages, which contained both the draft constitution and draft political programme, on arrival at the congress. Even among members of the government and other senior delegates – excluding those on the Organizing Committee who received their packages on 30 November – there were few who had read either document more than two days before the congress. Both documents were discussed and adopted by the congress as a whole, of course, and a very few minor revisions made in response to suggestions by delegates, but, as with other conference documents, popular participation in determining their content was minimal.
76. SWAPO's party constitution had last been amended and adopted by the Second Enlarged Central Committee Meeting, 17–20 April 1983, Cabuta, Kwanza Sul Province, People's Republic of Angola. The 1991 Constitution was drafted by a Subcommittee on Party Statutes, who made relatively few revisions to the 1983 version.
77. SWAPO, 'Constitution', December 1991, p. 1.
78. 'Closing Statement by H. E. Dr Sam Nujoma, President of SWAPO of Namibia and the Republic of Namibia, at the occasion of the first Congress of SWAPO of Namibia', Windhoek, 10 December 1991.
79. *Ibid.*, p. 6.
80. Journalists invited to a press conference (attended by the author) found the process extremely difficult to understand, despite patient and repeated attempts by Hamutenya to explain it, and expressed their doubt as to whether the delegates would find it any easier. The procedures had already been revised at least three times before the congress, and were to be revised twice more following the press conference. Originally, it appeared, any delegate who wished to be elected to the Central Committee was to have secured two seconders from each of the thirteen regions prior to the congress in order to run. This, of course, would have been virtually impossible for any delegate not already well known throughout the country, and in a position to travel widely. This was then revised to 26 seconders from seven regions, again prior to the Congress, and then to 20 seconders from seven regions within 24 hours of the convening of the Congress, which in theory eliminated the necessity to travel to solicit nominations, but was still heavily skewed toward party élites, giving candidates not already well known nationally little time to collect the necessary support.
81. In the final version, an absolute limit of 100 nominees for the 58 positions on the Central

Committee was set. (Of the remaining 12 positions on the 70-member Central Committee, the elections for President, Vice-President and Secretary General were held separately, as were elections for the heads of the three wings of the party, who were then admitted to the Central Committee as *ex officio* members, while 6 positions were reserved for persons appointed directly by the President.) Of these 100 nominations, the first 45 spots on the list were reserved for nominees of the outgoing Central Committee, which meant in effect that they could renominate themselves (and they did). The elections for President (Nujoma was acclaimed), Vice-President (Geingob withdrew at the last minute, allowing Witbooi to be acclaimed) and Secretary General (Garoeb defeated Toivo) were held first, and Geingob and Toivo subsequently individually nominated from the floor by special arrangement (a move which, if its procedural implications had been appreciated at the time, would have completely changed the whole election process). For the remaining positions on the ballot, nominations were solicited from the regions, which in practice encouraged a parochial outlook among delegates – encouraging regions to use their nominations to put forward local party élites, rather than people (union leaders, for example) whose constituencies were more representative and broadly based, and who almost certainly would have been nominated from the floor if such nominations had been permitted. Delegates were also not informed beforehand who the 45 nominees of the Central Committee were, with the result that some obvious names, popularly assumed to be on the list already, were not put forward.

82. As described in the new constitution, the position combined the responsibilities of Administrative Secretary, Garoeb's previous post, and the largely ceremonial role of Secretary General. Many delegates felt that the new post required a full-time commitment to the Party, and should thus be given to Garoeb rather than Toivo, who as Minister of Mines and Energy had other pressing obligations.

83. Minister of Defence Peter Mueshihange, Minister of Transport Richard Kapelwa, Deputy Chief Coordinator Festus Naholo, and Secretary for Information Kandi Nehova (all associated with the erstwhile 'securocratic arm' of the party) were, significantly, elected well down the list, while Dimo Hamaambo and Maxton Joseph were not elected at all. John Pandeni, of the Namibian Allied Food and Agricultural Union (NAFAU), Willem Konjore, Immanuel Ngatjizeko of the CCN, and Josephine Kandjambanga were among those cited as examples of exciting 'new blood'.

84. Ben Ulenga, Deputy Minister of Wildlife, Conservation and Tourism, interview with the author, 13 December 1991.

85. Bob Kandetu, interview with the author, 13 December 1991.

86. SWAPO, 'Resolutions of the First Congress of SWAPO, held in Windhoek, 6–11 December 1991.'

87. The SYL was told by congress officials that it had failed to register its submission properly as an official document, and that it could therefore not be tabled at the congress. Martin Kapewasha, SYL Deputy Secretary, interview with the author, 11 December 1991.

88. At the closing of the congress, Secretary General Moses Garoeb offered to read the 200-odd resolutions aloud but suggested that delegates might prefer to receive them later in written form, a proposal that exhausted participants gladly accepted.

89. A proposal to include a member of each branch of the party, that would have made the congress much more representative, was struck down.

90. SWAPO, 'Constitution', p. 6.

91. The congress elections, rather than assisting SWAPO to distinguish between its policies and structures as a party and its role as the nation's government, blurred the line by further conflating their respective personnel.

10

The Legacy
An Afterword

JOHN S. SAUL & COLIN LEYS

At independence Namibia presented a fundamental contradiction, familiar enough in the history of African decolonization, yet this time in a peculiarly dramatic form: the conditions that had allowed international capital to realize large, even vast profits, and were expected to do so again, were in contradiction with those for constructing an equitable and civilized society for its people. From the perspective of international capital, 'with a stable government, a multiparty system and potentially one of the most productive economies in sub-Saharan Africa, mineral-rich Namibia offers an attractive climate to foreign investors'.[1] To most of its own war-weary people, on the other hand, Namibia offered a bitter prospect: the population was growing at 3 per cent per annum (some estimates put the figure even higher in the north), leading to declining GNP *per capita* in the first three years of independence, after a 23 per cent decline over the previous decade; and more than half of the existing workforce was already unemployed.[2]

What was particularly striking was that none of the immediately foreseeable lines of economic development within the control of the government of Namibia seemed likely to offer employment to a significant portion of the unemployed, even though in absolute terms their numbers were not large – perhaps 300,000 people. The prospects for manufacturing employment were modest, since the local market was so small, existing and prospective industries were capital-intensive, and South Africa offered superior infrastructure, skills, markets and external economies.[3] Agriculture also offered only limited (mainly self-) employment prospects, especially owing to the shortage of land with adequate rainfall.[4] Most of the white-owned farms, including those owned by absentee foreigners which it was agreed at the 1991 Land Conference could be taken over for resettlement, were ranches, incapable of supporting agriculture (and at the end of 1992, after two years of drought and with declining prices for karakul pelts, white farmers were continuing to switch from cattle and sheep ranching to game management on their vast dry acreages).

New mining activities, including oil prospects, could generate substantial investment and income flows, leading to some employment (a large, though hard-to-exploit gas field has been discovered off Namibia's south-west shore, and offshore oil drilling by Norwegian and Anglo-Canadian companies was due to start in late 1992);[5] and considerable hopes attached to the fishery, which some believe could, with efficient management, become the country's chief private sector employer and foreign exchange earner – though this will come about slowly, if at all.[6] On the other hand, depressed markets were forcing the contraction and in some cases closure of marginal existing mines, while some of the country's biggest ones were nearing exhaustion (including the Tsumeb copper mine, with a resulting loss of 2,200 out of 2,400 jobs expected in the mid-1990s).[7] Big profits could still be made from mining, but the employment effects were not necessarily very promising.

Nonetheless, it was on such prospects that the government depended for economic expansion, and in its anxiety to do nothing to discourage investment in these sectors it went out of its way to pursue very conservative policies in all sensitive economic fields. It moved with extreme caution on land reform after the Land Conference,[8] on the new Labour Code, and in its budgets. Personal taxation remained essentially unchanged (though it was already relatively high and progressive), and government borrowing was kept to a minimum. This meant that services to the disadvantaged majority could not be rapidly expanded, except by redirecting them away from those – mainly whites – who had privileged access to them in the past. But the white population, whose interests were represented by an outspoken, not to say still arrogant Afrikaans and German press, served as a sort of litmus paper for foreign capital considering investing in Namibia: any strong criticism from them might well be taken as a sign that investment would be too risky, and so they had to be propitiated.[9] The government was also bound by the terms of the 1982 Constitutional Principles (produced by the Contact Group countries, agreed by SWAPO in exile and written into the independence constitution) which bound it not to expropriate private property without market price compensation; and also not to dismiss existing members of the civil service at independence, or reduce the terms of service of most of them. The result – reinforced by the government's overall policy of 'reconciliation' – was that a saving estimated at between R250 million and R400 million, had it been possible to shed unsuitable white personnel and replace them with black civil servants at less inflated salaries, was foregone. (At the same time it was clearly politically impossible to introduce a separate and lower pay scale for black Namibians, so a new caste of extremely highly paid black bureaucrats was also created.) In the short run, therefore, the best the government could do, within the framework of its dependence on private capital, was to put as much of its current revenue as possible into expanding health services and, above all, school places in the north, while trying as hard as possible to reassure and encourage private investment.

Of course many would argue that this was the only realistic strategy for the SWAPO government in the global conditions of the 1990s. It was also a strategy with a chance, albeit a slim chance, of success, given that the population needing to be supported was still so small. The discovery of oil or any other minerals on a large scale could, in the medium run, significantly alter the policy equation by giving rise to enough new spending. Above all, if peace and stability were to come to Angola, creating a major new market for exports from a South Africa also expanding economically in the conditions produced by a successful conclusion of its own transition to democracy, Namibia could find itself prospering as an entrepôt for the region's two largest economies – a role for which it seems destined by geography and climate, and which need not be a subordinate one.[10] Namibia deserves such good fortune.

In the shorter run, however, what most struck all observers was that with every passing month after independence, the inherited economic and social structure – with its extremes of inequality still largely following racial lines, and with large numbers close to the margin of existence and living in absolute poverty (not to mention those pauperized by the drought of 1992 and driven into dependence on food aid) – appeared increasingly likely to become incompatible with the continued stability, let alone popularity, of an elected SWAPO government.[11] The 3,000 unemployed youths seeking work and the 500 children begging on the streets in Windhoek; the thieves and burglars and dealers in stolen goods in the townships; the unemployed ex-combatants in their so-called 'Development Brigades' on former SWATF bases in the north; the great pool of underemployed people in the communal areas, especially in the north, including most of the 50,000 who had returned from exile: it was not hard to see that here were the roots of a potentially deep and dangerous political alienation from the regime.

And yet in November and December 1992 SWAPO not only won the country's regional and municipal elections (giving it control of the second chamber of parliament provided for in the independence constitution), but captured 67 per cent of the vote cast, up 17 per cent on its performance in the pre-independence elections of 1989 – a result that suggested that SWAPO might have taken as much as 70–80 per cent in a general election, given that seats in SWAPO's Ovambo heartland were uncontested.[12] This was achieved largely at the expense of the smaller, ethnically based parties, although the main opposition party, the DTA, would have suffered a bigger percentage drop (its vote fell 5 per cent compared with 1989) had there been contests in all areas. Some of SWAPO's gain was no doubt due to its having become the government. Smaller ethnic groups, whose leaders had tested the electoral waters with scant success in 1989, were now more inclined to come to terms with SWAPO and seek security or patronage under its umbrella. Nonetheless, the results showed that the SWAPO government was widely perceived by its core supporters, as well as by some former opponents, as having accomplished the potentially difficult transition from war to peace with considerable credit. Given the acuteness of the social problems SWAPO had inherited, and the very limited degree to which it had been able to address them, this was an achievement that needs explaining; and here the legacy of the armed struggle may well be seen as having been in several respects quite helpful.

In the first place, the struggle had produced many leaders of high administrative competence. It is true, as Dobell has pointed out in the previous chapter, that SWAPO in exile received exceptional volumes of aid. Nonetheless it was SWAPO that obtained and spent this aid, running the settlements in Zambia and Angola, the educational training programmes throughout the world, and the war itself. The leadership that was formed in this process was not perfect: many of the strictures of its internal critics were justified, even in its own eyes (as the admissions of the 1976 Ya-Otto Commission, noted in Chapter 3, testify). Yet the overall competence of the senior leadership as a whole, with their accumulated diplomatic and organizational experience, could bear comparison with that of governments in countries with populations many times the size of Namibia's, and with economies and educational systems far more advanced.

The construction of the government was also astute, the SWAPO 'old guard' being deftly combined with the more highly educated immediately succeeding generation of leaders, such as Hage Geingob, the Prime Minister, and Hidipo Hamutenya, the Minister of Information and Communications. Each member of the Cabinet was balanced by an appropriate team of deputy ministers and permanent secretaries, grafted onto the inherited civil service structure; the so-called 'hardliners' (such as Hamutenya) were counterpoised by 'soft guys' (such as Tjongarero, Hamutenya's Deputy Minister); and the 'securocrats' (defence and security personnel) were slotted into the defence and security branches where, in the short run at least, they appeared removed from mainstream policy making.

Policy making was not free from delays and errors, and implementation was often weak. Nonetheless, a good deal of new legislation did materialize, difficult problems such as policing and the court system were tackled, and corruption was curbed by some well-publicized dismissals and suspensions. Within the rather narrow limits set by the constitution and the government's pragmatic, market-oriented strategy, its performance was widely seen as satisfactory.

Not only did the exile experience produce a qualified government team: SWAPO's narrowing of the terms of resistance inside the country, described in Chapter 4, meant that there were no powerful and potentially critically minded internal SWAPO leaders to be accommodated. The most senior internal leader, SWAPO Vice-President Hendrik Witbooi, derived his authority as much from his standing among the Nama (a blend of his own option for SWAPO in 1976, and his family's historic record of anti-colonial resistance) as from his national role during the 1980s: in any case, he, like Tjongarero and the rest of the National Executive inside Namibia, fully accepted the pre-eminence of the returning exile leaders. This also allowed Nujoma and Geingob to co-opt into the government two prominent white businessmen in the key portfolios of Finance and Agriculture, and two prominent opposition leaders in the 1989 elections: Vekuui

Rukoro of the Herero-based SWANU, who became Deputy Minister of Justice, and Reggie Diergardt of the Labour Party (representing coloureds), who became Deputy Minister of Trade and Industry. Together with the SWAPO team's own notable ethnic diversity, including the preponderantly 'southern' leaders of the internal organization, but symbolized above all by the appointment of the Damara Hage Geingob as Prime Minister, this went far to pre-empt any tendency for the DTA, already an ethnic coalition, to widen its base by appealing to ethnic sentiment.

The new government was further aided by the massive loyalty of the Ovambo electorate. In the pre-independence elections turnout was almost 100 per cent in the Ovambo region, where SWAPO took 225,000 votes compared with 11,000 for the DTA. When it is remembered that during the war the South African regime had recruited two battalions of the South West Africa Territorial Force, and a large proportion of the 3,000-strong Koevoet, from the Ovambo, these are remarkable figures. And yet it was the Ovambo who were most affected, numerically and in many respects qualitatively, by the deprivations inherited from the racist regime. The Ovambo had the lowest *per capita* provision of school places, the poorest health services and the worst infrastructure.[13] It was also the Ovambo economy that was most inflated by military spending, and so, in strictly material terms, the most adversely affected by peace. Eighty-five per cent of the returning exiles went back to Ovambo country, where for most of them there were neither jobs nor land. Most of the unemployed youth in Windhoek in 1992, and most of the street children, were Ovambo. Yet the voting showed unequivocally that the Ovambo would be the last to desert SWAPO, and least of all for the DTA, given the DTA's past association with the racist regime. Significantly, it was the DTA that bore the brunt of the acute discontent of the unemployed former PLAN combatants in the election campaign in November 1992;[14] and, as Chapter 6 has already shown, when in 1991 the majority at the annual Congress of NANSO voted to disaffiliate from SWAPO, most of the Ovambo students left NANSO. In short, the massive and more or less automatic nature of SWAPO's Ovambo support underpinned the government, and might well continue to do so for some considerable time even if conditions deteriorated – although, as suggested below, this would then seem likely to entail a kind of ethnic politics that it has always been SWAPO's official policy to avoid.

The legacy of SWAPO's liberation struggle also operated in favour of the incoming government in the shape of the still undecided outcome of the struggle for liberation inside South Africa itself. So long as the government in Pretoria remained in the hands of the same racist party that had oppressed Namibians for almost half a century, SWAPO's call for unity against the Boer enemy would not lose its resonance. There were plenty of reminders, too, of Pretoria's continuing covert political influence, in addition to the sheer weight of the South African economy and South African ownership in all the SWAPO government's economic calculations. For example, during the 1989 election campaign Anton Lubowski, the most prominent white internal SWAPO leader, was assassinated by South African secret agents in circumstances that were never brought to light.[15] Subsequently a treason trial, in which the chief defendants were allowed bail and absconded, revealed a clumsy but still serious plot by an ex-policeman and various others, apparently with covert encouragement from within South Africa, to overthrow the new government. Furthermore, entire units of the former SWATF, including the Bushmen Battalion and 32 ('Buffalo') Battalion (composed of Angolans originally recruited from the defeated FNLA), were transported intact to bases in South Africa just before independence, together with significant numbers of ex-Koevoet members.[16] South Africa remained quite literally in Walvis Bay, where its presence included a large military base with a mechanized military unit stationed in it.[17] It was also disclosed in 1991 during the 'Inkathagate' scandal in South Africa that Pretoria had approved over R100 million to fund the anti-SWAPO parties in the 1989 elections;[18] according to spywatchers in South Africa in 1992, plans existed for intervening in the first post-independence elections in Namibia too.[19]

In these circumstances the SWAPO government's consistent call for 'national reconciliation' had strong undertones of the legacy of the struggle. It meant accepting, at least initially, the inherited structure of racial inequality. It also meant – in sharp contrast with the stance adopted by the ANC in South Africa – that SWAPO would not even discuss, let alone make any amends for, its own past abuses of power in exile; this was seen as a *quid pro quo* for not discussing or seeking any redress for abuses of power by South Africa's police and military officers, prison officers and other officials during the struggle. Whereas the ANC had not only confronted and tried to eliminate the abuse of prisoners in its own camps when in exile in the 1980s, but also committed itself to the fullest possible disclosure of them during and after the transition to democracy in South Africa, SWAPO did not even propose to investigate any of these wrongs; in other words, SWAPO did not adopt (and perhaps did not even consider) the principle that 'forgiveness and reconciliation depend on full disclosure', and that 'even the right to be magnanimous and the right to forgive … is dependent on acknowledgement of errors or wrongdoings on the part of whose who have been responsible [on both sides]' – a principle that was being insisted on by the ANC in the early 1990s.[20] A striking example of what this implied was the decision in 1990 to appoint Solomon Hawala, the former Chief of Security at Lubango, as Army Commander: a decision that stirred a strong public controversy.[21]

In short, so long as South African racism and military power, overt or covert, remained a significant element in the Namibian situation, a SWAPO government would enjoy an added degree of immunity from criticism for any shortcomings, real or imagined, in its handling of the country's acute economic, social or political problems.

Thus in the first three years of independence the legacy of SWAPO's 30-year struggle worked strongly to underpin its efforts as a government, producing a seeming paradox: a party whose own inner politics were markedly hierarchical or even authoritarian presided over the implementation of a constitution universally heralded as the most democratic in the continent. Yet the paradox was really only apparent. What Namibia had was a liberal constitution, rather than a democratic one: or more precisely, a liberal democracy of the specific type familiar in the West, to which modern scholars have given names like 'pluralism' and 'democratic élitism';[22] or, in the plain words of an American scholar by no means wholly unsympathetic to it, 'representative government, ultimately accountable to "the people" but not really under their control, combined with a fundamentally capitalist economy'.[23]

In reality, that is, liberal democracy does not imply that citizens rule themselves, but that rule by élites is made legitimate by periodic elections, and – very importantly – by various ancillary mechanisms, above all the mediation of political parties. People's desire for recognition, and for their interests to have some chance of being registered in government policy, is seen as largely being satisfied by the operation of parties; while on the other hand the fact that no significant political party offers a radical challenge to the capitalist economic system and the inequalities that go with it is guaranteed by the ability of that system at least to satisfy most people's minimum needs. On the other hand, if either – or in the worst case, both – of these requirements is missing, liberal democracy cannot work, as Africa's traumatic post-independence history has shown:[24] and it is in this context that the situation bequeathed by the liberation struggle must be carefully assessed. The question is whether liberal democracy had, or has, better prospects of surviving in Namibia than in other countries of the sub-continent.

On the one hand, the fact that Namibia not only had a liberal constitution, and that SWAPO in office gave every indication of wishing to abide by it, deserves emphasis. The existence of a diverse and partisan opposition press which frequently criticized the government (and by no means always 'responsibly') was in striking contrast with the situation in so many other African countries, as was the reaction of the government to cases of abuse of power as when, for example, it curbed the excesses of the Presidential Guard (alluded to in Chapter 7) or, to take another example, eventually suspended four senior (white) police officers responsible for an unprovoked assault on a group of demonstrating brewery workers.[25] Nor should the fact that free and fair regional elections were held in 1992, without the need for a corps of external 'monitors', be esteemed lightly.

That the SWAPO government showed respect for the constitution in these ways does not, however, remove the anxiety that an observer may reasonably feel about the threat that SWAPO's inherited inner-party political culture could pose in the slightly longer run, above all if economic growth is disappointing. If large numbers of people are not assured of the bare necessities of life, or the minimum means to participate fully in the national community and its culture, a different logic comes into play – either there is a tendency towards authoritarianism, typically reinforced by appeals to ethnicity, or a stronger bond has to be forged between the regime and the people, in which more is asked of citizens than their mark on a ballot sheet every four or five years, and more opportunity is given them to share in policy making than listening on the radio to the 'unveiling' of government plans. This is where SWAPO's 'democratic deficit' could become a serious problem: if it develops no more meaningful connection to its members and supporters, and no greater opportunity to share in policy formation and leadership selection than it has in the past (including the 1991 party congress described in Chapter 9 above), will it be able to supply the political stability, the national cohesion, needed to sustain liberalism and democracy in still harder times?

This question needs to be posed frankly because there is a tendency in recent writing to oversimplify the post-independence period and to see the convergence of liberal-democratic practices and capitalism in Namibia as unproblematically beneficient;[26] whereas the legacy of the events we have described in this volume, combined with Namibia's precarious economic circumstances in the post-independence period, are bound to give us pause. We have seen in Chapter 3 just how crowded with contingencies was the moment that 'drew forward SWAPO's UNIN team and diplomatic corps personnel to centre stage' in post-independence Namibia. It is also known that significant numbers – perhaps most – of the 'securocrats' from Lubango were, at the same time, installed in the new military and presidential security organizations. It needs to be remembered, too, that even the most liberal of the senior SWAPO leadership had not encouraged democratic practices, either within the ranks of SWAPO in exile or in the organization inside the country.

However, the 'democratic modernizers' knew, from their exile experience, that the consolidation in power of the more authoritarian SWAPO tendency could challenge their ascendancy, and perhaps even threaten their own security. Some of them undoubtedly felt quite comfortable with the emergence of a liberal economic as well as political dispensation in Namibia; and the narrowing of democracy to 'democratic élitism', involving as it did a tacit political demobilization, was not something they were particularly likely to question. Surrounded by the trappings of power, with its chauffeurs, large houses, 'power lunches' and embassy parties, and drawn into the circle of class privilege described in Chapter 8, they were not likely to rock the boat of the post-independence Namibian compromise by preaching popular empowerment or facilitating bottom-up democratization. In this fundamental sense – and without collapsing the relevant distinctions between them – the 'liberals' shared some of the same premises as their more authoritarian colleagues within the party.

It was not surprising, then, that SWAPO still showed itself little inclined to sanction the activism of various elements within civil society that might be expected to press against the apparent limits of the *status quo*. Consider the unease caused inside SWAPO by the debates within the National Union of Namibian Workers regarding the merits of possible disaffiliation from SWAPO (in order to be freer to press workers' demands upon capital and the state); and the difficulties the workers themselves have had not only in organizing their own activities but also in facing up to tough political questions (the contrast with the self-confidence of South African unions is quite striking).[27] Consider, too, the difficulties the SWAPO Women's Council had in bringing itself to enter into a broader coalition with other women's organizations to advance gender-based demands from across the political spectrum (difficulties first manifested in the Women's Voice controversy discussed in Chapters 4 and 5); or the subsequent disaffiliation from NANSO of a majority of its Ovambo students, already mentioned, when that organization also sought freedom to act independently of SWAPO on Namibian students' behalf.

Even within SWAPO's own structures, the notion of articulating and aggregating interests in order to build a mass base for counter-balancing the weight of established (white and capitalist) interests still tends to collapse into the goal, vaguely defined and focussed, of 'mobilization'. The similarity of this state of affairs to the kind of politics favoured by the internal leaders of SWAPO during the struggle itself is evident. Small wonder that the 1991 SWAPO congress described in the previous chapter, while allowing some lively debate, facilitated, in the end, no real grappling with questions of overall development strategy or of the contradictory situation in which Namibian society finds itself – for it was neither prepared for in such a way as to facilitate such an outcome, nor sufficiently self-conscious about the distinction between SWAPO as party (empowering, in theory, its base) and SWAPO as government (defending its record) to give space for that kind of fundamental debate on the floor. As Dobell observes, 'the traditional insularity of SWAPO's leadership was not fundamentally challenged'. President Nujoma's description of the congress as 'a practical demonstration of democracy in action' illustrates well the limited conception of democracy that still prevailed in SWAPO's official thinking.

There is a second dimension to this. As virtually all students of liberal democracy have pointed out, liberal democracy and capitalism have always been intimately linked. This means that, conversely, the kind of empowerment that a more significant kind of democratization would entail is only possible in the context of a political project that challenges the writ of capital. It would clearly be unrealistic to expect the Namibian leadership on its own to craft a policy for making global capital conform to the country's priorities when the left is so generally at a loss as to how this can be done anywhere else. But if, as seems all too possible, capitalism does not deliver development in Namibia, then responsible leaders will have to confront the task of trying to formulate an alternative strategy for development which frames alternative ways to meet human needs.

The history of SWAPO has hardly qualified it to undertake such a task. It has, on the contrary, not infrequently disempowered the activists and thinkers whose active participation in defining and implementing such a difficult project would be essential. This seems equally true at the level of ideology, where the movement has tended to undercut the very discursive ground upon which any real alternative – national, regional or global – to capital's hegemony might be conceptualized. Any practical conception of 'socialism' has been a casualty of the split within the movement between the 'hardliners' and 'democratic modernizers' that was carried from exile back to independent Namibia (see Chapter 3). For the so-called 'hardliners' were those most closely associated with 'socialism' of the Eastern European brand, on the one hand, and with authoritarian methods (of the same brand) on the other. Yet the 'pragmatism' now offered by many senior SWAPO leaders as the sole 'sensible' alternative to such 'socialism' leaves little space for defining any relevant and practicable alternative.[28]

In the last few paragraphs we may seem to have travelled a long way from the history of the liberation struggle. Yet if the liberation struggle has involved, besides one kind of empowerment of the people, another kind of disempowerment; and if socialism, even in its absence, has come to be associated with a brand of quasi-Stalinism, then the shadows of Mboroma and Lubango can be said still to fall sombrely across present-day Namibia.

For some of the same arrogance of power that scarred the liberation movement during the independence struggle remains, and hovers on the edge of the Namibian polity. When, in the teeth of a severe budgetary pinch, President Nujoma and his advisers rationalized the massive expenditure required to purchase him a private airplane, some saw the recrudesence of an all-too-familiar brand of 'presidentialism'.[29] And when, during the 1992 electoral campaign, an opposition DTA candidate was killed at Ondangua, observers noted that 'earlier that day SWAPO MP Nathaniel Maxuilili had said at a rally at Onashila, in the same region, that SWAPO youth should "eliminate puppets", and he also spoke of his desire to kill DTA leader Dirk Mudge though he was restrained in the name of national reconciliation'.[30] Notwithstanding the DTA's own brand of provocations, this strand of SWAPO rhetoric – its most aggressively populist strand – tends further to narrow the meaning of the radical alternative in Namibia to a kind of mere bullying, with potentially lethal consequences.

By 1993 there were also some disturbing indications that, in the absence of any significant internal party life in SWAPO, some SWAPO politicians were, in fact, already beginning to explore the possibilities of exploiting ethnic allegiances;[31] while on the other hand the old SWAPO security personnel – sidelined for the moment but, one fears, little transformed – were very far from being delegitimated, at least amongst the Ovambo, as the appointment of Hawala as army Chief of Staff showed. If the going were to get much tougher, and with so little basis having been established for any alternative response, might the new Namibia crack along ethnic and other fault-lines, as SWAPO itself once began to do when under severe pressure in Angola? And might the further effect of such a development be to pull the 'securocrats' back into the political arena?

Of course the legacy of the struggle does not boil down merely to this worry. The liberals – and the social democrats – in the senior SWAPO leadership are in no way *anti*-democratic, however narrow their conception of democracy has so far been; and in altered circumstances some of them might perhaps reach out for more democratic support. Nor can it be ruled out that a new generation of leaders might progressively modify SWAPO's traditions and inaugurate more active links to the party's rank and file, and seek to give them some significant power. For the liberation struggle developed strength and resilience in SWAPO, and a tradition of challenge to authority, as well as one of hierarchy and authoritarianism. All we can say is that what prevailed during the struggle was the latter tradition, rather than the former; and that this should not be forgotten or underestimated when the balance sheet of the struggle is drawn up and its implications for the future are assessed.

Notes

1. Annual report of the Namibian Banking Corporation, owned by South Africa's Nedcor, January 1993, quoted in Tom Minney, 'Miracle of hotels and fishes', *Africa South and East*, March 1993, p. 15.
2. Richard Chidowore, 'Namibia – Two Years After', Southern African Research and Documentation Centre, Harare, Zimbabwe, 16 March 1992. Unemployment statistics are inherently rough and ready in conditions like Namibia's. The waged and salaried workforce in 1992 was approximately 185,000. The ILO estimated that up to two-thirds of the labour force in the formal sector were unemployed, and two-thirds of those in the 'subsistence' sector were underemployed. Most commentators assume that the result is equivalent to more than half of the total available workforce being unemployed.
3. The government hoped for manufacturing investment in the processing of mineral, fish and agricultural products, and also established an Export Processing Zone at Arandis, near Swakop-

mund, in hopes of attracting manufacturers interested, for example, in exploiting Namibia's access to the European Community market through the Lomé convention. But as David Pieters and Cathy Blatt noted ('Namibia: guided by the politics of reconciliation', *Namibia Brief* No. 14, Windhoek, March 1992, p. 11), 'time is against Namibia's efforts at establishing an industrial manufacturing base as a route to economic diversification and import substitution' thanks to South Africa's head start and expanding export drive in the region.

4. The Agrarian Reforms programme of the Ministry of Agriculture aimed at creating 'earned livelihoods' for up to 50,000 people, although some intractable difficulties would have to be overcome to achieve this.

5. Rossing Uranium has a large graphite deposit in central Namibia and large low-grade copper ores have been proved at Otjihase. Increased prospecting combined with new technologies (such as CDM's new methods for recovering diamonds from the seabed and reworking old mine tailings) seemed likely to yield results.

6. Cf. Michael Stuttaford, 'The sea fishing industry', in E. Leistner and P. Esterhuysen, *Namibia 1990: an Africa Institute Country Survey* (Pretoria: Africa Institute of South Africa, 1991), pp. 131–2, whose careful analysis should be read as a caution against accepting the more extravagant projections of some external reports, including one for the World Bank which reportedly believed that the fishery could double the national income in five or six years (cited in Linda Freeman, 'Contradictions of independence: Namibia in transition', *Transformation*, 17 (1992), p. 32).

7. Rossing Uranium's workforce was cut back from 3,200 in the mid-1980s to 1,450 in early 1992 (Pieters and Blatt, *op. cit.*, pp. 14–15).

8. The conclusions of the conference were published in the *Namibian*, 2 July 1991. Tom Minney's summary ('Healing the wounds of war', *Africa South and East*, March 1992, p. 11) is of interest: the 600 delegates 'voted by consensus that despite past injustice over land it was too complicated to try to unravel it.... At a stroke, much of the core of the liberation struggle disappeared, to be replaced by a painfully slow process of loans to richer black farmers to help them buy land at market prices.'

9. For example, when the Minister of Finance expressed a wish for 'greater state involvement in the management of MEATCO, the marketing arm of the commercial beef barons', the Namibian Agricultural Union (the beef ranchers' lobby) stated: 'Incidents of interference like these send out the wrong signals, which will be generalised to include other areas as well, and Namibia cannot afford this!' *Namibia Development Briefing*, 1, 7 and 8, (January and February 1992). Letters to the newspapers by whites criticizing all aspects of government policy showed a consciousness of the protection given them by the presence of neighbouring South Africa, still under white control, and by the government's dependence on foreign investment and aid in the immediate post-independence years. Also, as Pieters and Blatt point out, 'the country's resident settler community is amongst the continent's largest relative to the indigenous population, despite their small number' (*op. cit.*, p. 8).

10. '[T]he country ... has so far mainly gained from its close proximity with the industrialized South African economy twenty-five times the size of its own ... as a useful and reliable link in the trade chain with other African countries' (Pieters and Blatt, *op. cit.*, p. 11).

11. The white 5 per cent of the population at independence enjoyed *per capita* incomes of $14,560 a year, accounting for 71 per cent of GDP, while the bottom 55 per cent of the population accounted for 3 per cent of GDP, with *per capita* incomes for rural blacks estimated at $63 a year (see Linda Freeman, 'Contradictions of independence' *op. cit.*, p. 31).

12. Tom Minney, 'Healing the wounds of war', *op. cit.*, pp. 10–11.

13. For some statistics and sources on the unequal distribution of services, and the levels of deprivation they implied, see Freeman, *op. cit.*, p. 36.

14. A DTA official was killed at Ondangwa by a '400-strong crowd, mainly from the development brigade which is made up of former SWAPO fighters'. *Southscan* , 7, 45 (27 November 1992).

15. Lubowski was gunned down outside his home on 12 September 1989 and an Irishman called Donald Acheson was arrested in Windhoek in connection with the crime, in which he was thought to be an accomplice of the actual assassin. In September 1989, in the Rand Supreme Court in South Africa, a South African police officer named Brigadier Mostert, who was investigating the so-called 'Brixton Murder and Robbery Squad', a 'hit squad' conducting assassinations and other crimes for the South African state, submitted an affidavit alleging that Acheson was working for one of the Squad's 'handlers', Calla Botha (who was then under arrest in South Africa), and that he had also been involved in other political murders including that of David Webster, a well-known anti-apartheid activist in Johannesburg. Acheson was eventually released, however, apparently for lack of sufficient evidence to prosecute him successfully.

16. The Angolans of the former 32 'Buffalo' Battalion were essentially mercenaries. Four thousand Namibian Bushmen (ex-SWATF soliders and their families) were reported as having been resettled in South Africa, while a further 1,800 were left at the former Omega base in Caprivi. About 500 former members of the SWATF's 101 Battalion (Ovambo) and 500 ex-members of 202 Battalion (Kavango) were reported as having fled to bases in Angola to escape persecution from the ex-PLAN 'Border Guard' that policed the Kavango and Caprivi regions in mid-1990. Former Koevoet members were also reported as being in bases in both Angola and South Africa. In late 1990 reports suggested that a stream of small groups of ex-SWATF and ex-Koevoet personnel (said by some sources to total as many as 2,000) had crossed into South Africa and had been moved through a SADF base at Upington to Pretoria (see the *Namibian*, 23 November 1990).

17. In early September 1993 it was agreed, following talks at the constitutional forum then in progress in Johannesburg, that Walvis Bay and the offshore islands hitherto claimed by South Africa would be handed over to Namibia on 1 March 1994, as duly happened. *Southscan* , 8, 33 (10 September 1993), p. 154.

18. Christopher Saunders, 'Transition in Namibia 1989–1990: and the South African case', *Transformation*, 17 (1992), pp. 53–4.

19. 'South Africa Plans', an edited version of an article in the German magazine *Top Secret*, published in *Namibia Development Briefing* 1, 7–8 (January–February 1992).

20. These formulations are cited from a summary of the ANC's record and policy on this issue given by the veteran ANC leader Albie Sachs in an interview in Toronto. 'Serious abuses: establishing a culture of truth', *Southern Africa Report*, 9, 2 (November 1993), pp. 13–19. Sachs states that in 1985 the National Council of the ANC devoted a full day at its Kabwe Conference to working out new statutes that would prevent any repetition of the abuses of power that had come to light in its own prison camps for suspected spies, leading to the implementation of 'systems of internal accountability, coupled with replacing the leadership of Security and developing some kind of inspection' that 'profoundly improved the situation'. The principle that mistreatment of 'counter-revolutionaries' was 'acceptable and good revolutionary practice' was rejected, and 'it was the young people who spoke most forcefully … on the issue and who were most insistent on preventing Security from having a free hand'. He notes that after the ANC was legalized inside South Africa there were two successive commissions of enquiry (the Skweyiya and Motsenyana commissions) into the ANC's past maltreatment of prisoners; but, he insists, while this was morally necessary for the ANC, for it to have a healing effect it had to be paralleled by similar enquiries into the abuses of power on the other side. For reconciliation to be possible, in the ANC's view, what is needed is not punishment but a general amnesty based on full dislosure of the misdeeds of both sides by a commission of truth; only then can there be compensation and forgiveness.

21. Many people voiced concern about this appointment because of Hawala's past role as Chief of Security at Lubango during the 'spy scandal'. In an interview with the authors, however, the editor of the *Namibian* stated that letters received by the paper ran overwhelmingly in support of Hawala's appointment, and in an editorial of 26 October the paper itself adopted the position that 'either every alleged "war criminal" should be tried by the courts, or none at all'. The alternative of a commission to establish the facts about the past abuse of power, already exemplified in Argentina following the end of military rule, was not entertained in the editorial, which raises the possibility that it was not considered by the SWAPO leadership either, in contrast to the leadership of the ANC two years later (see note 20).

22. A lucid summary of, and commentary on, the 'pluralist' analysis (and endorsement) of liberal democracy is contained in David Held, *Political Theory and the Modern State* (Cambridge: Polity Press, 1989), Chapter 2. Analyses of liberal democracy that criticize it include Alan Wolfe, *The Limits of Legitimacy: Political Contradictions of Contemporary Capitalism* (New York: Free Press, 1977); and Philip Green, *Retrieving Democracy: In Search of Civic Equality* (London: Methuen, 1989). The best-known brief historical overview of the subject is C. B. MacPherson, *The Life and Times of Liberal Democracy* (New York: Oxford University Press, 1977).

23. Green, *op. cit.*, p. 3. He adds that liberal representative democracy as it actually exists (which he calls 'pseudodemocracy') is 'preferable to most of the immediately available alternative ways of life of the contemporary nation-state. But it is not democracy; not really.'

24. A useful select bibliography on the fate of liberal democracy in Africa is to be found in Robert Fatton Jr., *Predatory Rule* (Boulder: Lynne Rienner, 1992); two influential surveys are Richard Sandbrook, *The Politics of Africa's Economic Stagnation* (New York: Cambridge University Press, 1985), and Jean-Francois Bayart, *The State in Africa: The Politics of the Belly* (London: Longmans, 1993; original French edition, 1989). Recent enthusiasm among Western 'aid donors' and journalists for the 'democratization' of Africa has been a somewhat startling

instance of wishful thinking: it was for a moment as if all that has been learned from over a century of study of the conditions for liberal representative democracy had been abruptly forgotten in the universal wish to see the impossible happen in Africa.

25. See William A. Lindeke, 'Namibia's second year of independence', *SAPEM*, May 1992, p. 2. This was the culmination of a series of similar police assaults on demonstrating workers after independence to which the government was actually rather slow to react – as the labour movement did not fail to notice.

26. For a particularly bald example of this kind of unreflective post-Cold War celebrationism as applied to Namibia see Joshua B. Forrest, 'The inauguration and consolidation of democracy in Namibia', paper presented to the 34th Annual Conference of the African Studies Association, St. Louis, 23–26 November 1991.

27. See Gretchen Bauer, 'Defining a role: trade unions in Namibia', *Southern Africa Report*, 8, 5 (May 1993).

28. This point was made to us most articulately by, among others, the Hon. Theo-Ben Gurirab, Minister of Foreign Affairs, in an interview on 24 June 1991. On the search for a very different alternative in South Africa, defined as 'structural reform', see John S. Saul, *Recolonization and Resistance: Southern Africa in the 1990s* (Trenton: Africa World Press, 1993), Chapters 4 and 5.

29. The Economist Intelligence Unit Country Report No. 3, 1992, *Namibia*, speaks of 'the furore that erupted over the government disclosure in May of the purchase of a presidential jet at a cost of Rand 75 million (US$27 million)... [with] running costs estimated at Rand 6 million annually, including depreciation. The timing of the announcement, on the eve of the drought appeal by President Sam Nujoma, together with the government's initial slowness in providing full details of the cost, fuelled criticism from SWAPO supporters as well as from opposition parties' (p. 9).

30. *Southscan*, 7, *loc. cit.* The article continues, 'the DTA asked for an interdict to stop him and Education and Culture Minister Nahas Angula, who spoke at the same meeting, from addressing any more campaign meetings, claiming they had incited the crowd'.

31. In 1993 not only were 'paramount' chiefs 'elected' by leading factions among the Damara and the Caprivians, but it was widely reported that a faction within the SWAPO leadership was planning to elect a new king of the Kwanyama (the largest Ovambo clan) who, it was believed, would then have the best claim to be the next President of SWAPO and hence, of Namibia.

Index